The dead alive and busy, the still voice
Of enlarged spirits, kind heaven's white decoys!

—Henry Vaughan "To His Books."

THE DEAD ALIVE AND BUSY

Selected Essays of Robert Morgan

EDITED BY
RANDALL WILHELM

The University of Tennessee Press / Knoxville

Library of Congress Cataloging-in-Publication Data

Names: Morgan, Robert, 1944– author | Wilhelm, Randall editor
Title: The dead alive and busy : selected essays of Robert Morgan / edited by Randall Wilhelm.
Description: First edition. | Knoxville : The University of Tennessee Press, 2026. | Includes bibliographical references and index. | Summary: "For six decades, Robert Morgan has been a preeminent voice in southern Appalachian literature. Growing up in Green River, North Carolina in the 1950s, he absorbed a variety of influences to inform his later work: his family's haunting stories, explorations of the mountainous landscape, paperbacks from a bookmobile, lessons from a kind elementary school teacher. *The Dead Alive and Busy* is a collection of essays on the author's personal history, masters of prose, and significant poets. Morgan's catalogue of literary interests is a melting pot of global traditions, from Leo Tolstoy to Appalachian writers such as Thomas Wolfe and Wilma Dykeman. His analysis covers writers "in a community across time"—including Poe, Hemingway, McCarthy, Carl Sandburg, and the Appalachian poets Jeff Daniel Marion and Jim Wayne Miller"—Provided by publisher.
Identifiers: LCCN 2025035319 (print) | LCCN 2025035320 (ebook) | ISBN 9798895270523 paperback | ISBN 9798895270547 adobe pdf | ISBN 9798895270530 epub
Subjects: LCSH: Morgan, Robert, 1944- | Poets, American—20th century—Biography | American literature—History and criticism
Classification: LCC PS3563.O87147 Z46 2026 (print) | LCC PS3563.O87147 (ebook)
LC record available at https://lccn.loc.gov/2025035319
LC ebook record available at https://lccn.loc.gov/2025035320

CONTENTS

Introduction   1
  Randall Wilhelm

PART ONE
Youthful Wonders: Life and Art in Green River

The Poetry of Place / The Place of Poetry   15
Nature Is a Stranger Yet   29
Work and Poetry: The Father Tongue   45
Fertile North Carolina   65
Reading Tolstoy's *War and Peace*   71
Wildacres   77
Leo's House   87

PART TWO
Fictional Forays: Landscape, Voice, and War

Thomas Wolfe and the Whole Wide World Catalogue   105
Albert Bierstadt and the Millennium: *The Sierras Near
    Lake Tahoe, California, 1865*   123
From the Blue Ridge to the Rocky Mountains:
    Thomas Wolfe and the American West   127
Wilma Dykeman's *Family of Earth:* This Was Peace   143
Cormac McCarthy: The Novel Raised from the Dead   161
The Wisest Book I Ever Read: *Doctor Zhivago*   173
James McConkey and the Quest for the Sacred   177
Hemingway and the True Poetry of War   189

PART THREE

Uncommon Meters: Vision, Craft, and the Authority of Poetry

The Mystery of Edgar Allan Poe   211
Carl Sandburg: Populist Among the Moderns   233
Concord Constructivist and Yankee Doodler:
    The Poetry of William Harmon   245
The Reign of King Stork: Geoffrey Hill's Early Poetry   253
Jeff Daniel Marion: Poet of the Holston   269
Jim Wayne Miller: A Radiating Presence   283
The Authority of Poetry   291

Afterword: Healing   313
    Robert Morgan
Bibliography   323
Index   333

INTRODUCTION

On October 3, 2019, Cornell University in Ithaca, New York, hosted "MorganFest," a seventy fifth year birthday celebration of the critically acclaimed poet, short story writer, novelist, historian, biographer, and essayist Robert Morgan. The occasion marked not only Morgan's birthday but also his forty eighth year teaching at the Ivy League university, where he became Kappa Alpha Professor of Literature in 1992, a position held until his retirement in 2022. Morgan takes his place among similarly distinguished professors and authors that have enriched the lives of those in Ithaca and beyond through their teachings and widely published literary work, writers such as M. H. Abrams, Walter Slatoff, Vladimir Nabokov, A. R. Ammons, and Baxter Hathaway, founding editor of *Epoch*, to name but a few.

Since publishing *Zirconia Poems* in 1969, Morgan has produced an astonishing range of work that testifies to his sweeping vision of history and the lives, objects, and land caught up in its inevitable tumults, travails, and tragedies. Helena Maria Viramontes has written about Morgan's "reverence" for his poetic and fictional worlds: "Sensually measured by objects of the past, by the regal sense of their shattering, both [Morgan's] stories and poems unspool between the marvelous and mundane, between the fantastic and fact, between memory and cross-generational history."[1] Morgan has produced seventeen volumes of award-winning poetry, seven novels, six collections of short fiction, three historical biographies, and a study of poetic craft, with more work steadily on the way. Morgan has taught and lectured countless audiences on writing and literary history in Ithaca and well beyond, through invited readings, lectures, and speaking engagements, a writing and teaching career that spans more than fifty-five years and confirms him as one of the nation's most venerable men of letters.

As an essayist, Morgan's path has followed a similar trajectory with a similar reach, following his personal and professional interests as his career developed and matured. "Some were written for private reasons, to understand my own past and memories better," he has said.[2] Others were composed for different occasions and different audiences, including important lectures at Cornell University, Mary Washington University, the University of North-Carolina at Chapel Hill, the Carl Sandburg Festival, and the United States Air Force Academy. Others were written to honor Morgan's poet-friends such as Jeff Daniel Marion, Jim Wayne Miller, and William Harmon, while others explore the prose influences of Thomas Wolfe, Wilma Dykeman, and Ernest Hemingway on Morgan's fictional aesthetic. For Morgan, writing essays, like all his work, is creative exploration:

> When asked if I consider myself primarily a fiction writer or a poet, I usually answer that I am a poet who also writes prose. And I have also worked to be an essay writer and a critic. Day after day and year after year I have stood in front of classes discussing the craft of writing, the glamor of Walt Whitman, the vigor of Emerson, Dickinson, Wallace Stevens, Frost, and Eliot. Formulating ideas in the classroom has aided me in getting down ideas and making connections on the page. We write essays to find out what we think.[3]

In his previous collection of essays, *Good Measure: Essays, Interviews and Notes on Poetry* (1993), Morgan offered readers a glimpse into the mind of the poet and the creative fire of the literary imagination. In "The Cubist of Memory," for instance, Morgan writes about his intimate connection to the physical terrain of the natural world, particularly his childhood in Green River, North Carolina, in the Blue Ridge Mountains. Morgan sees the land as a grand tableau, performing as material present that embodies geologic and human history, and as physical and textual palimpsest of deep time. "I like the sense that the continent has been written on by glaciers," Morgan writes, "earthquakes, floods, buffalo, Native Americans, and hunters. The soil is haunted by the Cherokee and Iroquois, extinct giant animals, ice tracks, frontier preachers. Looking for new ground to clear, we find Old Fields, scrublands opened by fire or ice storms or Indian hoe-farmers."[4] In discussing the "reach" of his poetry, Morgan has said "Perhaps I unconsciously seek out the heroic in poetry, connecting the humble and commonplace with the larger and more lasting, the temporary with the universal, connecting the moment with the everlasting, the near with the far. That is what I call the 'reach' in poetry: to see the large in the small, the infinite in the finite, the earthly with the heavenly, the ordinary with the eternal."[5]

Morgan's gift for finding correspondences between the most unlikely elements is not only his *ars poetica* but also provides his ethos as an essayist. In this sense Morgan performs as a grand unifier who reaches across gaps tenuously grasped through the magic of language:

> All is in fragments, and the recognition and gathering of those shards inspire the cubism of memory and imagination that implies the whole. All the best poetry is fragments joined in new ways, the broken edges sharp enough to cut as well as refract light and attention. At our best we recognize that we are just members of the chorus of language, that our voices, when most our own, are in concert with speakers past and present, with facts and their metaphorical fables.[6]

For Morgan, storytelling, as well as essay writing, is an intimate act, a recognition of the self, the reader, and the ties that bind in a universal, even sacred, view of literature as unifying human communication. For Morgan, differences between humans, societies, and cultures unite, rather than demarcate or repel. Morgan has said that "stories and poems make us feel less alone,"[7] and that "we read to connect with other people's lives, people often very different from ourselves, at least on the surface. And we write stories and poems to connect with others, to feel part of the larger community of humanity."[8] For Morgan, "one of the glories of storytelling is that narratives can reach across boundaries of gender, age, ethnicity, race, religion, geography, and even time, and, through translation, different languages. Stories and poems help us connect with a sense of community, even a community across time."[9] The essays that ensue are infused with this ethos of timeless community, that books, as Henry Vaughan writes in the epigraph, are spiritual gifts that reveal "the dead" as "alive and busy, the still voice / Of enlarged spirits, kind heaven's white decoys!"[10]

In this new selection of essays culled from over the last thirty years, Morgan speaks as a member of this chorus of language "in concert with speakers past and present," "the dead alive and busy"—family members and friends, poets and painters, short story writers and novelists, historians, and philosophers. While the topics and writers selected for this volume cross a spectrum of boundaries and historical epochs, the essays that follow are exhibited in three interpolating sections: "Youthful Wonders: Art and life in Green River"; "Fictional Forays: Landscape, Voice, and War," and "Uncommon Meters: Craft, Vision, and the Authority of Poetry." These major sections are followed by the distressing but inspirational afterword "Healing."

In Part One, Morgan showcases his skills at memoir, telling of the wonders of childhood and early adulthood, growing up in Green River, North Carolina, and his literary awakening and apprenticeship. Morgan makes clear the tremendous impact the land, especially the Blue Ridge Mountains, has made on him. In "Nature is a Stranger Yet," Morgan writes: "More like Emerson or Whitman than I realized at first, I have often seen nature itself as language, and the land as a text written on by runoff and wind, by floods, and by time."[11] An award-winning historian, Morgan charges his family memories with action and danger, kindness and love. The portraits of his family, including his mother, strong-willed and practical, and his father, stubborn and mysterious, are rendered in plainspoken beauty. In one account, Morgan recalls his earliest memory, waking up on his father's shoulder as he carried the child home from a prayer meeting where he had fallen asleep: "I must have been about eighteen months old. We were walking through the dewy pasture lit by starlight. My mother and sister were stepping through the dark beside us. The motion of my father's stride made the stars above rock and swim."[12]

The lyricism of memory yields to the furnace of poetic inspiration and craft in "Nature is a Stranger Yet," Morgan's 1998 Harder Lecture at Cornell University. Taking his cue from Emily Dickinson, Morgan explores the mystery at the heart of the poetic imagination, its elusiveness ever enthralling. The essay doubles as a workshop in writing poetry as Morgan recounts his early efforts to capture the essence of voice, meter, metaphor, line, and form, from *Red Owl* (1972) to *Sigodlin* (1990). Morgan humbly suggests that "[a]fter more than a quarter of a century of trying to fit language to landscape, and trying to fit word to thing, and to discover the natural world through language, I was as mystified as I had been starting out."[13]

In "Work and Poetry: The Father Tongue," Morgan writes about his father, Clyde Morgan, whose taciturn and difficult personality had been a mystery to him as a boy. But through the twinned acts of memory and writing, the adult Morgan learns to understand him through their shared catharsis of work. Other memory pieces yield insight into Morgan's early experiences with world literature via the county bookmobile that began to make rounds in Green River in the early 1960s. We learn of his enthusiasm when discovering Thomas Wolfe's *Look Homeward, Angel*, Boris Pasternak's *Doctor Zhivago*, and Leo Tolstoy's *War and Peace*. We also learn of Morgan's precocious youth, attending the summer camp "Wildacres" and discovering modern poetry and dance, before leaving home at sixteen to attend Emory at Oxford and later North Carolina State University where he would major in advanced mathematics and aerospace engineering. "Leo's House" concludes the memoir section, telling the story of Morgan's time in Hendersonville, North Carolina, from January 1970 to August 1971, before his full-time appointment to Cornell. Morgan, now with wife and young child, recounts the frustrations and fortitude of repairing his aunt's house and painting other homes in the area while thinking deeply about poetry, forms, line breaks, and meter, his only connection to the literary world the letters he received from William Matthews, his friend and confidant far north in Ithaca.

Part Two gathers a community of fiction writers with emphasis on the natural world, on novelistic styles and aesthetic developments, on voice in fiction, and on wartime experience renegotiated through language. The section opens with "Thomas Wolfe and the Whole World Catalogue," in which Morgan discusses Wolfe's masterpiece *Look Homeward, Angel*, perhaps the most significant novel of Morgan's early life and one that spurred him to imagine himself as a writer. Morgan discusses the controversies surrounding Wolfe's accumulative style, as the title somewhat humorously suggests, but makes a clear case for Wolfe's talent and unfulfilled promise as a writer. For Morgan, Wolfe's penchant for obsessive description and long passages of elevated rhetoric functions as a lyric strategy similar to Walt Whitman's catalogues in *Song of Myself*. Situating Wolfe in a long tradition of visionary writers, and even painters such as Albert Bierstadt. Morgan makes a compelling case for reading Wolfe's prose as language that bursts the bounds of even the most copious novelistic form.

Morgan's love of the natural world finds correspondence in the writings of Wolfe's western landscapes and in Wilma Dykeman's descriptions of the French Broad River in East Tennessee. For Morgan, Dykeman became a touchstone to his own mountain world in Green River. After moving to Ithaca, Morgan found himself often in Cornell's large research library drawn to the powerful and lyric prose of Dykeman's descriptions of the southern Appalachian Mountains. It was Dykeman's poetic eye which stirred Morgan's desire to write about the land and peoples of the Blue Ridge, as if in answer to the questions she often poses: "Which is the time to know the river?" . . . April along the French Broad is a swirl of sudden water beneath the bending buds of spice-wood bushes, ... August is a film of dust on purple asters along the country roads of the lower river, . . . October is a flame,

. . . the ripeness of harvest in husk and bin. It is the golden span between the dry rattle of September's end and November's beginning."[14]

Morgan's ability to penetrate the minds of writers, to see large patterns, intimate details, and big pictures charges each of these essays with potent and exciting clarity. Writing of Cormac McCarthy's East Tennessee novels, Morgan finds similar reverence for the land, however twisted the view through McCarthy's dark gothicism. But Morgan also addresses McCarthy's genius of voice, the pitch-perfect tone of country folk and mountain people that he heard one evening on a PBS station broadcasting McCarthy's play *The Gardener's Son*. Morgan recounts "as the story continued, I found tears in my eyes. Here were my people, people who had lived in the mountain hollers for generations and then gone down to the Piedmont to find work in the cotton mills."[15] Morgan also discusses the representation of Lester Ballad, the titular character of *Child of God*, whose necrophiliac tendencies do not deprive him of his spiritual status: "He moves in the dry chaff among the dust and slats of sunlight with a constrained truculence. Saxon and Celtic bloods. A child of God much like yourself perhaps."[16] Along with other writers, Morgan credits McCarthy for resurrecting the novel in the mid-to-late sixties, and also "oddly enough, in the horrors and cruelties, the misunderstandings and the grotesque humor, the paradoxes and absurdities in his fiction, Cormac McCarthy seemed to have made God alive too, whatever unspeakable deeds his children might commit."[17]

Part Two concludes with a triptych of war writers, Boris Pasternak, James McConkey, and Ernest Hemingway. Morgan's taste for the great Russian novelists such as Leo Tolstoy, Fyodor Dostoyevsky, and Pasternak is imbued with a youthful enthusiasm. As Morgan confesses when reading *Doctor Zhivago* at fourteen, "Even as I wrestled with the chopped-up narrative sections, the awkwardly joined chapters and the literary allusions beyond my understanding, I was thrilled by the details of the muddy roads, snowy vistas, clothing shops, ballrooms, and smoldering battlefields."[18] The character of Zhivago, especially his poems included at the end of the novel, leads Morgan to deem Pasternak's novel "the wisest book I've ever read." Of McConkey, one of his colleagues at Cornell, Morgan writes: "He was on a mission to search for truth, for meaning in modern life. . . . What made McConkey different from most contemporaries," Morgan believes, "was not only his soul-searching honesty, his self-lacerating confessions of failures and weakness, but, like [Saint] Augustine, he was on a quest to find the spiritual, to know the sacred, in a non-believing world."[19]

In the section's last essay, which Morgan wrote for the Keynote Address at the United States Air Force Academy in Colorado Springs, Morgan recalls the day in 1961 when he and his father learned from the local newspaper that Ernest Hemingway had died. For Morgan, Hemingway's muscular prose served as a model that approximated the rigor of science, providing Morgan with a crystalline hardness in which to shape words and sentences. Morgan links Hemingway's prose to Ezra Pound's imagism and focuses on the horrors of war through Hemingway's repeated use of ants as soldiers' bodies in *A Farewell to Arms* and in the masterful story "Big Two-Hearted River." As with many of these essays, an opening anecdote leads into new worlds, as memory unspools into a discussion of narrative style, emotive depth, and consummate control, qualities that led Morgan to connect Hemingway's work with "the true poetry of war."

The essays in Part Three begin with Morgan's lecture at Mary Washington University on "The Mystery of Edgar Allan Poe." Morgan paints Poe as a man of enormous talent and genius and situates Poe's life and work in the literary milieu of his time, seeing him as the dark side of the Emersonian coin. One would be hard pressed to find a more eloquent and insightful speaker on poetry than Morgan, who sees the art as a mysterious unifier with an infinite reach into the complexities of the human condition. Morgan makes a strong case for Poe's ambition, his stylistic, formal and conceptual innovations, claiming "Poe was a modernist writer long before the age of modernism. Compared to Poe's best work many of the stories of Hawthorne, his closest rival in American fiction, creak with heavy-handed moralism and allegory."[20]

In the following essays, Morgan recalls the childhood influence of Carl Sandburg, who lived close by in Flat Rock, North Carolina, and discusses the poetry of his longtime friend William Harmon. Morgan revels in the enormous range of Sandburg's ouevre, and how his interest in poetry and music led to under-heralded works such as *The American Songbag*. For Morgan, Sandburg "has the American love of fact, of the sciences, of the homemade. He was a minstrel, a humorist, a showman, and a philosopher, a phonographer of language. From the nation's heartland, he always wrote to and from the nation's heart. More than any of our poets since Whitman he seems to touch the collective wisdom of the people."[21] In the following essay Morgan discusses the poetry of fellow North Carolinian William Harmon, who Morgan winkingly calls a "Concord Constructivist and Yankee Doodler." Morgan praises Harmon's poetic voice as inspiringly "unique. No one else has quite his range of playfulness, improvisation, vastness of reference. He is a poet of thunderstorms and hymns, as well as 'the retail sublime.' He combines the vision and rhetoric of a revival preacher with the new high tech, high-rise, shopping mall world of the Sun Belt. He is one of the smartest, funniest, most serious poets I know."[22]

The discussion of poetry continues with Morgan's exploration of three poets, the notoriously difficult English poet Geoffrey Hill, and two pioneer poets of Appalachian literature, Jeff Daniel Marion and Jim Wayne Miller. While Hill's dense connotative textures have confused throngs of readers and critics, Morgan sees clearly through Hill's style to focus on major thematic strains such as drowning and (non) resurrection, a fate long pondered by many British poets. Despite the tenacity and violence in Hill's work, Morgan sees a genuine search for meaning and honesty: "Not only does Hill have an unromantic distrust of nature and 'generative process,' he seems suspicious, even ashamed, of art which cultivates and feeds on the violence, waste, and suffering of human experience."[23] And yet, Morgan tells us, "at the same time [Hill] keeps returning to the gesture of summoning time and drowning and decay. . . . The poem seems for him a kind of verbal garden where the expulsion is reversed by hard-won saying."[24]

Writing on Jeff Daniel Marion, Morgan fondly remembers the personal influence Marion and his journal *The Small Farm* had on his developing sense of poetry and place. Recalling their first meeting and their failures fly-fishing in Deep Creek at the edge of the Smokies, Morgan tells how Marion opened new territory—"Appalachia"—to explore through character voices instead of deep images. Of Marion's poems Morgan has high praise and finds in later work some of Marion's most penetrating verse: "I believe Danny reaches his deepest level of meditation and self-searching in the poems collected in *Father* (2009). These are poems of great affection, loyalty and bonds of kinship. But they are also poems of profound honesty and, less confessional than testimonial, poems of coming to terms with memory. There is a relentless clarity of vision."[25]

In the collection's penultimate essay, Morgan discusses the energy and "radiating presence" of Jim Wayne Miller, confessing that "Jim was the first person I ever heard talk about such a thing as Appalachian writing."[26] Like Marion, Miller's work is indistinguishable from his vision of an Appalachian Literature that he tirelessly promoted. In one passage, Morgan pictures Miller as a member of a community across time, a scene that could serve as illustration for this entire collection: "Whenever you saw Jim he was surrounded by friends, by students, by folks he had just met. If you listened you would hear outbursts of laughter from time to time, as he grinned and drew on a cigarette, and offered yet another story or anecdote from his vast and always growing memory hoard."[27]

With their interpolations of the personal with the professional, of memoir with literary history, of craft with interpretation, these essays perform as a blend of nontraditional biography and as critical treatise by Morgan, whose grand enthusiasm for life and art gleams on every page. The last essay in Part Three, the magisterial "The Authority of Poetry," offers a stunning discussion of the practical and philosophical powers of poetry for human civilizations. Poetry, for Morgan, performs many roles, from the personal to the political, from the memorial to the cultural, the humorous to the tragic, to the simplicity, the rightness of phrase and the assurance of wisdom: "Some might say it's important at times of crisis that familiar words be spoken, affirming identity and kinship, often lost in a materialistic and selfish culture. No doubt, that is one of the values of poetry, especially traditional poetry."[28] And yet,

> [o]thers might say it's the *oldness* of poetry that reassures, the continuity of a shared culture and language, in a society that often seems centrifugal and broken, without center, evolving so fast there is little confidence of stability. In that way poetry recalls the religious service, phrases and cadences that have been heard so many times over the centuries, in different places, words of prayer and comfort, words of dignity."[29]

Ultimately Morgan asserts that the authority of poems springs from their existence "for their own time, as well as for all time. The Greeks believed the muses were the daughters of Memory. The poet draws on memory to recreate the discoveries of childhood, of the past, but depends equally on imagination to create what has not been thought of before, and make it seem always there, authoritative, inevitable, timeless. When all else seems mere entertainment, poetry remains."[30]

Throughout this collection of essays, Morgan's discussions about art and life flare large with immense respect for and insight into the magic of language and the artists who create. We should celebrate Morgan, whose wisdom pours forth in giant syllables, enlightening with new perceptions and penetrating correspondences between the works of writers, poets, and thinkers who each seek to illumine the mysteries and vagaries of human experience with intensity, precision, and conviction. *The Dead Alive and Busy: Selected Essays of Robert Morgan* stands as testimony to the deep and enduring value of literary expression, and as a tribute to the life and work of this esteemed writer, scholar, teacher, historian, biographer, essayist, and friend.

NOTES

1. Helena Maria Viramontes. "Foreword." Robert Morgan, *The Oratorio That Was Time: Fourteen Poems and Three Stories*. New York: Audubon Terrace Press, 2022. vii–viii.

2. Personal Interview. Green River, North Carolina. November 2023.

3. Personal Interview. November 2023.

4. Robert Morgan. *Good Measure: Essays, Interviews and Notes on Poetry*. Baton Rouge: Louisiana State University Press, 1993. 10.

5. *Conversations with Robert Morgan*. eds. Randall Wilhelm and Jesse Graves. Jackson: University Press of Mississippi, 2019. 12.

6. Robert Morgan. *Good Measure*. 10.

7. Robert Morgan. *The Dead Alive and Busy: Selected Essays of Robert Morgan*. ed. Randall Wilhelm. Knoxville: University of Tennessee Press, 2026. 17.

8. Ibid.

9. Morgan, *Selected Essays*. Ibid.

10. Vaughan, *The Complete Poems*, 611.

11. Morgan, *Selected Essays*. 39.

12. Morgan, *Selected Essays*. 29.

13. Morgan, *Selected Essays*. 42.

14. Wilma Dykeman. *The French Broad*. Knoxville: University of Tennessee Press, 1965. 6.

15. Morgan, *Selected Essays*. 162.

16. Cormac McCarthy. *Child of God*. 1973. New York: Vintage, 1993. 4.

17. Morgan, *Selected Essays*. 170.

18. Morgan, *Selected Essays*. 174.

19. Morgan, *Selected Essays*. 179.

20. Morgan, *Selected Essays*. 225.

21. Morgan, *Selected Essays*. 242.

22. Morgan, *Selected Essays*. 245.

23. Morgan, *Selected Essays*. 255.

24. Ibid.

25. Morgan, *Selected Essays.* 277.
26. Morgan, *Selected Essays.* 284.
27. Morgan, *Selected Essays.* 283.
28. Morgan, *Selected Essays.* 295.
29. Morgan, *Selected Essays.* 295–96.
30. Morgan, *Selected Essays.* 310.

PART ONE

Youthful Wonders:
Life and Art in Green River

THE PLACE OF POETRY /
THE POETRY OF PLACE

Over the hills and a great way off
The wind will blow your topknot off.

Those lines delighted me when I was very young. I asked my mother to say them again and again. And I can remember my pleasure in the image of the hills, of crossing the hills to a faraway place, where the wind was so strong it thrilled through your hair and threatened to blow the top of your head away. To me, those windy hills suggested both the past and the future, a land of wonder I seemed to have forgotten, an ideal world I aspired to, that I was moving toward. Far beyond the everyday and ordinary, there was a luminous land of clouds over hills, of wind like music, a place of discovery, of possibility, but with a hint of danger that charged the image. And the repetition of the word "off" gave emphasis to the lines.

All of us are born with a sense of poetry, a taste for poetry. The rhythm of poetry is in the heartbeat, in the pulse, in the shaking of our first rattle. We do not have to be taught to love the chimes and lilt of nursery rhymes. Long before we know the names for meters, we recognize the stirring energy and strength of anapests, iambs, trochees, and dactyls. We may have to go to college to learn free verse, but from infancy we respond to "'Twas the night before Christmas when all through the house."

It is said that no one has discovered a language or a culture without poetry. Poetry seems to be an inherent part of the fabric of culture and humanity. The most powerful functions of language are naming and storytelling, and we seem wired from birth to relish both. Some have argued that the very origins of language lay in the poetic impulse, the love of word play, onomatopoeia, the excitement of narrative. When I published my third book of poems, *Land Diving,* a reviewer seized on the line, "A squirrel runs casting its tail on the sky,"[1] observing that the word squirrel comes from two Greek words meaning "shadow tail." I am not much of a Greek scholar, but I had noticed what some ancient Greek must have thought long ago, that a squirrel's tail looks like its shadow. We are born with a love for names that evoke, that fit, that seem to discover or re-discover a thing, person, idea, or experience.

Recently I was asked to describe my sense of place in connection with my writing. My sense of physical place is very specific, not just regional but local, not even a county, not even a township, but the Green River Valley in Henderson County, western North Carolina. It was about a square mile of land in the Blue Ridge Mountains, bought by my great-great-grandfather Daniel Pace in 1840. It stretched from the black loam along the riverbank across the pastures and hills to the rim of the Mount Olivet ridge. There was a peach orchard on top of the mountain, and apple, pear, cherry, and plum orchards on the hillsides. As a child I worked in the fields, hoeing corn and plowing with the horse in the loamy bottomlands. I hoed strawberries in the red clay upland patches and gathered leaves for cowbedding in the woods.

In my free time I could roam the pastures, climb trees in the woods, dig caves in the sides of the gullies, build ponds on the pasture branch, roll rocks off the mountaintop. I knew intimately every ditch and pine thicket, and the place on Kimble Branch where some Indian craftsman had left thousands of chips as he made arrowheads. I caught June bugs and tied threads to their legs and let them fly like model airplanes. I knew the pits on the mountainsides where my great-uncles had dug for zircons. My cousins and I slid down the mountainsides on boards polished by the leaves. I knew the swimming holes in the river, the places where trout lurked in the creek, the gloomy outhouse. For all my life since, that place has served as the touchstone with which I compare other landscapes.

As I worked in the fields, I found arrowheads and pieces of Indian pottery, a broken tomahawk. My dad told me the Cherokee and other Woodland tribes had lived there, and that Green River was a translation of the Indigenous name for the stream. The very ground seemed haunted by the ghosts of the Indians. The shoals in the river seemed to mutter Indian names; the shadows in the thickets were charged with their presence. The connection to Native Americans thrilled, deepened, and saddened my sense of place.

But for me there is an equally important sense of place, for which I have no name, in the landscape of language. When I heard a phrase such as "the valley of the shadow of death" or "death where is thy sting?" or "Before Abraham was I am," or "I am that I am," I knew it was a place I had to seek, where language had an intense luster, a strange and luminous vitality. I did not know how to get there, but I knew it was what I had to try for.

When I was older, I found guideposts to that place in lines from Walt Whitman, "I stand and look at them long and long"[2]; or Henry Wadsworth Longfellow, "A boy's will is the wind's will"[3]; or Carl Sandburg's "I listened to the wind counting its money and throwing it away."[4] In my search I found other guides in the music of Mozart, in Thomas Wolfe's *Look Homeward, Angel*, in the writing of Boris Pasternak. When my sister Evangeline returned from a year at college with her freshman English textbook, I looked through that anthology of American literature and found a poem by Wallace Stevens called "Domination of Black." In that poem Stevens talked about the fire turning inside a fireplace, and the leaves outside spinning, and the wheeling of the planets far overhead. I was stunned by the analogy of motion far and near, and the words, "I was afraid / And I heard the cry of the peacocks."[5] That was my first inkling of the connection between terror and the sublime. However scary it might be, I knew that was a place in the geography of language that I must make every effort to reach, however long it might take, whatever the cost.

It is important to remember that place primarily means people, the people on the land, the people who have been on the land. Our greatest interest in a place derives from those who live there, their struggles, failures, and joys. A place is about stories, and stories are about encounters, people encountering people, encountering the elements, or fate. It has been said that stories are about conflicts, and I would add that stories are less about conflicts of good versus bad, than conflicts of loyalty, one good versus another good. It has also been said that stories are about connection as well as conflict, connections between people, between people and land, people and cultures. We read stories to connect with other people's lives, people often very different from ourselves, at least on the surface. And we write stories and poems to connect with others, to feel part of the larger community of humanity. Stories and poems help us feel less alone. One of the glories of storytelling is that narratives can reach across boundaries of gender, age, ethnicity, race, religion, geography, and even time, and, through translation, different languages. Stories and poems help us connect with a sense of community, even a community across time.

Special phrases haunted me in my youth. I said them again and again in my head. Some were quotes from history I had learned from my dad, such as the description of George Washington as "First in war, first in peace, and first in the hearts of his countrymen." General MacArthur was quoted on the radio as saying, "Old soldiers never die, they just fade away." Such words quickened my pulse, suggesting grandeur, something heroic in life, beyond the habits and tedium of the familiar. "Life, liberty, and the pursuit of happiness" had the same ring, elevating the spirit. I attended rural schools that were so old-fashioned we were required to memorize poems and recite them to the class. In the fourth grade Miss Mary Sue Waters made us memorize the opening of Longfellow's *Evangeline,* and those dactyls washed like cool wind off the tongue. She also had us perform a section of Longfellow's *Hiawatha*, swaying as we chanted the trochaic lines:

> Should you ask me, whence these stories?
> Whence these legends and traditions,
> With the odors of the forest,
> With the dew and damp of meadows,
> With the curling smoke of wigwams,
> With the rushing of great rivers,
> With their frequent repetitions,
> And their wild reverberations,
> As of thunder in the mountains?[6]

When I began the ninth grade at Flat Rock High School in 1958, I was lucky to have Julia Lappin as my English teacher. Mrs. Lappin was just beginning her teaching career, and she had several new ideas for teaching writing and reading. She had no classroom of her own, and we met in a section of the school auditorium. She assigned us oral book reports, one each month. It was from her I first heard the names Faulkner and Pasternak. Her most radical idea was to have students write papers about their own experience, not about things they had read. I said to her, "All I know to write about is the farm where I grew up." She answered, "Someday you will be proud of that."

Mrs. Lappin's most ambitious project was the Poetry Notebook. Each student had to compile, write out, illustrate, and bind a booklet of poems. We were supposed to look in libraries, textbooks, anthologies, and encyclopedias, or any other place we could find, for poems on a particular theme, such as trees, flowers, butterflies, birds, or any subject that occurred to us.

While many of my fellow students had access to typewriters, and the library in town, and help, I suspect, from their mothers with illustrations for their Poetry Notebooks, I wrote out everything with pencil and crayon, on construction paper, and fastened the pages together with brads. The result looked somewhat like a booklet assembled by a mad surrealist.

But Mrs. Lappin would not let me end the year on a note of failure. She said I could write a paper, a book report, for extra credit, to shore up my good grade. I'd read the classic novel *Quo Vadis* that spring, and over the weekend I labored on a report, printed on lined paper with a green ink ball-point pen, writing more neatly than I ever had before, and handed it to Mrs. Lappin on the next to last day. On the final day she gave the paper back to me with an A+ written in the upper righthand corner.

When I began writing at North Carolina State, while studying applied mathematics and aerospace engineering, I wondered what I had to write about. My favorite authors wrote about London, Paris, and Moscow. All I knew was the farm in the Blue Ridge Mountains. It only came to me slowly, by trial and error, that I had a lot of material, the place and people I had known, the stories I'd heard while growing up, the stories of the Revolution and Civil War. And most important of all, I had the voices of those I had known, the living idiom, the many voices of witness and testimony.

My first modest breakthrough as a poet came in the summer of 1964 while I was working as a laborer at the General Electric plant near Hendersonville, North Carolina. My job was to help load the big trucks at the back of the plant. One afternoon a violent thunderstorm blew up, with claps so loud they shook the van we were loading. Lightning snapped so close you could hear the crackle in the air before the blast. As the storm passed, a shaft of sunlight shot down through the clouds at an angle. Pausing at my work I made up a haiku in my head:

> The shaft of light through
> clouds appears to be a brace
> holding up the sky.

I knew it was not an especially good haiku. I'd read Basho, Buson, and Issa. Yet I sensed there was something authentic about the little poem. It was a real observation, with a metaphoric truth my other experiments with poetry had not had. The simile seemed grounded in the natural world. It was a small beginning, but a beginning.

When I returned to Chapel Hill in September and registered for the honors class in writing, I met a group of students I hadn't known before. They were from the Northeast, and some had been kicked out of the finest prep schools in New England. They'd come to Chapel Hill to be beatniks and poets. They knew far more about poetry than I did and were certainly more sophisticated socially than I was. They could discuss Baudelaire and French poetry, metaphor and line breaks, and William Butler Yeats. The most talented of the group was Dudley Carroll, from Darien, Connecticut. Dudley was a great fan of Gary Snyder and Robert Bly. He urged me to show him some of my poems. Out of shyness I held back, but finally did type up some of my short poems on my second-hand typewriter and give them to him.

Around two or three o'clock the next morning there was a banging on my door on East Rosemary Street. I opened the door and there stood Dudley and his friend Tim Perkins. Almost shaking with excitement, Dudley said, "These are so good we had to come tell you." No honor since, no bestseller list, has meant more to me than that response from my fellow student. It was validation when I needed it most. I began to work more and more on poetry and less on fiction.

One afternoon in the fall of 1964 I sat in my room reading aloud T. S. Eliot's "Burnt Norton." I had bought a copy of Eliot's *Complete Poems and Plays* the summer before. I said the poem aloud and suddenly realized that Eliot had made the poem out of beautiful sentences broken into lines. It was the voice running through the measured lines that gave the poem such special energy. That may seem obvious, even trivial now, but at the time it was an epiphany. I had achieved a heightened sense of the progress, the forward motion, the voice of the sentences, in counterpoint to the repetition of the broken lines. Later, I would read Robert Frost talking about the cadence of the English sentence broken over the iambic pentameter line. But at the time I just had a stronger sense of how poetry was made, an almost physical sense of poetry as action, as acting, as drama and dance. I began to write longer poems with more confidence.

In the history of literature, especially poetry, writers seem to come in pairs or clusters. It is very rare that an important poet develops on his or her own. Even Emily Dickinson had mentors and readers, namely her sister-in-law Susan and Thomas Wentworth Higginson. Again and again we see in literary history the importance of the personal connection between writers: Wordsworth and Coleridge, Byron and Shelley, Goethe and Schiller, Emerson and Thoreau, Sherwood Anderson and Faulkner, Marianne Moore and Elizabeth Bishop, Ezra Pound and T. S. Eliot. It is as though we cannot become true writers until we have a true reader. Many writers search all their lives for their authentic reader. I was lucky: at UNC-Greensboro I found Fred Chappell.

Chappell was from Canton, just west of Asheville. He understood both the landscape of my writing and the language of my characters. Because I held two part-time jobs while in the graduate program at Greensboro, I was allowed to do much of my work in tutorials. I would give Fred a sheaf of poems and then meet him at a café off campus called "The Pickwick" to discuss the work. Fred was the best reader of poetry I'd ever encountered. He was deeply learned but carried his erudition lightly. He could be funny and critically sharp. "Big deal," he wrote at the top of one of my poems. But his enthusiasm for good writing was contagious and inspiring. "You got your emeralds from Wallace Stevens, who got them from Mallarmé," he once said. Fred knew poetry in several languages, including French, German, Italian, Latin. I didn't tell him I'd gotten my emeralds from James Wright. Fred's intense concentration on poetry, and his response to my poetry, helped turn me even more toward poetry making and less toward fiction. In the fall of 1967, I began to write the poems that would become my first book, *Zirconia Poems*, published in 1969.

In the meantime, three friends, including the poet William Matthews, began publishing a magazine in Chapel Hill called *Lillabulero*. I began to send Matthews most of the poems I wrote, and he published some in every issue of the magazine. I took a job teaching at Salem College in the fall of 1968. It was while teaching at Salem that I wrote what may be my first mature poem. It was called "Tool Shed":

> The sticky smell of rust breaking out in blisters
> after every wet spell and burning hoeblades, plows,
> crowds the eaves with dryness and wets the lower air.
> Dust is stuck to the greased singletree.
> Wasp nests like gray sunflowers
> hang from tin. The air here hasn't moved
> in thirty years, old snow hovering above ground.
> Pale weeds grow to cracks.
> Half-eaten shovels lean on plows
> caked with forty-year-old mud.
> Dust drifts crossed by snag zags. Broken clevis.
> Plow points are nailed like rusting leaves

to the rafters. Dauber combs dripping plaster.
A bird looks out of its nest in the corner like a dragon
lurking. 1936 license plate,
hames sucked weightless by dry rot.[7]

In the fall of 1970 Matthews arranged for me to give a poetry reading
at Cornell University. I'll never forget arriving on that campus on a dark
November evening, and going down into the basement of Goldwin Smith
Hall, to a coffee shop called *The Temple of Zeus* that was lined with plaster
casts of statues from the temple at Olympus. The reading seemed to go well,
but no one mentioned a job at Cornell. I returned to North Carolina, to
my work as a house painter, but the next May I received a letter from Barry
Adams, chair of the English Department at Cornell, inviting me to teach
for one year at Cornell as a visiting lecturer. It seemed too good to be true.
If I could have chosen any university in the country to teach at, I would
have chosen Cornell, because of its legacy of literature and science, gorges,
and lakes. I quickly wrote a letter accepting the offer. Teaching at Cornell and living in Ithaca were a cultural shock, after the relative isolation of
the mountains of North Carolina. But both colleagues and students were
welcoming. I concentrated on the art of teaching, as I never had before,
inspired by gifted and dedicated students.

At the same time, out of homesickness and nostalgia, I began to check
out books about western North Carolina and southern Appalachia from
Olin Library. I became a student of my native region in a way I never had
been when I lived there. I studied the settlement of the region, the geology
and geography, the Cherokee, the dialects, the flora, and fauna. And I began to write poems about my family, about the ecology of the mountains,
about farming. I'd gone to college in part to escape the hard work of the
farm, but far away in Ithaca I found myself inspired to write about the poetry of work, and the poetry of the soil. I could not stop writing about the
waterfalls, the churches, the seasons, the precarious living hacked out on
the mountainsides by my ancestors, and the many stories told to me by the
fireplace and on the porch. At a distance that world seemed larger than life.
I wrote several poems about the churches I'd grown up in, and about the
conflicts of "Southernness" and "Northernness" in my life, including one
called "Double Springs":

I used to wonder how
two springs could issue from the hill

a yard apart. Why not dig deeper
and unite their flow?

And later realized they
surfaced close from opposite
directions. The southern
sweeter, though the northern's steady

effluence came cold, even in the dry
months when its neighbor
slacked and almost stood, with
algae thickening the edges.

In the church nearby I've heard
sermons on the trinity describe
their separate currents merging to
one branch. The sweet uneven

head rose from the hillside leaning toward
Dark Corner, while the constant
icy thread emerged
from the farm county. In summer

they condemned the slow one and
when I came down to drink before
or after preaching its partner sure
enough ran clear, with ebullition

dimpling the surface above the pores,
and purifying lizards gripped
the sandy floor. But after swilling
there I'd dip the gourd

into the slightly silty left
embellished now with leaves and spiders
and aquatic mosses for a richer sip.
That ungodly taste I'd carry home.[8]

Though the community in which I had grown up was called Green
River, the nearby post office was named Zirconia. The name was given to
the post office in the late nineteenth century when a mineralogist named

William E. Hidden discovered industrial quality zircons on a local mountain. Mr. Hidden was an associate of Thomas A. Edison, and Edison had found that zirconium silicate could be used in the filaments of light bulbs. At that time Edison had a contract to light Philadelphia. When it was announced that Edison would be paying for zircons, there was a rush to find the stones. Local folks dug holes all over their woods and pastures looking for zircons. When I was a kid, I played in the pits dug in the hillsides and mountainsides by my great-uncles hoping to make their fortunes.

But the only zircons found were in the vein that ran through a mountain discovered by Hidden. Two different parties claimed the mineral rights to the mountain. They sued each other and began digging into the vein at either end of the mountain. And they sold several hundred pounds of stones to Edison. But just as their lawsuit was coming to trial, Edison discovered tungsten for his filaments, and no longer needed the North Carolina zircons. The lawsuit was moot. The antagonists became friends.

When I began writing poetry, I tried every subject that came to mind. The word "zircon" itself seemed especially poetic. The sound, the novelty of the letter "z" made it seem perfect for treatment in poetry. In the dictionary it said the name zircon came through Arabic from Persian. It was both a local and exotic word. Around 1966 I wrote a short poem called "Zirconia":

> Blue as mildew mountains break beyond the town
> and shadows swim the valley.
> Now filled with leaves the zircon mines
> bleed dirt into the lake.
> Further up, the millpond is a brain of mud
> and high in the bones of a chestnut
> crows watch the town
> until the moon lights
> the country like a TV screen.[9]

One can see and hear that I was just beginning to learn something about poetry, about fresh diction, and image. I wanted to show how the place looked, evoke the atmosphere. The mountains the color of mildew break like waves on a shore. Dirt from the zircon pits bleeds into the lake. Farther up the valley silt filling a pond is wrinkled like a brain. Dead chestnuts, killed by the blight of 1924, stand on the ridges. And I compared the moonlight to the glare of a TV screen, connecting, as I thought, past and present.

Later, as I wrote more and learned more, I returned to the theme of zircons from time to time, incorporating descriptive metaphor into narrative, into history. After I came to Cornell in 1971 and really began to discover the history of the place I had left, I continued to mine my memory for raw subjects I could refine into poetry. I returned to the theme of the Zircon Rush of the late nineteenth century. But now I addressed the subject from the perspective of personal narrative in a poem of the late 1970s called "Zircon Pit":

Just below the crest of Meeting House Hill
I used to climb the apron of soil
into a digging long abandoned. Leaves
and saplings hid the raw dirt and the hole,
half-filled in fall, fit like a nest
from which to drowse and look
down on the steepness and keep watch
on my century. One of the high places.
I spent hours there in late winter,
warmed by leaves and the solartrap, just
out of the summit winds compressing
across the rim. Caught the best sun, the new light
of February when the mountains
pressed clean by snow began to twitch
and trickle. From that blind
I watched the mailman on the creekroad
hours before he reached our box.
The only gem found where Great-Grandpa dug
was the many-facet thrill and vantage of remoteness.
Sometimes the whole forest seemed to river
up and over my lookout and burn
vivid, then drain into the present.
I listened close to the new sky.[10]

Notice how much more conversational this poem is than the earlier "Zirconia." The poem is autobiographical, not so impersonal in voice and point of view. It is a much more intimate poem, connecting the speaker with the reader or listener. The similes are more implicit than explicit.

Besides history and poetry, I have always been interested in science, including astronomy. In college I first studied mathematics and aerospace engineering. My latest attempt to write about the zircons in my native mountains was inspired by an article in *Scientific American* describing zircons as among the oldest minerals on our planet, a souvenir from the stellar furnace from which our world was baked, and an index of the age of the galaxy. With students I like to talk about the "reach" of a poem. In this example, I was excited by the reach associated with zircons, from the origins of the cosmos to the familiar dirt under my feet: "Zircon":

> When my great-uncles dug for zircons on
> the mountainside and on the pasture hill
> a hundred years ago they'd no idea
> the little crystal bit they sought would be
> a token from the planet's fiery birth.
> For zircons are almost as old as earth's
> creation in the conflagration from
> debris that formed the galaxies of suns.
> This tiny stone found in the family dirt's
> a kind of clock they say, a register
> of time from the beginning since it traps
> uranium and other elements
> decaying at a steady measured rate.
> The zircon lasts when mother rocks around
> have crumbled, worn away to sand. It keeps
> the fingerprints of isotopes from clouds
> of the original primordial dust,
> right here where spiders hide in rotting duff.[11]

It has been a surprise to me to discover that the more specific to a place, the more precisely local a poem or story is, the more accessible it is to others. Exact detail, well-chosen human struggle, and deep emotion are understandable to any literate reader, any listener. In that sense, all writing is local. As I have continued writing, I have discovered that in some important way Green River, Zirconia, is everywhere.

NOTES

1. Robert Morgan, "Squirrel. Shadow." *Land Diving*. Baton Rouge: Louisiana State University Press, 1976. 42.

2. Walt Whitman, "Song of Myself." *Poetry and Prose*. ed. Justin Kaplan. New York: Library of America, 1982. 188.

3. Henry Wadsworth Longfellow, "My Lost Youth." *Poems and Other Writings*. New York: Library of America, 2000. 337–339.

4. Carl Sandburg, "Wind Song." *Complete Poems of Carl Sandburg*. New York: Harcourt, Brace, 1950. 217–218.

5. Wallace Stevens, "Domination of Black." *The Collected Poems of Wallace Stevens*. 1954. New York: Vintage, 2011. 9.

6. Longfellow, *Poems. The Song of Hiawatha*. 144.

7. Robert Morgan. *Red Owl*. New York: W.W. Norton, 1972. 36.

8. Morgan, *Land Diving*. 5.

9. Robert Morgan. *Zirconia Poems*. Northwood Narrows, NH: Lillabulero Press, Limited, 1969. 33.

10. Robert Morgan. *Groundwork*. Frankfort, KY: Gnomon Press, 1979. 49.

11. Robert Morgan. *Dark Energy*. New York: Penguin, 2015. 72.

NATURE IS A STRANGER YET

What mystery pervades a well!
That water lives so far—
A neighbor from another world
Residing in a jar

Whose limit none have ever seen,
But just his lid of glass—
Like looking every time you please
In an abyss's face!

The grass does not appear afraid,
I often wonder he
Can stand so close and look so bold
At what is awe to me . . .

But nature is a stranger yet;
And those that cite her most
Have never passed her haunted house,
Nor simplified her ghost.

To pity those that know her not
Is helped by the regret
That those who know her, know her less
The nearer her they get.

—Emily Dickinson, Poem 1400[1]

My earliest memory, I think, is waking up on my father's shoulder as he carried me home from a prayer meeting where I'd fallen asleep. I must have been about eighteen months old. We were walking through the dewy pasture lit by starlight. My mother and sister were stepping through the dark beside us. The motion of my father's stride made the stars above rock and swim. Far out in the mountains, away from any streetlights, the stars were so bright they appeared close enough to touch. They washed back and forth and seemed to whisper, whirling around my head like fireflies. I may have fallen asleep again and dreamed the stars were speaking to me. But my memory is of being out of the hot church, and floating between the close, confiding stars and the glistening grass.

"The great book of nature is written in mathematical language," said Galileo.[2]

"An artist makes his region universal," said William Eastlake.[3] I have been described as a Southern writer, and though I am proud to be associated with the South and the southern Appalachians and Blue Ridge Mountains, the real focus of my poetry and much of my fiction has been on one particular place, not even a county, just a community, part of the Green River valley in western North Carolina. And really not even the whole community, but about a square mile of land on the banks of Green River bought by my great-great-grandfather Daniel Pace in 1840.

My connection with this piece of earth where I lived the first sixteen years of my life is so close that, in a way, I have never left it. As a child I ran in its pastures, fished in its streams, explored its thickets and gullies, sweated in its fields, climbed the trees and ridges, rolled rocks off the mountaintops, gathered its chinquapins and blackberries. I was terrified by the rattlesnakes and black widow spiders, by flash floods and lightning storms. In the almost forty years since I left, I have continued to live there in the imagination, in the geography and landscape of language, the geometry of poetry.

I was raised among storytellers. My dad's formal education had stopped at the sixth grade, but he was a great reader and gifted talker and storyteller. My grandfather was a tireless teller of tales who had attended school only a few months in the 1880s, though he also had done a good deal of reading on his own. In the summer evenings, before television, we often sat on the porch after supper. As crickets sparked their notes in the grass, and later katydids set up their mating roar in the woods beyond the yard, my grandpa told ghost stories, stories of panthers that climbed down chimneys, of giant rattlesnakes that got into attics, stories of people who died a long time ago. There were stories of children marked in the womb because the mother had stared into the eyes of a snake or mad dog. As darkness gradually enveloped us, we children listened in thrall as my grandpa told us about Cold Friday when the world was frozen and the sun never came up, about the Confederate times when children left alone in remote cabins were robbed and tortured by bushwhackers, about the skeleton of a bride who had disappeared on her wedding night, found in a trunk in the attic eighty years later. One

of his scariest and most memorable stories, showing nature's revenge on
human meddling, I later made into the poem "Mountain Bride":

> They say Revis found a flatrock
> on the ridge just
> perfect for a natural hearth
> and built his cabin with a stick
>
> and clay chimney right over it.
> On their wedding night he lit
> the fireplace to dry away the mountain
> chill of late spring, and flung on
>
> applewood to dye
> the room with molten color while
> he and Martha that was a Parrish
> warmed the sheets between the tick
>
> stuffed with leaves and its feather
> cover. Under that wide hearth
> a nest of rattlers,
> they'll knot a hundred together,
>
> had wintered and were coming awake.
> The warming rock
> Flushed them out early.
> It was she
>
> Who wakened to their singing near
> the embers and roused him to go look.
> Before he reached the fire
> more than a dozen struck
>
> and he died yelling her to stay
> on the big four-poster.
> Her uncle coming up the hollow
> with a gift bearham two days later
>
> found her shivering there
> marooned above a pool
> of hungry snakes,
> and the body beginning to swell.[4]

I was taught to read by my mother before I attended school, and around the age of twelve I became addicted to reading adventure stories. I sat in my room without a lamp on rainy days gorging my imagination on Laura Ingalls Wilder's *Farmer Boy* and the Hardy Boys, whatever I could lay my hands on from the bookshelf at the elementary school or borrow from friends. A transformation in my life occurred when Henderson County began sending a bookmobile to the parking lot of Green River Baptist Church the first Monday afternoon of every month. It was an old utility repair truck outfitted with bookshelves. I had never seen so many books. I quickly searched out the westerns of Zane Grey and the Royal Canadian Mounted Police stories of James Oliver Curwood. It was the latter I fell most in love with. For months I dogsledded and snowshoed and canoed and galloped my way through the Yukon and Klondike and Northwest Territories, to Native American camps and trapper cabins. I lived and dreamed under fantasias of northern lights and midnight sun. I discovered the arctic stories of Jack London and paddled and panned and hunted my way through the northern wilderness propelled by London's vigorous prose.

I loved to read the Arctic adventure stories so much that I took the books to school and read them in class, inside a textbook. Once my sixth-grade teacher, Mr. Ward, walking around the class as he lectured, lifted the book out of my hands and laid it on the shelf without pausing in his lesson. He was onto my game, but not entirely disapproving. I did my first writing for this same teacher. The class was taking a day off in spring to visit the Biltmore House near Asheville. George Vanderbilt's improbable chateau was and is a favorite tourist attraction in western North Carolina. The trip cost three dollars, which I did not have.

Rather than let me sit idle in the classroom all day while the other students were gone, Mr. Ward suggested I write a story. Knowing how my tastes ran, he gave me a plot: a man is lost in the Canadian Rockies without a gun or even a knife. How does he find his way back to civilization? I sat at the desk with loose sheets of paper and a pencil in front of me for an hour, puzzled about how to begin a story. Finally, I thought it might be done with *details,* details about the landscape and weather, the trees and streams. As I began putting down the details the story started to unfold. The hero has no knife, so he must sharpen a stick by rubbing it on a rock. He has no matches, so he starts a fire by rubbing dry sticks together, and he hardens the point of his spear by holding it over the flames. He improvises a fishhook by fitting a worm on a thorn. I found that the life of the story was in the details, in the description of his efforts to catch fish and small animals, as he navigates by following streams and the North Star. I got so involved in the details of his escape from the wilderness that I lost track of time and was surprised when the other students returned from their excursion.

From the very beginning I connected wilderness and writing. One of the most exciting things about writing was that it enabled me to see the wilderness better, to create wildernesses I could never otherwise know, to live on the frontier. Text and wilderness mirrored each other and informed each other. The wilderness was a poem, and poems had the mystery and splendor and perhaps the danger of the wilderness.

As I got into my teens I read and read and thought about writing. I took piano lessons and studied music theory and harmony on my own. I listened to the New York Philharmonic on the AM radio on Saturday nights, and fell under the spell of Baroque music, especially Bach and Handel. Before that, from infancy, I had been exposed to hymn and ballad singing. I grew up among people who could sing shaped notes and old mountain ballads. My grandpa had been a banjo picker before he got married and joined the church. One of my great-great-grandpas had been the most famous fiddle player in upper South Carolina in the 1850s and 60s. Before I could read, before I had ever studied music, I heard music in my head much of the time. When I looked at a mountain, or at a tree in the wind, or at the sun on tall grass, I heard a musical equivalent to the scene in my head. As best I can remember, it was music made up of snatches of things heard on the radio and in church. I could play the music in my mind for hours. There was a musical correlative to everything I saw or thought about, a melodic accompaniment, a harmonic enhancement, to every mood or image. I looked at the clouds and heard the sweep of music. I thought of old, sad stories and heard music. As I grew older, I lost that ability to compose mentally and spontaneously. But in my teens, I became convinced that I wanted to compose music.

As I looked across the Green River valley at the Cicero Mountain looming dark lavender in winter and tipped with ice on its cliff, I knew I wanted to compose a poem or piece of music as grand as the mountain. It would be an epic, or something like an oratorio, or fantasia and fugue for organ. I heard vast deep chords like engines and heavy machinery inside the earth, and crisp notes sparkling in the high registers as though from beyond the Milky Way. My composition would be heroic, and it would be in the measure and wavelength of the mountain.

Though I had memorized poems in elementary school, Poe's "The Raven," Wordsworth's "I Wandered Lonely as a Cloud," Lanier's "The Marshes of Glyn," Bryant's "Thanatopsis," Holmes's "Old Ironsides," and parts of Longfellow's "Hiawatha," I had never read poetry on my own until my sister returned from her freshman year at Bob Jones University with the anthology used in her English class, Cleanth Brooks's textbook of American literature. I pored through it from cover to cover and came across the beginning of Walt Whitman's "Song of Myself." Never had I encountered anything like Whitman's lines. I would have thought it was illegal to talk that way. The long flowing verses, the sense of freedom and exuberance, the wildness, were exhilarating. I read and re-read the lines, and soon knew many by heart:

> I celebrate myself, and sing myself,
> And what I assume you shall assume,
> For every atom belonging to me as good belongs to you.
>
> I loafe and invite my soul,
> I lean and loaf at my ease observing a spear of summer grass.[5]

Reading Whitman, I saw possibilities in language and life I had not thought of before. As I continued to browse through the textbook, I discovered dozens of other poets and poems also. But the one that made the deepest impression was Wallace Stevens' poem "Domination of Black." Looking out a window, the speaker sees the planets gathering "[l]ike the leaves themselves / Turning in the wind," and how night "[c]ame striding like the color of the heavy hemlocks."[6] The repetitions and music of the poem thrilled me. The synesthesia of cry and color, the onomatopoeia of the rhymes, the connection between the close-up fire and the faraway motion of the planets were an epiphany. But it was the weirdness, the wonder of the sense of doom in the poem that moved me most. Here was a poet who understood how fearful nature was, how threatening and mysterious its signs and sounds. Here was a poet who understood the cruelty of experience, the ambiguity of omens, the sadness of pleasure, the strangeness of the familiar. The poem haunted me then as it haunts me still.

Paradoxically, the more we study a place, the longer we know a place, the more mysterious it becomes. The more we respond to experience, the more we discover there is to respond to. When I began writing in my late teens, like everyone else I had no idea what I wanted to write about. My favorite writer was Tolstoy, but his subjects were the Napoleonic wars and high society in Tsarist Moscow. By comparison I had no subject at all. I knew a little about history, but nothing at all about high society, except what I had read. Besides the small farm in the Blue Ridge Mountains, my only home had been the university campus. And I had spent more time thinking about how to escape the small farm than going back to it. I wanted to be a writer the way Baudelaire was a writer in Paris or Pasternak in Moscow.

Imagine my surprise as I began to write story after story and poem after poem, at engineering school at North Carolina State, to find myself returning again and again to the work of a small mountain farm, to the intimate landscape along Green River, to the church where I had attended Pentecostal services. Had I escaped those things only to return to them in my imagination? To live there again through language?

I found that I did not choose subjects: they chose me. And for the next fifteen years I wrote hundreds of poems and dozens of stories in which I tried to communicate the mystery and fear, the terror and resentment, the harshness and futility, the contradictions and cruelties, as well as the loyalties and kinships and beauties, of the world I had grown up in. I was never interested in portraying a pastoral world, a simpler world, but in dramatizing the complexities of the seemingly plain: the sharpness of the everyday, the cruelties of the conventional, the isolation of the rural. I wanted to show the thresholds of the theatrical in the ordinary. One of my earlier published poems was "Cellar":

> The air moves as if something just left.
> Snake breath.
> Cool razors circulate
> touching the skin with wet silk.
> Breathing clear cheese.
> Mold flowers grow like plastered snowballs
> on the walls, rust-lacquered pipes.
> The heads of translucent shoots crawl out of the potato bin
> and run like wires to the window.
> Once cut straight and firm
> the walls have dripped and rotted to black jelly.
> Jam grows blue fur.
> The light bulb flickers as if circled by moths

fanning its coolness
and lighting on my neck.
Walls sweating mercury, straining
to the weight.[7]

As I continued to write, I found myself returning again and again to the poetry and poetics of work. I who had longed to escape the hard labor of pole-bean farming and pulp wood cutting, of house painting and carpentry and masonry, explored and relived those efforts again and again in language. I fell in love with work through words. I looked again and again at the details and discipline of work, at the drama of digging and hoeing, sawing and chopping, I had performed as a boy. The catharsis of work in the hot Southern sun, became the central experience in much of my writing. I came to see that work was a purifying ritual, and the baptism of sweat a sacrament in the quest for meaning. The meaning of life on the small farm was its hard work. The most significant gift of labor was the ritual of labor itself.

From the time I was very young, I was fascinated by the presence of the Native Americans in and on the ground where I lived and worked. Arrowheads and pieces of pottery turned up in the fields where we plowed and hoed. A flood washing away sandy loam by the river exposed the charred sticks of an ancient campfire. The river and waterfalls and ridges had had Cherokee names. And before the Cherokee, the Catawbas had been there. And before the Catawbas, and other Woodland tribes. A scree of chipped quartz on the mountainside above the river showed where there had once been an arrowhead workshop. Graves on the pasture hill were said to be Native American graves. The knowledge of herbs passed down from the first settlers was known to come from medicine men: snakeroot and tincture of lobelia for rattlesnake bite, foxglove for the heart, ginseng for old age, pennyroyal tea for fevers. And for my father and Uncle William, the treasure of the wilderness was not the metals and gemstones that could be dug there, but the fur of mink and muskrat, fox, and raccoon, as the Native Americans had taught the first settlers. This is my poem called "Visitors":

The ground is haunted by the Cherokees.
Ashes, teeth of arrows, pottery
work up in the Old Fields. Digging
for ginseng I'm afraid of cutting
a rotted hand. Half the boulders seem

scratched with messages. Over the rim
of the Craggies clouds lift signals.
In company with word and star all
weeds are medicine. The rivers
have names they repeat forever
just out of hearing. A doe
shows her thigh through the shadows.
The names Saluda, Oklawaha run
a secret stairway of the spine.
What one deity shall we
raise to speak to their powerful many.[8]

Many of the things I have written contain images of the land as text. More like Emerson or Whitman than I realized at first, I have often seen nature itself as language, and the land as a text written on by runoff and wind, by floods, and by time. And I have been intrigued by the way people inscribe their ambitions and greed, their dreams and pretensions on the landscape. But just as mysterious are the ways we interpret the signs and signatures of nature. It is the essence of the human to see the accidental and incidental, the arbitrary and coincidental, as a correspondence, as message. When we read nature, we often over-read. We do not want to think anything is merely what it is. Everything may be taken as a sign. Everything is speaking to us. In the world where I grew up people often talked of the "Writing Spider":

When Uncle Wass had found the spider's
W woven between the limbs
of a dead chestnut over on
the Squirrel Hill, he said he knew
there would be war. But even before
Pearl Harbor he was gone himself
and my Grandpa, his brother, told
how the writing spider's runes could spell
a message to the world, or warn
of the individual reader's own
end with an initial. That web
was strung significant as lines
in a palm and the little webster,
spinning out its monogram like

the fates, put the whole dictionary
of a life in one elaborate
letter to be abstracted from
the Jacob's ladder of floss and dew
in the eye of the beholder,
a lifetime's work for it and all.[9]

When I moved to Cornell in 1971 it did not occur to me that I was moving from the southern tip of Appalachia to the northern tip. I knew I was coming to the university of Hans Bethe and William Strunk, Vladimir Nabokov and Baxter Hathaway. If I could have chosen any university in the world, Cornell would probably have been my first choice. Because of its outstanding agricultural school, its renowned physics and chemistry and engineering programs, its combination of state university and Ivy League intellectual tradition, Cornell seemed the ideal community to join: a stimulating cultural environment in a rural landscape.

When I began gardening in Tompkins County, I discovered a soil new to me, a soil with little sand or loam, clayey and hard when it dried, and infested with rocks that appeared, were carried away, and reappeared the next year. I discovered the ground was haunted by the Cayugas, by the Iroquois, and the lake was haunted by the boom and echo of General Sullivan's drummer boy. I found farming a greater challenge than I had ever dreamed it could be, in a short, cool growing season, under a low northern sun, where the raccoons made free with the sweet corn, the deer ate the peas, and groundhogs feasted on lettuce just before it was ready to gather.

It was in my first year at Cornell that I discovered Emerson. I had been circling Emerson for years, reading Thoreau and Whitman and Dickinson. It was as though the landscape of Upstate New York, and the climate, not unlike New England, demanded the white heat of Emerson's prose and poetry to temper its coolness and hardness. Reading Emerson at Cornell was like breathing pure oxygen. I was intoxicated in my first years here by the New Testament rhetoric, by the scientific imagery, by the Neoplatonic metaphors, by the love of the natural world in his sentences. Every sentence was a work of art in-itself.

In "Nature," Emerson writes: "Have mountains, and waves, and skies, no significance but what we consciously give them when we employ them as emblems of our thoughts? The world is emblematic. Parts of speech are metaphors, because the whole of nature is a metaphor of the human mind.

The laws of moral nature answer those of matter as face to face in a glass.
The visible world and the relation of its parts is a dial plate of the invisible."[10] In "Self-Reliance," Emerson tells us "Prayer is the contemplation of
the facts of life from the highest point of view. It is the soliloquy of a beholding and jubilant soul."[11] And in "The Poet," he declares "The people
fancy they hate poetry, and they are all poets and mystics! . . . there is no
fact in nature which does not carry the whole sense of nature. . . . Every
word was once a poem. Every new relation is a new word."[12]

In the early 1970s I got one further idea about mind and nature from
reading Emerson's twentieth century heir, Robert Frost. I'm sure many
readers think of Frost as a pastoral poet, and so he is in some instances. And
he is certainly our most accomplished and memorable poet of the century.
But he is very much the poet of relativism, of pragmatism, of pluralism,
and even skepticism and rebellion. And sometimes he is almost the poet
of anti-nature, or of nature against itself, what he prefers to call contraries.
In the poem "West-Running Brook" Frost has the couple observing the
stream spot a white wave that appears to reach back upstream, against the
flow: ". . . see how the brook / In that white wave runs counter to itself," the
man named Fred says. "It is from that in water we were from / Long, long
before we were from any creature."[13]

It was almost two years after coming to Cornell before I really began to
write poems again. The shock of living out of the South for the first time, of
teaching full-time, of leaving the isolation of the mountains for a community where everyone I knew was a writer or literary scholar, took my voice
away. If everybody else was writing poetry, there was no need for me to add
to the surplus. When I did begin to write again, it was in a new voice, more
conversational, more narrative, more formal, sometimes even discursive.
And oddly enough, I discovered that I still wanted to write about the Blue
Ridge Mountains of North Carolina. I expected to write about Cornell,
about my life in the Finger Lakes, about English Departments, but kept
postponing those projects until I had done more preliminary work about
the farm where I had grown up, about erosion and the geology of the mountains, about family stories and ghost stories. The more I walked among the
red pines and battlement-like gorges of Treman Park, in awe of the drama of
that landscape, the more I wrote about Green River, about the speech of the
Southern highlands. Cornell gave me a perspective from which to see and
explore the world I had left. The more I resolved to write about the North,
the more I could only write about the South. And the more I wrote about

family history and folklore, the more I discovered there was yet to write. The more I resisted those subjects, the more they claimed and possessed me. The poetry of the Blue Ridge stuck to me like an infection that I could not shake off. I could only cool my fever by writing more.

But suddenly in the late 1970s, I discovered that I could write about the landscape of Upstate New York. Maybe I had lived there long enough for the place to enter my blood and my dreams. One of the first Upstate poems was "Yellow":

> May is the yellow month. At this
> latitude the woods are a fog of different
> yellow-greens as first leaves
> open pages and new twigs on the willows
> grow bright as chicken fat.
> In every yard the daffodils and dandelions,
> and clouds of wild mustard light
> the open fields, even as wind
> bruises cowlicks in the rye. Along
> highways and parks forsythia
> sprays its heat, and fire rinses seedbeds
> in a golden antiquity, flushing
> the ridges so they echo inside the room
> where flesh stretches into flower, where
> even the interior of night is saffroned
> the most erotic color of touch and know.[14]

For the first ten years I lived in Tompkins County and walked the trails and fields here, I wanted to write about the splendors of the purple asters that appear in such profusion in the autumn. Their colors are so intense, majestic; it is a privilege to be out among the asters and goldenrods and drying weeds under a hard autumn sky. Finally, in the late 1970s I wrote this poem called "Purple Asters":

> In the months of lavender, late summer
> and early fall, you notice the first purple
> puffs on thistles, and out along
> the creek and high banks of weeds the joe-pyes
> lean like giraffes above the undergrowth
> into tree level. Down by the branch, grass

darkens the same color Charlemagne had
his Irish scholars dye their pages for
jeweled lettering to play on like cities
in the desert sky. A purple butterfly
rolls its dice from chicory to burdock
to morning glory. And in the aging fields
ironweed opens bright fur to nectar moths.
Almost hidden at the edge of upland swamps,
lobelia and foxglove shake their sexual
pockets around bees. So much royalty
and ripeness! Foxgrapes fume the river woods,
and summer clots its ink in pokeberries
in the kingly time of sunsets and honey
trees and goldenrod. But all charge and color
are concentrated in this northern flower
the shade of the underworld and deep space
where stars begin, where the violent
and ultraviolet become seen dark.[15]

As I turned more to fiction writing in the late 1980s, and wrote less poetry, the spark and life of poetry became more mysterious, and the intense
experience of the natural world I had felt when young more elusive. As I
grew obsessed with voices, with accents, with lives and relationships, with
narrative and characterization, the natural world lost none of its power
over me. If anything, it gained drama and evocativeness. And seemed less
and less renderable in language. In the novel *The Truest Pleasure* the character Ginny walks down by the river and looks at the water:

The day I fell in love with the shoals I was standing with my feet in
water below the big rock. It was like the water was talking, quoting
scripture or muttering a poem. The river pulled at my feet heavy
and powerful. The surface appeared to sort and resort a puzzle,
scattering the pieces and gathering them again.

But I was looking at the tall hemlocks pointing straight up on
the side of the mountain. I looked through the tops of the lower
trees toward the pines further up, right to those on top of the
ridge. And then I saw a cloud moving. It was just a little cloud in
the clear sky, but white as snow. And it was like I was standing and
looking right up the ladder of trees into heaven.[16]

After more than a quarter of a century of trying to fit language to land-scape, and trying to fit word to thing, and to discover the natural world through language, I was as mystified as I had been starting out. The natural world in all its multiplicity eluded me. I had failed to seize and fix its evolutions and processes in the crystal of lines. As I turned more to storytelling, I was proud of my attempts to be intimate with loam and puddles, flowers and clouds, but saw how far short I had fallen from my original intentions. I had looked into the well and seen the splash of a pebble shatter my reflection, but I had not been able to see what was under the water. I knew there were veins and secret passages, shelves of rock and metal ores and lairs of great animals and serpents beyond, which I had not touched. And I had not written a poem as grand as the Cicero Mountain.

But the recognition of my failure was a gift. I came to see my previous work had only been a preparation. The more I studied my earlier writing the more hopeful I became. Far from being finished, my work had hardly begun. The real work remained to be done.

> But nature is a stranger yet;
> And those who cite her most
> Have never passed her haunted house
> Nor simplified her ghost.
>
> To pity those who know her not
> Is helped by the regret
> That those who know her, know her less
> The nearer her they get.

NOTES

1. Emily Dickinson, "Poem 1400." *The Complete Poems of Emily Dickinson.* ed. Thomas H. Johnson. 1890. Boston: Little, Brown and Company, 1952. 599–600.

2. Galileo Galilei, quoted in David Herbert Donald. *Look Homeward: A Life of Thomas Wolfe.* Boston: Little, Brown, 1987. 34.

3. William Eastlake. "Sense of Place." *South Dakota Review.* Volume 36, Number 1 (Spring) 1998. 144.

4. Robert Morgan, *Groundwork.* 8–9.

5. Walt Whitman. *Poetry and Prose.* 188.

6. Stevens, *Collected.* 9.

7. Morgan, *Red Owl.* 4.

8. Robert Morgan. *At the Edge of the Orchard Country*. 1987. Winston-Salem: Press 53, 2014. 62.

9. Robert Morgan. *Sigodlin*. 1990. Winston-Salem, NC: Press 53, 2014. 49.

10. Ralph Waldo Emerson. *Essays & Lectures*. ed. Joel Porte. New York: Library of America, 1983. 24.

11. Emerson, *Essays & Lectures*. 275–76.

12. Emerson, *Essays & Lectures*. 454–55.

13. Robert Frost. *Collected Poems, Prose, & Plays*. eds. Richard Poirier and Mark Richardson. New York: Library of America, 1995. 236–38.

14. Morgan, *At the Edge of the Orchard Country*. 20.

15. Morgan, *Sigodlin*. 5.

16. Robert Morgan. *The Truest Pleasure*. Chapel Hill: Algonquin Books, 1996. 125.

WORK AND POETRY

THE FATHER TONGUE

A few years ago, a critic pointed out, in *Poetry*, that more of my poems are about male characters than about women. I remember being surprised because at that time I was writing a series of prose stories often narrated by women characters and primarily concerned with women's lives. I looked back at my books of poetry and saw that sure enough, while I had written several poems about my grandmothers and great-grandmothers, the preponderance of poems about people concentrated on men, and stories of men. And the majority of the better poems were concerned either directly or indirectly with my father.

After Daddy died in June of 1991 at the age of eighty-six, I began to think of writing a prose memoir about him. This took me back to the poems I had written in the 1970s and 1980s, especially "Mowing," "The Gift of Tongues," "Sunday Toilet," and "When He Spoke Out of the Dark." I saw that I had already caught the essence of what I had to say about him in verse. What was left to be described in prose were the details of his long life on a farm in the Blue Ridge Mountains, the frustrations and failures, the descriptions of his manners and speech, his clothes and habits. What was large and most memorable about him I had already gotten down either explicitly or implicitly in the poems.

The more I made notes and wrote drafts for a memoir, the more clearly I saw how different the persona of a prose portrait would be from that evoked in the poems. A literal telling of the circumstances of his life could easily be misleading, for I would keep circling back to the frustrations and conflicts of his personality, his attempts to escape the farm and mountains, his energies and curiosities thwarted by failure of nerve, bad luck, lack of opportunity. But in the poems, because they isolated certain moments and magnified important traits, the effect was not only truer but heroic and elegiac.

As I reviewed the poems I had written about Daddy, I had a new respect for the power of poetry to reveal. It is in the very nature of poetry to seize on the large and celebratory, the elegiac and symbolic. The dignity of poetry enabled me to speak and see far better than I could in the prose memoir. The figure in the poems was larger than the actual and yet more accurate. The very elevation of poetry helped me get to the heart of the character.

Daddy was a person of contradictions and extremes without much middle ground. He lived in terms of all or nothing. It was as though he had been born without the ability to shade or blend the different aspects of himself. He rushed from one pole to the other, with little pause or diverting complication. When he was feeling good, he had a relish and enthusiasm that were astonishing. Each person, each fact, each book kindled his attention. He seemed thrilled by the world in all its difficulty, variety, and surprise.

But when he was frustrated or disappointed, he kept to himself. In general, he preferred to work alone and daydream without interruption. When he was broke, or worried about church quarrels, he stayed away from the house, and from the rest of us, for most of the day. In summer he would be out working for hours before the others got up. Sometimes I could hear the swoosh of his scythe in the big weeds along the road as I woke.

In fact, mowing was the work he preferred to all other. Scything weeds along the road bank and around the barn and outbuildings seemed both a pleasure and an obsession with him. Frustrated by his farming, and by the fussing in the church, and by the disapproval of his relatives, he sought the control and order of mowing. From spring until late autumn, he mowed continually, every chance he got. In the years I knew him Daddy must have worn out twenty scythe blades. By the time he was an old man scythes were no longer easy to buy, and those he did find were forged in Austria or Czechoslovakia. The new blades were wide and thin as razors. He carried a whetrock in his hip pocket and sharpened the blade every half hour or so.

Since he was a boy he had mowed the family graveyard and the churchyard, as well as the banks of the dirt road. It was a community service he performed year after year, though I don't think anybody ever thanked him for it. It was work he did for love of the community, and for love of the work itself. I was mystified by his persistent mowing. It seemed a waste of time, and the more broke he was the more effort he gave to the unpaid labor. One of the poems I wrote about Daddy was "Mowing":

> A summer-long ritual for my father.
> Half-dancing and half-rowing into the weedbank,
> he gripped the handles of the snath

and swung, beginning high and back, and followed
through, running the blade true
to the ground and then up to winnow
away the cut ends. Snakes and fieldmice
and my mother's flowers got beheaded
in his rage to mow, and pokeweeds, briars
around the pasture, were subdued to his measure.
He even cut the shoulders of the public road,
exposing beer cans and bags of trash,
and once each season cleaned off the church yard
and cemetery acre. Mowing met his first requirements:
solitude and no monetary gain. As he swung
he must have seen the heads of neighbors,
deacons, wife and son, topple,
and the stubble bleed, for their intrusion
on his long reverie. That blade,
a wide wing of metal, tempered in Czechoslovakia,
soared around and back, making its deadly time
regular as a pendulum, touching its flame
with a hiss to the green stampede.
But there was no end, except frost, to the siege
of tender growth. Suddenly he'd stop
and, holding the scythe upright, take the stone
from his hip pocket and whet the blade brilliant,
spit on his hands, and return to the lone war.
I see him there now, wading in rampant vines,
turning quick as a matador in overalls and wrecked hat,
reaching back with his instrument to let
the next wave of summer plunge past and wilt.[1]

Only as an adult did I begin to understand the satisfaction he took in felling the big weeds around the barn and hog pen. By midsummer those vegetables were rampant and bush-sized. They seemed to radiate heat in the middle of the day. He cut them down and exposed the ground. He made the field margins and back areas look trim as a Flat Rock estate. Through mowing he kept some control over the property and turned all his land into a kind of garden.

Daddy was by instinct and inclination a gardener. He was happiest when working for the pleasure of the work. If money was involved, things got crossed and awkward for him. He avoided the subject of money, and when he had any he spent it quickly. He did not want the responsibility of cash, and he never had a bank account as long as I knew him. I believe money made him feel guilty, as though he was touching something tainted. It was as though he belonged to an earlier, frontier world where people helped each other and shared whatever they raised or traded by barter. The more broke he was, the more he needed cash, the less able he was to think about ways of getting it. If payments were due, or if there were groceries to be bought, he would disappear from the house in the early morning and stay away until after dark. A pressing need of money confused and disoriented him. Only after my mother had gone back to the cotton mill, or taken another job as a salesclerk, would we see much of him again. He had no desire to shirk responsibilities or work. He was anything but lazy. The need for money simply dazed him. There were demons he never learned to face, and the need for money was one of them.

There were other tasks Daddy liked that were no more remunerative than mowing. After a heavy rain he took his shovel and opened clogged culverts along the county road. Before the rain had completely stopped, he would be out draining puddles and filling in places where the gravel had washed away. He shoveled and raked the roadbed until it was smooth again. He could not stand to see trapped or stagnant water. He opened pools of standing water around the barn with his pitchfork.

Not only did Daddy solace himself through digging and mowing; in work he found an asylum from family and the modern world. It was the solitude of work he sought. He mesmerized himself through the rhythm of mowing or hoeing, chopping or raking. Through work he reached a contemplative plane of his own creation. Sometimes he worked on his own until long after dark. He preferred to be outside on rainy days because no one else was about and he had the countryside to himself. The most recent poem I have written about Daddy is "Working in the Rain":

> My father loved more than anything to
> work outside in wet weather. Beginning
> at daylight he'd go out in dripping brush
> to mow or pull weeds for hog and chickens.
> First his shoulders got damp and the drops from
> his hat ran down his back. When even his

armpits were soaked he came in to dry out
by the fire, make coffee, read a little.
But if the rain continued he'd soon be
restless, and go out to sharpen tools in
the shed or carry wood in from the pile,
then open up a puddle to the drain,
working by steps back into the downpour.
I think he sought the privacy of rain,
the one time no one was likely to be
out and he was left to the intimacy
of drops touching every leaf and tree in
the woods and the easy muttering of
drip and runoff, the shine of pools behind
grass dams. He could not resist the long
ritual, the companionship and freedom
of falling weather, or even the cold
drenching, the heavy soak and chill of clothes
and sobbing of fingers and sacrifice
of shoes that earned a baking by the fire
and washed fatigue after the wandering
and loneliness in the country of rain.[2]

Among the things that frustrated Daddy most were the quarrels at church. There had been a feud at Green River Baptist Church, going all the way back to Confederate times, between the Old Regular Baptists and the Missionary Baptists. The Old Regulars, or the Hardshells, believed it a sin to have musical instruments in church. They also believed in predestination and thought it futile to try to win converts among the lost. The Missionary Baptists understood their primary mission was to save souls, and they considered music and musical instruments an important asset of their ministry. The argument became a kind of family quarrel, passed down through the generations, and each faction had tried at least once to expel the other from membership. The conflict was aggravated even more when my great-grandfather and one of his daughters and one of his sons began attending Pentecostal Holiness meetings held by a visiting preacher in a brush arbor by the river. My grandmother, Sarah Matilda, spoke in tongues and performed holy dances at the services. Her sister and several of her cousins bitterly disapproved. The argument over doctrine and manner of worship, baptism of fire versus the traditional baptism of water, was passed down to Daddy's generation. Though his mother died in 1912, when he was seven, he followed her example to the Holiness services when they were held, even though he remained a member of the Baptist church.

My grandfather Morgan was violently opposed to the Holiness meetings and furious when his wife kept attending after she was married. One evening he was so angry she had gone to a prayer meeting at her brother's house that he got out his shotgun and fired repeatedly across the pasture. Not only did she attend the services, but she gave money to the visiting evangelists. My grandfather Morgan was an especially frugal man, raised during the hard years of Reconstruction, and he resented her openhandedness most of all.

The aftershocks of that quarrel were felt in the family long after my grandmother died of measles. Daddy used to point out to me the apple tree below the house where he had gone to cry when his mother died. He always took her side, and blamed his father, I think, for her death. In his teens he began attending Pentecostal services, and participating in the shouting and speaking in tongues.

As a boy I was taken to both Baptist and Pentecostal meetings and was always aware of the tension revolving around the conflict in the family and community. I was ashamed and frightened by the Pentecostal services, but they also thrilled me. It was many years before I could bring myself to write about my experiences in "The Gift of Tongues":

> The whole church got hot and vivid
> with the rush of unhuman chatter
> above the congregation,
> and I saw my father looking at
> the altar as though electrocuted.
> It was a voice I'd never heard
> but knew as from other centuries.
> It was the voice of awful fire.
> 'What's he saying?' Ronald hissed
> and jabbed my arm. 'Probably Hebrew.'
> The preacher called out another
> hymn, and the glissade came again,
> high syllables not from my father's
> lips but elsewhere, the flare of
> higher language, sentences of light.

> And we sang and sang again, but
> no one rose as if from sleep to
> be interpreter, explain the writing
> on the air that still shone there like
> blindness. None volunteered a gloss
> or translation or receiver
> of the message. My hands hurt
> when pulled from the pew's varnish
> they'd gripped and sweated so. Later,
> standing under the high and plain-
> sung pines on the mountain I clenched
> my jaws like pliers, holding in
> and savoring the gift of silence.[3]

I believe Daddy's involvement with the Pentecostal movement aggravated the conflicts within him. It was rumored that he had been "marked" by his mother's emotional worship before he was born. The extremes of the services made him more confused and unsure of himself in the everyday world. He had a taste for the ecstasy and intensity, but he had no way of reconciling his religious experience with other facets of his life such as his interest in history and geography, his love of the wilderness, his ambition to be extraordinary. Many of his family had ridiculed his religious fervor and bookishness. To them, he must have seemed unstable and eccentric. Their disdain helped undermine his confidence.

The conflicts within Daddy were at least as deep and as painful as those between him and his family and community. Though without formal education—he had gone through the sixth grade in school—he read widely in history, theology, biography. His favorite reading was the *National Geographic* magazine and his Bible. I have never known another person whose thought had as little to do with his actions. He loved to talk and would stop on the road bank or in the middle of a field to converse with whomever passed by. But while he stood dripping in overalls among ragweeds and hogweeds he would talk about George Washington, or his hero, Teddy Roosevelt, or evangelists he had heard or whose tracts he had read. There seemed no connection between his work and what was on his mind. In later years he liked to imagine he would build a Scottish castle in the field beside the house. But even while he entertained such fantasies, he was usually able to joke about them.

Yet his frustrations and dividedness were very real. I think he worked furiously at times to forget, to sweat out, to block out his anger and disappointment. When he was young, he had made several attempts to escape the community and the mountains. Once he bought a train ticket to Duluth, Minnesota, hoping to go on to Canada to become a trapper. After waiting all day in the train station at Asheville he finally cashed in his ticket and returned to Green River. In the fall of 1927, he drove his Model T Ford, loaded with steel traps, guns, and winter clothes, all the way to Toledo on the way to Canada. Crossing the Cumberland Gap into Kentucky he was thrilled by the great horse farms of the bluegrass country. Cincinnati with its spectacular bridge was the most impressive city he had ever seen. On Highway 25 just north of Lima, Ohio, he was flagged down by a man standing near a shiny Packard.

"Could you give me a lift?" the man in the dark suit said. "We have broken a fan belt."

The man got in and as they drove along, he said to Daddy, "Say, Carolina, you going up to Canada to get a load of hooch?"

Daddy told him he didn't drink and was certainly no bootlegger.

"Come on, Carolina, you can level with me," the stranger said.

In his rearview mirror Daddy saw the Packard coming up behind. The big black car swung around and passed. "I thought your fan belt was broken?" Daddy said.

"Ah, they must have fixed it," his passenger said. They drove on through the sweeping farmland of western Ohio, but Daddy was no longer admiring the teams of great Percheron and Belgian horses doing the fall plowing.

"Sure you ain't going after a load of booze?" the man said. "I wouldn't want you to get in trouble, you being a nice kid from Carolina and all."

They came over a rise, and there the big Packard sat beside the highway. "Let me out," the man said. Even before the Model T rolled to a stop, he opened the door and jumped out. "Stay out of trouble, Carolina," he said.

As Daddy drove on the big car appeared behind him and then roared past. He heard laughter from the Packard. That evening he drove on to Toledo and spent the night in a motor lodge. But the incident changed his mind about going to Canada. The next morning, he pulled back onto Highway 25 and headed south.

Exactly sixty years later to the month, I was visiting the campus of Ohio State at Lima and told the story of Daddy and the Packard. A member of the English department informed me that Lima had been a major hangout for Chicago gangsters on the run in the 1920s. When she bought her house, the professor said, the real estate agent had told her it had once belonged to Dillinger, and not to dig up the yard.

A year after the trip to Toledo, Daddy took the train for eastern North Carolina and spent all his money in Rocky Mount on a boat for trapping along the Tar River. He had read there were many muskrats on that river. But after nearly drowning in high water, he was grateful to pawn his rifle for train fare home. By the time I was born he was no longer trying to leave the mountains, but he was escaping in daydreams and fatalism. He was especially fatalistic about his attempts at farming. Every year he planted a new crop of pole beans, and almost every year ended in debt. It was mainly my mother's wages in the cotton mill and beauty parlor that kept us going.

No crop, unless it is tobacco, is as labor-intensive as pole beans. Besides plowing and planting and cultivating, every field required poles that had to be cut in the pine thickets. Every year we seemed to wait till summer to get the poles, and had to go into the scratchy thickets, risking snakes, ticks, chiggers, and hornets' nests. As soon as you worked up a sweat bits of bark and needles stuck to your skin, causing a rash. After the holes were dug and poles put in place in the field, wire had to be stretched from end to end and strings tied every foot for vines to climb. But even after all the work was done, and the rows strung up, hoed and side-dressed and culti-vated, a drought could destroy the vines, or in a rainy season root fungus, called "sore shin," could stunt the yield. The harshness of my memories about bean farming surprised even me when I wrote the poem "Soreshin" in 1976:

> Buying tools or implements when flush
> Uncle Alvin asked for the highest priced.
> He donated to the church then
> in nothing less than hundreds, and for
> weddings gave only silver.
> Young beans he'd over-fertilize and over-
> plow, ripping out the tender roots with
> a cultivator just when they should be
> banked and left alone. To support his
> extravagance every spring he
> took out a hefty loan on the land
> just like a big farmer, and ran through
> it in a week or two of paying the

highest wages in the valley.
Jesus said seek first the kingdom
of God and all the rest would be added;
he meant to hold him to it.
I've seen him throw away good beans
to get a few bushels of fancies.
In small things like wire
He'd sometimes go stingy and use
any old bale, knowing when the vines
loaded with maturity both wire
and poles would break, which meant
going into the snaky thickets in
July to hack out new poles
almost too gummy to chop for
propping the toppled rows.
The fields too big to pick at once
left beans swelling to culls
in wet weather. At the end we'd
have the fun of cutting with machetes
the smut-dusty vines and pulling out
the stakes from late summer's adobe.
And where we planted beans for long
the ground itself got sneaky.
Alright in a dry year, even
through prolonged drought, but
come the least rainy spell on the
running vines and trillions of spores
revived and had at the roots. Within a week
each tap was swollen red and scaly,
dissolving in the soil, and the plants
set adrift in scalding sun would
make a last attempt to grow
a collar of white rootlets at the surface
then wilt yellow. That would be the end of
his hopes of paying back the bank that year.
Weeds immune to the subterranean
mold buried all signs of his work
with expedition, thanks to the

over-fertilizing with the borrowed
cash. With only one money crop it
meant for him oddjobs and housepainting
just to pay the interest on the
privilege of wading muddy rows lugging hampers,
breathing parathion while rasped in the face
and neck by runners. His footing
on the land in ruptured shoes and on
skinny knees that showed through torn
overalls was mushy and unsteady
as the shoring of his mangled rows.
He'd mow off the road banks for
miles to work off anger,
and scythe the cemetery, churchyard,
and the big pokeweeds below the hogpen.[4]

Perhaps the worst frustration of bean farming was the fact that Daddy did not have a truck until 1953. Before that he had to depend on his brother and brother-in-law or some other neighbor to get his beans to market. This was a source of humiliation to both my parents. They had to rely on others to get to town, to the market, and, most importantly, to go to the doctor when my sister or I was sick. Whenever they needed transportation they had to ask, to beg, to hire, to cajole a way, and this more than any other thing made them feel vulnerable, defensive. After we picked our beans in mud and rain, or in the heat and dust, and carried them out of the long rows, wired the lids in the hampers and stacked them at the end of the field, we had to wait for someone else, after they had picked their own beans, to come and load ours on top of theirs. At that time, I don't think we appreciated how irritating that must have been for the uncles and neighbors, tired after a long day's work and in a hurry to get to market, to have to stop and take on an additional load and be responsible for our beans getting counted and ticketed at the packing house. Sometimes there wasn't room for our beans on the truck, and the hampers had to sit there by the road until the next day. By then they had begun to wilt and would not bring the best price.

Even when I was a little child Daddy seemed an anachronism. He appeared to belong to an earlier century, to a world of hunting and trapping, of storytelling. Gesturing with huge hands as he described events in the

Bible or in history, he seemed almost a figure out of legend. He did not have a car or truck, and he could not stand to be in offices. As he grew older, and I grew older, he seemed increasingly to belong to the frontier past. "When He Spoke Out of the Dark" was written a few years before his death, but it already sounds like an elegy, an encounter with a memory. In it, I tried to re-create a sense of the enormous amount of work and physical energy of his life:

> When he spoke out of the dark I
> had not seen him sitting there in
> a lawn chair on the grass resting
> in his white painter's overalls
> and gray sweatshirt and cap, gray hands,
> easing after the long workday.
> For the milking was over, and
> weeds pulled for the hog, kindling had
> been cut and the painting done,
> the masonry and carpentry,
> the holes had been dug, the corn hoed,
> beans carried out of mud, the ditch
> opened, the corn gathered and heaved
> into the barn loft and shelled and
> carried to mill. And there he sat,
> tired, where I had not seen him,
> looming to my dark-adjusting eyes
> white and smokelike out of the depths
> of night, and spoke close as anyone
> in the after supper darkness,
> rest-happy after the long workday.[5]

Since children spend so much more time with their mothers than with their fathers, it surprises me still that so many of my poems of childhood concern my father rather than my mother or aunts. Over the past few years, I have thought about this often, and I think it has something to do with the stance or scale of poetry. It is connected with the way poetry creates or seizes on the heroic and finds grandeur in the most unexpected places. My father became the subject of so many of my poems because he was such a fit subject for poems. His frustrations and failures, his gestures and his joys, were on a vast scale. He was a person of conflicts and extremes, paradox and contradiction. Lives of common sense and frugality, of small success and carefulness, do not lend themselves so much to poetry. His hard life was a gift to me as a poet, though I did not recognize it for years.

Though my Daddy's family had been small farmers in the Blue Ridge Mountains since the eighteenth century, and none had ever attended college, many of them had been bookish. Each year when they hauled produce down to Greenville and Augusta they bought books, especially history books. These men are hard to portray and explain partly because of this combination of dirt farming and isolation with literacy and even intellectuality. They do not fit anyone's notion of Blue Ridge Mountain farmers. One of the truest poems I've ever written is "Books in the Attic":

> Sunday afternoons we crossed the branch
> and climbed by the molasses furnace
> to the springhouse with its melodic
> pipe, past the smokehouse full of spider-
> shrouded jars, to the Morgan house.
> Dozens had been born and died there,
> but it stood a husk of sagging sills
> and porch and damp echoing rooms
> waiting to be wrecked. A barn lantern
> had rusted crisp, the glass held by
> a crust of metal. All of Daddy's
> renovations before the war
> for his bride were peeling, moldy.
> In the closet we pulled ourselves
> up the green-stepped ladder into
> attic light. There, scattered by owls
> and nesting squirrels whose cobs remained,
> sprawled the books of the family
> smelling of must and old tobacco,
> silverfish and pages singed by time,
> the fat histories Great-grandpa
> got in Augusta when he wagoned
> hams and produce down the Winding Stairs.
> Loose sheets spiced the floor with pale ink:
> vague photographs of Teddy
> Rough Rider, worm-hollowed magazines
> and rifle catalogues, pencil

accounts. Boots molded to the corns
and toes of dead plowmen slouched in
a bronzing of dust. The pages seemed
to hover, unfolding wings and
facets to the light. A stout
Assyrian lion reared on the back
of an ancient history. We turned
the aromatic leaves like flakes
of boiled down and pressed extract
of the last century, until
my nose began to drip with the
so-far-unnoticed cold and there
was just light to see the ladder
down to the trail and milking time.[6]

One of the things that embarrassed me as a boy was the way Daddy sometimes let his brother and nephew browbeat him. My cousin Luther was especially obnoxious when he was drinking, which was every weekend. Then he would drive up into the yard in his pickup and honk his horn. Daddy always went out to talk to him. It was considered inhospitable not to go out when someone drove up. Daddy sometimes stood for hours while Luther rambled on in a drunken sentimental way. But sometimes my cousin would circle around to old grudges and family quarrels. As he got worked up, he would cuss and holler so you could hear him all the way down the valley. A few times Daddy walked away and left Luther shouting from his truck. On one occasion he dropped to his knees and began to pray. That was the incident that embarrassed me most of all, and I burned with shame whenever I remembered it. But in fact, Daddy's method was very effective and to the point, for Luther jerked his truck in gear and backed up in the driveway and roared away. And he didn't return for weeks.

The poetry I wrote about Daddy taught me to view him in an entirely new way. Through the poems I came to see that he was not just a failure, even though I had seen him as such in my teens and twenties. I did not set out to heroize him, but that was the way the poems seemed naturally to reveal him. The poems discovered for me the things about him I could not have seen otherwise. The nature of poetry was operating far beyond my intentions and awakening ambitions. Through the poems I came to understand that even Daddy's humblest work had a grandeur about it that belonged not just to him, but to the work itself, to me, to the reader, and to language. Nowhere was this better illustrated than in "Sunday Toilet":

> On the hottest Sundays of the year,
> in the morning shift of bird hymn
> and dew song, before the church-bell
> split the poised whole, Daddy raked
> a waterbucket full of lime
> from the pile beside the toolshed
> and flung comets and smoking hands
> on the walls of the hogpen.
> The young shoat's feet sucked mud as he
> ran to corners from the fog that
> flurried over sty and ripening
> puddles and drifted on the spillage
> of cobs rotting on the downhill side.
> The dusting finished, the pen looked
> white as confectioner's sugar
> in the cooling talc, the whiteness
> somehow medicinal if not
> opiate, and the air was
> sweeter floating up to the house
> where the preacher would come to dinner.
> After the hogpen Daddy sprinkled
> the chicken yard and floor of the
> brooder house, dropped what was left
> down the holes of the two-seat
> toilet. When the make-up was hit
> by early sun the mire looked
> pristine and cool as the tops of
> cumulus reaching to heaven
> while women powdered their faces
> for church and flies got chalk on their
> feet to write on the back screen door.[7]

Daddy, while not a reader of poetry, could recite even in his old age poems he had memorized in school. These included Tennyson's "Crossing the Bar" and John Burrough's "Waiting." An important part of elementary education in the South when he was a boy was the memorization and recitation of poems. In the one-room schoolhouse beside the church he learned and declaimed the beginning of *The Song of Hiawatha* and the prelude to *Evangeline,* as well as prose texts such as the Gettysburg Address and the Preamble to the Constitution. As a result, he carried around in his memory more poems than most college graduates and English majors do these days. Forty years later I had to memorize the same poems in the successor to the one-room school in the cotton-mill village of Tuxedo. In the 1950s we learned by heart and declaimed "The Raven" and "Annabel Lee," as well as Sidney Lanier's "The Marshes of Glynn" and "Song of the Chattahoochee." I am certain that the teaching of poetry and the recitation of poetry in grammar school give a lifelong taste for poetry. Memory and recitation are essential features of poetry.

Looking back at the poems I wrote about Daddy I can see that they are almost all about work. This must be in part because I am fascinated by work, by the process and psychology and ethos of work. But I am sure that it also has something to do with the fact that I grew up on a small farm where work filled the day every day except Sunday. We were working class people in the most literal sense. As a child I never knew anyone who took vacations or went away for holidays. Even on Sundays the cows had to be milked, the stock fed and watered, eggs gathered, the horse led out to the pasture.

I think Daddy felt guilty that he never made enough money to support the family, and hard work was a penance and expiation as well as an escape. The repetitions and rituals of work functioned like poetry, distracting him from worry but also deepening his satisfaction and experience of time. Through the rhythm of work, he lifted himself to other, freer states of mind.

One of the wonderful things about poetry is the way that even at its most innovative it harks back to the past. This seems to have always been so. Sir Thomas Wyatt radically changed poetry in English by going back to models in French and Italian for translation and imitation. A century later English poets looked back to Pindar and Horace for their models. Not only do poets seek the authority of the past, but also the newness of the past, and the truth of the past. Ezra Pound created an important free-verse tradition in the twentieth century by translating and imitating Tang poetry of eighth-century China. Even at its most experimental, poetry seems to derive much of its power from the revival of ancient gestures and knowledge. In a sense, the phrase "modern poetry" is an oxymoron, for poetry is the least modern of all the arts, while in some ways the most experimental. At its best poetry recovers for us a sense of ancient and permanent insights and connections. Even as poetry seems to be doing new things, it is really doing very old things. The choral ode was already an anachronism in Pindar's time, yet he raised it to a new level of accomplishment and preserved it in written texts.

Poetry takes us back to forgotten ceremonies, buried connections, archaic, therefore radical, recognitions. Poetry through its rituals excavates and reenacts the visceral and subliminal. Because of its strong sense of the past and its love of language and storytelling, the South still seems especially suited to the reading and writing of poetry. Many of the best poets working today are in the South and of the South. The best audiences I have encountered for poetry readings are in the South. At the moment we lack the support of a strong critical tradition for the reading and writing of poetry, but I am hoping and assuming this condition is only temporary. Creative writing courses and workshops have distracted us into thinking more about the intentions of people writing poetry than the experience of poetry. As a result, the sense of what poetry might be has been diminished. If we concentrated more on the reading of poetry, the hard craft of poetry would probably take care of itself. I would like to see our classes become more reader-oriented and less writer-oriented. I see no reason why we can't make this slight but crucial shift.

I have never met a person who loved the wilderness more than Daddy. It seemed to me, and possibly to him, that he had been born far out of his time. His birthday was June 13, 1905, but, in spirit, it might as well have been 1805. As a boy he absorbed from his grandpa and uncles a tradition of trapping and hunting and wood lore that went back to the time of the Cherokee, when the woods were full of deer, the creeks flashing with trout, a wilderness of bears and panthers, gold nuggets in stream branches, ginseng plants everywhere. Many of the stories he liked to tell were set "way back yonder," and it was as though he was talking of some distant, special land he had known himself.

I was born too late to understand his love of trapping. When he and my uncles talked about mink and muskrat it was as though they were describing gold. And in a way they were, for at one time fur was the most dependable source of money for mountain boys. It was a tradition that went back to the first settlers, and beyond, to the first traders and explorers, and beyond that to the Native peoples. Talk of trapping made old timers' eyes fire up: gray fox and red fox, muskrat, mink, coon and bobcat. Trapping required skill and hardship and cunning. It was an art too elusive and difficult, and perhaps too cruel, to be passed on to my generation. Daddy and my uncles talked of trapping as though it were a secret ritual, with restrictions and pleasures beyond the understanding of the young. But through them I touched some of the thrill and intoxication the old hunters must have felt. There was the excitement of gleaning the luxury and treasure of fur from the hinterlands. The furs themselves were beautiful beyond description and served as tangible reward for the pleasure of walking to the headcreeks and remote coves and back of the horizon. I don't think Daddy ever felt truly at ease except outdoors. His real home was the fields and woods and riverbank.

In the late summer of 1956, my parents bought a new Studebaker truck. That must have been one of the few years he actually made anything out of his farming. I know that most of the eighteen hundred dollars the truck cost were paid by my mother, but at least some of the money must have come from Daddy's bean farming. He was exuberant. He had not owned a new vehicle since 1927.

One cool, overcast Saturday in October of that year he and I started off to town. I assumed we were just going to the feed and seed store to pay our bills and get a new sack of dairy feed. But after we got out of the store he said, "Let's go up to Pisgah and look for deer sign." He turned on Highway 64 out toward Brevard and the high Pisgah mountains. Deer season would open in about six weeks, and though I was too young to hunt on government land, he wanted to show me where to look for deer runs and likely stands. It was a gray day, but I began to catch his mood as we headed toward the high mountains covered with clouds.

Everything seemed new about that trip. The truck was new, and the road to Brevard had just been rebuilt. It was the first modern highway, wide and contoured and straight, that I had ever seen. I was interested in becoming a civil engineer, and the trip seemed like a new beginning for me.

"That's the way to the Pink Beds," Daddy said, as we started to climb higher and higher into the national forest. He showed me the valleys where he had hunted and killed bucks, and he pointed out the trail he had followed when he came camping in his late teens to Black Balsam. I never saw Daddy happier than he was on that trip. It was as though he rose above his worries and frustrations. These peaks were part of our mountains, but they were also strange and grand, and they had Canadian balsams on the tops that had been there since the last Ice Age.

As we climbed the overcast grew closer and the foliage brighter. The beech trees and hickories were a luminous gold. Suddenly we entered the clouds. "We'll go on a little ways to see if it clears up," Daddy said.

But as we climbed the fog got thicker. We were closed in, and we slowed to fifteen, ten, five miles per hour. Our exuberance turned to fear. The fog was so thick we could not see any place to turn around. The fog was in motion. Not only were droplets attaching themselves to the windshield, but the air boiled in fits. I opened the window, and high wind cut into the cab.

We came to a plateau and saw a parking place ahead. At the same instant we smelled steam from the overheated engine. Daddy pulled off the Parkway, and we got out and opened the hood. The engine was smoking and steaming. It made a crackling sound and smelled like a new stove scorching its paint and polish. I shivered, wondering if the truck had been ruined by the hard climb. The fog moved closer, pouring up the slope and through the beech trees.

But after a few minutes the motor seemed to have cooled off. We got back in and started again. The fog was so thick now we could make out nothing in front of the headlights. I don't know how Daddy could see to stay on the road. We inched along in the whiteness that did not seem to have any direction. We were on the tops of some of the highest mountains in the state, but we might as well have been in a tunnel for all we could tell.

Suddenly I saw ahead the entrance to a real tunnel. There was a stone arch, and it looked as though the road shot right into the mountainside. Daddy kept going, and soon we could see further because there was no fog inside. It felt as though we were curving into the heart of the mountain. The stone walls and ceiling were shiny with dripping moisture. The road curved on and on.

And then there was a white wall ahead. I wondered what it was as we got closer and seemed to be running right into it. And then I saw it was the end of the tunnel. We drove out of the side of the mountain, but the fog wasn't as thick there as it had been on the south side. I saw pointed forests of balsam and spruce stretching far up the ridge. Wind tore fog in strips and wisps. "That's Black Balsam," Daddy said, pointing ahead to where ridge rose behind ridge to an awesome summit. "That's where I camped in 1922." He turned into a parking lot on the left.

The fog had opened up completely, and we were facing the afternoon sun. Before us a gorge dropped out of sight, and above the chasm a cliff loomed up and up all the way to where the sun broke through. The cliff, shaped like a face, had balsams on top like horns or feathers of a headdress.

"That's Devil's Courthouse," Daddy said, shouting with excitement. "That's what the Indian's called it." From far down the valley, and all the way up to the cliff itself, I saw the many-colored trees in autumn sun. It looked as though war paint had been spilled below the black spruces. The air was so clear that every tree, every leaf and stick stood out in biting focus. "That's the way it looked in 1922," Daddy said.

It seemed as though the ridge dropped away for miles into the mauve and magenta of oak forests. I shivered to think how hard it would be to climb all that way with a sixty-pound pack. Just as quickly as it had opened up, the fog began closing in again. Vapor streamed through the gap and across the view. Clouds poured up the slope from the north, covering first the lower trees, then the balsams and cliff, snuffing out the sun. When fog filled the air completely, we got back in the truck and started home.

NOTES

1. Robert Morgan, *Topsoil Road*. Baton Rouge: Louisiana State University Press. 15–16.

2. Morgan, *Topsoil Road*. 14.

3. Morgan, *At the Edge of the Orchard Country*. 29.

4. Robert Morgan. *The Iowa Review*. Volume 8, Issue 1 (Winter) 1977. 41–43.

5. Morgan, *Sigodlin*. 64.

6. Morgan, *At the Edge of the Orchard Country*. 17–18.

7. Morgan, *At the Edge of the Orchard Country*. 33–34.

FERTILE NORTH CAROLINA

What I am as a writer I owe mostly to the good fortune to have been born and raised in North Carolina. Almost all my poetry and fiction is set in the mountains in the western part of the state, and the voices I have heard and written belong to the Old North State and the Southern highlands.

I have been asked many times by people in the North why there are so many outstanding writers associated with North Carolina. The flippant answer is: because there ain't nothing else to do down there. But the more serious answer is because of Thomas Wolfe. Once Wolfe became such a celebrated writer and international celebrity, and his fiction made such an impact on young readers, inspiring passionate admirers, it was inevitable that the talented youth of North Carolina would think of following his career path. The state became, from the 1930s on, a seedbed and hotbed for young writers, and the University of North Carolina was the forcing house.

But there are many other factors besides the fame of Thomas Wolfe that have contributed to the bumper crop of writers from North Carolina over the years. When I was a student at North Carolina State University in 1962–63, Sam Ragan had a feature in the Raleigh *News & Observer* every Sunday celebrating one North Carolina author or another, usually with pictures and an interview. It was obvious that writers were important and recognized in the state.

A few years ago, I was interviewed on the farm where I grew up on Green River in Henderson County. The reporter looked at the cornfield and old barn and said, "Tell me, I'm curious, how did you ever get from here to Cornell University, because practically speaking, you can't get there from here." I told him I could understand why he would ask that question. After all, my parents were poor, without a lot of formal education. We didn't have a car or truck or tractor. We plowed our land with a horse and kept our milk and butter in the springhouse when I was small. But, in fact, I had some distinct advantages for a future writer.

I grew up among great storytellers. My grandpa had a thousand stories about ghosts and panthers, snakes and mad dogs, bears, haunted places.

We talked on the porch in summer and by the fire in winter. He sent us to bed many times terrified by his yarns of panthers coming down chimneys, snakes long as a man was tall. He'd polished those tales over his lifetime. My dad had gone only to the sixth grade in school, but he was an avid reader. He subscribed to the *National Geographic Magazine*, and he read history and biography. He had absorbed an enormous amount of history from his grandfather who was a veteran of the Confederate army and Elmira prisoner of war camp. My dad had an extraordinary memory for detail, and loved to tell about George Washington at Valley Forge and Daniel Boone in Kentucky, Teddy Roosevelt on San Juan Hill. I drank in his stories and acquired a love of history from him. He could make the past come alive. My mother was a gifted talker also, preferring stories about witches, babies marked in the womb, women charmed by rattlesnakes. It was she who told me the many family stories about Gap Creek and the old days on Mount Olivet where my Grandma Levi had grown up.

I was also fortunate to explore the woods and fields and pastures around our house. My great-great-grandpa, Daniel Pace, had bought a square mile of land on Green River in 1840, and I knew virtually every foot of it, from the riverbank to the top of the mountain. I built ponds on the pasture branch, dug caves in the walls of the gully, caught rabbits in a rabbit gum, and slid on a plank on leaves down the mountainside. I knew the weeds and thickets, the different kinds of soils and clays, the rocks, and sinkholes. I climbed the trees and knew trees like friends. That sense of intimacy with the place is so strong I have compared every other place I've seen to it, to this day.

Every day we read the Bible aloud and I was exposed to the majesty of the King James scripture. We attended church and prayer meetings four times a week and sang hymns and gospel songs. From the first, I loved music. When I was two or three and resisted taking a nap, all my mother had to do was sit down and start singing. It could be any song at all, a hymn, carol, Stephen Foster. As soon as I heard the first note I dropped whatever I was doing and ran to her lap. Pressing my cheek to her breast I could hear the voice through the flesh, and the measure of her heartbeat. Every time I floated away into an arcadia of melody and dreams.

As I got older, I listened to the radio, to church choirs, country music, Christmas carols, and even classical music. Longines watches sponsored the Philadelphia Orchestra every Sunday afternoon, and I thrilled to the grandeur of that polyphony. I made up music in my head to accompany whatever I was doing. It was tunes based on what I had heard. One special tune I played in my head over and over. Only years later did I discover that it came from Bach's Fifth Brandenberg Concerto.

My parents read to me as an infant, and my mother taught me to read before I ever went to school. I was always interested in reading and writing. As I grew older, I wanted to write something grand, an epic poem, an oratorio, grand as the Cicero Mountain across the river. I wanted to write something as powerful as a thunderstorm or the procession of the seasons. I wanted to find language radiant as sunlight on pine needles.

Two wonderful things happened to me the year I was in the sixth grade. I had Dean Ward, principal of Tuxedo Elementary School, as a teacher, and the Henderson County bookmobile began coming to Green River Baptist Church every first Monday afternoon of the month. Mr. Ward was a relative who had grown up on Bob's Creek and gone off to Chapel Hill. He also was a wonderful storyteller, and regaled us with stories of the old days, of the Roaring Twenties, ancient history, the plots of *The Iliad* and *The Odyssey, Silas Marner, Paradise Lost.* He drilled us in grammar and for the first time I began to have a firmer sense of the structure of language. I became self-conscious about the way I spoke, the way I pronounced words.

I will never forget my first sight of the bookmobile. It was an old utility truck outfitted with bookshelves. I'd never seen so many books. There I discovered *Farmer Boy* and *Little House on the Prairie.* In the future, I would discover Thomas Wolfe's *Look Homeward, Angel* there, and *War and Peace.* I was so enthralled by Wolfe's story, I thought I was Eugene Gant and his family were my family. I knew he had grown up in Asheville thirty miles away, and I began to think that if Wolfe could write a book about Asheville and sell it to Yankees maybe I could write something and get it published.

When I was sixteen, I wanted to be many things. I wanted to compose music, and I wanted to study science and mathematics. I wanted to attend West Point, and I wanted to build highways. As it turned out I attended North Carolina State University to study aerospace engineering and applied mathematics. In those days, we were supposed to do our part in beating the Russians in the space race. I wanted to be a rocket scientist.

I had been writing all along, and I had entered college without graduating from high school. My first encounter with a writer happened that fall of 1962 when I attended a workshop taught Monday evenings by the playwright and actor Romulus Linney. Anyone could attend and I listened to Rom talk about his work in the theater, as well as fiction writing. He sometimes brought famous writers to the class, including Reynolds Price and Edward Albee. It was from Rom Linney that I first got some idea about how a professional writer might speak and act. Things were going so well in my math classes I decided to accelerate and take an advanced class in differential equations. My advisor looked at my transcript and said, "Why, you never graduated from high school." He refused to let me accelerate. I was disappointed, but discovered I could take English 222, Creative Writing, in the time slot freed up. The professor was the novelist, Guy Owen.

Owen's class was so much fun I began to think less and less about differential equations and the Bernoulli Effect, and more about how to write a decent English sentence. Guy Owen said things the first day of the class that I'm still passing on to my students. He said learn to use the precise names for things. Don't say, "tree," say "oak tree," or better yet "chestnut oak" or "water oak." (This is what Henry James called "solidity of specification.") He told us to listen to the way people actually speak, to get the living inflections that will make a character come alive in dialogue and narration.

About the third or fourth week of the semester I gave Guy a little story I'd written about my great-grandmother Delia Johnson Capps. As a small girl in 1862, she had been taken out of the dangerous mountains of North Carolina to Walterboro, South Carolina, to be safe. She was safe there until Sherman's army reached Savannah and turned north, devastating central South Carolina. She could remember bodies being piled on their porch, and dogs climbing up on the bodies licking the blood.

Guy brought the story into class and said he wept when he read it. None of my math teachers had said anything like that to me. I was hooked on writing and never looked back. I began to think less about the space race and more about the textures and power of words.

Transferring to the University of North Carolina at Chapel Hill in 1963, I intended to study both literature and pure mathematics, and write fiction. But I soon fell in with a group of students from the Northeast who were obsessed with contemporary poetry. They could talk about Baudelaire, Rimbaud, and line breaks. They knew a great deal more than I did about poetry. We lived and breathed poetry that year. I had been writing poems all along, but I began to concentrate on the craft of poetry in a new way, exploring contemporary idioms, finding evocative phrases, writing about the Blue Ridge Mountains and the farm where I had grown up. I thought more and more about lines of poetry and less about writing stories. I read Robert Lowell, James Wright, Gary Snyder, and many others.

In the fall of 1964 several things happened that deeply influenced my writing. I became aware of the sound of words, the textures of words, the resonance of words, in a new way. I saw a shaft of sunlight break through the clouds after a storm and thought of a timber of light bracing the sky. I wrote a haiku-like poem about that beam, my first authentic effort in poetry. I began to write more and more poems.

At the same time, I was taking a writing class with the fiction writer Jessie Rehder, who was a wonderful, generous teacher, and I wrote both poems and stories for her class. One day I was crossing the parking lot to the Wilson Library, and she was driving out of the lot. She stopped her car, rolled down the window, and said, "You're the most talented writer I've ever taught," then drove away. She may have said that to all her students, for all I know, but I walked on into the library that day about three feet off the ground.

The MFA program in writing had been started at the University of North Carolina at Greensboro, and it was my good fortune to study there in 1967–68. Writers, not scholars, were the stars in that English Department, a tradition started by Allen Tate and Randall Jarrell. I was lucky to work with both Robert Watson and Fred Chappell. Each wrote both fiction and poetry, as I did. I soon discovered that Fred Chappell was the best reader of poetry I had ever encountered.

Because I was married and had a child, and held two part-time jobs, I was excused from most of the workshops. Instead, I would meet Fred for tutorials. I would give him poems and we met every week or two at a café called "The Pickwick" in late afternoon to go over the work I had submitted. Fred's erudition, his critical eye, his generosity, and enthusiasm were inspiring. I remember thinking, "He really understands how these poems are written." The honesty of the man was impressive. I began to concentrate more and more on poetry, and less on fiction. And I began to get some sense of my own voice and subject matter. Fred was from Haywood County, in the mountains, and he knew the world and the voices I knew. I believe a poet cannot come into his or her own until he or she has a true reader, an authentic reader. For me, Fred was the true reader. All you need is one, and I was damn lucky to find him at the University of North Carolina at Greensboro.

I owe a great deal to North Carolina and the people who taught me and encouraged me, the land there, the blue valleys and mountains, the rich soil of the bottomlands, the waterfalls and remote coves, the people who wrung a living from the rocky ridges, the ancient hunting ranges of the Cherokee. When I was a boy hoeing corn, I often turned up arrowheads and pieces of Indian pottery. It seemed the ground itself was haunted by the Cherokee and the other Woodland tribes who had come before them. It was a world brimming with history, with poetry, with stories. It was my legacy, waiting to be written down.

READING *WAR AND PEACE*

The fall of 1958 was the last time we grew sorghum cane and made our own molasses on our small farm in the Blue Ridge Mountains. After school, I worked long hours cutting and stripping the stalks, then feeding them into the mill while Daddy and Uncle Abe boiled the molasses syrup over the furnace. The sweet steam mixed with the sour smell of leaves in ditches and marshy places along the creek. I had been reading Charles Dickens, and I was thinking of pickpockets and back alleys of London. I was also thinking of tramping the woods with my squirrel rifle. I was looking forward to high school, and I had a sense my world was about to change.

In the fall of 1958 my eyes, searching through the shelves of the bookmobile parked at the Green River Baptist Church, fell on a book in maroon cloth with *War and Peace* stamped in gold on the spine. It was the thickest tome I'd ever seen, except for the Bible and the dictionary. I lifted it off the shelf and felt the weight, the substance of it. I had seen *War and Peace* advertised in the Sears & Roebuck catalogue as "the greatest novel ever written." It was the book I had been looking for.

I don't ever remember being without books. We didn't have enough money to buy a car or truck or tractor, and we had to borrow a horse for farming, but we had a few novels and history books and copies of *National Geographic* on the mantel. Some religious tracts and pamphlets had been sent by radio preachers after Mama or Daddy had mailed them a dollar. There was a big dictionary that my great-grandpa must have bought, along with a few other books that were in boxes in the attic, when he wagoned hams and produce and sourwood honey down to Greenville, South Carolina, or Augusta, Georgia, in the days before the railroad reached into the mountains.

The Bible was the book grown-ups talked about most in our house. Daddy and my grandpa argued constantly about which prophecies had been fulfilled.

"I figure Stalin is the anti-Christ," my grandpa said.

"Hitler was the anti-Christ," Daddy said, "And I figure the Rapture will come by the end of this century."

"It says the world will end in fire," my grandpa said. "I reckon Stalin will blow it up with the A-bomb."

When my sister and I were little, Mama and Daddy read to us every night by the fireplace. They read from the Bible and from a book of children's stories that included *No Penny* and *The Little Red Hen*. The year before I was to begin school, Mama bought a primer and taught me to read about Dick and Jane and Sally, and their dog Spot. I was impressed that their daddy left every morning for work in his Sunday suit.

When I began school, I was bored because I already knew how to read and write and count. As a result, I wasted my time daydreaming or teasing the other students. There was no library at Tuxedo Elementary School, but there was a small shelf of books at the back of each classroom in grades four and above. When I reached the fourth grade, I started checking out books and reading one each day. I read *Old Yeller* and *The Yearling*. I read the Hardy Boys books, and I found it hard to believe there were so many stories in the world.

There had been a lot of talk lately about "beating the Russians." In the aftermath of the first Sputnik, we had been told by our teachers that it was our duty to study science and math to help the Free World compete with Soviet Communism. I took the exhortation seriously and knew that I would study engineering or physics someday if I could get a scholarship. But already, secretly, I was thinking of other ambitions. I had begun taking piano lessons, and practiced Mozart and Bach on the piano for longer and longer hours. I wrote poems and stories in my school notebook.

But once I got Tolstoy's big novel in my hands, I seemed to think of nothing else that fall. I did not have a reading lamp, so I read sitting on my bed in the light of one overhead bulb. Once I started *War and Peace*, I knew this was a different kind of novel from any I had read before. It was a story about people, and the minds of people, but also about history and the logic of history. It had to be read slowly, and it rewarded the reader sentence-by-sentence and paragraph-by-paragraph, and not just through the unfolding of the plot. It was a story of insight as well as action.

The novel had a different pace and scale. Some scenes were in ballrooms and drawing rooms, and the characters included counts and princesses and army officers. But the details were so vivid and real I felt intimate with the Imperial world spread out so slowly and thoroughly:

> The young Princess Bolkonsky had come with her work in a
> gold-embroidered velvet bag. Her pretty little upper lip faintly
> darkened with down, was very short over her teeth, but was all
> the more charming when it was at times drawn down to meet the
> lower lip. As is always the case with perfectly charming women,
> her defect—the shortness of the lip and the half-opened mouth—
> seemed her peculiar, her characteristic beauty.[1]

Each day that fall I could hardly wait to get the cows milked, and
the corn shelled for the chickens, so I could run back to read about the
Bolkonsky estate outside Moscow, or the party where Pierre ties a police-
man on the back of a bear. Sitting in the cold bedroom with only the dim
light above me, with rain tapping on the oak trees outside, I wandered over
the Napoleonic battlefield with Pierre, among the confusion and carnage.

We are told that before Tolstoy and Stendhal, all portraits of war had
been heroic: Homer and Vergil, Milton and Tasso. But Tolstoy showed us
the panic and disorientation, the helplessness of the individual in battle.
The sarcastic portrait of Napoleon is a kind of comic relief, balancing the
sympathy for Pierre, Prince Andrey, the young Rostov. One of the passages
I have never forgotten is the vision of the deep blue sky above the battlefield
that Prince Andrey sees when he is wounded:

> Above him there was nothing but sky—the lofty sky, not clear
> but still immensely lofty, with gray clouds creeping quietly over
> it. 'How quietly, peacefully and triumphantly, and not like us
> running, shouting, and fighting, not like the Frenchman and artil-
> leryman dragging the mop from one another with frightened and
> frantic faces, how differently are those clouds creeping over that
> lofty, limitless sky. How was it I did not see that lofty sky before?'[2]

The greatest writers never lose sight of eternity, it has been said, no
matter how loud or twisted the events in the foreground. Tolstoy's ability to describe life in drawing rooms and country houses, city clubs and
army barracks and headquarters, answered a hunger I had not known I had
about how the world works, or had worked. His society women, politicians
and generals, rakes and spongers, were more real to me than most of the
people I saw every day in Green River.

The essay chapters on history and destiny—the very passages that more
mature readers often skip over—were among those that stirred me most

profoundly. Even so, I was unprepared for anything as romantic as the scene where Prince Andrey hears Natasha at her window in the moonlight:

> She was evidently leaning right out of the window, for he could hear the rustle of her garments and even her breathing. All was hushed and stonily still, like the moon and its lights and shadows. Prince Andrey dared not stir for fear of betraying his unintentional presence: 'Sonya! Sonya' he heard the first voice again. 'Oh how can you sleep! Do look how exquisite! Oh, how exquisite! Do wake up, Sonya!' she said, almost with tears in her voice. 'Do you know such an exquisite night has never, never been before?'[3]

As I chopped wood or picked corn in the cool October afternoons, I was really thinking of Natasha and Sonya, of the down on the little princess's upper lip, of old Prince Bolkonsky working at his lathe, and of the exhilarating hunt over the steppes that lasted all day. Each afternoon and weekend that fall I hoped it would rain, so I could stay in my room and read. Sometimes I rested my eyes by practicing on the old piano. But mostly I sat cross-legged on the bed reading Tolstoy in the gray light of our house in the woods. The best part of the story was still to come.

Near the end of the novel, while Pierre is being led away as a prisoner of the French as they flee Russia, he comes to know a fellow prisoner, an old peasant named Platon Karataev. Even as they are cold and hungry and force-marched day after day, the old man never loses his liveliness and friendliness. The reader shares Pierre's wonder at the old peasant's resilience. Platon Karataev is a kind of philosopher; he encourages Pierre to see meaning in the simple details of his life, in eating and sleeping and talking, in the living of life day by day. Pierre has spent his previous years searching for meaning and self-knowledge:

> He had sought for it in philanthropy, in freemasonry, in the dissipations of society, in wine, in heroic feats of self-sacrifice, in his romantic love for Natasha; he had sought it by the path of thought; and all his researches and all his efforts had failed him. And now without any thought of his own, he had gained that peace and that harmony with himself simply through the horror of death, through hardships, through what he had seen in Karataev. Pierre recognized the truth of the main idea. The absence of suffering, the satisfaction of needs, and following upon that, freedom in the choice of occupa-

tion, that is of one's manner of life, seemed to Pierre the highest and most certain happiness of man. Only here and now for the first time in his life Pierre fully appreciated the enjoyment of eating when he was hungry, of drinking when he was thirsty, of sleep when he was sleepy, of warmth when he was cold, of talking to a fellow creature when he wanted to talk and to hear men's voices.[4]

This seemed like the best wisdom I had encountered at the age of 14. It still does to the 51-year-old reader today.

In the concluding section of the book, Tolstoy shows us the married couples, Pierre and Natasha, Nicolay and Marya, long after the Napoleonic wars are over. They are raising their families, looking after their estates, worrying about the details of their households. These chapters reinforce the insight of the old peasant, that the meaning of things is in the living of our lives day by day. Still, Pierre is not satisfied. He wants to do more. He would like to influence the reform of society: "All my idea really is that if vicious people are united and form a power, honest men must do the same. It is so simple, you see."[5]

Reading *War and Peace* suggested to me that I did not live just in the Green River valley, in the Blue Ridge Mountains, but in the world, in the stream of history, and my thoughts and ambitions were much like those of people everywhere. I saw that the Blue Ridge Mountains were everywhere, and that the gift of fiction was to connect me to everybody.

NOTES

1. Leo Tolstoy. *War and Peace*. 1869. Trans. Constance Garnett. New York: Modern Library, 1962. 123.

2. Tolstoy, *War and Peace*. 336.

3. Tolstoy, *War and Peace*. 573.

4. Tolstoy, *War and Peace*. 712.

5. Tolstoy, *War and Peace*. 930.

WILDACRES

In the spring of 1961, a number of strange and exciting things happened to me. I applied to the early admissions program at Emory College at Oxford, Georgia and was accepted. Emory at Oxford admitted students after their junior year in high school if they had good SAT scores. I had saved enough money from bean farming and selling my cow Ginger to pay for a year of college, with the help of a small work scholarship. In September I would be leaving home for Oxford, Georgia. Emory was best known as a medical university. My vague plans were to study something having to do with science, and perhaps pursue a career in medical research.

Also, in the spring of 1961 the principal of East Henderson High School announced over the intercom that one student from the school would be selected to attend a Civitan Club camp at Wildacres, near Little Switzerland, in the mountains east of Asheville. Those interested should come to the school office to apply. Uncharacteristically I hurried to the office and submitted my name. I was in a mood to try new things but thought it unlikely I would be chosen.

Much to my surprise I was selected. Perhaps no one else applied. In any case, after school was out in early June, I found I was headed to Wildacres for a week. I'd never been away from home before. Attending the Civitan Club camp seemed good practice for going away to college in the fall. I bought a duffel bag in which to carry my things, and new chukka boots made of heavy green corduroy cloth. I was a little scared, but mostly I was curious.

The Civitan Clubs in those days supported a number of charitable activities. Their mission at that time was to improve human relations, and the stated goal of the camp, in the literature sent to me, was to study human relations and the issues of equality, citizenship, and civil rights in the context of contemporary society. The conference at Wildacres would consist of counselors and teachers, and about a hundred campers. Classes would be offered in history, especially Southern history, race relations, music, modern dance, literature, folklore, and nature study. Recreational activities would include hiking on mountain trails. In the evenings there would be lectures and concerts.

Each participant was asked to write a letter ahead of time stating his or her particular interests and reasons for attending the conference. At the time I had so many interests I completely filled the available space on the form, describing my work in music, in composing, in writing poetry and fiction, and my ambition to study science. I also mentioned that I was superintendent of the Sunday School at Green River Baptist Church. And I stated that I was on my way to college in the fall. Later I was told that the camp was intended for rising seniors who would return to their high schools in the fall and tell others what they'd learned at the retreat.

Having never been away from home before, I had no idea what to expect. The brochure said Wildacres was owned by the Blumenthal family of Charlotte. Mr. Blumenthal had bought the camp in the 1930s and it was used for many conferences, retreats, and programs on human rights. The trip to Wildacres in early June was going to be an adventure for all my family. Daddy would drive us in the green Studebaker pickup, and Mama would pack a picnic lunch to eat on the way. My sister Evangeline went along also. We left on Sunday morning, all of us packed into the cab of the truck, my duffel bag in the back. I'd never been east of Asheville before, and the trip was exhilarating; we passed through Oteen and Swannanoa, then Black Mountain, and descended out of the mountains on Highway 70 through one curve after another to Old Fort at the edge of the Piedmont. I kept thinking of Thomas Wolfe's description of making the same journey by train in *Of Time and the River*. Wolfe's rhetoric soared in my head. I too had a feeling of release, of escaping over the wall of the Blue Ridge Mountains into the wider spaces of the foothills, through the little towns with water tanks, furniture factories, the wide river bottoms.

Near Marion we turned north on Highway 221 and headed back into the mountains. As noon approached, we wondered where we might stop to eat our picnic lunch. Then, a little past noon, we spotted a picnic area in a small park on the left side of the road. There were tables, grills, even a bathroom. It seemed too good to be true, as though the rest area had been built with us in mind. This was before the days of superhighways when rest areas would become a common sight. Daddy turned aside into the parking lot and Mama spread her tablecloth on one of the concrete tables. We ate fried chicken, macaroni and cheese, green beans, apple pie, and drank lemonade.

Our trip seemed blessed. It was a warm sunny day, but not too hot. Bright clouds drifted overhead in majestic flotillas.

The climb back into the mountains toward Little Switzerland and the Blue Ridge Parkway was impressive. Mountain rose above mountain. We drove higher and higher, then turned off onto a smaller highway, and on top of the ridge found the driveway to Wildacres. The brochure had said we should arrive by four o'clock. It was only a little after two. I was glad to be coming early, before others, for I was a little ashamed to be arriving in a pickup truck. As it turned out, only two counselors were there ahead of me. I unloaded my duffel bag and said goodbye to Mama and Daddy and Evangeline. As they drove away and disappeared down the winding driveway, I felt I'd crossed a threshold into a new phase of my life.

Checking in with the counselors (they were seniors from Pfeiffer College in Misenheimer, North Carolina) I toured the grounds, checking out the cafeteria, the dormitories, classrooms, auditorium. I was indeed the first camper to arrive. The campus seemed on top of the world. There were benches around a fire pit for bonfire gatherings. Through the trees I could see the deep valleys below on either side. After scouting out the place, I sat on the porch watching others arrive in limousines and convertibles, on buses from Marion.

A beautiful girl from Winston-Salem arrived with her father. He carried her bags in, looked around at all the boys, and said, "I understand this conference is about human relations," and burst out laughing, like he understood what was really meant by the term. I struck up conversations with new arrivals from Charlotte, Raleigh, Greensboro, Chapel Hill, Durham. It was clear that the other participants were from more affluent backgrounds than me and were more socially sophisticated.

Mrs. Blumenthal arrived with her husband. They introduced themselves and welcomed us. Mrs. Blumenthal was very tall and willowy; her husband was shorter. And then a couple from Chicago arrived, Mr. and Mrs. James Dodman Nobel. They were the senior counselors and instructors. She was a modern dancer, and he was a poet. They sought me out immediately and took me aside to ask if I would lead in prayer before supper that evening. They also asked if I would play the piano while Mrs. Nobel danced, and Mr. Nobel read his poems. I was so surprised I hesitated, and then agreed to both requests. I was not used to being singled out that way. The Nobels had read my statement of interests. Apparently, I was the only camper who claimed to compose music, write stories, and play a role in a local Sunday School. I was flattered and a little dazed.

That evening I did indeed say grace before supper in the big dining room, and I did improvise on the piano at the evening program while Mrs. Nobel danced, and Mr. Nobel read poems to the assembly. It seemed odd that I was asked to do these things while surrounded by many who were probably better qualified to lead in prayer and play the piano.

Mrs. Nobel's dancing was a surprise and a discovery for me. I knew little about dance, formal, modern, or otherwise. I'd been taught that dancing was a sin and had never even taken part in a square dance. Mrs. Nobel wore black leotards and moved in irregular and unpredictable ways, with little repetition. She rolled on the floor and tied herself in knots, ran forward and back, dropped in a heap, spread her arms, circled, backtracked, plunged sideways, and turned like the hands of a clock. It was all spontaneous and fascinating. I saw there was no way to go wrong at the piano, for her moves were independent of the music.

Mr. Nobel's poetry was in free verse, not unlike the poetry of Sandburg or Walt Whitman. Only later would I realize how deeply influenced Mr. Nobel's poetry was by the Eliot of "The Hollow Men" and "Gerontion." He had a little book of poems with handsome woodcuts, called *Modern Trilogy*. One of his phrases that stuck in my mind was "implicitly immortal." He also used the word "hecatomb," which I'd never heard before. The first section, or "refrain," began:

> We are a generation confounded,
> Misdirected and disillusioned,
> Treading, with slow uneager steps
> Familiar paths
> Of popular convention,
> Weakly despising ourselves,
> Weakly conforming.
> We are a public hecatomb,
> Innocent victims
> Of a slow transition,
> Cast in the mold of hypocrisy...[1]

In my conversations with Mr. and Mrs. Nobel over the next few days I learned more about their background. Mr. Nobel had graduated from Cornell University in 1925 and done graduate work there, but never completed his PhD. His advisor had retired, and his dissertation had been left unfinished. In the 1930s the Nobels had become involved with an arts collective in Chicago called Park House where she danced and taught dance. He offered classes in politics and poetry, and also taught at a junior college. Their son was about to graduate from Cornell. The Nobels were a handsome, athletic couple. They had been political activists, involved in civil rights, and union organizing. I'd never met anyone with so much energy and elan. They were my introduction to what I learned later was called "the Old Left."

I was excited because of the way the Nobels singled me out and made a fuss over me. Surely, I would be found out later as an imposter among all the better-educated campers from cities and university towns. Surely others must compose music and write stories and poems. That the Nobels showed so much interest in me was a revelation and a validation. Their encouragement gave me at once more confidence as well as fear that my all too obvious limitations would be revealed.

The counselor in charge of our dormitory was a recent graduate of Pfeiffer College who had majored in philosophy and theater. I engaged in several conversations with him about Nietzsche and Schopenhauer and George Bernard Shaw, one of my favorites at the time. Most of what I knew about German philosophy was from encyclopedias, though I had read selections from *Thus Spake Zarathustra* and *The Birth of Tragedy from the Spirit of Music.* I didn't even know how to pronounce Nietzsche's name, calling him "Nitch," and was corrected by the counselor. I had also read Colin Wilson's *The Outsider* and was anxious to talk about existentialism and Camus and Sartre. It was thrilling to pick the counselor's brain.

Shaw appealed to me for his wit and surprising opinions, his Fabianism, his love of Wagner, his radical ideas about spelling. At home I would have been tying bean strings and hoeing corn in the hot fields. Instead, I was sitting on the porch high in the Blue Ridge Mountains talking about German philosophy and drama. The big world out there was opening its doors, and I was getting a taste of the future.

One of the classes I attended each day was taught by a professor of music from Pfeiffer, Dr. Brewer. He lectured to us on music from different periods, and played records, illustrating Baroque, Classical, Romantic, Impressionist, and Modern music. He had a special enthusiasm for Edvard Grieg and played the "Peer Gynt" suite for us. He reserved his highest praise for Joseph Haydn, father of the symphony and string quartet. I discovered I knew more about classical music than the other students. I asked question after question about composition, counterpoint, harmony, orchestration. I'd read Leonard Bernstein's book, *The Joy of Music*, and knew some of the terms of music criticism and theory.

The main emphasis at Wildacres was the discussion of current events, civil rights, Southern history, union organizing, and the history of Judaism. We were addressed by a rabbi from Charlotte who talked about Reform Judaism. I'd never seen a rabbi before and asked many questions as we stood on the steps to the porch after the session. The rabbi was patient, dignified, casual, answering all my questions.

One of the best discussions that week was about the play *The Octoroon* by Dion Boucicault. I had never heard before of the author or the play. Boucicault was an Irishman who had come to America and written more than a hundred plays. I'd heard the term "mulatto," but not "quadroon" and "octoroon." And I'd certainly never heard a discussion of miscegenation. The examination of the whole issue seemed daring. It was pointed out that one drop of "black blood" made a person in the South labeled black. The play was a thriller, with murder, a purloined letter, a steamboat explosion, and Native Americans. It was my introduction to the issues of abolition and miscegenation, and the serious discussion of race.

The other camper at Wildacres from Henderson County was named Linda. She was a great basketball star and very pretty, well over six feet tall. I'd met her the year before in a debate between my East High team and her West High team. Since we were the only people at Wildacres we already knew we often fell into conversation. She was very bright and friendly. During the week I also met a number of other interesting campers. One named Peter would go on to become an authority on Italian Literature and film. John from Charlotte I would later see at Chapel Hill. A very smart guy from Greensboro named Sam was into logic and the parsing of grammar and vocabulary.

It was on the fourth night, after I played again for Mrs. Nobel's dancing, that a stunning copper-haired, brown-eyed beauty from Chapel Hill congratulated me. I'd noticed her before but hadn't spoken to her. She was tall and mature, serious, and very friendly. We talked until it was time for lights out. We seemed to share so many enthusiasms it was astonishing. I'd never met a girl who seemed so perfect. Later that night I lay in bed feeling my life had acquired a new brightness.

We sought each other out at breakfast the next morning and stayed together all that day, attending the same discussions, sitting together at lunch. One of the afternoon classes was about nature hikes on mountain trails. Instead of attending the music class, I accompanied her on the afternoon jaunt. The purple rhododendrons were still blooming at that elevation, and other wild flowers were vivid in the woods along the trail. The very air seemed to have a new sparkle. We paused on the trail, letting others go ahead of us. The ground, the leaves, the rocks, everything, seemed different. We listened to the tinkle of a cowbell in a mountain pasture. I pointed out the many kinds of shrubs and trees, the ones I knew.

Everything seemed perfect that afternoon, the trail, the mountain pastures, the flowers, the crisp mountain air, and the attentions of this intellectual beauty from Chapel Hill. It seemed impossible that she was so attentive to me, that she even appeared to be impressed with me. I wondered what I had done to deserve such approval.

We stayed together all that afternoon and at dinner. I knew Linda felt isolated, but I did not pay her the attention that I should have. I couldn't help myself. That evening I played the piano again for Mrs. Nobel to dance and for Mr. Nobel while he read his poems. Immediately after the last assembly the Nobels were leaving to drive overnight to their son's graduation in Ithaca, New York. The Chapel Hill girl and I accompanied them to their station wagon, exchanged handshakes and hugs, and Mr. Nobel gave me a signed copy of his book of poems, *Modern Trilogy*. The Chapel Hill girl and I watched the car until the taillights disappeared around a bend down the mountain. Then we rested on a bench and talked until it was time to return to the dormitories.

The next morning, we sat together at breakfast and exchanged addresses. We promised to write to each other and keep alive "the spirit of Wildacres." A photograph of the whole group had been taken earlier and we signed each other's copy. I saw her off on the bus to Marion and then Chapel Hill.

All that morning I talked with departing campers as parents arrived to drive their sons and daughters home. I chatted with counselors who were anxious to get away. My duffel bag was packed. I passed Mrs. Blumenthal and she smiled at me and wished me a good day. Still my dad did not come in his pickup truck. I was still glowing with the inspiration of the week, but there was inevitably an air of anti-climax, of aftermath, as the camp emptied out. I was standing on the porch with two counselors when the green Studebaker pickup finally appeared.

"Now who could that be?" one of the counselors said.

"Probably someone looking for work," the other answered.

Without saying any more, I grabbed my bag and ran for the truck.

My dad had brought my cousin Paul with him. And Daddy announced we were driving back on the Blue Ridge Parkway and stopping to visit Mount Mitchell. There was so much to tell about my week at Wildacres I didn't know where to start, so I said little. The Parkway was dazzling with its lookouts and vistas, balsam forests, and looming cliffs. And the climb to the top of Mount Mitchell, the highest peak east of the Mississippi, was exhilarating. I stood on the tower drinking in the gathering remoteness. But all the time, on the way home, I was thinking a new stage in my life had begun.

A month later I was asked to report on my week at Wildacres to the Civitan Club in Hendersonville. The meeting was held in the ballroom of the Skyland Hotel, the hotel where F. Scott Fitzgerald had written *The Crack-Up*. I drove to town in the pickup truck, and got my hair cut. I was tanned from working in the fields and my hair was bleached to a light blond. Linda and I had lunch on the dais with the Civitan officers. And then it was my turn to address the crowd. Though nervous before, I was surprised at how easy it was to tell that large crowd about the week at Wildacres, about the modern dance and poetry, the discussion of race and human relations, *The Octoroon*, Southern history, music, Mrs. Nobel's dancing and Mr. Nobel's poetry, and the rabbi's lectures. Standing before that group I shed my shyness and found new strength in my voice. Afterward a well-known lawyer came up to me and said, "That was such a good speech. You would be a fine lawyer."

All that summer I pondered the concluding lines of Mr. Nobel's *Modern Trilogy*. They seemed to strike a theme for the next stage of my life:

Now we gaze on new horizons--
Pioneers among us,
Conservers of the good,
Moral optimists,
Men and women
Who have made the effort
To clear their minds of rubbish,

Who see a new dignity for man,
Greater self-realization for woman,

New and simpler re-creation,
New modes to peace,
A living religion,
And a quality of life
Implicitly immortal.[2]

NOTES

1. James Dodman Nobel. "Refrain One." *Modern Trilogy*. Chicago: Broadside Press, 1940. 1.
2. Nobel, "Refrain Six." *Modern Trilogy*. 33.

LEO'S HOUSE

There are many stories of how lives may be radically changed. Some transformations seem to happen instantly, like Pascal's vision of "Fire, Fire, Fire!" and Paul's blinding illumination on the road to Damascus. It was Darwin's voyage on the *Beagle* to the South Seas that made him the great scientist that we honor. It was Goethe's two years in Italy that fired him to become a seminal thinker and poet of *Faust*. Two years in the cabin by Walden Pond enabled Thoreau to become the author and thinker we celebrate. In my own more modest case, it was nineteen months, January 8, 1970, to August 8, 1971, in an old farmhouse outside Hendersonville, North Carolina, with my wife Nancy and son Ben, that made a noticeable difference in my life and work.

In the fall of 1969, I was twenty-five years old. I'd published my first book, *Zirconia Poems,* on July 20, 1969, the day Neil Armstrong stepped onto the moon. In the academic year 1968–1969 I'd served as an instructor in English at Salem College in Winston-Salem. I had also been given, out of the blue, a creative writing fellowship by the National Endowment for the Arts. (In those days you didn't apply for a grant but had to be nominated by others.) In the late summer Nancy, Ben, and I took a camping trip across the country, stopping at Yellowstone, Glacier, Yosemite, and Sequoya National Parks.

Between the grant money, and savings from the year of teaching, we had a tiny nest egg. Because teaching jobs were so easy to come by in the late 1960s, when colleges and universities were expanding to accommodate Baby Boomers reaching college age, I'd resigned my post at Salem, assuming I could always return to teaching when I chose. The plan was to spend a year or two back in the mountains where I'd grown up, working on poems and a novel.

One advantage of being back home was that I could work part-time with my dad, who took various jobs in winter as house painter, carpenter, and rock mason. Working one week each month, I could earn just enough to get by.

Western North Carolina is a resort area and rentals are expensive in summer, but cheaper in winter. We looked at a number of houses, hoping to find something we could afford. Finally, on January 8, 1970, we took a house owned by my cousin Leo Levi, located just off the Brevard Road, US Highway 64, about three miles west of Hendersonville. The rent was $75.00 a month. It was a one-story farmhouse, built late in the nineteenth century, with a wide porch overlooking the valley. Even then many new ranch houses were scattered over that part of suburban Hendersonville, and many more were under construction. There was a pasture on one side of the house with maybe a dozen cows, and a forest on Long John Mountain came down to the rental cottage behind the house.

Next door was a summer home owned by an elderly couple, the Ritchies, from Delaware. The Ritchie yard extended over several acres down to the branch. In winter there was no one close by, and Ben and I could run and play kickball on the large lawn. On clear days I would lie in the grass watching clouds convoy above. There were woods and a small stream along the driveway running downhill to the road and mailbox. For a writer in those days a mailbox was a lifeline to the larger world, and the walk to the mailbox and back became an essential feature of each day.

When I was not working with my dad on some house painting job in Flat Rock or Mills River, I had more free time than I'd known for years. After rising each morning, I could read or work on poems. I made long lists of words new to me and looked them up in the Random House dictionary. I could walk in the woods along the driveway or follow a trail up Long John Mountain. There was an old couch sitting deep in the woods that fascinated me. How did it get there, and why? It was while walking that I often got the best ideas for poems.

I also strolled along the dusty gravel road that swung in a bow shape from Highway 64 through the country and back to the highway closer to town. On that walk I could travel from deep in the countryside to the very edge of Hendersonville. It was appealing to come out of the woods to the busy highway and a shopping center and textile plant.

As the early flowers appeared I became a student of plants in a way I'd never been before, finding a new intimacy with weeds and shrubs and wildflowers. I bought and borrowed books on botany and identified flowers as they appeared by the driveway and trails in the woods, along the stream: arbutus, spring beauties, hepatica, trillium. Like Thoreau, I began to keep a kind of calendar of blooms for the area. I read Thoreau's essays, "Walking," "Wild Apples," "Autumnal Tints," and "The Natural Succession of Forest Trees." As the days passed, I became more and more focused on the flora, weeds as much as flowers.

I savored Whitman's *Specimen Days*, and relished his observations about birds, trees, weeds, insects, clouds, and life at the pond-side. Every day I sauntered to the mailbox and back. More often than not there was nothing in the dusty box, and I couldn't tell whether the mailman had come and left nothing or was running late. As best I could surmise, the mailman usually came around noon, or just before noon, but I never actually spotted him. Much of the tenor of the day was determined by the jaunt to the mailbox. I was sending out a few poems and if there was an acceptance my steps were light back up the hill. If there were rejections I tended to loiter, watching bees in clover, noticing snake eggs sucked by rodents. Large water snakes and black snakes lurked in the thicket by the stream.

As the days and weeks wore on, my steady correspondent was Bill Matthews. I sent him poems and he mailed me the poems he wrote. I made comments on his work by return letter. He also wrote critiques of my poems and chose some for the magazine *Lillabulero*. A letter from Bill could keep me buoyed up for days, and his comments were always helpful. His criticism could be tough but bracing. The longer we stayed in Leo's house, isolated from the academic and literary worlds, the more I came to depend on a response from Matthews.

How can I best describe the days and weeks and months in Leo's House? Maybe one way is to list what I was reading. Poetry magazines and new volumes of poetry were sometimes sent to me by Bill Matthews and others, so I saw a good bit of contemporary poetry, James Wright, W. S. Merwin, Robert Lowell. But from my teaching at Salem College, I'd saved the Norton anthologies of English Literature, and for the first time ever I began a sustained study of British poetry from Sir Thomas Wyatt to Philip Larkin. I'd taught some of Larkin's poems at Salem and noticed that permission to reprint the poems from the volume *The Less Deceived* came from the Marvell Press in East Hessle, Yorkshire. I wrote to the Marvell Press asking the price of a copy, and two weeks later the book arrived with a note: "Please pay by cheque, $2.95."

It was from the *Norton Anthology* that I began to grasp something of the shape and sequence of writing in English, especially the lyric poetry from Ben Jonson, Shakespeare, Herrick, and Marvell, to Coleridge, Keats, and Arnold. The introductions and notes in the anthologies were a source of delight almost as much as the texts themselves. The general editor of the second volume was M. H. Abrams of Cornell University. Hayden Carruth published his paperback anthology of modern American poetry in 1970,

The Voice That is Great Within Us. That volume was a treasure of poems new to me. There I discovered the work of Robert Francis, and the plain, crystalline perfection of the poems of Yvor Winters and J. V. Cunningham. I became more inspired with an idea of mathematical precision and tightness in poetry. (In fact, I had once been a math major.)

By the summer of 1970 most of our savings were exhausted. We had spent some on hospital treatments for Nancy's asthma. What had seemed plenty of money when I left Salem had slipped away. As our budget for groceries dwindled, it seemed impossible we'd indulged ourselves in leisurely wandering across the continent the summer before. As the farming season began, my dad took no more painting jobs. From time to time, I helped him cultivate his fields of pole beans, a labor-intensive crop to say the least. Often, we had Sunday dinner with my parents, and my dad and I spent part of the afternoon discussing local history, family history, American history. My parents gave us potatoes and cans of beans, peaches, peas, and beets from their cellar.

When I'd left for college in 1961, I never thought I'd return to farming. But in my new circumstances, with medicine to buy and doctor bills to pay, I was glad to help in the bean fields, even though Daddy couldn't pay me much. My Uncle William Levi plowed the fields with his Ford tractor, but Dad and I opened the furrows with the horse and single-foot plow, dropped fertilizer and seeds by hand. One of the hardest jobs was cutting new poles in the pine thicket above the pasture and digging post holes at the ends and every thirty feet along the rows. When the poles were set in the holes, dirt filled in around them was tamped firm with another pole. The bean field looked like the pikes on a medieval battlefield. We had to stretch and nail wires along every row. Then strings would have to be tied to the wires a foot apart and twine strung along the ground. As a child I had tied the lower ends of the strings.

I had a new appreciation for days free to roam in the fields and woods, identifying day flowers, ironweed, cardinal flowers by the branch. A shrub near the stream below Leo's house yielded immaculate white blossoms, luminous in the swampy shade. I discovered the shrub was a marsh mallow, for which the puffy white candy had been named. Sometimes when I walked along the road, I passed a neighbor at work in his garden. More than once he called me over and handed me a half dozen ears of sweet corn.

Another destination of my walks was the cemetery of Shaw's Creek Church on the hill above the highway. Shaw's Creek was one of the first churches in Henderson County. I enjoyed showing Ben the graves of his great-great grandparents, George W. (1824–1900) and Rebecca Ann (1832–1924) Johnson. In the 1850s Rebecca Ann had been sent from South Carolina to the mountains for her health. It was thought she had consumption. The treatment must have been effective, for she eloped with George, a cabinet maker, and lived to be ninety-two.

In the summer of 1970, as I worried about paying bills, alternating between labor in the fields on Green River and rambling and dreaming in the woods and fields, a new rigor and dedication emerged in my writing. I bought a spiral notebook at a drugstore and scribbled poems about the sun and fields and flowers, about soil and weeds. I grew more and more focused on exactness, economy, compression, suggesting much in little, with an almost mathematical density, finding a phrase or image that was precise, but with wide implications.

I'd always written poems through several drafts, but now I revised obsessively, through version after version in the notebook, experimenting with effective line-breaks, to give emphasis to certain phrases, surprise the reader as the sentence continued on the next line, suggesting a meaning unanticipated. Day after day I copied and re-copied short poems, hoping to make them vividly real, surprising. A typical poem, worked on through many drafts that summer, would be "Thaw," later published in the volume *Red Owl*:

> Rods and cones
> at the ends of fingers held up to the sun.
> Snakes work in their roots of sleep
> and dirt shows through
> a huge fingerprint in the field.
> Hiss of crystals breaking
> as sun renders out the fat in snow
> to run and be drawn to the sky again.[1]

Looking back at these poems now, I can see I was learning to incorporate phrases and concepts from science into lines of visual observation and unexpected connections, fresh diction, while celebrating cycles, of seasons, ice to water, sleep to waking, synesthesia of touch and light. I hoped to make the poems both calm and explosive little packages that gave the reader new ways of seeing the ordinary.

When I was a boy my friend Ronald and I loved to dislodge rocks on the mountaintop above our house and send them rolling down the slope. One of the poems I worked on through dozens of drafts was called "Speaking," in which I equated rolling rocks down a mountainside with expression, inspiration:

To roll rocks off mountains
you set them up like monuments and push.
They start out slow,
staggering, out of alignment,
then generate stability,
blurring over logs,
crashing, bobbing
up again like deer till out of sight.
And still you hear them running away all the way
to the bottom and stop, coin like, in the leaves.[2]

From my reading of poets, especially Baudelaire, and from the experience of honing and condensing sentences, I evolved an ideal of crystalline hardness, lattice-like perfection, but with freshness and spontaneity of voice, always a little unpredictable, yet clicking into place with a sense of inevitability. Even though I could not live up to that ideal, I was excited to have something to strive for, the thrill of searching for the precise phrase and image, the right cadence and implied metaphor, to lift me above worries about bills, prospects, isolation.

Even so, my isolation was not total. The Henderson County Public Library was only three or four miles away. While growing up, my best source of books had been the bookmobile the library sent out to rural communities in the county. The first Monday afternoon of every month the van, named "Ridge Runner," arrived at the parking lot of the Green River Baptist Church. One of the staff with the bookmobile was Mrs. Mary Keeling. Month after month she brought books, starting with Wilder's *Farmer Boy*, and moving on to Dickens, Jack London, Thomas Wolfe, *War and Peace*, Hemingway, and later Jean-Paul Sartre.

In 1970 Henderson County had a new library on Third Avenue West, much bigger than the old Carnegie Library on King Street. Once a week Nancy, Ben, and I indulged ourselves by driving to the library to return titles and check out other volumes and records. We had discovered a love of *bel canto* opera from the Saturday afternoon program on public radio, and brought home albums of Maria Callas singing *Lucia di Lammermoor*, *Norma*, as well as others performing *Rigoletto* and *Tosca*. (At certain hours we could also listen to a classical music station from Greenville, South Carolina). In the library I found histories of the Natchez Trace, Mountain Men, journals of Lewis and Clark, and the *Travels* of William Bartram. It was the Highlands poet Jonathan Williams who had introduced me to Bartram, to Objectivist poetics, to the Black Mountain School.

Many books I wanted were not to be found in the Henderson County Library. I felt a special need to study Ezra Pound at that time, as well as Carl Jung's writings on alchemy, praised by the poet Robert Bly. Mrs. Keeling still worked at the check-out counter of the library, and she informed me that she could acquire almost any book through interlibrary loan. All I had to do was fill out a form and pay postage for the delivery of the book. Through Mrs. Keeling I got Pound's *Selected Essays*, *The ABC of Reading*, *Guide to Kulchur*, and the anthology *Confucius to Cummings*. I was also able to read Jung's extended work on alchemy, and a number of studies of Baudelaire. With the *Norton Anthology* and the books acquired by Mrs. Keeling, I was educating myself, and was excited, despite poverty and uncertainty.

A happy event of the fall of 1970 was that Bill Matthews invited me to give a reading at Cornell University. I would be paid $150 and cover my own travel. It was an exciting and intimidating prospect. I'd been living in isolation and had not given a reading for more than a year. I've never known a more intense combination of exuberance and dread than we felt heading north in mid-November. After the months of seclusion, sickness, and worry about money and the future, it was exhilarating to be on the road again in late autumn.

We stopped in Greensboro for Mary Feeney, Bill Matthews' former student, who was translating the poems of Jean Follain with him. Mary's wit added to the liveliness of the trip. We drove straight through, leaving the colorful trees in the North Carolina Piedmont for the bare forests of northern Virginia and Pennsylvania, arriving at the Matthews house near Ithaca after midnight on November 20.

The visit to Cornell was all that I could have hoped for, however daunting it seemed to read poems at the Ivy League university. The Cornell appearance occurred on a dark and foggy night, and Bill led me downstairs in Goldwin Smith Hall to the coffee shop in the basement called *The Temple of Zeus*. I spoke my short poems beneath the statue of Zeus himself.

Sitting directly in front of me was Baxter Hathaway, famed editor of *Epoch* magazine, and founder of the Cornell creative writing program. After the reading, Baxter came up to me and, following some hesitation, asked, "Do you like farming?" (I later discovered that when Baxter worked in a paper mill in his youth that was the question that he asked farm boys who came to work at the mill.) I also met the Faulkner critic Walter Slatoff and the poet Archie Ammons, each cordial and less enigmatic. I had met the writer James McConkey the year before at the party for the publication of *Zirconia Poems*. The next day I visited one of Ammons' classes, and met a graduate student who asked to print a chapbook of my poems on his fine letter press. In my conversation with Ammons, I discovered that he had grown up on a farm in eastern North Carolina and had attended both Baptist and Pentecostal churches as I had. We had each studied science as undergraduates. The Cornell campus with its gorges and Agriculture School, the Ithaca landscape with its waterfalls, lake, and vineyards, was especially haunting. It never occurred to me that I might be invited to teach there.

After the Cornell visit, we stayed with Nancy's mother near Syracuse through Thanksgiving, and watched the first snows arrive, before heading home to more house painting and a winter of isolation. To say the least, I was buoyed by meeting the writers and students in Ithaca. To know that my poems were read and respected that far from home gave me new energy and confidence.

In the winter of 1970–71 my father and I did renovation work and painting on a three-story farmhouse in the Mills River section of Henderson County, near the foothills of Pisgah Forest. The house was owned by the Bergin family. The late Mr. Bergin was a regional leader who served in the state legislature. His widow, living in the house with her daughter, was a spirited, educated woman who, before her marriage, had traveled as a missionary to the Tlingit and Kwakiutl Indians of the Pacific Northwest. During breaks in our work, I often talked with Mrs. Bergin about geography and Native American history.

My work on the Bergin house was probably the most difficult and dangerous I did that year. We scraped and painted the outside, me working from the high ladder on gables and dormers. Harsh, icy wind swept across the Mills River Valley, making my balance on the ladder even more precarious. Exposure to wind and fumes of paint gave me a sinus infection that made me even less stable far above the ground. I was lucky not to suffer a fall in the brutal air. The Bergin house was under the glide path to the Asheville airport, and every few minutes a jet thundered over on take-off or approach, so close I could smell the oily exhaust.

Besides painting, my dad and I replaced plaster on the walls of the parlor, knocking the old coat loose and raising such a fog of dust we had to run outside and wait while the cloud settled. That was the first time I'd ever worked with plaster and the experience gave me a new respect for those who mixed and applied multiple coats over laths.

Through every hour, as we painted, plastered, and repaired tall white columns at the front of the house, I thought about poems underway in my notebook, considering additions and excisions, new line-breaks, ideas for new poems. I ran phrases and lines through my head, so focused on words, and sounds of words, it's a miracle I had no serious accidents on the ladder or standing among falling plaster.

The most intense loneliness felt during that time occurred on New Year's Eve, 1970. I had had no letters, no greetings. The night seemed a void, a blank. There appeared to be nothing to celebrate. Luckily the mood passed with the night, and next morning sunlight of the new year came raw and fresh as new-sawed lumber.

One of the things that had impressed me about Archie Ammons was that he seemed so much at home in the ordinary, middle-class world. I knew he'd been a businessman in the glass industry in South Jersey. In conversation he was both folksy and articulate, attuned to speech and everyday things. His poems sounded the same way, very prose-like, observing and commenting on the most quotidian things. I wrote him a letter, thanking him for his cordiality at Cornell, and describing my work on the Bergin house and my plans for gardening and growing cucumbers in the summer ahead. Ammons was a model of how someone could live in the practical world successfully while also pursuing poetry.

That year I was much influenced by the work of Jonathan Williams, especially the poems based on quotations from mountain speech in the volume *Blues & Roots/Rue and Bluets*. Williams had a lively appreciation of the lyricism of everyday Appalachian parlance, of language as a living thing. His work introduced me to the writing of William Bartram, as well as the music of Frederick Delius and the paintings of Blake's friend, Samuel Palmer. Most important, Williams published a small selection of poems based on anagrams, called "Slow Owls." I wrote a short review of Williams' volume *An Ear in Bartram's Tree* and published it in *The Nation*.

After we finished work on the Bergin house in the late winter of 1971,

I'd saved enough cash for a few weeks of leisure. As early spring approached, I sat on the porch of Leo's house with notebook in hand, listening to birds in the maples, cows grazing in the pasture nearby and calls of crows, viewing a line of trees against the sky on a far hill, and scribbling anagrams that came to mind. Many were obvious: coin/ icon; ten/net; state/taste, etc. I made list after list, and then selected six pairs for a tiny poem called "Mountain Graveyard":

stones	notes
slate	tales
sacred	cedars
heart	earth
asleep	please
hated	death[3]

There was something both astonishing and ordinary about anagrams, at once so arbitrary and accidental, yet evocative. I spent afternoon after afternoon on the porch, listening to distant traffic on the Brevard Road, jotting down unlike words containing the same letters.

One day I found in the dusty mailbox a postcard from Richard Howard, poetry editor of the *New American Review* in New York. He said he had recently visited Ithaca and both A. R. Ammons and Bill Matthews suggested he ask me to submit poems to his prestigious publication. I stopped on the driveway to read and re-read the typed postcard. The branch beside the driveway seemed to murmur poetry. Since before the publication of *Zirconia Poems* I'd often received invitations from editors of little magazines to send poems. Sometimes they mentioned they had seen my work in other magazines, but more often they wrote that Bill Matthews had urged them to publish something by me. It was as though Matthews was my agent. (Later, Peter Davison, poetry editor of *The Atlantic*, told me that every time he had ever met Matthews my friend had mentioned my poetry.)

I took great care in typing poems to send to Richard Howard, expecting them to be rejected. When he accepted a longish poem and sent me a substantial check it seemed too good to be true. I'd already been published in *The Nation* and *The American Scholar* but was especially elated to be included in a mass-market, popular publication.

I knew that unless I wanted to spend the rest of my life as a part-time house painter, I needed to find another teaching job. We were so poor at one point in the spring of 1971 that when Nancy's Auntie Marjorie in Boston sent her a check for $10 it was like a windfall. Marjorie had been an actress and speech teacher, and she must have had some idea of how young artists struggle. Once I was so frustrated by an unpaid bill that I slammed my fist through the dry wall. Before leaving Leo's house I knew I'd have to repair the hole with spackling and match the paint exactly. One cold night in early spring the oil for the furnace ran out. The next morning, I had to ask the oil company to refill the tank. The company was owned by a distant cousin, and, luckily, he did not ask me to pay at once.

Gathering my slim credentials, I wrote letters to community colleges and junior colleges in the region. I applied to private schools and called chairs of English Departments. After the boom years of the 1960s, the bottom had fallen out of the teaching market, in part because of the disruptive demonstrations of the anti-war movement in 1969–70. I actually visited some local colleges and pestered deans, but never got an offer. Departments had over-expanded and were cutting back among the unrest and interruptions. Three years before, jobs could be had for the asking. In 1971 new positions seemed non-existent. I began to think of freelance writing and applied for a job with the Tennessee Valley Authority.

But even with all the uncertainties and financial worries, and doctor bills outstanding, the spring of 1971 was glorious. I discovered that at a certain stage worries seem to cut off, as I pursued my writing. It was writing that gave meaning to days. Much of the time I would put the uncertainty aside and proceed with my work.

One satisfaction that spring was that UNC-Greensboro invited me to give a poetry reading. To be invited to your alma mater is a special pleasure. Fred Chappell said they would pay me $50. It was my first poetry reading in the South in two years. (Later I guessed the $50 had come out of Fred's own pocket.) We drove to Greensboro as though in triumph. I was surprised to find Allen Tate there serving a short residency as visiting writer, and rooming at the Alumni House where we were put up. That was my only opportunity to meet the renowned poet and critic. He was gracious and witty, but I only saw him for a few minutes. We talked about Tate's former colleague at the University of Minnesota, James Wright. I regret that I didn't question him about a lot of things, including his long friendship with Robert Penn Warren.

The audience at UNC-G included a new crop of MFA students. It was my first reading since Cornell. The next day I visited Fred Chappell's poetry class and discussed the issue of "sincerity" in the poems of Thomas Hardy and Ezra Pound. North Carolina was bursting with luminous new green and blossoms. As we drove back into the mountains we passed from full spring to early spring and late winter in the higher mountains. Ben had stayed with my sister Evangeline in Winston-Salem. I returned to Leo's old farmhouse with a $50 check in my pocket and a reaffirmed sense of connection to the literary world.

As spring advanced Nancy, Ben, and I repeated our walks in the woods and on the mountain. Because of the challenges we had faced and survived, the spring beauties and trillium seemed more vivid, and the succession of blooms of the redbud and sarvis, the dogwood and apple trees. We took longer walks than ever on the sides and along the top of Long John Mountain. Sometimes I held Ben on my lap, and we slid on leaves down the steep sides of a ravine.

One day as we strolled far out on the ridge we heard a dull roar, like trucks on the highway. We ignored the noise until it grew louder and seemed to reverberate from the mountainside. Curious, we paused as the howls came closer, so harsh they seemed to come out of the ground. Suddenly a machine burst into view, and then another, and another behind it. A man bent over the handlebars of each vehicle, as though racing up the rough trail. The engines barked and boomed and spewed blue smoke into the cool mountain air. The leaves on trees around us seemed to tremble with the sound.

In April my Aunt Wessie asked me to paint the interior of her house. She and Allen were living on Social Security, and she could pay only $2.00 an hour, but I accepted, both because I wanted to help her, and because I needed money. I already planned to plant an acre of cucumbers as a money crop, but that would be done later, in May.

I was lucky to be hired to paint only the inside of Wessie's house, for it rained steadily that week. Wessie fixed "dinner" for me each day, and I became familiar with her soap operas, listening to the TV turned up loud throughout much of the day. I was surprised by the subjects addressed in the daytime dramas, not only adultery, divorce, drug addiction, but child abuse, embezzlement. That was my introduction to a new world of daily entertainment as I painted and thought about poems and wondered about my future.

On the next-to-last day of that job I drove home in heavy rain and found a letter from Cornell University. Barry Adams, chair of the English

Department, wrote asking if I would like to teach for a year as a visiting lecturer, conducting poetry workshops while A. R. Ammons was on sabbatical. The letter was typed on crisp letterhead. It seemed unlikely, an offer from the most prestigious university I had ever visited.

Peeling off my painting clothes and washing up, I dressed and began typing letters asking for transcripts and letters of recommendation to be sent to Cornell. I asked Fred Chappell at UNC-Greensboro, and Guy Owen at NC State, and Carroll Hollis at UNC-Chapel Hill to write on my behalf. By the time I went to bed I had all the letters typed on my old typewriter. Of course, I could hardly sleep.

Many nights I'd lain awake in Leo's house, listening to owls in the trees, wondering if I would ever find another teaching job or be able to pay bills. I told myself that, of course, I would not get the position at Cornell. Professor Adams had explained in his letter that the appointment was only for nine months. I should not expect further employment at Cornell. I persuaded myself that his candor could be a good sign, that the invitation might be genuine.

Next morning on my way to work I stopped at a filling station on Highway 64 where money orders were sold. I didn't have a checking account and needed to enclose $2.00 with each request for a transcript. With the money orders sealed in the envelopes I drove straight to the post office before heading on to Wessie's house. It was still raining, but the letter from Cornell made the light seem altered. A door to the future had opened a little.

Our plan for earning money that summer was to plant an acre of cucumbers on the land on Green River. I got my Uncle William to break a patch with his tractor, then I cut poles in the pine thicket and hauled them to the field in my dad's pickup. I bought seed and fertilizer, and we planted the acre. I dug post holes, stretched wire, and strung the rows up. It was a dry spring, and in June we carried buckets of water to encourage the young vines.

About ten days later Barry Adams called to say I had the job teaching poetry workshops at Cornell. With enhanced confidence, I continued writing poems, between making plans to move to Ithaca for nine months and coaxing the cucumber patch to thrive and yield. The clods, the weeds, the vines around the field, appeared bitingly vivid. I felt I was looking at things as through magnification. One of the poems I wrote in the days after accepting the lectureship was called "Wire Grass." It had a more fluent voice, greater range of reference, with a plainer surface, than many of my earlier descriptive poems:

A star explosion, and the streamers, debris,
set off new stages where they touch
and are nailed down by roots.
To leap off again
skipping over ground.
Each new base fires out filaments
that overlap and dive under
the parent systems,
weaving a wire mat over
dirt, a web trapping sunlight
and area, not halting at water
but throwing its tendrils
across, floating
them out until they catch
or get washed back by the current.[4]

By then I'd learned that poetry, like alchemy, was "the art of far and near," weeds and stars, now and the past.

All summer I drafted poems and worked in the cucumber field, plowing, weeding, then picking. We had to wash the cucumbers in a tub, then rub them with cooking oil to make them shine, before taking them to market. We made little money from that field, but it was an exuberant summer, nevertheless. I spackled and painted the hole I'd punched in Leo's wall. We moved out of the house on August 8, 1971, exactly nineteen months after moving in. I took care to leave my painting clothes at my parents' house, assuming I'd be back the next summer. I didn't know that I'd worked with my dad for the last time. We borrowed $400.00 from my mother-in-law to pay for the move. I paid $1.95 for a pair of blue sneakers at a thrift store, my first new shoes in years.

In a sense, little had changed while living in the old farmhouse. I'd expected the world of poetry to come to me, and it hadn't. Yet in another way, it had, and much had changed in me. Through the long days of walking to the empty mailbox and back, climbing on the mountain, studying ironweed, mullein, the swamp mallow, day lilies, and crab grass, writing draft after draft in the notebook, reading Baudelaire, getting letters from Bill Matthews, lying in the winter grass inspecting clouds, I'd found something essential in myself not recognized before. I was at once tougher, more confident, yet more alert, receptive.

I had learned to look and listen to language more closely, to take advantage of the happy accidents of writing, to think of the "reach" of implicit metaphors. I'd learned something about persistence and patient revision, about giving a poem a second and third (and tenth) chance to find its ultimate potential. I'd also learned that no one was responsible for me but me. I'd learned that the world owed me nothing. But I had also learned the importance of close friends, and learned that the most essential talent is the willingness to persist, to listen and attend. I'd learned that we can revise ourselves the way we revise poems. And I'd learned that as we get older, we can accomplish things impossible to imagine a year or two before. I'd found that the universal is more likely to be discovered in the local and specific, and that the extraordinary is to be located in the ordinary. I'd found that for a poet in the act of writing, everything is alive and connected, that to find a subject is to find a voice, and that just when there seems no way out, suddenly there is. I'd found that boredom can be a muse, as well as reverie. For the rest of my life, I knew I'd be forgetting and relearning these things.

If I had to return to house painting, I could, and would continue writing poems. I knew something of the strength of curiosity and openness to change. I'd learned about making the most of opportunities and uncertainty, and to recognize potential in the blank, unwritten pages of time ahead.

NOTES

1. Robert Morgan, *Red Owl*. 18.
2. Morgan, *Red Owl*. 19.
3. Morgan, *Sigodlin*. 27.
4. Morgan, *Red Owl*. 16.

PART TWO

Fictional Forays:
Landscape, Voice, and War

THOMAS WOLFE AND THE WHOLE WIDE WORLD CATALOGUE

In the year 2000, for the centennial celebration of Thomas Wolfe's birth, I wrote a tribute titled "O Lost, and Found." In that address, I said that one of the great events of my teen years occurred one Monday afternoon in 1959 when I saw on the shelf of the Henderson County bookmobile a thick volume in gray cloth with *Look Homeward, Angel* printed on the spine. I'd seen Thomas Wolfe's picture in the Hendersonville newspaper, and also a photograph of the stone angel in the local cemetery that was supposed to have inspired his most famous work. Wolfe was often mentioned in the newspaper in those days. There was still an air of scandal and mystery about him. He was a local legend, having grown up in Asheville just thirty miles away, and having written his notorious book about Asheville, and about his family.

When I took *Look Homeward, Angel* home and began reading it, and studying the Gorsline illustrations, I felt this was the book I had always been looking for. It was a novel about me, and it was more than a novel. It was a revelation about how ambitious and thrilled and scared I was, and also how "lost" I felt at times. Eugene Gant's parents seemed like my parents, and his anxieties, frustrations and sense of destiny were my own. As so many other American boys had before and since, I discovered a version of myself in *Look Homeward, Angel*, and I became intoxicated with the elevated, poetic prose. I felt I had discovered a new poetry in the choral sections, in the soliloquies: "*Which of us has known his brother? Which of us has looked into his father's heart? Which of us has not remained forever prison-pent? Which of us is not forever a stranger and alone? . . . . Remembering speechlessly we seek the great forgotten language, the lost lane-end into heaven, a stone, a leaf, an unfound door.*"[1]

This sounded to me better than Homer and Shakespeare combined. I didn't really know Homer or very much Shakespeare, but I was sure this was what was meant by great writing, and by tragic poetry. I read passages from the book so many times I had them by heart: "Each of us is all the sums he has not counted: subtract us into nothingness and night again, and you shall see begin in Crete four thousand years ago the love that ended yesterday in Texas."[2]

Imagine my exhilaration when I discovered Thomas Wolfe was born on October 3, 1900, the same day on which I was born forty-four years later in nearby Hendersonville, North Carolina. Our kinship appeared even stronger than I had guessed before. No wonder the language and longing of his book felt so much my own. It appeared to me that Thomas Wolfe had captured for all time the essence and the rage, the fear and poetry of what it meant to be young and alive in western North Carolina in the twentieth century. After describing the long slow painful death of Eugene Gant's brother Ben from consumption, Wolfe writes:

> We can believe in the nothingness of life, we can believe in the nothingness of death and of the life after death—but who can believe in the nothingness of Ben? Like Apollo who did his penance in the sad house of King Admetus, he came, a god with broken feet, into the gray hovel of this world. And he lived here, a stranger ... trying to recall the great forgotten language, the lost faces, the stone, the leaf, the door.[3]

At the end of the novel, as Eugene Gant is about to set out for the world beyond Altamont, or Asheville, as he walks in the square at sunrise after hallucinating that the stone angels in his father's shop have come alive and that Ben has returned as a ghost to talk with him, he exhorts himself to set out on his journey, paraphrasing Stephen Dedalus. "I shall find no door in any city. But in the city of myself, upon the continent of my soul, I shall find the forgotten language, the lost world, a door where I may enter, and music strange as any ever sounded; I shall haunt you, ghost, along the labyrinthine ways ..."[4]

The theme of the lost language, and the lost world to be recovered, haunted me as much as any other motif in the novel. Reading Wolfe, I felt I was recovering a lost language of vision and of the self. The impact of *Look Homeward, Angel* was a sense of self-discovery and of doom at once. It was similar to what I felt when reading Poe and Whitman, and Tolstoy and Dostoevsky all wrapped up in one book. The intensity, the sadness, and the sense of thrilling grief, and of the fallen-ness from a higher world and a higher language, inspired me to dream of writing my own book.

After that first euphoric encounter I did not re-read Thomas Wolfe for almost twenty years. I had gone on to discover the precise understatement of Hemingway, the fury of Faulkner, the tragic romance of Fitzgerald. But when I returned to *Look Homeward, Angel* in the early 1980s I was pleased to discover the novel still worked its spell on me. The cadence of the language, the richness of diction, the passion of the narration, the details of boyhood and small-town life in the South, were just as vivid as they had been in my teens. But what was different in my re-reading were the emphases. At the age of thirty-six the choral sections, the rhapsodic interludes, seemed less interesting than the realism and satire. Wolfe was particularly good at pinpointing absurd features of small-town life, the hypocrisy, the sentiment, and capturing the speech of store clerks, local politicians, reporters, blowzy widows. It seemed in many ways a different book from what I had read in my teens.

I am often asked why there are so many important writers from North Carolina. A few years ago, a reviewer in the *Times* of London, commenting on an encyclopedia of American literature, said there seemed to be "an inordinate number of American writers who were born in North Carolina." There may be more, well known fiction writers and poets per capita from North Carolina than any other state, unless it's Mississippi. My short answer to the question is: Thomas Wolfe. Once Wolfe achieved such great fame in the 1930s and beyond, other young North Carolinians got the idea that writing was an opportunity, a real possibility. The same is probably true of Faulkner and Mississippi. Once a region or a state has an extremely famous author, other writers are likely to follow. But the recognition and encouragement North Carolina has given to its writers is a factor also. In the 1960s, there was a feature almost every Sunday in the Raleigh *News and Observer* about one North Carolina writer or another: Paul Green, Frances Grey Patton, Guy Owen, Reynolds Price, Doris Betts, Romulus Linney, Fred Chappell. It was assumed at both the University of North Carolina-Chapel Hill and the University of North Carolina-Greensboro that among the students there would be important future writers.

When I re-read Thomas Wolfe in the 1980s, I was reminded how much he is the poet of the town, the city of Asheville, and the university campus, and in his later work, Boston and New York. The mountains themselves are in the distant background. The mountain folk are the mother Eliza Pentland Gant's gaunt and somewhat sinister relatives in the hills back of beyond. The mountains' coves and peaks are glimpsed from the train window or from the city square. Here is a passage describing the father of Eugene Gant arriving in the mountains: "Dusk came. The huge bulk of the hills was foggily emergent. Small smokey lights went up in the hillside shacks. The train crawled dizzily across high trestles spanning ghostly hawsers of water. Far up, far down, plumed with wisps of smoke, toy cabins stuck to bank and gulch and hillside."[5]

And once Gant enters the remote beauty of the mountains and settles in the village of Altamont, he meets Eliza Pentland from far back in those mysterious hills. They become engaged and he was taken to meet the Pentland family:

> ... and finally Greeley the youngest, a boy with lapping idiot grins, full of strange squealing noises at which they laughed. He was eleven, degenerate, scrofulous, but his white moist hands could draw from a violin music that had in it something unearthly and untaught.
>
> And as they sat there in the hot little room with its warm odor of mellowing apples, the vast winds howled down from the hills, there was a roaring in the pines, remote and demented, the bare boughs clashed. And as they peeled, pared, whittled, their talk slid from its rude jocularity to death and burial: they drawled monotonously, with evil hunger, their gossip of destiny, and of men newly laid in the earth.[6]

In 1960 I had been struck by the accuracy of Wolfe's portrait of certain aspects of the mountain people. I had grown up listening to my elders tell stories of grief and sickness and somebody that died a long time ago. But I had never thought the habit peculiar to mountain people until Wolfe pointed it out with his satire and caricature. Wolfe was particularly good at evoking real traits and characteristics by exaggerating them. The mournfulness, the relish for tales of misery and sickness and death, were so much a part of the world I grew up in I never thought them notable. Reading Wolfe again in the 1980s I saw that instead of the Byronic observer I thought I was at fifteen, I was really one of those whittling by the fire and telling those stories of sickness and grief. Those people were my people, and their stories were my stories. I had learned from Wolfe almost the opposite of what I had wanted to learn. It was not Wolfe's "poetry" that had inspired me. I had learned more about accuracy, understatement, implicitness and indirection from Hemingway. It was the world of his mountain people, so haunted and sinister to Wolfe, which I wanted to write about from inside, in those people's own voices. I wanted to let the mountain folk tell their stories in their own idiom. The lost language I wanted to recover was the living speech of a culture almost vanished when I was a child. I wanted to capture that lost language with the artistry and seeming naturalness with which young Greeley played the violin.

Wolfe, and his character Eugene Gant, had felt imprisoned by the mountains and the provincial town of Altamont/Asheville. They dreamed of escaping by train to the larger world, to the great cities of New York and London and Paris. Wolfe's language was a soaring vehicle of escape toward a dimly perceived destiny and glory. For me, growing up in a mountain valley thirty miles away in Henderson County, Asheville itself seemed a glorious place, a city set on a hill, that I wanted to reach and know in its mystery, its strangeness and complexity. I got to go there once a year, some years, to buy Christmas presents.

Among Wolfe's shorter works is a novella called "The Web of Earth." This story is spoken entirely by a woman narrator talking to her son about their family, about gossip from home, about the late father. Wolfe wrote it after a visit from his mother in New York, and it is different from almost anything else he published, for it is without a third person narrator or editorial comment. Reading "The Web of Earth" in the early 1980s helped steer me toward writing in the voice of a woman character, toward letting the character tell her own story. That connection with the living voice is, for me, at the heart of fiction writing. We read novels, and we write them, to know and touch other lives, and to listen to other voices:

> That was the year the locusts came: it seemed so long ago since the
> year the locusts came, and all the earth was eaten bare, it seems
> so long ago. But no (I thought) the thing kept puzzlin' me, you
> know—it can't be that, there hasn't been time enough for that, it
> was only the year before in January—Lord! Lord! I often think of
> all I've been through, and wonder that I'm here to tell it. I reckon
> for a fact I had the power of Nature in me; why! No more trouble
> than the earth takes bearing corn, all the children, the eight who
> lived, and all the others that you never heard about . . .[7]

One of the special things I learned from "The Web of Earth" was that it is the unpredictableness of that narrator that makes the voice come alive. The speaker keeps surprising us, but the sentences seem inevitable once we hear them. I also saw the advantages of a woman narrator, for women are usually closer observers of detail than men are, and they are more willing to talk about their feelings and relationships. The novella was an inspiration about intimacy, paradox of characterization, and toughness.

Re-reading *Look Homeward, Angel* in 2008, I am most impressed by Wolfe's overarching ambition and achievement in his twenties, his drive for largeness and inclusiveness. It has been said that one feature of a great novel is that it keeps revealing new facets and dimensions each time it is read. The earlier delights are still there, but new ones appear. Reading the story of Eugene Gant in my sixties, I am struck by the rage to document and record, to get down the whole of experience, and by the depth of Wolfe's learning, both implicit and explicit, and his passion to list, to enumerate, to catalogue the whole wide world of fact and emotion. Reading his first novel again I can see why Wolfe became dissatisfied with the novel form and spent the last several years of his life turning out reams of writing, reaching for something beyond, some other kind of work, something wider, deeper, and at once more innovative and yet ancient as Homer. *Look Homeward, Angel* is filled with long catalogues, inventories, chains of association.

Wolfe's use of the catalogue is of course not unique. Certainly, other novelists before him, including Melville, and after him, including Cormac McCarthy, have used long strings of names and details to create richer, more various fictive worlds. But more often the catalogue is a feature of poetry, epic poetry. In the second book of *The Iliad* Homer gives us a great roll call of the armies and warriors setting off to attack Troy. It is a muster list of heroes and would-be heroes.

In the second book of *Paradise Lost* Milton does something similar, calling up and quoting one by one Satan and his fallen angels. For Homer and Milton, the catalogue is a means of creating a sense of scale and grandeur, majestic pacing and vast perspective. The Russian film director Sergei Eisenstein claimed to have gotten the idea of the montage sequence from Milton's poetry. Certainly, the bird's-eye view and zoom-out or -in in film remind us of many passages in *The Iliad* where the poet describes huge movements of ships or complex maneuvers on a battlefield.

In American literature the most famous examples of catalogues are in the poetry of Walt Whitman. In all of *Leaves of Grass*, and especially in "Song of Myself," we encounter list after list, in section after section, name after name, image after image. Whitman lists and enumerates as though he wants to incorporate into his poem the whole of American life, in its complexity and range, including the ugly, the ordinary, the cruel, and the sublime. Section 15 of "Song of Myself" begins:

> The pure contralto sings in the organ loft,
> The carpenter dresses his plank, the tongue of his foreplane
> whistles its wild ascending lisp,
> The married and unmarried children ride home . . .
> . . . The pilot seizes the king-pin, he heaves down with a
> strong arm,
> The mate stands braced in the whaleboat, lance and harpoon
> ready,
> The duck shooter walks by silent and cautious stretches,
> The deacons are ordained with crossed hands at the altar.[8]

The effect of a Whitman catalogue depends on its textures, contrasts, surprises, and the sense of aggregation. While each increment should not be predictable, it must add to the accumulation of the whole. *E Pluribus Unum* would be Whitman's rule of thumb. Out of the many details and individuals he would create a sense of wholeness and unity, of humanity, history, country. It has also been pointed out that for Whitman there is something Edenic and Adamic in his long lists of images and details. In his great essay of 1841 "The Poet," Emerson had said,

> The Poet is the Namer or Language-maker, naming things some-
> times after their appearance, sometimes after their essence, giving
> to every one its own name and not another's, thereby rejoicing the
> intellect, which delights in detachment or boundary.
>
> The poets made all the words, and therefore language is the
> archives of history. . . .
>
> For though the origin of most of our words is forgotten, each
> word was at first a stroke of genius, and obtained currency because
> for the moment it symbolized the world to the first speaker and to
> the hearer. The etymologist finds the deadest word to have once
> been a brilliant picture. Language is fossil poetry.[9]

In the garden of the New World, in the promised land of North America, Walt Whitman, the persona and seer and bard, goes abroad like Adam naming the plants and animals, the landforms and occupations and preoccupations of the people. Like a colossus he wants to know and name, assimilate, and absorb the whole of the geography and history, and call forth a population to its greatness. It is almost certainly Whitman who inspired Wolfe in his own euphoria of naming and accounting for the vivid multiplicity of his world.

From the beginning of *Look Homeward, Angel* Wolfe thrills us with his listing of details, names, and individuals. He exhilarates with the range and contrasts, the multeity of experience. He even throws in Coleridge's word "esemplastic," referring to the power of the imagination to fuse unity out of the disparate elements of experience. His catalogues have a primal energy and a sense of visionary totality, a reach for encyclopedic completeness. Whitman described himself as "large, containing multitudes."[10]

Wolfe is no less inspired by hunger and relish, a gourmand of all sensation. Early in *Look Homeward, Angel* he writes:

> They fed stupendously. Eugene began to observe the food and
> the seasons. In autumn, they barrelled huge frosty apples in the
> cellar. Gant bought whole hogs from the butcher, returning home
> early to salt them, wearing a long work apron, rolling his sleeves
> half-way up his lean, hairy arms. Smoked bacon hung in the pantry,
> the great bins were full of flour, the dark recessed shelves groaned
> with preserved cherries, peaches, plums, quinces, apples, pears.
> All that he touched waxed in rich pungent life. . . . The earth was
> spermy for him like a big woman. . . . In the morning they rose in a
> house pungent with breakfast cooking, and they sat at a smoking
> table loaded with brains and eggs, ham, hot biscuits, fried apples
> seething in their gummed syrups, honey, golden butter, fried steak,
> scalding coffee.[11]

There is exuberance in Wolfe's catalogues, as he invites the reader to share in Eugene's discovery of the delights and pains and mysteries of the world around him. *Look Homeward, Angel* has been described as an outstanding apprenticeship novel, or *bildungsroman*, which it certainly is. But in many passages, it seems as clearly related to the poetry of Wordsworth's *The Prelude*, Byron's *Childe Harold*, and Whitman's *Leaves of Grass*, as to any work of fiction, with the possible exception of the long ledgers of details in parts of Dickens's *Bleak House* or *Great Expectations*.

Wolfe especially delights in cataloguing smells. He enumerates Eugene's memory of the St. Louis World's Fair of 1904:

Yes, and the exciting smell of chalk and varnished desks; the smell of heavy bread-sandwiches of cold fried meat and butter; the smell of new leather in a saddler's shop, or of a warm leather chair; of honey and of unground coffee; of barrelled sweet-pickles and cheese and all the fragrant compost of the grocers . . . or pine-sap and green pine-needles; of a horse's pared hoof . . . and of the rank slow river. . . ."[12]

There is something elemental and elementary about poetry. It is the oldest literary art. It is primal and primeval. The poetic instinct is the springhead of language itself. Poetry is at once simple and infinitely subtle. We can recognize and respond to poetry long before we understand it. Ezra Pound exhorted his generation to "Make it New." But as Pound himself illustrated, we often make it new by making it very old. A good poem seems to clear away the clutter and take us back to fresh beginnings. As Frost said, it is the discovery of what we had forgotten that we know that is at the heart of the delight of poetry. Synesthesia helps us recover the awe and wonder of infancy when the senses were not yet differentiated and the world was all mystery. The writer Madison Smartt Bell has said the essence of the poetic imagination is a sense of "universal animism."[13] Universal because the poet sees the connections between all things. Animistic because the imagination sees that all is alive, animal, vegetable, mineral, time, and memory.

While both readers and writers have been delighted *by Look Homeward, Angel* from 1929 to this day, critics overall have not been so kind to Wolfe. Even those who admire him concede that in the books published after *Look Homeward, Angel* there is a prolixity, repetition, with long flat sections that frustrate the reader. And at the other extreme are critics such as Harold Bloom who asserts, "One cannot discuss the literary merits of Thomas Wolfe; he has none.[14] The charge usually laid at Wolfe's door is that his fiction, especially the later fiction, lacks form, lacks novelistic ordonnance, control, and focus. He is also accused of over-writing, of using three words where one will do.

Re-reading his work now I have come to feel that Wolfe, after the great success of *Look Homeward, Angel*, grew dissatisfied, even bored, by the idea of a novel. What he yearned for, what he was reaching for, was something different. With Maxwell Perkins's help he had presented to the world a narrative of great distinction. But he was unsure how to go on from there. For one thing, he had little talent or interest in making up characters and events. His gift was for recording, remembering, re-imagining and commenting on his own experience. Where a Faulkner or Henry James would immerse themselves in characters and events and times they had never seen, Wolfe kept circling back to his own experience, emotions, memories. The fact that he was a famous novelist, and had been declared a great novelist, had left him in a cruel dilemma. He was expected to go on writing novels, and he expected himself to go on writing novels. But his passion, his vision, his erudition, often failed to cooperate. He was very young, and after writing furiously for eight more years he died in 1938 at the age of thirty-seven.

One explanation for his later failure has been that Wolfe was essentially a one book author who tried unsuccessfully to keep from repeating himself. With his considerable ambition and gifts and fame he refused to accept the fact that he had done what he was capable of. In the famous exchange of letters with F. Scott Fitzgerald in the 1930s, the author of *The Great Gatsby*, admiring Wolfe's talent and ambition, warned the author of *Of Time and the River* that he should learn to revise and exercise greater control over his narrative, and appealed to the model of Flaubert as the exemplary artist. Wolfe rarely answered his critics directly, but this time, he told Hamilton Basso, he let Fitzgerald "have it with both barrels." "Don't forget," he wrote, "that a greater writer is not only a leaver outer but also a putter-inner, and that Shakespeare and Cervantes and Dostoevsky were great putter-inners— remembered for what they put in— remembered . . . as long as Monsieur Flaubert will be remembered for what he left out."[15]

It is ironic and perhaps significant that the most sustained attack on Wolfe's writing in his lifetime came from the novelist, editor, critic, and historian Bernard DeVoto, in an article called "Genius is Not Enough," published in *The Saturday Review* in 1936. Ostensibly a review of *The Story of a Novel*, it was a blistering criticism of Wolfe's work in general, cruel and unrelenting. DeVoto accused Wolfe of publishing books encumbered with "placental" material, "long, whirling discharges of words, unabsorbed in the novel, unrelated to the proper business of fiction, badly if not altogether unacceptably written, raw gobs of emotion, aimless and quite meaningless jabber, claptrap, belches, grunts, and Tarzan-like screams."[16] He went on to mock the characters in Wolfe's novels and to assert that Wolfe had "mastered neither the psychic material out of which a novel is made nor the technique of writing fiction."[17] He added that Wolfe was hopelessly handicapped by a lack of critical intelligence.

Some have said that DeVoto was bitter because he himself had failed as a novelist to find an audience. And DeVoto's biographer Wallace Stegner points out, DeVoto often did not know when to stop his sarcasm and vituperation, either in his writing or in his social life. He was for the most part a generous and gentle man. I find DeVoto's attack on Wolfe's writing particularly interesting because DeVoto is a historian I deeply admire. He was not a Southern Agrarian offended by Wolfe's satiric and vulgar portrait of the American South, and he was not a New Critic espousing objectivity and autonomy of art, nor a fastidious devotee of Flaubertian aesthetics. The fact is that DeVoto had very much in common with Thomas Wolfe. Both were from small towns far from the northeast—Ogden, Utah in DeVoto's case. Both, through relentless reading, great intelligence, and ambition, had made it to Harvard. Both had failed at their first choice of careers, novel writing in DeVoto's case, play writing in Wolfe's, but both had succeeded in New York. Both had vast erudition and superb memories, encyclopedic knowledge, verbal eloquence, and a passion for history, for the American landscape, and the American West.

Some years after his blast at Wolfe, De Voto would publish his masterpiece on the Westward Expansion, *1846: Year of Decision*. One has only to read a few paragraphs in that work to see his kinship with Wolfe, in the vivid detail, the sense of space and landscape, the sense of time, the love of place names, the sweeping sense of history unfolding, the breath-taking range of reference and vocabulary. Wolfe was learned in a way no other famous novelist of his time was, in Greek and Latin, ancient history, geography, the sciences, the theater, classical music, the history of ideas and architecture. So was Bernard DeVoto. Reading both Wolfe and DeVoto, I constantly ask myself how one human being could know and marshal in writing so much information.

I believe that DeVoto's anger at Wolfe's writing was inspired by a deep sense of kinship and frustration. He must have recognized in Wolfe a gift very much like his own, greater than his own, but misapplied and misunderstood. Besides *1846: Year of Decision*, published in 1943, DeVoto would go on to complete his great trilogy on the exploration and settlement of North America, with *Across the Wide Missouri* in 1947, and *The Course of Empire* in 1952. In the catalogues, in the detail, in the unexpected extremes of biting sarcasm and satire, DeVoto's history writing often indeed reminds one of Wolfe's fiction.

It is a fact that in the last few years of his life Thomas Wolfe was drawn to the American West. One of the high points of his professional life was his participation in the Rocky Mountain Writers Conference at Boulder in the summer of 1935. He was the keynote speaker and the star of the conference. Halting at first in his lecture, he found his voice and kept the audience spellbound for two hours with his eloquence, his candor and generosity toward other writers. After the conference he spent weeks touring the West, and he would return for an even more extensive tour of the national parks, from Grand Canyon to Glacier National Park, right at the end of his life, keeping a diary that he planned to turn into a book about the West. It was said that he stood silent before a giant tree in Sequoyah National Forest in California for more than an hour, as though in communion with the colossus. He was studying and absorbing the landscape and the culture and history of the West, the way he had studied Asheville and New York earlier.

One of the most astute scholars of Wolfe's work is Louis D. Rubin. In his book *Thomas Wolfe: The Weather of His Youth*, Rubin writes "If *Look Homeward, Angel* is a book involving the wholeness, harmony, and radiance of a completed remembered time, what of the three subsequent novels? They are certainly not complete entities; the total impact is far from harmonious; and luminous passages are mixed in with opaque and soggy passages."[18] Yet for all its flaws, both DeVoto and Rubin admit that *Of Time and the River* contains some of Wolfe's finest writing, the finest of its era. But as a novel it is flat and uninspiring. At the end of his study Rubin observes that in the future Wolfe may well be viewed as a one-book author, though that book is a mighty masterpiece "alive in space and color and time."[19]

All biographers and scholars of Wolfe's work seem to agree that in his last years he had come to a new social awareness, a concern for the poor, the struggle for civil rights, for political issues of fairness and equality. He had matured and acquired a new kind of intelligence.

What I want to suggest is that had Wolfe not died of tuberculosis of the brain in his 38th year his work might well have gone in a direction that would have surprised many of his admirers. Frustrated by the expectations of critics and reviewers, perhaps bored by the whole idea of a novel, he seemed to be working his way toward another genre in his journals and notebooks, perhaps toward something like what Truman Capote would one day call a "nonfiction novel," or like Norman Mailer's nonfiction masterpiece *Armies of the Night*. Wolfe's passion for detail, for documenting, for witness and testimony and candor, would have lent itself to such a work.

The writer on whom Wolfe had the most profound influence was almost certainly James Agee. Three years after Wolfe's death, Agee published his classic nonfiction work *Let Us Now Praise Famous Men*. In its extended catalogues, in the vivid detail, in the passages of Biblical and Elizabethan language, and quotes woven into the narration, in the acute attention to sounds and smells, clothes and furniture, Agee's work reminds us from first to last of Wolfe's writing. *Let Us Now Praise Famous Men* suggests a documentary and testimonial direction Wolfe might well have taken himself had he lived a little longer.

Two years after Wolfe's death John Steinbeck published *The Grapes of Wrath* with its catalogues and cinematic montages of the Dust Bowl landscape, the highway, the hordes of migrants swept aside by history and trying to find a way to survive, to secure a mouthful of nourishment. The impact of Wolfe's writing can be found in passage after passage of Steinbeck's classic work. With his new social and political awareness, Wolfe might well have researched and written such a story, as he began to think beyond himself, beyond his own emotions and sense of destiny, to the sensibilities and struggles of others.

There is in Thomas Wolfe, the person and the written work, a relentless honesty and candor about himself and others that made both readers and friends uncomfortable. Had he lived longer he might well have written a memoir as shocking and merciless and thrilling as Rousseau's *Confessions*, or Benvenuto Cellini's *Autobiography*. We cannot imagine Faulkner or Hemingway or Fitzgerald attempting such a book. Faulkner once said reading Wolfe's writing was like watching "an elephant trying to do the hoochie-coochie."[20] But it is not much of a stretch to visualize Wolfe taking on such a project of self-analysis, confession, and catharsis. His obsession with recording, a full accounting, his erudition, his vast ambition, would have stood him in good stead in such a self-revealing enterprise.

But Wolfe might well have taken his genius in the direction Henry Adams did in *The Education of Henry Adams*, creating a memoir that is part history, part novel, part photographic detail, an elegy for a kind of innocence, an *Ecclesiastes*, subtle as quantum electro-dynamics or string theory.

Since I have said that as a fiction writer myself I have been more deeply influenced by Hemingway than by my great fellow Tarheel, I will conclude by quoting two passages from my most recent book, a nonfiction work, where some of the writing may owe a considerable debt to Thomas Wolfe

and my reading of *Look Homeward Angel* over the past fifty years. The first
is a passage from *Boone: A Biography* where I discuss Boone's exploration of
the Bluegrass region of Kentucky in 1769–1770:

The caves of Kentucky are one of the most spectacular features of
the region. Indians had taken shelter in them and explored the co-
vert passages for thousands of years, and animals had lived in them
long before that. Underneath the surface of much of Kentucky,
including some of the Bluegrass area, conditions were perfect for
cave formation, beginning with a water-soluble layer of limestone.
With plenty of rainfall, runoff picked up carbon dioxide from the
air and soil to make carbonic acid that seeped downward through
faults and crevices, eating away the rock, to reach a base water
level where pools and streams gathered. Rotting vegetation on the
surface produced even more acid to cut away at the limestone.

The pools and streams that collected underground made tubes
and tunnels, draining toward river basins, creating gutters, a maze
of abandoned drains. Because of the many colors of the salts and
stone, the underground chambers and corridors lit up like flower
gardens, chapels, sculpture salons, when a torch was brought into
the whispering, dripping passages, opening into one another like
chains of buried memories, half-suppressed dreams. Besides bats,
crickets, rats, turtles, and salamanders, animals that came in and
left the caves, there were permanent residents of the dark hallways,
alcoves, and grottoes: white eyeless fish, crayfish, flatworms, bee-
tles, and spiders.

The water and minerals made their own decorations, stalag-
mites and stalactites that resembled trees, statues, drapery. Colorful streaks called bacon festooned the walls. Cave pearls were
made by the tumbling action of dripping water. Other formations
were called snowballs, gypsum flowers, angel hair, cave cotton, cave
grass. Some stalactites were as translucent as flesh.

The shadow world of the caves was no less a wonderland than
the landscape above. Boone lived in many caves and carved his ini-
tials on several, as did other white hunters. Indians before them had
left their talismanic signs on the hidden surfaces. The caves were a
refuge, a secret world, sanctuary for the wet and cold, the pursued
and frightened. It was a land beneath the threshold of hunting and
settlement, multiplying the mysteries that Kentucky offered."[21]

When I came to write about the death of Daniel Boone in Missouri in 1820, I planned to describe his end succinctly and then move on to a final chapter on Boone's influence on Romantic literary culture. But as I studied the scene, and began to write about the frontiersman's final hours, I knew I had to do a little more than just state the fact of his passing. As I slowed the pace and began to put in details from the documents and depositions we have, I thought of other death scenes I had read. The most memorable is the death of Ben in *Look Homeward, Angel*. I knew I would not write a scene that extended and poetic—I would stick to the facts as I found them. But nevertheless, I decided to give the passing of my subject its due, having long ago learned from Wolfe the importance of describing the fate we all must one day face:

In the nineteenth century people talked about a 'beautiful death.' It was as though one's death was a work of art, something to be crafted, an achievement. Deaths were described and critiqued, commented on, compared to others', admired. A beautiful death was one's final accomplishment. In modern times, most people, except those who are killed in accidents or by sudden heart attacks, die in hospitals or hospices, often far from family and home. Usually, the old have been isolated for years in nursing homes and hospitals, in an air-conditioned and sterilized world of care by professionals. Death is hidden away in its own proper sphere. Too often, the last place modern people see is an equipped room in a large institution of care and dying.

Before the age of retirement homes and hospitals and nursing homes, the old died at home. If they were lucky to have a large caring family, children and grandchildren, friends and cousins, gathered around in a death vigil. In a world without modern medicine, the old felt death coming on, recognized it. People gathered in the bedroom and said their farewells, and the one dying had his or her final say. There were kisses and hugs and sharing of memories. Quarrels and grudges were resolved, grievances aired, forgiveness offered and received. Final requests were made. There were prayers and hymn singing, visits by the minister as well as the local doctor. The subject might describe the sensations of dying, the gathering of stillness and ease, the feeling of weightlessness and coolness. Sometimes the dying heard music or saw a pleasing light that might take the shape of an angel. Sometimes family members saw a dove or other bird light at a window, or heard the scrape of wood being planed, as if a coffin were being made.

If the dying person was very lucky, he just closed his eyes and stopped breathing, as the soothing rest closed in or opened out into an infinite stillness. But for some, there was a long death struggle as lungs tried to keep breathing and heart failed and struggled to restart, kicking in again and again, always getting weaker. Breath rasped in the throat and got shorter, until instead of breath there was only the rattle of air.

On his last day, Boone, who knew he was dying, said, 'I am about worn out.' The acute burning around his heart was worse than he had felt before. He asked for his coffin to be brought down from the attic, and he touched the polished wood with his cane to reassure himself of its strength. He described the kind of funeral he wanted and reminded them to bury him beside Rebecca on the hill overlooking the bottomlands to the river. A servant shaved the old man and Jemima cut his hair to suit him. Granddaughter Delinda even brushed his teeth. Boone asked his daughter-in-law Olive to sing some of his favorite songs. He expressed pleasure in his long life and health, his attempts to do good and not harm others, his faith in the mercy of God.

As morning approached, Boone asked for a bowl of warm milk, which he drank with relish. Then all the family members, including the slaves, filed in to say a final good-bye and receive his farewell. He told each one not to be sad, for he had lived a long and fruitful life. As Nathan and Jemima held a hand on either side, he said, 'I am going; don't grieve for me, my time has come.' He died just after the sun had risen, September 26, 1820.

Boone's body was carried in his fine coffin to Jemima's house and a large crowd assembled for the funeral there two days later. James Craig preached the funeral in the barn, which was the only building large enough to hold the number who had gathered. In the sermon Nathan's son-in-law saluted Boone for his explorations and development of the West, and for his defense of the settlements. It is not mentioned whether or not any Shawnees attended the funeral. Boone's nephew Daniel Bryan later told Draper:—Daniel Boone died . . . in the state of Missouri not owning as Much land as would make his grave—.

The crowd then followed the coffin and an American flag
to the hill-top a mile away where Boone was placed in the earth
beside Rebecca. The long hunt and pilgrimage to the west that had
started almost eighty-six years earlier in Pennsylvania were over.
Now there were only memories, stories, and legends.[22]

NOTES

1. Thomas Wolfe. *Look Homeward, Angel.* 1929. New York: Scribner, 2006. 3.

2. Wolfe, *Look Homeward, Angel.* 5.

3. Wolfe, *Look Homeward, Angel.* 454.

4. Wolfe, *Look Homeward, Angel.* 508.

5. Wolfe, *Look Homeward, Angel.* 8.

6. Wolfe, *Look Homeward, Angel.* 15.

7. Thomas Wolfe, *The Web and the Rock.* New York: Grosset & Dunlap, 1939. 148.

8. Walt Whitman. *Poetry and Prose.* 200.

9. Ralph Waldo Emerson. *Essays & Lectures.* 456–57.

10. Whitman, *Poetry and Prose.* 247.

11 Wolfe, *Look Homeward, Angel.* 55–56.

12. Wolfe, *Look Homeward, Angel.* 69.

13. Madison Smartt Bell, "Lecture." Chattanooga, Tennessee. Spring 1991.

14. Harold Bloom. "Passionate Beholder of America in Trouble." *The New York Times.* 8 February 1987. Section 7, Page 13. www.nytimes.com/1987/02/08/books/passionate-beholder-of-america-in-trouble.html. Accessed 25 July 2024.

15. Thomas Wolfe, quoted in David Herbert Donald. *Look Homeward: A Life of Thomas Wolfe.* Boston: Little, Brown, 1987. 416.

16. Bernard DeVoto. "Genius is Not Enough." *The Saturday Review of Literature* 13. April 25, 1936. 3–4. www.degruyter.com/document/doi/10.4159/harvard.9780674865488.c16/html. Accessed 11 July 2024.

17. DeVoto. 14–15.

18. Louis D. Rubin. *Thomas Wolfe: The Weather of His Youth.* Baton Rouge: Louisiana State University Press, 1955. 149–50.

19. Rubin. 166.

20. Joseph Blotner. *Faulkner: A Biography.* One Volume Edition. New York: Vintage, 1991. 483.

21. Robert Morgan. *Boone: A Biography.* Chapel Hill: Algonquin Books, 2007. 112–13.

22. Morgan, *Boone: A Biography.* 443–45.

ALBERT BIERSTADT AND THE MILLENNIUM

"Geography has no superior to this glorious sea, this chalice of divine cloud-wine held sublimely up against the very press whence it was wrung," wrote Fitz Hugh Ludlow of Lake Tahoe.[1] Ludlow accompanied Albert Bierstadt on his second tour of the West in 1863, and in articles sent back to eastern magazines gave written tributes to many scenes that Bierstadt painted. It is interesting to compare Ludlow's words with Bierstadt's vistas, for I suspect that the writer wrote as the painter may have spoken of the subjects of his work.

Bierstadt had learned his art both from his teachers at the Dusseldorf school of landscape painting and from the American masters of the Hudson River School such as Thomas Cole and Asher B. Durand. It is traditional to talk about how Bierstadt took the Edenic vision with him to the West, to "the land with no history,"[2] applying that vision to the vaster, more sublime landscapes of the Rocky Mountains and the Sierras. Ludlow described their travel as "going to the original site of the garden of Eden."[3] In this view the painter served as the new Adam, imaging if not naming, the mountains and rivers, trees and animals, geysers and chasms, of the fresh new world.

But I believe this vision of an original garden is only a part of the appeal and genius of Bierstadt in his best work. His later paintings have often been described as heroic panoramas, a term that fits those works in the Capitol in Washington. But in his greatest paintings done on the second western trip, such as "The Sierras Near Lake Tahoe," there is something intimate in the foreground, and something hazy, even dreamy, in the atmosphere. And the scale suggests intimacy more than spectacle.

It is a special feature of many of Bierstadt's best works that the viewer feels in the middle of the scene, not standing back from it. This is certainly true of "The Sierras Near Lake Tahoe." The viewer can almost taste the air over the pondweeds and flowers beside the water. The boulders in the foreground interrupt and complicate the scene in a lively way. The meadow appears to surround and continue behind us as we look.

But Bierstadt's art, like alchemy, is the art of far and near. What is so immediate and touchable in the foreground slides right into the farther meadow with the deer and sunlit, luminous grass. As we look at the valley floor, we see a lighted plane stretching from the four bold trees on the left to the more distant clump of trees on the right. And from the base of the trees on the right we see the plane reach up over the background trees into the lit haze over the mountain flank. And from that spiritual haze on the left an even bigger plane shoots up to the snow caps and into the radiant clouds. The painter has led us in a zigzagging pattern from the humble weeds beside the still water up into the mists and celestial vapors. The painting draws us from the close and detailed to the remote and transcendental.

I do not believe the experience of this painting is essentially Edenic. I do not get a sense of looking at origins, at the past, at a lost paradise. The vision is less Adamic than prophetic. I believe Bierstadt's work is so stirring because it suggests the future, not the past. It is a painting of Pisgah vision. The viewer is looking toward the Promised Land. For Bierstadt and his contemporaries, the West was destiny, the place of becoming. His paintings have the fullness of revelation. They are more Apocalyptic than nostalgic. The West is the New Jerusalem, not the lost Eden. It is a landscape lit with the becoming future, haunted by possibility. He is looking at a world where the lion shall lie down with the lamb, in the words of Daniel. There is the sense of the culmination of a quest, not of going back to beginnings.

The painting has an air of impending fulfillment, near the end of a long journey. Ludlow wrote of Lake Tahoe, "here, virtually at the end of our long journey, since our feet pressed the green borders of the Golden State, we sat down to rest, feeling that one short hour, one little league, had translated us out of the infernal world into heaven."[4]

As we look across the buzzing meadow at the great ramp of the mountain slope and lighted air, we feel something of the same translation, in the space haunted by haze of altar smoke catching sunlight, as if we are dreaming at the threshold of an apocalypse, at the golden frontier of the manifest Millennium. A pilgrimage that began thousands of miles to the east, and thousands of years ago, has almost reached the final goal of its destiny.

NOTES

1. Albert Bierstadt. "The Sierras Near Lake Tahoe, California." Oil on panel. 1865. https://www.wikiart.org/en/albert-bierstadt/the-sierras-near-lake-tahoe-1865. Accessed 11 June 2024.
2. Fitz Hugh Ludlow. "Among the Mormons." *Atlantic Monthly* (April 1864. 495. https://www.theatlantic.com/magazine/archive/1864/04/among-the-mormons/306013/ Accessed 25 July 2024.
3. Ludlow. 495.
4. Ludlow. 495.

FROM THE BLUE RIDGE
TO THE ROCKY MOUNTAINS

THOMAS WOLFE
AND THE AMERICAN WEST

Thomas Wolfe was passionate about many things. He loved to describe the sound of trains in the night and the thrill of journeys to far places. He loved to celebrate the lure of great cities and the lordly power of rivers. He delighted in catalogues of food, giant feasts, and the faces of thousands of nameless people. More than any other American novelist he attempted to gather up in one epic catalogue the whole of life, the sum of experiences he had had and the experiences he imagined. Wolfe exhibited in all his work a particularly intense and complex interest in mountains. He was passionate about big things, colossal things, and mountains were among the biggest things he had encountered, along with oceans and great rivers, and giant teeming cities.

I share at least three things with Thomas Wolfe, an October 3rd birthday, the Blue Ridge Mountains of western North Carolina, and a love of words and storytelling. When I was almost fifteen, I discovered *Look Homeward, Angel* and learned chunks of the novel by heart. It was *Look Homeward, Angel* that gave me the idea that I too might write something big and intense. But where Eugene Gant dreamed of escaping Altamont (Asheville) to the great cities of the east and Europe, I dreamed of escaping from the small farm to Asheville, the shining city on a hill.

Wolfe was, after all, a city boy and there is something sinister in his portrayals of the mountains around Asheville and the mountain people in the coves and hollows. They were his mountains and his kin, yet he feels a deep alienation from them, especially in his earlier writing. They belong to the world he was trying to escape. Near the beginning of *Look Homeward, Angel* he describes Oliver Gant's first sight of the Blue Ridge Mountains:

Far up, far down, plumed with wisps of smoke, toy cabins stuck to bank and gulch and hillside. The train toiled sinuously up among gouged red cuts with slow labor. As darkness came, Oliver descended at the little town of Old Stockade where the rails ended. The last great wall of the hills lay stark above him. As he left the dreary little station and stared into the greasy lamplight of a country store, Oliver felt he was crawling, like a great beast, into the circle of those enormous hills to die.[1]

In Wolfe's descriptions of the Blue Ridge Mountains there is almost always a sense of hauntedness, of lostness. More often than not his tone is elegiac. When Oliver visits his fiancée's family, the Pentlands, he feels he has entered an alien world: "they drawled monotonously, with evil hunger, their gossip of destiny, and of men but newly laid in the earth. And as their talk wore on, and Gant heard the spectre moan in the wind, he was entombed in loss and darkness, and his soul plunged downward in the pit of night, for he saw that he must die a stranger—that all, all but these triumphant Pentlands, who banqueted on death—must die."[2]

This sense of doom, of curse, of hauntedness in the mountains, can be found in Wolfe's second novel, *Of Time and the River*, also. Preparing to leave Eugene Gant exults that "in another hour he would be speeding world-ward, life-ward, North-ward out of the enchanted, time-far hills, out of the dark heart and mournful mystery of the South forever."[3]

The train that carries him away winds through the mountain pass:

The great shapes of the hills, embrowned and glowing with molten hues of autumn, are all about him: the towering summits, wild and lonely, full of joy and strangeness and their haunting premonitions of oncoming winter soar above him, the gulches, gorges, gaps, and wild ravines, fall sheer and suddenly away with dizzy terrifying steepness, and all the time the great train toils slowly down from the mountain summits with the sinuous turnings of an enormous snake.[4]

As he flees the mountains on the train Eugene looks out the window and sees a switchman "looking at the train with the slow wondering gaze of the mountaineer. The little shack in which he lives is stuck to the very edge of the track above the steep and perilous ravine. His wife, a slattern with a hank of tight drawn hair, a snuff-stick in her mouth, and the same gaunt, slow wondering stare her husband has, stands in the doorway of the shack, holding a dirty little baby in her arms.[5]

Though Wolfe changed the name of his main character and the town in *The Web and the Rock*, the mountains remain pretty much the same. George Webber:

> heard lost voices in the mountains long ago, the wind-torn rawness, the desolate bleakness of lost days in March along clay-rutted roads in the bleak hills a hundred years ago.
>
> Someone was dead in a hill cabin long ago. It was night. He heard the howling of the wind about the eaves of March. He was within the cabin. The rude, bare boards creaked to the tread of feet. There was no light except the flickering light of pine, the soft, swift flare of resinous wood, the crumbling ash. Against the wall, upon a bed, lay a sheeted figure of someone who had died. . . .
>
> From every intonation of Aunt Maw's life and memory, he heard lost voices in the hills long, long ago, saw clouds passing in the wilderness, listened to the rude and wintry desolation of March winds that howled through the grasses of the mountain meadows. . . . Aunt Maw sat with other rusty, aged crones of her own blood and kin, with their unceasing chronicle of death and doom and terror and lost people in the hills long, long ago.[6]

The dream of Wolfe's character is always escape from the sinister hills: "And the heart of the hill boy will know joy because he knows, all world-remote, lonely as he is, that some day he will meet the world and know those cities too."[7]

For George Webber, life in "the great bulk of the Blue Ridge . . . is near, as common as your breath, as strange as time."[8]

Even in *You Can't Go Home Again* the older George Webber is still haunted by the hills as he returns to his native city. But now the mountains do not seem quite as sinister:

> When he looked from the windows of the train next morning the hills were there. They towered immense and magical into the blue weather, and suddenly the coolness was there, the windy sparkle of the air, and the shining brightness. Above him loomed huge shapes, the dense massed green of the wilderness, the cloven cuts and gulches of the mountain passes, the dizzy steepness, with the sudden drops below. He could see the little huts stuck to the edge

of bank and hollow, toy-small, far below him in the gorges. The everlasting stillness of the earth now met the intimate, toiling slowness of the train as it climbed up round the sinuous curves, and he had an instant sense of something refound that he had always known—something far, near, strange, and so familiar—and it seemed to him that he had never left the hills, and all that had passed in the years between was like a dream.[9]

Wolfe, as he grew older, developed a romantic fascination with the West. It was the westness of the Blue Ridge Mountains in the state of North Carolina that gave them a special aura. He had traveled in Europe, lived in Boston, New York, and London. He had celebrated Octoberfest in Bavaria.

In 1935, around the time Wolfe first visited Boulder, Colorado and discovered the American West, he conceived a vast, poetic and documentary project, recording and celebrating America, the night in America, called "The Hound of Darkness." It would be a cinematic catalogue, a series of vignettes, dramatic scenes, passages of dialogue, different voices. As he worked his way across the West from Colorado to California he collected details, quotes, descriptions, for this "great tone-symphony of night—railway yards, engines, freights, dynamos, bridges, men and women, the wilderness, plains, rivers, deserts, a clopping hoof."[10] Using the film techniques of parallel cutting, panorama, zoom-in, montage, sound bites, he would create a "prodigious sense of simultaneity and omnipresence,"[11] evoking the "chemistry of darkness, the strange and magic thing it does in our lives, about America and the night."[12] The sound-track would be in part the voice of the train that goes "stroking the night with the pistoned velocity of its full speed" going "chucka-lucka, chucka-lucka, chucka-lucka," the *Pacific Nine* "like a lighted thunderbolt . . . smashing westward through Nebraska" hooting "Ho-Idaho! Ho Idaho! Ho Idaho! Ho ho ho ho ho ho ho ho ho," moving "through the planetary distance of the continent."[13]

My guess is Wolfe was inspired by Whitman's poem "The Sleepers," and Hart Crane's *The Bridge*, as well as film technique, and perhaps Carl Sandburg's *The People, Yes*, and his exhilarating encounter with the splendor of the Rocky Mountains. He believed "The Hound of Darkness" would be a "great and original book,"[14] an experimental breakthrough. But when he returned to New York his editor Maxwell Perkins did not encourage the project, and he resumed work on his fiction. A portion of "The Hound of Darkness" material was later published in *Vogue* under the title "A Prologue to America."

But in his thirty-eighth year Wolfe became more and more curious and excited again about the American West. The western mountains were big, bigger than anything he had ever known. The mountain West would be his new subject, as he returned to the earlier inspiration of "The Hound of Darkness."

In 1938 Wolfe still had the curiosity and wonder of a young man. Traveling to Portland, Oregon, in the early summer he met a newspaperman named Edward M. Miller and Ray Conway, director of the Oregon Automobile Association. The two men were planning an automobile trip through the National Parks of the Far West. They invited Wolfe to travel with them in Conway's white Ford. Though he was exhausted from just delivering a manuscript to his editor of over a million words, material that would become *The Web and the Rock* and *You Can't Go Home Again*, Wolfe could not resist the opportunity to see parts of the country he had never visited. It was a whirlwind trip lasting only twelve days, from June 20 to July 2. Each day Wolfe would make notes as he rode in the back seat of the Ford, and in his hotel room at night. The notebook of about twelve thousand words became known as *A Western Journal*: "Starting out from Portland the party drove South by East through farmlands of upper Willamette and around base of Mount Hood, which was glowing in brilliant sun. Then climbed and crossed Cascades, and came down with suddenness of a knife into the dry land of the Eastern slope."[15]

Every day Wolfe would record the number of miles they had covered, as well as his impressions of the landscape, people, buildings, and the quality of the light. He was dazzled by the brightness of the mountain West: "Unapproachable the great line of the Cascades with the snowspired sentinels Hood, Adams, Jefferson, 3 sisters, etc. . . . then down through the noble pines to the vast plain like valley of the Klamath, "the virgin land of Canaan all again" the far-off ranges—infinite."[16] Throughout the notebook Wolfe keeps referring to parts of the West as Canaan, or the Promised Land. And though he mentions in passing Native Americans and reservations he seems not to see the irony of his observations. The West had been their Promised Land too.

At Crater Lake he sees "the incredible crater . . . the great crater fading into incredible cold light."[17] Having driven 404 miles the first day, Wolfe fears "the gigantic unconscious humor of the situation . . . 'making every national park' without seeing any of them."[18] On June 21 Wolfe is dragged out of bed at 5:30 AM to start the journey south. He wakes up slowly, but once he is awake in the car he begins to make more detailed notes, as though he was just warming up the first day: "The desert, sage brush, and bare, naked, hills, giant-molded, craterous, cupreous [one of his favorite words] glaciated, blasted—a demonic heath with reaches of great pine, and volcanic glaciation, cupreous, fiendish, desert, blasted."[19] And then Wolfe is much taken with Mount Shasta looming above it all: "the naked crateric hills and the volcanic lava masses and then Mount Shasta omnipresent— Mount Shasta all the time . . . to Mount Shasta at 8:15 . . ."[20]

Farther south he sees "the lovely timbered Siskiyous . . . and all through the morning down and down and down the canyon, the road snaking, snaking always with a thousand little punctual gashes."[21] They drive through the wide Sacramento Valley, through "a dry land, with a strange hot heady fragrance and fertility" and "across the great, hot, straw light plain, and great fields mown new and scattered with infinite bundles of baled hay."[22] A gourmand, Wolfe lists the BQ and Greek restaurants where they stop, and then "the San Joaquin Valley . . . bursting with God's plenty—orchards—peaches—apricots—and vineyards."[23] They arrive late at Yosemite and find it already crowded with campers and tourists, though he is awed by the landscape, the "terrific mountain folds, close packed, precipitous . . . . And down again along the breathtaking curves."[24]

Even in 1938 Yosemite with its "gigantic cliff walls" was teeming with visitors: "hundreds of young faces and voices—the offices, buildings stores, the dance floor crowded with its weary hundreds and hundreds of tents and cabins and the absurdity of life and the immensity of all—and 1200 little shop girls and stenogs and new-weds and schoolteachers and boys . . . necking, dancing, kissing, feeling, and embracing in the great darkness of the giant redwood trees –all laughing and getting loved tonight—and the sound of the gigantic fall of water—so to bed! And 535 miles today!"[25]

The next day they hurry on in the white Ford to Sequoia National Park where Wolfe notes, "the great view back across the vast tangle of the Sierras—then Gen. Grant and the giant trees—the pretty little girls."[26] [Wolfe always has an eye for the girls.] After visiting the General Sherman tree, they hurry on to Bakersfield where Wolfe is impressed by an "enormous electric sign—Frosted Milk-shakes—A Drive-Inn—and girls in white sailor pantys serving drinks—I drank Frosted lime, Miller a Coca-Cola float, etc."[27]

On June 23 they stay at a hotel in Mohave and the next day drive through blinding brightness and blistering heat to Barstow: "Hotter and more fiendish—through fried hills— cupreous, ferrous, and denuded as slag heaps."[28] They reach Needles where it is 106 degrees in the shade and 116 to 120 degrees in the sun. Then drive through the desert and blasted landscape toward Grand Canyon:

> The blazing crater of the desert sky snakes on, snakes on its mono-
> tone of forever and of now—moveless Immediate and at last the
> rim and down down through blasted slopes, volcanic 'pipes' and
> ancient sea erosions, mesa table heads, columnar swathes, stratifica-
> tions, and the fiendish wind, and below the vast, pale lemon-mystic
> plain. . . .Immense plain backed by more immensities of fiendish
> mountain slopes.[29]

Wolfe appears intoxicated by the desert as they approach the Grand Canyon: "Fried blasted slopes and the enormous lemon magic of the desert plains, fiend mountain slopes pure lemon heat mist as from magic seas aris-ing."[30] And then he is taken by the pine forests as they approach the can-yon, which they reach after dark. For some reason Wolfe calls the canyon "the Big Gorgooby." Like everyone else he lacks words to communicate the experience of that natural wonder: "The Big Gorgooby there immensely, dark, almost weirdly there—a fathomless darkness peered at from the very edge of hell with abysmal starlight—almost unseen."[31]

The next day, June 24th, they tour around the canyon, but Wolfe has surprisingly little to say about the splendor. Instead, he notes a "cowgirl with broad hat, and wet red mouth, blonde locks and riding breeches filled with buttock," as well as "four small Indian girls in rags and petticoats be-side the road awaiting pennies (dimes they got) two upon a burro."[32] Later he writes: "the tremendous twilight of the Big Gorgooby—more concise and more collected here (from the north rim)."[33] At the lodge that evening the waitresses and bellhops perform "Hiawatha" and there are clog danc-ers, a slide show, and scotch with his companions. The next morning as visitors depart, some tearful, Wolfe writes, "the view from the terrace of the Big Gorgooby in first light—and glorious!—and glorious."[34]

On June 25th as they head north toward Utah Wolfe observes "quiv-ering the aspen leaves in the bright air, and down and down and then the bottomland spread below us over again, the fierce red earth, the tortured buttes and the Vermillion Cliffs, the Painted Desert and on."[35] They will visit Zion National Park and Bryce Canyon. It is the colors that seem to impress Wolfe the most: "And now pink rock again, strange shapes and scarrings in the rock, and even vertices upon huge swathes of stone, and plunging down now in stiff canyon folds the sheer solid beetling soapstone block of salmon red again—deeper yet not so fierce and strange (as I thought) as Grand Canyon earth."[36] And later, he writes of the "Sheer soapstone blocks of red capped by pinnacles of blazing white!—pool in cottonwoods surrounded by fierce blocks of red and temples and kings thrones and the sheer smoothness of the bloody vertices of soapstone red."[37]

Wolfe was impressed by the Mormon farmlands as they drove toward Salt Lake City: "A greener land, and grass in semi-desert fields, and stock and cattle grazing, and now timbered hills in contour not unlike the fields at home, and now farms and green incredible of fields and hay and mowing and things growing and green trees and Canaan pleasantness and a river flowing. . . .[38] A man says, "We have no deserts here in Utah." Wolfe asks, "Is Zion then a flowering prairie?"[39]

At a ranger's house he sees "the stick-candy whipping of the flag."[40] There are still more mountains before they reach the city: "A million wind-blown pinnacles of salmon pink and fiery white all fused together like stick candy—all suggestive of a child's fantasy of heaven and beyond the open semi-green and semi-desert plain."[41]

He is depressed by the tourist shops and the tourists at Bryce Canyon: "Feeling more and more desolate in this most unreal state of Utah."[42] He strikes up a conversation with a "quaint old blondined wag named Florence who imitates bird calls and a dark rather attractive woman, Canadian probably French, who sold curios and had life in her. . . . Young people coming out looking rather lost and vaguely eager, I thought, as if they wanted something that wasn't there and didn't know how to find it. . . . Americans in search of gaiety."[43]

Wolfe cheers up the next morning when he views Bryce Canyon: "Looked fragile when compared to other giant canyons 'like filigree work' of fantastic loveliness. . . . Great shouldering bulwarks of eroded sand going down to it . . . erodes at the rate of 1 inch a year—something the effect of sugar candy at a carnival—powdery—whitey—melting away."[44] Later he reports, "Talked with waitress who was from Purdue—studying 'home economics' and dress designing and hopes to be a 'buyer' for a Chicago store."[45] The waitresses, maids, bellboys gather in front of the lodge and sing to groups departing on a bus. Many of the women schoolteachers departing weep. One of the workers brags: "We got tears out of four of 'em this morning. Oh, I love to see 'em cry; it means business."[46]

The morning of June 26 they drive rapidly toward Salt Lake City. Wolfe observes the Mormon farmers: "sickling reaping, mowing hay with reaping machines and fields strewn with cut mounds of green lemon hay, and water—the miraculousness of water in the west, the muddy viscousness of irrigation...."[47] He is less impressed by the little towns they drive through: "villages—blazing and blistered in that hot dry heat—and the forlorn little houses—and sometimes just little cramped and warped wooden boxes, all unpainted ... the blistered little storefronts."[48]

But the fact is Wolfe spends more effort and more words describing the Mormon country than any other single place on their journey. He cannot say enough about the miracle in the desert: "the hackled ridges on both sides—denuded and half barren, curiously thrilling in their nakedness – and Canaan magical, the vale irriguous below—the marvellous freshness and fecundity of the great Sevier valley..."[49]

But Wolfe was disappointed when he finally got to Salt Lake City. He thought he saw "a denuded absence of humanity."[50] The place had "an appearance of a City greater than its growth ..." in "Sunday hotness, brightness, emptiness—the old feeling of Mormon coldness, desolation—the cruel, the devoted, the fanatic, and the warped and dead."[51] They observe "the harsh ugly temple, the temple sacrosanct, by us unvisited, unvisitable, so ugly, grim, grotesque, and blah."[52] Wolfe writes: "Enough, enough, of all this folly, this cruelty and this superstition."[53]

Wolfe feels much better as they get beyond the city, heading north, and he sees "The orchards lusty with their fruit, their vineyards growing with their cherries, and greenery, lushness, watery fertility, the like of which was never seen before."[54] They pass through Ogden, Brigham, Logan, and Wolfe is back in his element. It is the land that thrills him: "The great valley around Logan—a valley that makes all that has gone before fade to nothing—the very core and fruit of Canaan—a vast sweet plain of unimaginable riches.... A land of peace and promises of plenty."[55]

On June 26 they drive 467 miles to reach Pocatello, Idaho. The next day they follow the Snake River up toward the Tetons and then Yellowstone, and Wolfe delights in the potato farms: "the most fertile we had seen perhaps."[56] And then the climb toward Jackson Hole and the Tetons. Spectacular as the mountains are he sees the town of Jackson as "beduded."[57]

Too many dude ranches around it. After spending so much effort describing Utah it is as though Wolfe has no words for "the vastness and the sweetness of the Tetons."[58] Perhaps he was overwhelmed by their grandeur.

As they drive on to Yellowstone he begins to write more descriptively again, about "the Paint Pots and the boiling waters, sinister, grotesque, curved like a rhinoceros imbedded moving through hot oatmeal."[59] Like everyone else Wolfe is much taken by Old Faithful: "the hot boiling overslopping of the pot, and then the vast hot plume of steam and water—and the people watching. . . . The tons of water falling and the hot plume dipping."[60]

There is partying in the lodge that evening. Before leaving the next morning, they witness Old Faithful again and drive on to Sapphire Pool and other wonders: "Enchanted country, and green meadows, and pine—hemlock—spruce—aspen forests, bears upon the road . . . and the Elk feasting."[61] Toward Mammoth Hot Springs, Wolfe writes "Enchanted mountain country now and great peaks to the west and the climb, the patched dirty snow beneath trees, and then the rising eminence of Mount Washburn."[62]

Wolfe spends several pages describing the Yellowstone country, including the Northern Pacific station "and the waitress with the tired face, and yet with charm, sedateness and intelligence."[63] Livingston is "a blaze of neon, bars, and the bold hills about."[64] At Bozeman they encounter the Lewis and Clark Trail. In Bozeman he goes barhopping before writing in his journal: "The Great American Plain opening with infinite lift and rise and vastness to the fore—so towards the Rockies and the lift and rise and heaving of the Earth Mass—so the Blackfoot reservation turn and Browning—all confused disorderly and Indian."[65]

On June 29th they reach Glacier National Park. "The shining and bright austerity of the mountains and through the big barks and into the canyon. . . . Going to the Sun Pass and the stupendous hackled peaks now—the sheer basaltic wall of glaciation, the steep scoopings down below, the dense vertices of glacial valley slopes and forest."[66]

On the morning of June 30 Wolfe watches a "woman feeding deer and laughing before the hotel: 'Talked to waitress sitting in grass with deer nestling to her.'"[67] He sees "The lake marvelous in morning shadow and the Alpine sheerness of the granite peaks."[68] They drive on to Flathead Lake and observe "The lumber mills and trains of logs . . . ,[69] driving on to Missoula and then along Clark's Fork, a lovely ride along a valley, "the scenery often almost Appalachian (save for the darkness of the trees)."[70]

At Thompson's Falls he observes "three little girls dancing in front of the place where we eat,"[71] and further speculates "on the route of Lewis and Clark, whose ghosts have haunted us and this country since Three Forks and the upper reaches of the Missouri."[72]

In Spokane he settles his accounts for the trip ("less that, $50") and enjoys a bottle of scotch.[73] On July 1, they drive through "the Grand Coulee down, down, down and the tremendous size and glacial greenness of the Columbia River sweeping round the bend and the basal ramparts of the terrific dam, and the crews with red helmets working."[74]

After the drive down the spectacular Columbia River gorge there was one final stop in the mountains—through the Chinook Pass and on to Mount Rainier: "Mist blowing in in floods of spume and up and up to timber line and to the Sunrise Lodge and light playing marvelously, and blue cerulean, struggling to break through, and the glaciers level to the eye and visible but the great mountain massif and the peak obscured."[75] The next day "the mist ocean below us—but the great mass of Rainier clearly defined now . . . . And all of its perilous overwhelming majesty, and with its tremendous shoulders, the long terrific sweep of its hackling ridges. . . . A universe of mountain, a continent of mountain—and nothing else but mountain itself to compare mountain to."[76]

The whirlwind journey ends in Olympia, among "strings of market stores, hot dog stands, filling stations, taverns, etc. so down into the crowded streets of Olympia choked with giant tides of traffic for the Fourth, the sidewalks crowded with throngs of people—farmers, seamen, lumberjacks in town for the Fourth."[77] After a hearty lunch at "Crane's famous seafood Restaurant" Wolfe says goodbye to his traveling companions. They give him the map and Tour Book as souvenirs, write their names in the book, and are gone: "A curiously hollow feeling in me as I stand there in the streets of Olympia and watch the white Ford flash away."[78] He catches the bus to Seattle, collects his mail and gets money from a bank, buys a bottle of scotch, and the trip is over.

I believe that in 1938 Wolfe was about to take a new direction that would have surprised many of his readers. Frustrated by the expectations of critics and reviewers, perhaps dissatisfied with the whole idea of a novel, of fiction, he seemed to be ready to return to something like "The Hound of Darkness," working toward another genre in his journals and notebooks, perhaps toward some epic documentary kind of book, a Walt Whitman kind of work. Wolfe's passion for detail, documentation, for witness and testimony and candor, would have lent itself to such a bold new work.

A giant of a man himself, Wolfe had hankered for a literary form adequate to his vision of America. So far, he had not found it. But in the West, he witnessed a landscape commensurate with the scale of his passion and vision, his love of both wonder and the real. In his notes from the western journey, we begin to see the hint and outline of that future kind of writing.

Of course, we will never know what Wolfe might have done with his fascination and passion for the grandeur of the West. Within days of his return to Seattle he became ill. Thinking he could throw off the cold he took a ferry to Victoria. But instead of throwing it off he got worse and worse. A doctor diagnosed pneumonia, and then tuberculosis. His brother Fred came out to stay with him. Instead of getting well he grew weaker, suffering thundering headaches.

Wolfe was just strong enough to write a last letter to Maxwell Perkins, saying he had a "hunch":

> I've made a long journey and been to a strange country, and I've
> seen the dark man very close; and I don't think I was too much
> afraid of him, but so much of mortality still clings to me—I
> wanted most desperately to live and still do, and I thought about
> you all a 1000 times, and wanted to see you all again, and there was
> the impossible anguish and regret of all the work I had not done,
> of all the work I had to do—and I know now I'm just a grain of
> dust, and I feel as if a great window has been opened on life I did
> not know about before—and if I come through this, I hope to
> God I am a better man, and in some strange way I can't explain I
> know I am a deeper and wiser one.[79]

Wolfe did not improve. His sister Mabel came out to stay with him. It was decided to take Wolfe all the way across the country to Johns Hopkins. Admitted to the Baltimore hospital on September 10, 1938, his skull was trephined to release the fluid under pressure on his brain. On September 12 he was operated on for a brain tumor. Tuberculosis of the brain was discovered. Wolfe never regained consciousness, and died September fifteenth, only a few days short of his thirty-eighth birthday. He was buried in Asheville at Riverside Cemetery.

Thomas Wolfe was one of the most influential and imitated writers of his time. The verve and vision, the passion of his style, inspired many writers of his generation and the next. James Agee's *Let Us Now Praise Famous Men* clearly owes a debt to Wolfe's detailed, intense, poetic, often photographic, narratives. More than any other American author Wolfe inspired the young Jack Kerouac. For that matter there are passages in John Steinbeck's *The Grapes of Wrath*, published in 1939, which echo Wolfe's vivid cinematic prose. The same is true for certain passages in Robert Penn Warren's *All the King's Men*.

All my life I have felt the influence of Thomas Wolfe, especially in the voices of his narratives, in particular *The Web of Earth,* inspired by his mother's monologue. The way Wolfe lets the old woman tell her story to the son was a revelation to me when I began to work on fiction again in the 1980s. Letting the character Sharon tell her own story in the novella *The Mountains Won't Remember Us* was *my* greatest breakthrough as a fiction writer. It was Wolfe more than anyone else who showed me how that was done.

NOTES

1. Thomas Wolfe, *Look Homeward, Angel.* 1929. New York: Scribner, 2006. 8–9.

2. Wolfe, *Look Homeward, Angel.* 15.

3. Wolfe, *Look Homeward, Angel.* 51.

4. Wolfe, *Look Homeward, Angel.* 52.

5. Wolfe, *Look Homeward, Angel.* 53.

6. Thomas Wolfe, *The Web and the Rock.* New York: Grosset & Dunlap, 1939. 8–9.

7. Wolfe, *The Web and the Rock.* 13.

8. Wolfe, *The Web and the Rock.* 16.

9. Thomas Wolfe. *You Can't Go Home Again.* New York: Dell, 1960. 99–100.

10. John L. Idol. *A Thomas Wolfe Companion.* New York: Greenwood, 1987. 6. **16?**

11. David Herbert Donald. *Look Homeward: A Life of Thomas Wolfe.* Boston: Little, Brown, 1987. 348.

12. Donald, *Look Homeward.* 347.

13. Thomas Wolfe. *The Complete Stories of Thomas Wolfe.* New York: Scribner, 1987. 409–10.

14. Donald, *Look Homeward.* 347.

15. Thomas Wolfe. *A Western Journal.* Pittsburgh: University of Pittsburgh Press, 1951. 1.

16. Wolfe, *A Western Journal.* 1–2.

17. Wolfe, *A Western Journal.* Ibid.

18. Wolfe, *A Western Journal*. 3.

19. Wolfe, *A Western Journal*. Ibid.

20. Wolfe, *A Western Journal*. 3–4.

21. Wolfe, *A Western Journal*. Ibid.

22. Wolfe, *A Western Journal*. 5.

23. Wolfe, *A Western Journal*. 6–7.

24. Wolfe, *A Western Journal*. 8.

25. Wolfe, *A Western Journal*. 9–10.

26. Wolfe, *A Western Journal*. Ibid.

27. Wolfe, *A Western Journal*. 11.

28. Wolfe, *A Western Journal*. 12.

29. Wolfe, *A Western Journal*. 14.

30. Wolfe, *A Western Journal*. 14–15.

31. Wolfe, *A Western Journal*. 16.

32. Wolfe, *A Western Journal*. 18.

33. Wolfe, *A Western Journal*. 20.

34. Wolfe, *A Western Journal*. 21.

35. Wolfe, *A Western Journal*. 22.

36. Wolfe, *A Western Journal*. 23.

37. Wolfe, *A Western Journal*. 24.

38. Wolfe, *A Western Journal*. 25–26.

39. Wolfe, *A Western Journal*. Ibid.

40. Wolfe, *A Western Journal*. 27.

41. Wolfe, *A Western Journal*. Ibid.

42. Wolfe, *A Western Journal*. 28.

43. Wolfe, *A Western Journal*. 28–29.

44. Wolfe, *A Western Journal*. Ibid.

45. Wolfe, *A Western Journal*. 30.

46. Wolfe, *A Western Journal*. 31.

47. Wolfe, *A Western Journal*. 32.

48. Wolfe, *A Western Journal*. 33.

49. Wolfe, *A Western Journal*. 34.

50. Wolfe, *A Western Journal*. 36.

51. Wolfe, *A Western Journal*. 37.

52. Wolfe, *A Western Journal*. 38.

53. Wolfe, *A Western Journal*. Ibid.

54. Wolfe, *A Western Journal*. 38–39.

55. Wolfe, *A Western Journal*. 40.

56. Wolfe, *A Western Journal*. 43.

57. Wolfe, *A Western Journal*. 44.

58. Wolfe, *A Western Journal*. 45.

59. Wolfe, *A Western Journal*. Ibid.

60. Wolfe, *A Western Journal*. 46.

61. Wolfe, *A Western Journal*. 48.

62. Wolfe, *A Western Journal*. 48–49.

63. Wolfe, *A Western Journal*. 51.

64. Wolfe, *A Western Journal*. Ibid.

65. Wolfe, *A Western Journal*. 53.

66. Wolfe, *A Western Journal*. 53–54.

67. Wolfe, *A Western Journal*. 55.

68. Wolfe, *A Western Journal*. Ibid.

69. Wolfe, *A Western Journal*. 56.

70. Wolfe, *A Western Journal*. Ibid.

71. Wolfe, *A Western Journal*. 57.

72. Wolfe, *A Western Journal*. 58.

73. Wolfe, *A Western Journal*. 59.

74. Wolfe, *A Western Journal*. Ibid.

75. Wolfe, *A Western Journal*. 62.

76. Wolfe, *A Western Journal*. 64.

77. Wolfe, *A Western Journal*. 66–67.

78. Wolfe, *A Western Journal*. 67.

79. Donald, *Look Homeward*. 458.

WILMA DYKEMAN'S
FAMILY OF EARTH

THIS WAS PEACE

After Wilma Dykeman's death in December 2006, her son, Jim Stokely III, searching through papers in her house in Newport, Tennessee, found a box labeled "Northwestern." Under material relating to Dykeman's graduation from Northwestern University in 1940, he discovered a two hundred page-memoir which the author had either lost or forgotten. It would appear the manuscript was written during World War Two, when the author was in her early to mid-twenties, probably after the return to her native Asheville, North Carolina. This memoir, *Family of Earth,* adds significantly to her legacy of fiction and nonfiction. It is clear that from the first Dykeman was a very accomplished writer.

Wilma Dykeman (May 1920-December 2006) belonged to a second generation of gifted Southern and Southern Appalachian writers, following the literary renaissance of Faulkner, Thomas Wolfe, Eudora Welty, James Still, Margaret Mitchell, Erskine Caldwell, etc. Along with Mary Lee Settle, Harriette Arnow, and John Ehle, she furthered and deepened the literary heritage of the Southern Appalachian region. In both fiction and nonfiction, in workshops, lectures, classes at the University of Tennessee, in reviews and newspaper columns, she enriched the cultural life of the region for half a century. And with her husband James Stokely, Jr. she played a significant part in the discussion of the social, environmental, and racial issues of her time.

For those of us who have known Dykeman's work for decades, and for those just discovering her fiction and nonfiction, the memoir *Family of Earth* is a treasure. Here we encounter an unusually gifted and observant young writer, exploring her voice, meditating with eloquence and lyrical passion on her life and family and the world from which she came. The writing is alive, with a fresh sense of wonder. The detail is intimate, sensuous, sometimes cinematic. In this memoir there is a special sense of thresholds connecting the past, the traditional, with the modern present.

The two themes that stand out in the memoir are the closeness to the natural world of trees, streams, butterflies, flowers, the progress of the seasons, and the closeness to family and a great variety of other people, including Aunt Maude, the Preacher, and Old Man Milligan. As Dykeman writes: "The life of one human is the life of every other living thing on earth."[1] It is thrilling to watch the young Dykeman explore the "fresh, papyrus of memory."[2] The narrative reveals an unusually intense recall of infancy, the discovery of the self as a "triumph of lone splendor."[3] The truth is Wilma Dykeman was a poet as well as a prose writer, evoking the rumble of stones in a flooded stream, moments of hush, the many varieties of wildflowers, the "Aladdin's lantern"[4] of childhood imagination, the death in nature that feeds life, the beauty of forest fires, butter making, tent caterpillars, dirt daubers and katydids, hounds baying on the mountain, a rooster crowing in the middle of the night.

Dykeman writes: "I do not believe that any true realist . . . can help being a romantic."[5] Yet for all the romance and magic in her memories, there is a great deal of realism also as she recounts the pain of the Land Boom collapse in Asheville and the Great Depression, the "leanness" of mountain children, the loss of childhood imagination, the hurt of missed connections with those we know and love. The portrait of her father, and the account of his illness and death are especially poignant.

In this early work Dykeman does not turn away from the tragic, the harsh, the essential loneliness of the human condition. She admits to a sense of not fitting in, either in the mountain community or the society of Asheville, caught somewhere between two worlds and not belonging wholly to either. At dance lessons she feels like an intruder. Her social conscience is awakened when she realizes that sometimes when one gained, "somebody, somewhere paid a price."[6]

Significantly, Dykeman writes: "I have no talent for boredom," which can serve as the theme of this memoir and all her writing.[7] This long-lost book is her testimony of "tasting the fire"[8] of poetry and the world around her. She speaks of an infinite curiosity for history, biography, for gardening and the rhythms and routines of the natural world, for travel, for exploration of solitude, for the "singularity of homelife."[9] Her words serve as both telescope and microscope, making the distant in time close, enlarging the minute fact until it is luminous.

My first encounter with the writing of Wilma Dykeman was with her nonfiction classic *The French Broad*. Reading that book was an important event in my discovery of the history of the Southern Appalachian region. *The French Broad* is such a vivid book and such a loving book, packed with information and insight, memorable writing, and environmental consciousness. It gives us a living sense of the land, the watershed of the French Broad, the geology and geography, the Cherokee, and the development of the culture of the area.

In 1971, I was invited to Cornell University to teach poetry workshops for one year, while A. R. Ammons was on sabbatical. For the past two years I had lived with my family outside Hendersonville, North Carolina, in an old farmhouse and worked part-time has a house painter and farm laborer while writing poetry. It was a culture shock to be suddenly living in Ithaca, New York, surrounded by other writers and scholars and scientists, and wondered how I would ever have the courage to speak in such company.

As it turned out, Cornell was very welcoming, and instead of one year I have stayed there now forty-five years. But as I worked to make myself an effective teacher at an Ivy League university, to take part in the discourse with bright students and faculty, I found myself thinking more and more about the southern Appalachian Mountains from which I had come. Out of homesickness and nostalgia I began to go to the large research library on campus to check out book after book about the history of Western North Carolina and Eastern Tennessee. I studied the geography and geology of the region, and the history of the Cherokee, and the exploration and settlement of the mountains. I read articles on the dialects of the southern highlands, speech patterns I had grown up speaking and shed when I went off to college. At Cornell, I became a student of my home region in a way I never had been when I lived there.

Of all the books I found in the library and read at that time, the one that had the deepest impact on me was *The French Broad* by Wilma Dykeman. I had grown up just one mile south of the continental divide that marked the limits of the French Broad watershed. As I devoured the first chapters of Dykeman's story of the river, I could hardly believe my good fortune. There was such clarity to the writing, and the depth of research and scholarship was obvious. The author was a poet, with a deep sympathy for the people of the region, and for the land and environmental issues. The book had been published in 1955, yet in most ways it seemed completely up-to-date. The range of knowledge and subjects was impressive. Dykeman had studied the history of the place, the streams and forests, the soils and rocks, the flora and fauna. She wrote about exactly what I needed to know: the early explorers, the missionaries, the stock drives and taverns on the Buncombe Turnpike that passed along my family land in Henderson County. She wrote about moonshining, which had been an avocation of certain members of my family. (One of my cousins used to refer to the time he had spent in the penitentiary for moonshining as "back when I was going to school for the government.")

Dykeman told me the Cherokee had called the French Broad River "The Long Man," with his head in the high mountains and his legs in the valley. Like the Cherokee, she caught a sense of the sweep of the watershed in time and the vast interior of the continent. She asks:

> Which is the time to know the river? April along the French Broad is a swirl of sudden water beneath the bending buds of spice-wood bushes, a burst of spring and breath of sweetness between the snows of winter and summer's sun. August is a film of dust on purple asters along the country roads of the lower river, and the green stillness of heavy shade splattered with sunlight beside the upper river. October is a flame, a Renaissance richness of red and amber, the ripeness of harvest in husk and bin. It is the golden span between the dry rattle of September's end and November's beginning.[10]

One of the powerful motifs in all Dykeman's writing, fiction and nonfiction, is water, especially springs as sources of life sustaining water. Early in *The French Broad* we find this passage:

> The cold sweet springs of these mountains, the springs which feed thousands of steady streams to make a river, have been valued for generations by the families they feed. If halfway up a hillside or deep in the head of some remote cove you see a house and wonder why its people built there rather than on easier slopes, the answer is probably the water. Cupped in a clear steady pool under a thicket of blackberry vines and old shade trees, their spring bubbles from the earth like a rare gift for the taking.
>
> When buyers for the Great Smoky Park were appraising some of the small holdings on the Tennessee boundary, an old fellow would come down from his little farm each day. 'When'll you be a-getting to my place?,' he'd demand of the buyers.
>
> 'We'll be up there as soon as we can,' they'd reply.

'Well, I'm just aiming to make sure you see my spring. You'd have to see it afore you could know the worth of my place.'

'At last, after these urgings had interrupted work every morning for a week, one of the appraisers asked, 'And what is it that's so special about this spring?'

'Everything,' the old man retorted. 'But mainly its cold. Year round it stays the same: two degrees colder than ice.'[11]

I had grown up drinking from and looking into just such a spring, as had my ancestors more than a hundred years before me.

Dykeman spends a great deal of time in *The French Broad* portraying the people who drove the Cherokee out of the mountains and replaced them in the river valleys:

Over the mountains, through the gaps, down the watersheds they came, Scotch-Irish, English, Germans, low Dutch, and occasionally French Huguenots, overcoming the Blue Ridge barrier in their search and settlement of what they called the Southwest. No wilderness they found was more isolated than the valley of the French Broad and its tributaries. Because of the barriers against the outside world and the 'money' poverty of the people, it came to be called 'the land of do without.' More accurately it was the land of 'make do'. . . .

Tired and eager, they found their place, each his own cove or mountain slope or river field, and found their first tremendous task: that of destroying the most precious resource on the continent with all the vigor and recklessness of necessity which had been behind their forward push to this very place. They attacked the forests of primeval pine and poplar, walnut and oak, chestnut and maple. With axe and fire they laid the giants low. The bitterest irony of all the years of settlement is in this process by which a people so frugal they utilized every element of nature, animal, vegetable and mineral, to its least portion, made every scrap count, scraped and pinched and survived only by the closest economy, could waste, with prodigal abandon, the vast harvest of centuries as if it were not only useless but actually an enemy.[12]

Dykeman's portraits of the mountain people are indelible. One subject she celebrates is John C. Smathers who lived at the head of Hominy Creek:

As late as 1912, when he was eighty-six years old, John Smathers was still called a good rock and brick mason, carpenter, shoemaker, tinner, painter, blacksmith, plumber, harness and saddle maker, candle maker, farmer, hunter, storekeeper, bee raiser, glazier, butcher, fruit grower, hotel-keeper, merchant, physician, poulterer, lawyer, rail-splitter, politician, cook, school master, gardener, Bible scholar, and stable man . . . . he can still run a foot race and 'throw' most men in a wrestle 'catch as catch can.'[13]

One of the most riveting stories of *The French Broad* is the account of Big Tom Wilson the bear hunter finding the body of Professor Elisha Mitchell, the man who first measured the elevation of Mount Mitchell, the highest peak east of the Mississippi. For several days a posse of men searched for the lost professor on the slopes of the mountain. Finally Big Tom Wilson led them to a stream below the summit: "Only a short distance farther they came to the precipice over which the stream plunged forty feet. Crawling to its edge Big Tom looked over into the pool. The dark water was impenetrable, but on a driftwood log lodged at the side lay a familiar fur hat. Crumpled and water-soaked, it lay like a black period marking the end of a search and a life."[14]

Dykeman does a particularly good job of describing the complexities and contradictions of loyalties in the mountains during the Civil War:

And so, while the larger part of each state turned a united front toward the war, felt its ebb and flow and frequently followed its shifts of fortune from afar, along the French Broad the war was civil and daily, and every man looked to his own conscience and his own musket. The soldiers were neighbors, and the betrayer might be in a man's own family. Food and lack of it were weapons sure as guns, and age or youth knew no mercy, for this war was fratricidal in both the larger and the more specific meaning.[15]

Later, she writes "Zeb Vance knew what Richmond never learned: You can lead a man into battle, but you can't drive him there."[16]

One of the finest chapters of *The French Broad* describes the great stock drives over the mountains before the railroad reached into the southern highlands:

To the north and west of the French Broad gorge lay the grasslands and cornfields of Kentucky and Tennessee. To the south and east waited the ready markets of South Carolina and Georgia. Between them stretched North Carolina and two hundred or more miles of transportation, depending on the point of departure; most difficult, most picturesque, and most challenging, waited the seventy-odd miles of the French Broad River canyon.[17]

Besides herds of horses, cattle, hogs, the drives over the mountains included many turkeys. Dykeman writes:

Thousands of turkeys were driven up the French Broad every year, and these passages were a sight to behold. Four or five or six hundred turkeys to a flock, led by an old master gobbler who strutted and gobbled his way through the dust and rocks and mud, making way for the other high-stepping noisy birds to follow. The column they made might be four hundred yards long, but it was kept in line by the owner who rode horseback in front, and two or three drivers who followed behind or on each side with long whips decorated at the end with pieces of red cloth, usually flannel.[18]

No matter what the subject, Dykeman always returns in each chapter to her central theme, the fragility of the ecology of the French Broad Valley. After the unforgettable narrative of the stock droves of the nineteenth century she concludes:

With no system of crop rotation, little money to invest in fertilizer and the dwindling of corn yield after the first couple of harvests, much of this land so quickly and indiscriminately cleared was left to wash away in the quick-melting snows of winter and the sudden beating rains of summer. The French Broad still runs red with its second and third topsoil. Only in recent years have the people begun to understand that this water reddened from the butchered earth is draining away life blood as precious as was once the blood in the livestock which trampled along this route on their great half-remembered drives.[19]

Another especially dramatic chapter describes the building of the first railroad up the mountain to Asheville. Again, Dykeman demonstrates her novelist skill with narrative:

Another problem was the embankment area that came to be known as the Mud Cut. Excavating a passage through one of the sharp promontories of the mountains, the workers had drilled through hard rock and removed nearly eighty thousand cubic yards, when the great slide occurred. One hundred and ten thousand cubic yards of soft rock and earth, loosened by the removal of its hard rock foundation, rolled down in a thunder of devastation and wiped out all signs of human labor at that spot. They began again. The loose earth, soaked by rains, became a jelly-like mass; in addition, mud seemed to boil up from under the tracks. Sometimes in the morning the level of the tracks was raised as much as twenty feet higher than it had been the night before. It was spirit-breaking and backbreaking work.[20]

In *The French Broad*, Dykeman discovered a special talent for portraying entrepreneurship and business organization, which would be developed further in the later novels. In *The French Broad* she tells the story of the development of the timber industry in the valley, of the Stokely-Van Camp canning empire, and of the tourist industry. None is more memorable than her story of the first timber boom in the mountains in the 1880s. The business depended on a log boom in the river to hold the thousands of logs cut on the slopes. She puns on the word "boom":

> When the band sawmill came into the wild domain of the French Broad, a cycle began that is not yet concluded. When the big boom on the Pigeon broke that Saturday night in 1886, it could have been a prophecy: There was no boom built by man that nature could not break; there was no waste practiced by man that could not be matched by a greater complementary waste to follow. Unfortunately, there was no one equipped to hear the prophecy. The time of cutting of the trees had come. It is still here.[21]

No section of *The French Broad* contains more affectionate humor than the chapter on religion in the mountains, titled "No Cokes in Hell." She quotes an eloquent street preacher holding forth in a county seat on a hot summer afternoon. He shouts:

> There's a many of you going to be a-weeping and hollering and begging for mercy—but brother the time to beg is now. Get right now, pull your feet out of the muck and mire of hell, cause hit's a place of pain and sorrow everlasting, burning forever, and, brother, when you're burning and sweating down there let me tell you ain't

no relief. There ain't no fans nor no rest and, brother, there ain't no Cokes in hell."[22]

Asked by a tourist what the altitude of Buncombe County is, a native answers: "Baptist, by a damn sight."[23] Another story tells of "A traveling preacher in the early days . . . asked one of the mountain women if there were any ministers in the county, to which the woman replied, 'You can go round the gable end of the house and see for yourself. John's got the hides of ever' kind of varmint in this county tacked up there."[24]

When the first bishop of the Episcopalian Church visited the area, there was a lot of curiosity about his services: "The general lack of understanding with which his services were attended was illustrated by the man who invited a friend to 'come on, let's go down and hear the feller read and his wife jaw back at him,' referring to the fact that the bishop's wife was sometimes the only member of the congregation who could serve as a respondent during the litany."[25]

When I was a young writer, I had wondered what I had to write about. My favorite authors set their stories in London, Paris, Moscow. What did I know that was interesting enough to write about? Wilma Dykeman's *The French Broad* helped to show me that I had an endless store of material in the stories I'd heard on the porch in summer or by the fireplace in winter, in the arrowheads I'd turned up while hoeing corn, in the history I'd grown up hearing, and in the threatened beauty of the mountains themselves.

A little later, when I read her fiction, I made equally significant discoveries about western North Carolina and about writing. I saw that the inevitable focus of fiction about the region was about the land and the seasons, and the strong women who struggled on the land to raise children and feed large families, to keep families together over the generations, through wars and natural disasters, sickness and poverty. There could be no better model for a young writer than Dykeman's first novel, *The Tall Woman*. Lydia Moore McQueen is the glue and the inspiration that hold her family and community together across the years of war, sickness, outliers, greed, disappointment, and prejudice. Lydia is very much an individual, but also a personification of the culture at its best. And her interest in springs, and the loving description of springs, are among the most memorable passages in the novel. Dykeman describes the spring on her property in passionate detail:

'And what are you doing on this bleak day on this godforsaken mountain?' Dr. Hornsby asked.

'She laughed at the gloom of his words, belied in part by the heartiness of his smile: 'Cleaning my spring.'

'And pray tell me, Lydia McQueen,' he said, 'how do you clean a spring? Do you wash the water?'

'Don't be making fun of me! There!—she pointed with the hoe—look under the ledge where the roots of those poplar trees are, and tell me if you ever set eyes on a bolder, finer spring than this? Or a cleaner one?'

He went and looked. The natural bowl of water, surrounded on three sides and overhead by a ledge of rock and tangled web of roots and earth, stood clear and cold as glass. Around the spring and beside the stream that flowed from it were beds of moss and galax, a luxuriant winter green, and the vines of other carefully preserved plants that bloomed in summer. On the far side and overhanging the spring, were a dozen wild blackberry stalks. There were no other briers or dead weeds or fallen limbs around the spot. Someone had worked here lovingly and well.

'I've never set eyes on a bolder, finer spring,' he repeated. 'Or a cleaner one.'

'This is my favorite place on our farm,' she said.[26]

Water is an important theme in Dykeman's second novel, *The Far Family*, as well:

'One thing about this jumping-off-place your sawmilling dragged us to, Tom Thurston,' Aunt Tildy said, 'it's got as good water as ever I tasted.'

'Now that's a fact,' Tom agreed, pleased.

'Only better water I know of anywhere,' Martha said quietly, 'is the spring on Grandpa Moore's farm.'[27]

This second novel follows the heirs of Lydia Moore McQueen far beyond the small farms in the mountains. It is a novel of growth, development, education, politics, finance, and power, as Dykeman tells the story of this particular family in the twentieth-century mountains and beyond. It is a story of family dynamics, of loyalty and conflict, of betrayal and sacrifice. Two generations later, Ivy visits the Moore homestead and feels the bond of blood and kinship across time:

Two stone steps surrounded by moss and ferns and tiny wild

flowers led down to the natural bowl of water, scooped deep in the sparkling sand, chilled by the secret depths from which it flowed. The spring's overflow ran under a stone slab into the springhouse where a long wooden trough held crocks, pitchers of milk, pans of butter in the cool constant stream of water . . . .

There was more than land and buildings to the farm, however. There was a past, the presence of those who had turned this ground before, swept these floors and cleaned this springhouse during many yesterdays. Ivy had never before been part of this feeling of aged places, familiar paths. Her mother involved them in this sense of continuity and the children were captivated.[28]

In this second novel, as in *The French Broad* and *The Tall Woman*, Dykeman shows a considerable knowledge and affection for rural mountain life. She demonstrates how much the sense of who we are comes from memory. But she also reveals an equally acute understanding of modern city life, of the worlds of business, politics, and affluent families. There is a knowing satiric edge to her portraits of country clubs and cocktail parties, the chemistry of political events, romance among the upper classes. In *The Far Family* she takes us from Jesse Moore's springhouse to the champagne at a country club bash three generations later.

Phil Cortland, the young senator and descendant of Lydia McQueen, returns to his hometown at a moment of family crisis, and attends a dinner party with his old flame Sherry: "Phil talked with them all, effortlessly using the attentive interest of other people which was his greatest political asset. There were the middle-aged young, the middle-aged old, natives and newcomers, the pleasantly wined and dined and the outright drunk, the ones on the way up, the ones on the way down, and those who were holding on. The chief fact that struck him about them was how much alike they were."[29]

One of the themes Dykeman dramatizes in *The Far Family* is the standardization of modern life. With the coming of roads and railroads, mass communication, outside investment and industry, the mountain region becomes more and more like every other part of the country. With the gains of prosperity come the loss of character, distinctiveness. Identity is increasingly a matter of money:

Phil felt that he might be in the state capital or Washington or
any other city—for these were not unique Nantahala people;
they were as standardized as identical hairstyles, clothes, jokes,

food, newspapers and rebellious offspring could make them. But although they were not unique, neither were they universal. Paradoxically, just as Ivy and the family were unique—exasperatingly, humorously, sadly so—they were also touched by universality and Phil knew that his mother could have walked among the people in the foreign lands he had visited and won their friendship.[30]

I know of no work of fiction that reveals more effectively the loneliness and emptiness in the lives of so many of the prosperous and powerful, the outstandingly successful, than *The Far Family* does. In the post-war boom the region has risen to undreamed of affluence. The families with memories and roots in dirt farms are living in mansions, managing banks, mingling with factory owners, senators, and governors. Yet, Phil is overwhelmed by a feeling of emptiness and pointlessness. The political world is not at all what he imagined it would be:

> As he went to get the car, Phil sighed in exasperation both with himself and with the evening. He had never seen a lonelier, more desperate, group of people. They held on to their little club to show how closely they were bound together, and essentially they were as uncommitted to one another as the lion and impala of the jungle were uncommitted to each other. They made up for a lack of true community with the trappings of 'community spirit.' Words replaced actions. Symbols passed for realities.[31]

One of the special things about Dykeman's third novel, *Return the Innocent Earth*, is that the first-person narrative sections are spoken by a contemporary male character, Jonathan Clayburn, Jr. Jon is a senior vice-president of Clayburn-Durant Foods, and he is the presiding conscience and consciousness of the story. Readers and reviewers are often surprised when women authors write from a male perspective, or when male authors write from a woman's point of view. But one of the glories of fiction writing, and reading, is the discovery of the world through other eyes, other voices. The way stories connect with other lives keeps us reading, and writing them. One of the rewards of fiction is this reaching across the boundaries of gender, geography, class, race, ethnicity, religion, even language through translation. And not least is the way fiction can give us a window on the past, stretching across generations to bring us a sense of kinship and community with those who have come before us.

Return the Innocent Earth is a dynastic story, the story of the building of a canning corporation in East Tennessee and then across the nation. It is a story of seedtime and harvest, from mountain spring to the boardroom of a corporation. Most of all it is the story of a family, the Clayburn family, beginning with Elisha and Mary on their farm in the mountains, and the extended family of community and business. It is a story of growth, from pumpkin patch to preferred stock.

Return the Innocent Earth reveals an impressive knowledge of business, the methods of business and organization, the cultures of business, the ethics of business. I know of no other novel that gives such an intimate and sweeping view of the process of business growth, the setbacks and triumphs, the uncertainties and vision, decision making, and how personalities define policies as much as rules and principles. The novel should be required reading in every MBA program.

As Dykeman exhibited a considerable insight into the political world in *The Far Family*, the country club and the courthouse, she shows a special understanding of the process of manufacturing, development, research, and marketing in *Return the Innocent Earth*. She illustrates with precision and clarity the technology and experiment that go into modern business. The novel is an education in the methods of research, quality control, labor studies, and environmental concerns. The novel is a portrait of industry, including both the horrors and the industrial sublime. There is a special feeling for the thrill of enterprise, competitiveness, growth, and the drive toward excellence and winning.

The character Stull is the embodiment of ruthless ambition, blind ambition. Rather than cooperation, communication, team play, he relishes the fight itself, and victory, whatever the cost. His instincts are those of a killer: "Stull wanted something. And whatever it was, he wanted it exclusively and totally and at the cheapest price possible. Whoever sat opposite him was automatically an adversary. Winning was all."[32]

But Stull's cousin Jon, the narrator of much of the book and the leading character, sees competition and industry in another way. He views the company not only as its products and profits, but as the people who contribute, who do the daily work. The company includes the soil from which the crops grow, and the food to nourish and nurture a society:

This mid-town, five-story brick building grew from the wide flat cornfields surrounding this midwestern metropolis where the

Durants had built a food empire, and grew from the river-bottom acres in the mountain South where the Clayburns had built their business, and grew from cool acres of clear chartreuse spring peas in Wisconsin. . . . The fragrance of ketchup gathered all up on one bouquet.[33]

A major theme in *Return the Innocent Earth* is the need and importance of remembering. Men like Stull have no interest in the past. They only want to move forward, toward the bigger and richer, the more powerful. But Jon Clayburn, Jr. wants to keep in touch with the past, his family past, with its roots in land and place. He says, "I could remember. I needed to remember."[34] Later he realizes that "Canning is part of two worlds and there is no escaping either. Land and computers. Seeds and machinery. Weather and sales charts. The gone-before and yet-to-come are by-products of every can we fill. Yet in those big, sleek central offices in the midwestern metropolis where I live we lose touch."[35]

Return the Innocent Earth is Jon's act of remembering, of reconnecting. He knows that to know himself he must keep in contact with the past, with his family past, and the region's past. To lose the past is to lose the self, and to lose the present and future also. We know who we are because we know what has come before us: "I come from a line of remembering people. In generations past we built churches and ballads and a way of life out of our remembering, handing down words the way others pass along designs woven into coverlets, carved in wood, or worked into clay. But now that is going too—the woven words and the cloth and all."[36]

Clear water is a motif in *Return the Innocent Earth,* just as it is in the two novels that precede it. When Jonathan Clayburn, Sr. tells his dream to Cebo, he describes darkness, and narrowness, lostness and fear. It is a dream of anxiety and confusion, until he hears the sound of water: "I heard an unbelievable sound. It was running water. When I looked, I found the boldest, clearest river seen on this round globe. And I lay right down in its swift, deep current and it carried me through a passage in the mountains and out near home."[37] After he describes his dream, Cebo, the ancient voice of folklore and wisdom, responds: "That about the best luck can come, a dream of clear water."[38] Water is always a sign of continuity, of health, of renewal in Dykeman's fiction. It is almost a Biblical symbol of life.

Dykeman has a special understanding of the code of maleness. I cannot think of a contemporary fiction writer who has portrayed better the masculine sense of self. As Jon Clayburn describes his own growth, his own recognition of what it means to become a man, to act like a man in a man's world, we recognize the accuracy of his account, the truth of his realization:

> But I knew the code I had broken with Stull. Even then I knew, although I could not have put it into words. We (especially we boys, we men) were not supposed to discuss the innerness of life. We were supposed to observe true division of Sunday from Monday. We were splintered into a half-dozen fragments and our maturity was measured not by trying to make the parts into a whole but by juggling the pieces cleverly, separately, so that no one saw the empty spaces. . . . I remained acutely aware of the embarrassment most Clayburns felt in confronting or discussing the creative, spiritual, moral, sexual, intangible forces of our lives.[39]

Perhaps the most moving scene in the novel is when the brother Dan has let slip an obscene phrase in front of his mother, Mary Clayburn. He and his siblings are paralyzed by the embarrassment. All wait in terror to see what the strict Mary Clayburn will do to punish him. She surprises them, and us, by ordering Dan to go out and break a hickory, then sends him back to get a larger switch, and then orders him to whip *her*, since if he has done wrong, it is her fault. She is the mother, and she is responsible. He breaks down in tears, but she will not let him off:

> The sigh of the supple bough echoed down the hall.
> 'Again, Daniel. Harder.'
> The sound of the striking and the crying mingled.
> 'Much harder.'
> Eventually the ordeal was finished. They heard the switch strike against the wall and fall to the floor as Dan flung it away from him. They heard him run upstairs.[40]

Besides her fiction and *The French Broad* Wilma Dykeman published more than a dozen books of nonfiction. With her husband, James Stokely, Jr., she gave us sensitive and progressive studies of the modern South, and with her sons, Dykeman Stokely and James Stokely III, haunting portraits of the people of the Great Smokies. She enriched us with a memorable history of the battle of Kings Mountain, and the poetry of the volume called *Haunting Memories*.

It is an honor to celebrate Wilma Dykeman, who contributed so much to the state and region with her writing. She was a grand woman of letters of a kind we don't see much anymore. She was equally at home talking with governors or rural mountain people. She served as an ambassador of history and literature to countless communities, and she was an enthusiastic champion of contemporary writers. Like a mountain spring, she gave us a bold, steady stream of sparkling words for over half a century. Her presence was an inspiration to many young writers, and she was certainly an inspiration to me. I am proud to say she is one of our region's treasures, and I am proud that she belongs to us here, in the mountains. Her work will continue to refresh, inform, delight, and inspire us for years and generations to come.

NOTES

1. Wilma Dykeman. *Family of Earth: A Southern Mountain Childhood.* Chapel Hill: University of North Carolina Press, 2016. 13.
2. Dykeman, *Family of Earth.* 14.
3. Dykeman, *Family of Earth.* 19.
4. Dykeman, *Family of Earth.* 45.
5. Dykeman, *Family of Earth.* 74.
6. Dykeman, *Family of Earth.* 111.
7. Dykeman, *Family of Earth.* 102.
8. Dykeman, *Family of Earth.* 134.
9. Dykeman, *Family of Earth.* 109.
10. Wilma Dykeman, *The French Broad.* Knoxville: University of Tennessee Press, 1965. 6.
11. Dykeman, *The French Broad.* 11–12.
12. Dykeman, *The French Broad.* 50–51.
13. Dykeman, *The French Broad.* 61.
14. Dykeman, *The French Broad.* 72.
15. Dykeman, *The French Broad.* 81–82.
16. Dykeman, *The French Broad.* 85.
17. Dykeman, *The French Broad.* 137.
18. Dykeman, *The French Broad.* 140.
19. Dykeman, *The French Broad.* 151.
20. Dykeman, *The French Broad.* 160–161.
21. Dykeman, *The French Broad.* 171.
22. Dykeman, *The French Broad.* 312–313.
23. Dykeman, *The French Broad.* 315.

24. Dykeman, *The French Broad*. Ibid.

25. Dykeman, *The French Broad*. 318.

26. Wilma Dykeman. *The Tall Woman*. New York: Holt, Rinehart and Winston, 1962. 176–77.

27. Wilma Dykeman. *The Far Family*. New York: Holt, Rinehart and Winston. 1966. 52.

28. Dykeman, *The Far Family*. 104.

29. Dykeman, *The Far Family*. 311.

30. Dykeman, *The Far Family*. 314.

31. Dykeman, *The Far Family*. 315.

32. Wilma Dykeman. *Return the Innocent Earth*. New York: Holt, Rinehart and Winston, 1973. 8.

33. Dykeman, *Return the Innocent Earth*. 20–21.

34. Dykeman, *Return the Innocent Earth*. 21.

35. Dykeman, *Return the Innocent Earth*. 35.

36. Dykeman, *Return the Innocent Earth*. 36.

37. Dykeman, *Return the Innocent Earth*. 99.

38. Dykeman, *Return the Innocent Earth*. Ibid.

39. Dykeman, *Return the Innocent Earth*. 161–62.

40. Dykeman, *Return the Innocent Earth*. 188–89.

CORMAC MCCARTHY

The Novel Raised from the Dead

One evening in 1977 I turned on the television to the PBS *Vision* series. The program was already in progress, and I missed the title and credits. But my attention was quickly drawn to the screen as I began to notice the accents of the actors. The inflections were not what I was used to hearing in television dramas. I became aware that the story was set in a Southern cotton-mill town and that the actors really spoke like working-class people of the Piedmont and mountain South.

> TIMEKEEPER: Did they not learn you to sir at your home?
> ROBERT: Sir.
> TIMEKEEPER: If Mr. Gregg was to hear he'd flop in his grave like a fish, God rest his soul. Good manners are never out of place. What he used to say. Well. Tell you what. You can start in by cleanin this here place up some. Right yonder through that door and on the right is a closet and you'll find a broom in it if I'm not bad mistaken. We'd best get the heaviest dirt out fore cotton starts to volunteer in here. Little as the roof leaks it never would grow noway.[1]

Suddenly my full attention was on the television screen. I was a native of western North Carolina whose mother had worked for years in a cotton mill when I was a boy. I had already spent five years teaching in Upstate New York and was homesick and hungry to hear the speech of my native region. And here it was, on public television, done with such accuracy I was astounded. As the story unfolded, I watched and listened closely.

> JAMES GREGG: How many altogether?
> RAGGED MAN: They was twenty-six of us come down.
> TIMEKEEPER: In one family?

RAGGED MAN: Lord God no, not in no one family. They aint but
five in my family. They's three families of us. Some of us is cross kin.[2]

As the story continued, I found tears in my eyes. Here were my people, people who had lived in the mountain hollers for generations and then
gone down to the Piedmont to find work in the cotton mills. The accuracy
of the African American speech was equally revealing:

1st BLACK: You wants to take dinner with us you gots to ast. I aint
goin to ast you. You liable to shoot me. . . .
1st BLACK: Everybody that aint got a say so, don't mean they dont
care. In this life or out of it.[3]

And then I saw the image of the McEvoy home where Mrs. McEvoy
was lying in her coffin. The mirrors in the house were covered with cloth.
I thought: who in Hollywood would know to do this? Who has done that
much research on the rural South in the nineteenth century? Who would
know that mirrors were sometimes covered when a family, especially an
Irish immigrant family, was in mourning? And a few minutes later the sister
Martha said to Bobby McEvoy: "We went up there last year. He and Mama.
We seen our old place up at Pickens and we went to Greenville and I seen
Captain, Bobby. He was harnessed to a wagon in the street and he knowed
me, Bobby. And we was up there three days . . ."[4]

Not only did I hear the names of towns I was familiar with, where
my own family had come from in the nineteenth century, but I heard a
character call a horse by name, revealing the sense of intimacy and loss in
the detail of Captain harnessed to a stranger's wagon, but still recognizing
Martha years after being sold.

Further on there is a scene in a ramshackle barn that serves as a tavern.
The men are playing cards and drinking corn liquor. The publican is called
Pinky. When Robert McEvoy appears there, Pinky says: "Thought you'd
quit these parts, young buddy."

McEVOY: My mama died.
PINKY: Well honey I didnt know that. Come here and set and get
ye a drink. I'm sorry to hear it.[5]

The dialogue at the tavern is some of the best in the play: "Here Ed, let's
see a little of that muleshoe," Pinky says, asking for the liquor. They drink

and eat slices of raw potato for chasers. "Here, honey. Get ye a drink. Ed, let's see that tater here."[6]

Later the men discuss the mill owner:

THIRD MAN: Thing about James. He never did want to put the jam on the lower shelf where the little man could get some.
FIRST MAN: Get ye a little old drink there, Housecat.
THIRD MAN: They's plenty of rhubarb all around the farm. And another little drink wont do us any harm.[7]

The actual scene of the murder of the mill owner by Robert McEvoy is done with economy and understatement. And later—after the stark drama of the trial, and after the bleak scene of the hanging of Robert McEvoy for murdering the mill owner, who Robert thinks once propositioned his sister, and after we see the coroner filling out the death report—we are given one final scene in the published screenplay, though not in the film. A young man, descended from the mill owner's family, is doing research on his family history many years later. He comes to the state hospital in Columbia to interview McEvoy's sister Martha, now an old woman. He brings her a bouquet and Martha replies: "I was always a fool about flowers. I guess I take after my daddy thataway. He was a nurseryman. He had peach orchards. . . You never seen the like of peaches. They used to ship em out by train. Just carloads of em. He had a touch with anything growin. Just had a sleight for it. He never did have no luck about people."[8]

The young man asks a series of questions, most of which she can't answer. There is such a sense of waste in the scene, of enormous loss, and of long time passing. Martha tells the young man: "I dont even know where he's buried at. Daddy never told us. He never put up no marker. Just a nameless grave somewheres. He was afraid they'd come and dig him up. Them doctors. They'd come and dig up anybody like that and get they head. They'd take it and study it. Daddy said that God would know where to hunt him."[9]

As the play closes, Martha is talking once more about the horse named Captain:

Me and Mama went back up to Pickens about a year fore she died.
I was just a young girl. Went up on the train. We'd had this horse
and his name was Captain and I used to ride him just everwheres

and he'd foller me around like a dog and I remember whenever
we got ready to leave from up there why they sent me over to
Mamaw's because the feller was fixing to come and get him. They
had done sold him, you see. But me and Mama went up there. We
went up there and we was in Greenville that Saturday afternoon
and I looked and there in the street was old Captain. He was
harnessed up in an express wagon standin there in front of a store
and whenever I seen him I just run across the street and throwed
my arms around his neck and kissed him and I reckon everbody
thought I was crazy standin there in the middle of the street and
me about growed, huggin and kissin an old horse and just a bawlin
to beat the band.[10]

And then she looks down at the faded tintype of her brother in her hand:
"Sometimes I wish I'd not even kept it. That lawyer said that the image of
God was blotted out of his face. That's what he said about Bobby. I ort not
even to of kept it. I think a person's memory serves better. Sometimes I can
almost talk to him. I caint see him no more. In my mind. I just see this old
pitcher."[11]

It has been said that the greatest writers evoke a sense of the poise and
scale of eternity in their work, no matter how cluttered or twisted or violent the scenes in the foreground. No matter how grotesque, repugnant,
tragic, or ridiculous the human story, there is always a parallel and contrasting narrative of the natural processes and cycles, seasons and years and
lifetimes, even of geological and astronomical time. A great poet can contrast and even superimpose these different senses of time so they both clash
and complement each other.

When the credits began to roll that night in 1977 and I saw the name
of the film was *The Gardner's Son*, I knew I had witnessed a story I would
never forget. And when I saw the name Cormac McCarthy as writer, I
knew I had found an author I would never stop reading. Friends had mentioned McCarthy's work to me before, but I had not read any of it. That
night I knew I would.

I had begun writing fiction while an engineering and math student at
North Carolina State in 1963, taking a course with the novelist Guy Owen.
Owen encouraged me to write stories using the speech and details of the
rural world I knew. I even published some stories as an undergraduate. But
in the excitement of the mid-1960s I discovered poetry.

Many critics and teachers at that time said the novel was dead, or at least dying. It was understood that poetry, like rock music, was the medium of the future. Perhaps I should say that poetry discovered me. I wrote more and more poems and fewer and fewer stories over the next few years. I fell in love with image and metaphor and compact lines. The poetry writing was rewarded with publication in national magazines, with fellowships, and with a job teaching poetry at Cornell University in 1971. I lived and dreamed and read and wrote poetry every hour of every day for more than ten years. I thought of language in terms of metaphor and cadence, line break and rhyme. I loved the compression and indirection of poetry, the implicitness of poetry. But after moving to Cornell and teaching poetry and writing about poetry, and writing many new poems, I knew in the back of my mind I wanted to write narratives also. I wrote several long narrative poems, but they did not seem to turn out as well as the shorter poems. With narrative I lost the richness and subtlety of language. There were stories I wanted to tell and subjects I wanted to write about, but I was unable to do them adequately in verse.

It was after seeing *The Gardner's Son* that I began to realize what I had been missing. I won't pretend it was a sudden revelation, a road to Damascus clarification. It took me years to sort out what I wanted to do. But seeing the film was the beginning of a process that enabled me, over the next decade, to understand that what I wanted to write was *voices*. I began to see that a writer can bring back a lost world, can make the dead live again, by finding the voices, creating the living voices. I guess it was the sense of "raising the dead" in speech that attracted me most to prose in the 1980s. It took me years of practice to even begin to learn how to do it. But watching *The Gardner's Son*, I saw what was possible and why it was so worth doing.

Reading the novels of Cormac McCarthy over the years since, I have been struck by the craft, by the unforgettable sentences, by the exact phrasing and imagery, as everyone else has. No other American writer has a more vivid, more colorful, various, and accurate vocabulary. Reading McCarthy's novels one has to look up words every few pages. His sense of the textures of words is unsurpassed. It was while reading the early Tennessee novels that I realized how extensively he had used *Webster's Third New International Dictionary* and the *OED*. Again and again, the word I was looking up could be found only there (spalpeens, clotpolls, lobcoks, runagates, anneloid, blueflocced, jowter, etc.). It gave me a special sense of relish and connection that McCarthy used the same dictionaries I did. It seemed to me that McCarthy owned the language in part because he owned *Webster's Third* and the *OED*.

As I grew as a writer myself, and as I continued to read and reread Cormac McCarthy, I decided my favorite of his early novels was *Child of God*. I was drawn to this short book because of its spareness, its precision, its macabre details and mad central character. It contains some of McCarthy's finest humor, as well as some of his most chilling and grotesque scenes. As the title implies, with and without irony, the novel explores the outer, and inner, reaches of humanity. The murderer and necrophile Lester Ballard stretches but does not break the definition of the human.

Child of God is very much a novel of voices, voices alternating with authorial narration. Here is the description of Ballard, the main character: "He moves in the dry chaff among the dust and slats of sunlight with a constrained truculence. Saxon and Celtic bloods. A child of God much like yourself perhaps.... The man stands straddlelegged, has made in the dark humus a darker pool wherein swirls a pale foam with bits of straw. Buttoning his jeans he moves along the barn wall, himself fiddlebacked with light, a petty annoyance flickering across the wall-ward eye."[12] In Romans 8:16 Paul says, "The Spirit itself beareth witness with our spirit, that we are the children of God ... And if the children, then heirs, heirs of God, and joint-heirs with Christ." And in Romans 9:26 he goes on to say, "There shall they be called children of the living God." And the author of the epistle First John 3:10 says, "In this the children of God are manifest, and the children of the devil: whosoever doeth not righteousness is not of God, neither he that loveth not his brother."

There is a voice running through the narration of *Child of God* that sounds much like a chorus in a Greek tragedy. I have quoted an early example of this voice where the narrator addresses the reader and compares us as children of God with a man who becomes a murderer and monster. We will hear that voice again from time to time in the novel. It adds an extra dimension to the story. When the narrator describes waking in a hospital room with his hand amputated, the narrator becomes respondent to the action of the story, becomes commentator:

> Woke in a room at dawn or dusk he knew not which where motes
> of dust passing through an unseen bar of light incandesced briefly
> and random and drifted like the smallest fireflies. He studied them
> for a while and then raised his hand. No hand came up ... Ballard

in a thin white gown in a thin white room, false acolyte or antiseptic felon, a practitioner of ghastliness, a part-time ghoul.[13]

The choral effect helps illustrate how far McCarthy is from what in the 1980s was called minimalist fiction. In fact, he could be called an anti-minimalist in the way he adds response and comment, choral poetry, background and description. This choral voice connects McCarthy's early fiction with the novels of the eighteenth and nineteenth centuries. One of the most famous examples is the ending of *Suttree* where he leaves the reader with a kind of choral exhortation: "Somewhere in the gray wood by the river is the huntsman and in the brooming corn and in the castellated press of cities. His work lies all wheres and his hounds tire not. I have seen them in a dream, slaverous and wild and their eyes crazed with ravening for souls in this world. Fly them."[14]

McCarthy is an anti-minimalist also in the way he sets the scenes of his stories. Few writers in prose can match his ability to evoke place and season. He achieves a precise, photographic lyricism. But McCarthy can also evoke the extraordinary place, the macabre landscape of nightmare, as in this description of the cave Ballard has retreated to: "Here the walls with their softlooking convolutions, slavered over as they were with wet and bloodred mud, had an organic look to them, like the innards of some great beast. Here in the bowels of the mountain Ballard turned his light on ledges or pallets of stone where dead people lay like saints."[15]

I know there has been a lot of critical comment about caves in McCarthy's work. Caves figure extensively in the landscapes of *Child of God* and *Suttree*. And caves under Graniteville, South Carolina, are even mentioned in *The Gardner's Son*. Because his Tennessee fiction is set in limestone country, McCarthy finds a ready-made symbol in his geography, and because he is such a resourceful artist, he knows how to put it to good use. Lester Ballard's retreat into the cave as an adult reverts to the hidden world of the unconscious, to repressed passions and reptile-like cruelty. It is a retreat into deep pain and the deep past. Ballard descends into the world of cave dwellers, rodents, snakes. He comes across bones from ancient times and the bones of extinct animals. There the posse tries to follow him down into the slimy guts of the earth, but he loses them. It is a world of darkness and madness with which Ballard feels an ancient and awful kinship. He has become a reptile, a rodent in his den. In the cave he has reverted to the world just under the consciousness of all of us children of God, a world of murder, rape, incest, filth. He has gone down by stages from an abandoned house to county dump to cave underneath it all. He is a sewer rat, and yet he is a child of God.

Besides the voice of the narrator, there are several other speakers telling the story of *Child of God*. Most of the speakers are never named or identified. But their voices are one of the most alive, most effective parts of the novel. They give humor, daylight, sanity to an otherwise almost unbearable story. They give depth and poise and perspective to the narrow world of Lester Ballard. Without these voices the novel would have less effect because we would be numbed by the unrelieved horror of Ballard's activities. As I reread the novel, I kept hearing those passages as voice-overs in a movie.

It is the alternating narrators who fill in the portrait of Lester Ballard, who give the background. McCarthy chooses a device from oral history methods to expand and clarify his story. Some of the voices sound like they were taken down by WPA writers. They are one of the glories of the novel. Many of the monologues contain anecdotes seemingly unrelated to the main narrative of Lester Ballard. But they are memorable and effective in grounding the main story in the greater world of the region and time. Without the monologues the reader would lose touch with humanity and become inured to the repetition of Ballard's crimes. We would become lost in the labyrinth of perverse actions. The other speakers allow us to pause and breathe.

McCarthy not only lets us hear characters speaking in their own idiom, he lets us see the work they do and how they do it. He especially exults in the way mechanical work gets done. A blacksmith, like the artist that he is, like the alchemist that he is, tells Ballard to watch the steel in the fire until the color turns a thin blue on the edges. It is a measure of Ballard's loss of humanity that he shows no interest or understanding of what the blacksmith tells him. The precision and pleasure and sacramental nature of the work are lost on him. Many of McCarthy's sentences are like little poems. They appear to be cut, machined, tempered for toughness. Many sentences astonish with a turn, a word choice, and then appear to be inevitable. McCarthy can move quickly from the epigrammatic and compact to an elevated and polyrhythmic prose. Here are three sentences from near the end of *Child of God*:

> He watched an empty wagon come up the valley below him,
> distant clatter of it, the mule pausing in the ford and the clatter of
> the immobile wagon rolling on regardless as if the sound authored

the substance, until it had all reached his ears . . . Squatting there
he let his head drop between his knees and he began to cry. . . He
had resolved himself to ride on for he could not turn back and the
world that day was as lovely as any day that ever was and he was
riding to his death.[16]

Notice the movement from an almost baroque style to a crisp imagist style,
to a balladic, even elegiac tone of voice. It is the quick shifts of pace and tone
that characterize McCarthy's touch in the novel.

Much has been made of the influence of Faulkner on McCarthy's early
writing. But rereading *Child of God* I was rarely reminded of Faulkner. The
book seems to be distinctive and original in both style and characterization.
If this book resonates with any of the classic modernists it would be with
Hemingway in the hard bare lyrical voice of his early stories, in the photographic accuracy of "Big Two-Hearted River" and "Up in Michigan," and
in the hard clinical objectivity of the narrator. The objectivity and poise of
McCarthy's writing, the care with which he avoids pretending to get into
the minds of his characters, remind me of Hemingway's early fiction again
and again.

But as I continued reading *Child of God*, I kept thinking of Camus and
Sartre and the talk about existentialism and the death of God in the 1950s.
Lester Ballard fits perhaps as much into the esthetic and spiritual world of
The Stranger and *Nausea* as into the world of Colonel Sartoris and French-
man's Bend. There is a tight focus on the present in *Child of God*, not an
engagement with the culture of the past. Because of the overwhelming
presence of Faulkner in modern Southern writing, we have trouble seeing
clearly some of the things that are distinctive in other writers.

When I began writing fiction again in the 1980s, Faulkner seemed too
remote to be an aid. A great writer of the past, he was no more useful with
his special manners and difficulties than *The Waste Land* was to writing
contemporary poetry. But Cormac McCarthy's work reflected the great
changes in the world, and in fiction, since the 1950s. The rigor, the surprise,
the craft of his fiction, were a usable model. Furthermore, he was not just
a Southern writer; he was also an Appalachian writer, from just across the
mountains in Tennessee. As I began to read and reread him, I saw new
possibilities in fiction and in the region.

In the 1960s many critics and teachers said the novel was dead, as others
in the 1950s said God was dead. I remember someone in Chapel Hill about

1966 saying the novel was a middle-class form about the middle range of experience, and that it had been replaced by psychedelic poetry and rock and roll music. But those critics could not have been more wrong. In the past thirty years we have witnessed a rebirth of realistic and naturalistic fiction in the work of women writers and minority writers, in Tim O'Brien and Lee Smith and Louise Erdrich and many others.

And especially in the work of Cormac McCarthy, I found the novel was very much alive. If it had been dead, it was resurrected. And oddly enough, in the horrors and cruelties, the misunderstandings and the grotesque humor, the paradoxes and absurdities in his fiction, Cormac McCarthy seemed to have made God alive too, whatever unspeakable deeds his children might commit. In one of the rare accounts of a conversation with McCarthy, Garry Wallace describes the author's response to a skeptical remark Wallace had made about Christian belief: "He appeared to be a very patient listener. He said he felt sorry for me because I was unable to grasp this concept of spiritual experience. He said that people all over the world, in every religion, were familiar with this experience. He asked if I'd ever read William James's *The Varieties of Religious Experience.* I had not."[17]

As McCarthy moved on to the peak of his early career, or shall we say the twin peaks, of *Suttree* and *Blood Meridian*, he achieved a new Joycean, urban density in the first, and a Homeric intensity and sweep in the latter. And he continued to use voices just as effectively in these larger, more complex works as he had in the earlier stories. *Suttree* is a polyphonic work, and a great part of its glory is in the narration: "He paused at some trash in the corner where a warfarined rat writhed. Small beast so occupied with the bad news in his belly. It must have been something you ate. Harrogate crouched on his heels and watched with interest.... He looked down at the rat again. It was moving one rear leg in circles as if to music."[18]

It is hard to predict, and harder still to analyze, the things that trigger and enable artistic work. But I know that hearing the voices in Cormac McCarthy's writing gave me a new sense of potential in my own writing, allowed me to imagine again what was possible in writing about the Appalachian world I knew and had forgotten that I knew. By hearing the truth of living voices, I was able to return to storytelling, to the rural world where I had grown up, and to the stories I had heard by the fireplace as a child. And in those voices, I was able to confront a range of human experience, from the horrible and shameful, the absurd and petty, the almost unbearably painful, to the compassionate, the large of spirit, the sublime.

NOTES

1. Cormac McCarthy. *The Gardener's Son: A Screenplay.* 1976. Hopewell, NJ: The Ecco Press, 1996. 20.

2. McCarthy, *The Gardener's Son.* 22.

3. McCarthy, *The Gardener's Son.* 33–34.

4. McCarthy, *The Gardener's Son.* 39.

5. McCarthy, *The Gardener's Son.* 45.

6. McCarthy, *The Gardener's Son.* 47.

7. McCarthy, *The Gardener's Son.* 50.

8. McCarthy, *The Gardener's Son.* 89.

9. McCarthy, *The Gardener's Son.* 91.

10. McCarthy, *The Gardener's Son.* 93.

11. McCarthy, *The Gardener's Son.* Ibid.

12. Cormac McCarthy. *Child of God.* 1973. New York: Vintage International, 1993. 4.

13. McCarthy, *Child of God.* 174.

14. Cormac McCarthy. *Suttree.* 1979. New York: Vintage International, 1992. 471.

15. McCarthy, *Child of God.* 135.

16. McCarthy, *Child of God.* 169–70.

17. Garry Wallace. "Meeting McCarthy." *Southern Quarterly.* Vol. 30, No. 4 (Summer 1992). 138.

18. McCarthy, *Suttree.* 100.

THE WISEST BOOK
I EVER READ

In the late summer of 1959, I was preparing to enter the tenth grade at Flat Rock High in Henderson County, North Carolina. My sister was getting ready to enter college, and my parents drove us down to Greenville, South Carolina, in the pickup truck to buy school clothes. I had saved money from selling pole beans, and in the air-conditioned stores I bought new pants with buckles in the back, new shirts, a pair of white buck loafers, and a belt as thin as a shoelace. Before driving back to the mountains, we stopped in a drugstore near the parking lot for soft drinks. Near the marble fountain counter stood a rack of paperback books.

While sipping my Coke, I turned the rack, reading titles. One black and red Mentor paperback caught my attention: *Doctor Zhivago* by Boris Pasternak, a book that had been much in the news during the past year. There had been a scandal about Pasternak being forced to refuse the Nobel Prize. I had heard the book was a love story, critical of the Russian Revolution and the Soviet regime. Before leaving the drugstore, I paid ninety-five cents for the volume, the first book I ever bought.

I had already fallen in love with Tolstoy's fiction, devouring a copy of *War and Peace* borrowed from the Henderson County bookmobile. And I had read Dostoyevsky's *Crime and Punishment* in a tattered paperback sent to a friend by his brother in college. I had also written my first paper the year before on *Quo Vadis*. I was in awe of Russian fiction, of Slavic romance. I could hardly wait to get home with the inky smelling paperback.

I was not disappointed by Pasternak's novel. I read it at odd moments between fieldwork and homework, milking the cow and helping to cut winter firewood. I thought it was the wisest story I'd ever read. It was a love story, and the poetic prose, the sweeping scenes of the countryside and the city, train rides and devastated towns, were so real it hurt to read them. The feeling for field and forest, river and ravine, the decaying house, and ruined backstreets, seemed a revelation. Even as I wrestled with the chopped-up narrative sections, the awkwardly joined chapters and the literary allusions beyond my understanding, I was thrilled by the details of the muddy roads, snowy vistas, clothing shops, ballrooms, and smoldering battlefields.

And over the chaos of the revolution, the threatened lives of Yuri the poet and Tonia his wife, and Lara his muse and lover, there hung a spell of sacredness, of destiny. I couldn't have described the sense of luminous presence in the story then, but I recognized it and was thrilled by it. The details of the novel, the pain of the story, the entwined lives of the heroes, had a special meaning, beyond anything I could have defined. I understood something about the political history the book revealed and implied. But it was the lives and loves of the individuals projected against that cataclysmic history that enthralled me. History was a beast that devoured those precious lives. I missed the references to Baudelaire and Mayakovski, but I understood the celebration of poetry as simplicity, the immanence of the everyday, the complex textures of modern life illuminated by goodness, simple purity of heart.

More than any book I had ever read, *Doctor Zhivago* made me feel I was touching real life. I saw that the true subject of fiction, and poetry, was the dignity and spirituality of human life in harsh circumstances. Other writers had said the same thing, but it was Pasternak who drove home the lesson to me, in his uneven and somewhat disjointed masterpiece.

Doctor Zhivago was my first encounter with that special genre, the flawed masterwork. Later I would come to know *The Adventures of Huckleberry Finn*, *The Charterhouse of Parma*, and *Tender is the Night*. But then I believed what a teacher had told me, that great art was about perfection of form. *Doctor Zhivago* showed me that great writing can succeed despite its imperfections. No other work would touch me in quite the same way. I read Pasternak at just the right time.

One of the special messages *Doctor Zhivago* sent to me was that poetry and prose fiction were complementary, not antithetical. In American writing, the two genres are almost always separate. Of the classic American prose writers only Melville and Poe wrote notable poetry. But the hero of Pasternak's novel is a poet, like the author, and a great poet. And many of the discussions in the story are about poetry and the place of poetry in modern life. The novel might be the first work of literary criticism I ever read. It is still one of the best discussions of poetry I know. More important, the book ended with a selection of Zhivago's poems. I will never forget reading "Hamlet," "Bad Roads in Spring," and "Hopbines" there. The concluding poem, "Garden of Gethsemane," taught me something about the possibilities of poetry, just when I was most impressionistic. The poem ends:

Seest thou, the passing of the ages is like a parable
And in its passing it may burst to flame.
In the name then, of its awesome majesty
I shall, in voluntary torments, descend into my grave.

I shall descend into my grave. And on the third day rise again.
And even as rafts float down a river,
So shall the centuries drift, trailing like a caravan,
Coming for judgment, out of the dark, to me.[1]

I might have missed many of the literary allusions, but I certainly got the biblical references. I had been raised by fundamentalists who read the Bible to my sister and me every day. I understood that the poems were an homage to a church and belief that had been virtually wiped out by the Soviet regime. The novel was a monument, in part, to a world now lost, to the church, to artists and thinkers purged and lost, to the poet/Christ figure of Zhivago.

I realized that Pasternak had written, not only to honor those now lost, but to celebrate sanity and health, the human potential, against the devastation of totalitarianism and ideology. It was only later, as I studied Russian poetry and history that I saw what an elegy Pasternak had written for specific Russian futurists and symbolists, such as Blok and Mayakovski. I also came to see the book as a lament for the legacy of the church, the culture that had been preserved and handed down by so many generations until 1917. Pasternak's feeling for the meaning of tradition moved me more than T. S. Eliot's essays and poems would.

Reading *Doctor Zhivago* helped me see how fiction and poetry make the world, and history, immediate, palpable. I saw that novels were about details, surprise, unexpected truths. More important, they were about lives, and they helped us see the gift of family legacy and church that so many had worked to create for us. The story of loss and suffering was really a celebration of the things around me I hadn't noticed before. The novel showed me the privileges I had enjoyed and the importance of humility and compassion. The book showed me something of my own failures and limitations.

I never forgot the description of revising a poem on page 453 of the novel. Pasternak describes how Zhivago's poems to Lara, written in the most desperate, hopeless time, after Lara has been lost, go through draft after draft, until they are no longer just a personal statement but a work of art that speaks to all. Of this essential paradox about writing, the narrator says:

> As a result, his feeling, still pulsing and warm, was gradually eliminated from his poems, and romantic morbidity yielded to a broad and serene vision that lifted the particular to a level of the universal and familiar. He was not deliberately striving for such a goal, but this broad vision came of its own accord as a consolation, like a message sent to him by Lara from her travels, like a distant greeting.[2]

Oddly enough, the passage that made the deepest impression on me was one of the most obscure, the section describing Zhivago's return to Moscow by foot and rail across a Russia ruined by war and revolution. The chapters are a catalog of towns and countryside torn by fighting, disease, dislocation. I read it again and again for its detail and panoramic sweep. I felt in my heart that Pasternak was teaching me about history and culture and what it means to be human, more than any textbook or Sunday school had: "In unharvested fields the ripe grain spilled and trickled on the ground. Yet Andreievich gathered it in handfuls, and at the worst, if he had no means of boiling it and making gruel, he stuffed it into his mouth and chewed it with great difficulty. The raw, half-chewed grain was almost indigestible."[3]

Particular books affect us at particular times. Each of us finds our own literary canon. I found *Doctor Zhivago* at just the right time, for it showed me how fiction brings the world to our own eyes and breath and connects us intensely with those so different, so distant, and yet so much like ourselves. I saw how much I had to learn and, just as important, I saw how much I already knew without knowing it.

NOTES

1. Boris Pasternak. *Doctor Zhivago*. 1959. New York: Pantheon, 2011. 652–53.
2. Pasternak, *Doctor Zhivago*. 453.
3. Pasternak, *Doctor Zhivago*. 388.

JAMES MCCONKEY AND THE QUEST FOR THE SACRED

"Moreover, I, on my side, require of every writer, first or last, a simple
and sincere account of his own life . . . "

—Henry David Thoreau[1]

When I came to Cornell in 1971, I already knew the work of some of my
colleagues. I was familiar with the *Norton Anthology of English Literature*
edited by M.H. Abrams, the poems of A.R. Ammons, Robert H. Elias's
study of Theodore Dreiser, *Apostle of Nature*, Walter Slatoff's *With Respect
to Readers*, and Baxter Hathaway and *Epoch* magazine. The great surprise to
me was the writing of James McConkey. I had been told that McConkey
was a fiction writer, but early on in my reading of the book called *Crossroads*
I came on this passage:

> One night more than seven years ago, as I sat in my darkened
> basement study, I became conscious to a heightened degree of
> the details of my surroundings and life. A piece of fiction I had
> just written was contrived and thin, measured against the sight
> of a long-vacated bird's nest mounded with snow in the backyard
> maple and faintly illuminated by starlight, or against the feel of
> a dog's cold and moist nose on my skin. My relationship with
> my family and children was suddenly of such consequence to me
> that I wondered how any of my days had ever seemed routine or
> commonplace.
>
> For I thought the world, at least as I had known it, was likely to
> end fairly soon. . . . I needed that night to impose order upon my
> own experience, and to communicate what I felt to anybody who

would listen; and so I began the first of a series of accounts that make up this autobiographical novel.[2]

Later, in the book called *Court of Memory,* McConkey would again describe this profound turning point in his life again: "The story I had written was unsatisfactory because it was 'made up,' a fiction, one devoid of the sacredness I saw everywhere around me. The only way open to me to communicate the strength of my feelings was through myself—through my intimate experiences, through memory, and personal observation. . . . At that moment in my own life I began an autobiographical account of the meaning implicit in one of the humblest objects imaginable . . . a botched-up nightstand I had built as a child for my mother."[3]

I discovered that McConkey's first book of stories was called *Night Stand* and the memory of that little table was the trigger for the abundance of memory that followed. McConkey explained that he decided to give up writing about imagined characters and write only about his own experiences because he was disturbed by the events and threats of the early 1960s, such as the Cuban Missile Crisis, by:

> a sense of desperation at the folly of public affairs, by a sense of the human irrationality demonstrated in present history and the history of the recent past, including the evil of Auschwitz. One either went inward, striving to testify to the meaning that still existed for the individual . . . or one went outward, beyond the personal truth, to the region in which the sacred apparently no longer existed: the outer world in which the individual had lost his uniqueness, that world which lacked apparent logic or causality or even substance.[4]

As I read McConkey's stories about himself and his family and his memories, I discovered his ongoing fascination with the *Confessions* of St. Augustine. This surprised me at first, because McConkey was so clearly a modern and a secular writer, an authority on the novels of E. M. Forster and a student of moderns such as Joseph Conrad. But as I continued to read McConkey I began to understand more his affinity with the Bishop of Hippo. In his *Confessions* Augustine is relentless in his examination of his own faults and failings, his weaknesses and vanities, his talents and delusions. Augustine pays homage to his mother Monica for her faith and steadfastness. His mother's unwavering presence and affection lead him ultimately toward salvation and truth. Augustine is determined to witness to the reader the depth and paradoxes of his struggle and his victory. "All this I do inside me, in the huge court of memory," Augustine writes. "There I have by me the sky, the earth, the sea, and all things in them which I have been able to perceive. . . . There too I encounter myself."[5]

As I continued to read McConkey's stories in his books and in *The New Yorker*, I felt the uniqueness of his enterprise. He was on a mission to search for truth, for meaning in modern life. But ultimately, he was attempting to discover, if possible, what was still sacred in a world that seemed determined to be profane and to destroy itself. What made McConkey different from most contemporaries was not only his soul-searching honesty, his self-lacerating confessions of failures and weakness, but, like Augustine, he was on a quest to find the spiritual, to know the sacred, in a non-believing world.

In former times James McConkey would almost certainly have been a theological writer, probably a clergyman. But in a post-Darwin, post-Freudian, post-Holocaust world, he attempted to touch and communicate the divine in authentic experience of himself, other people, and the world around him. It is a quest whose grandeur is counter-balanced by the ordinariness of his details, the plainness and directness of his voice, the humility of his claims. But again and again through his writing McConkey *finds* the extraordinary in the ordinary. The casual detail or overheard comment becomes a revelation. McConkey is a poet without verse and a churchman without a creed.

McConkey's stories are so memorable that when I go back to them thirty-some years later I am astonished at how clearly I have remembered them. As a native of the southern Appalachians, I was inspired by the accuracy and affection of his portraits of the people of eastern Kentucky where he taught at Morehead State College before coming to Cornell. McConkey has a special feeling for working people, for the poor and disadvantaged. I will never forget his description of the poor boyhood friend in Arkansas who bites off his toenails in bed for fear of scratching the young Jim during a sleep-over: "'You scratched me. Your toenails are too long,' I said. He quickly said, 'I'm sorry,' and sat up in the dark. I heard a nibbling sound. 'What are you doing?' I said. . . . But he held one foot in his mouth, and then the other, nibbling and tearing at his nails."[6] And then there is the wonderful account of living in a trailer in Iowa City, while Jim was in graduate school, listening to a reading in the evening on the Philco radio of Francis Parkman's *La Salle and the Discovery of the Great West*. That was *my* introduction to Parkman's masterpiece.

By my count Jim has published ten books, and there are far too many wonderful scenes in them for me to mention more than a fraction. Among my favorites is the account of the filling station attendant in Sicily who wants so badly to give the McConkey family a souvenir he thrusts the rag with which he wipes windshields into Jim's hand. And then there is the account of the race across Germany in a Jeep near the end of WWII to find a substance called *fischleim* for printing an Army publication and being wounded when the vehicle hits a booby trap and wrecks. The German woman who attends the wounded McConkey is a never-to-be-forgotten instance of humanity and human connection in the least expected place. Only a writer of McConkey's integrity and candor would admit the connection he felt with the blue-eyed Nazi soldier who shouts "Heil Hitler" and then waits to be shot by his captors.

But in the short time I have here I think the most effective way to celebrate the writing of James McConkey is to quote some short passages from the story that set his imagination off on its quest for art, for understanding, for the sacred, the story of the night stand and the chain of events leading up to that significant memory.

As the madeleine was for Proust, opening the sluice gate of memory and artistry, so the little night stand was for McConkey in 1960: "Wretched little night stand, acting as if its turn had come, as if it won't be satisfied until given its due . . . :

I made it in the ninth grade. In the previous summer despair had settled upon my family; sudden poverty—for the depression had reached us at last—was the cause. I shall say only that my parents were so distracted that they moved here and there and finally to Arkansas, and that my father—a Northern businessman—seriously considered pig raising as an occupation and ordered the proper leaflet from the government. An impossibility, of course, but so was everything else; in their chaos, my parents were separated. My father headed even further south, while my brother, my mother, and I sold all the furniture for gasoline and traveled halfway across the continent in the old Packard—symbol of former opulence—to knock, without warning or invitation, one midnight upon the door of the nearest relatives too tender to deny us admission. They took us in, that most kind uncle and aunt—took not only us, the three of us prickled and small with shame, but my dog as well, a thin and ravenous German shepherd not unlike the one sleeping on the couch as I recall the past on another midnight.

For months thereafter, I was continually drowsy, my mind occupied with lassitudinous dreams. Full of humiliation and self-pity, I was pleased whenever someone spoke to me harshly for having neglected an assigned task. But let me pass over this year with my uncle and aunt simply by saying that my two semesters of ninth-grade manual training produced only that one wobbly night stand, its legs spindlier than any previous night stand had been known to be. I had planed them down, down, down, day after day, with eyes shut: once I opened them to see the instructor and the rest of the class standing in a half-circle before my bench, laughing silently. The blueprint called for a drawer which I had neither the time nor the aptitude to build. Nor, after the legs had been screwed to the top, did I even have time for paint or stain. I gave the night stand to my mother on her birthday: my gift, a year's toil; she—do you believe it?—cried.

Keep your eyes, whoever you are who may be following this reminiscence, keep your eyes on the night stand; some sudden travels take place, but the night stand is the theme of these chronicles of my youth; never lose sight of it. My mother certainly didn't. After this year with my relatives, my brother took a job in Michigan; we accompanied him. The dog, the night stand, and my mother occupied the back of the car during the journey. Misfortune ensues once more, and once more as the result of insufficient cash. The finance company—the old opulence, after all, had been based on credit—took the Packard: a relative in Ohio, the dog. I cried when he was carted off in his Railway Express cage. (Note how fully I am concerned with myself in these recollections: no mention of the perpetual grief and loneliness of my mother; no mention of my brother, four years my elder, who assumed the burdens of a father and who thus, instead of going to college, sold hamburgers at a dime store lunch counter; no mention of my still-distracted father, who was traveling about the country, holding this job or that, sending us whatever money he could.)

My mother, always strongly religious, now went with unfailing regularity to church for spiritual counsel; as one less benighted, I refused to accompany her. I would make us rich by writing fiction;

on Saturdays and Sundays, all weekend long, even after school during the week, I would furiously write—sometimes one story a week, sometimes two, sometimes three or even more. I would make us rich, yes—but even more than that I was playing God, creating little dream worlds in which I could impose the pattern, in which I would bring love to hate, peace to violence, unity to chaos. The paper, the pencils, and the typewriter ribbons took money from food, and the stories—ten-page thrillers, tales of suicide, rape and murder, but all with happy endings—never sold; even I knew they were poor. Such a succession of failures only made me increasingly belligerent when my mother continued to ask me to attend Sunday services with her.

And so we would quarrel; I was incensed by her mild, even meek, determination to salvage my soul. Hiding behind the curtains of our second-story apartment—a small apartment in a frame dwelling on the fringes of the downtown area—I would watch as she stepped off the curb (Careful of that car, little momma!), and walked quickly, without a backward look, toward the Presbyterian church six or eight blocks away. But not until early morning—in those gray and heavy hours before sunrise when a child, awakening, can sense death waiting for others, if not for himself—would I feel truly contrite, alone and frightened. I would tiptoe into her room, then wake her gently: "Mother, I'm sorry. Next Sunday I'll go." She would smile, clasp my hand and fall back into sleep. The clock by her bed stood on the miserable nightstand I had made.

This little idyll of my youth came to an end when we were no longer able to pay the modest rent for our apartment. My brother found other lodgings in town; eventually, after visits with those second cousins that would have me, I returned to live with my uncle and aunt; my mother (how it anguished me at the time!) took employment as a maid with still another relative, one insufferably rich and inexcusably distant in the blood line. I need not comment on my intense loneliness, my bitterness; indeed, they soon began to vanish, for my uncle and aunt gave me the love and care of parents. And then, finally, the depression began to retreat, to disperse, the way a shrouding cloud does before the moist winds of spring; pockets slowly filled with cash again, madness departed the world, and my parents, as in my happy endings, were reunited. Yet I still recall a letter from my mother, one written soon after she took her job as a maid: My room is cheerful, in a separate wing above the garage, and with private bath. It is a home for me though. I look forward to the time our whole family can be together again. The photographs of you, your father and your brother are on my bureau; the night stand you made is of course by the bed. . . .

That wretched, miserable night stand: wobbly, unpainted, without a drawer! I read the letter as many times as it was capable of imparting pain; I carried it in my pocket to my high-school classes, it lay under my pillow at night. In my dreams I saw my mother's face in sleep at the moment before I had wakened her in my remorse; I had visions of tortured tables with twisted tops, with legs warped and wobbly as bent pins. And I tried to imagine her long bus trip from Michigan: where had she put the night stand? Would the driver have argued that she couldn't take it, that it could travel with propriety neither in the luggage compartment nor in the racks? Later, I discovered that he had argued, and that she, in her mild perseverance, her gentle and maddening obstinacy, had won. It had occupied the seat next to her the entire trip.[7]

James Rodney McConkey was born in 1921 in Lakewood, Ohio. His father, Clayton, a salesman and businessman, moved the family again and again as he followed jobs and business opportunities all over the Midwest, and to Long Island and Arkansas. During the 1930s McConkey's parents were divorced, and he lived alternately with relatives, with his father and his second wife, and with his mother and brother. McConkey began his career as a journalist with the *Cleveland Press*, and graduated from Western Reserve University, met and married Gladys, served in the Army in WWII. Wounded in a jeep wreck in Germany on April 13, 1945, he returned to the United States and attended graduate school at the University of Iowa. His first teaching position was at Morehead State College in eastern Kentucky and his first book was a study of the novels of E. M. Forster. The McConkeys and their three sons moved to Ithaca, New York, in 1956 when Jim joined the English faculty at Cornell. Here Jim continued writing his splendid short stories, but as mentioned earlier, he decided in 1960 that instead of creating fictional narratives which seemed beside the point as the Cold War heated up, he would write about his own life and the world he knew first-hand. The result was the books for which he is best known: *Night Stand*,

Crossroads, Court of Memory, To a Distant Island, Rowan's Progress, My Life With Other Animals, The Telescope in the Parlor. In addition, he has published several related fictional narratives, including *Journey to Sahalin, The Treehouse Confessions,* and *Kayo.* Much of Jim's finest writing has been published in *The New Yorker.*

At Cornell Jim taught classes in writing, literature, especially the Modern European Novel, and he directed the creative writing program, as well as serving on many college and university committees. In the late 1970s he organized the two-year Chekhov Festival, still the most outstanding literary event I have witnessed in my time at Cornell, bringing to campus many luminaries such as Eudora Welty, Walker Percy, John Cheever, and Denise Levertov. As an editor of *Epoch* Jim helped make it one of the nation's pre-eminent literary journals.

A theme that runs through McConkey's work from beginning to end is the search for human connection, for brotherhood. In *Court of Memory,* he writes:

> Possibly brotherhood can be found in nobility of action and the virtuous cause; but I have discovered it—as these episodes suggest—chiefly in feelings of shared helplessness, impurity. And guilt. Caught in periods of depression by the sense not only of my own unsatisfactory nature but of the equally unsatisfactory nature of the world of men about me, I have thought brotherhood—that ostensible touching of wings—a circling flight from and back to the dark box of my ego. Angered with myself for crying Brother! wherever I meet up with my own flaws. I have on occasion thought, the blue-eyed puppet Nazi in your guts wants a comrade.[8]

Like James Agee in *Now Let Us Praise Famous Men,* McConkey has a special affinity for the poor and struggling, but is untiring in his examination of himself, his motives and actions. He cuts himself little slack as he probes his own intentions, integrity, conscience and memory. He is gentle with everybody but himself. Yet after years of vivid, dramatic, memorable reporting and meditation on his own life, he came to the recognition that he had not escaped fiction, as he realized that autobiography is also an imaginative construct, another kind of fiction, as all art includes selection, suppression, distortion for emphasis, shaping for clarity. As with the stories of his beloved Chekhov, there is something at once deeply satisfying and deeply unsettling about McConkey's narratives. He delights us with the clarity of his exposition, his sentences honed to lapidary brightness. There is an intense integrity, a clear-headed sense of responsibility to the language and to the reader. The stories have poignance, poise and gravitas. When I read his account of visiting Mammoth Cave with his fiancée at Christmas 1943 before shipping out for war, I wept. The vividness of his memory of the train station, old hotel, countryside, the tour of the cave, dread of the future and of leaving Gladys, is so powerful it hurts. His account of almost consummating their marriage before the ceremony reveals the times and the people in both comic and breathtaking brevity.

McConkey shares with the great Anton Pavlovich a concern with complexity, paradox, the surprise that suddenly shifts the paradigm. Like the Russian master, he is rarely judgmental— except with himself. There is a wholeness to McConkey's vision that echoes the breadth of Chekhov's world. On the evidence of the fictional stories printed in *Night Stand* I regret that McConkey gave up writing short stories. But on the other hand, he has given us the richness and insights of the unforgettable nonfiction narratives. The world would be poorer without *Court of Memory* and the other books.

What is unsettling about McConkey's writing is, I think, the intensity of his quest for the spiritual, colliding with the toughness of his honesty and skeptical self-revelation. It would be hard to think of another writer more sensitive to those around him, humans and animals, and the environment. McConkey has a deep sense of responsibility to attend, to witness, to report and to testify. So much of his writing is what would be called in the Baptist churches I attended when young a "testimonial," which could be either a confession of failure or of victory. In *Court of Memory,* he describes sitting on a tin roof with Gladys at night watching a display of the northern lights:

> It was very still that night, and we heard the faint honking of
> geese long before we saw them. And so, when we did see them, we
> were prepared for the patterned flight, for the high birds outlined
> against the pulsating streams of red and yellow and green. They
> entered the crown directly above us and passed into the dark,
> heading not due south but southeast; for they were following the
> waterways, and below our house, beyond the park, Six Mile Creek,
> heavy with autumnal rains, was rushing southwestward and over
> Van Nattas Dam. I had not heard the sound of the water until the
> geese flew by, but then the roar was steady and strong.

My wife held my hand. "I don't think I've ever been so happy," she said. 'I'm happy enough to die."

"And so was I; at that moment. I thought myself capable of soaring off that tin roof, to impale myself without regret on my neighbor's white-painted and most proper picket fence ten feet below."[9]

Occupied with the thorniest existential and theological questions, McConkey imposes no answers. He gives us facts and poses questions; he relates and speculates. Writing about Augustine and Bishop Spong and the challenges of belief in our times he observes:

In the current neurobiological view, the "mind" is created by the brain, but—unlike the brain—it is clearly not a substance but a quality. The Testimony describes Augustine's long labor before his own reason made it clear to him that God is not a substance existing everywhere and at every moment in the observable universe of space and time. God, then, is Mind. However circumscribed or otherwise limited it is, the human mind is an image of the Divine Mind, containing more than it can know it knows.[10]

We are told that Chekhov's favorite of all his stories was "The Student." Chekhov was a known agnostic, but his character here is a theology student who has been hunting on Good Friday. Suddenly the wind turns cold and depressing and as he returns to the village the student doubts himself and the purpose of his calling. Passing a widow and her daughter heating water over a fire in their yard, he comments to them that it was over such a fire that Peter warmed his hands after denying Christ three times. The widow and her daughter are deeply affected by the mention of that story. As he walks on the student is struck by the power of a narrative to reach like a chain across nineteen hundred years and touch people that deeply. As he nears the ferry, he feels a return of his confidence and sense of purpose. It is stories that give meaning to our chaotic lives.

A truly modern, as well as a classical, writer, McConkey offers us no sure answers beyond the power of narrative and human connection and the miracle of being. Rather than preach, he is a witness to his own quest and failures, connections, and recognitions. He is unsettling because he peels the layers of experience deeper and deeper. He is satisfying because he proves by example that the sacredness will always be in the journey, in the struggle, in the quest itself.

NOTES

1. Thoreau, Henry David. *A Week on the Concord and Merrimack Rivers, Walden; or Life in the Woods, The Maine Woods, Cape Cod.* ed. Robert F. Sayre. New York: Library of America, 1985. 325.
2. James McConkey. *Crossroads.* New York: Dutton, 1968. 5.
3. James McConkey. *Court of Memory.* New York: Dutton, 1983. 2.
4. James McConkey. *Night Stand: A Book of Stories.* Ithaca: Cornell University Press, 1965. 3.
5. Augustine. *Confessions.* Translated by F.J. Sheed. Indianapolis: Hackett Publishing Company, 1993. 196.
6. McConkey, *Night Stand.* 110.
7. McConkey, *Night Stand.* 69–73.
8. McConkey, *Court of Memory.* 57.
9. McConkey, *Court of Memory.* 21
10. James McConkey. *The Telescope in the Parlor.* Philadelphia: Paul Dry Books, 2004. 122–23.

HEMINGWAY AND THE TRUE POETRY OF WAR

In Flanders fields the poppies blow
Between the crosses row on row,
That mark our places; and in the sky
The larks, still bravely singing, fly
Scarce heard amid the guns below.

We are the dead. Short days ago
We lived, felt dawn, saw sunset glow,
Loved and were loved, and now we lie
In Flanders fields.

Take up our quarrel with the foe:
To you from failing hands we throw
The torch; be yours to hold it high.
If ye break faith with us who die
We shall not sleep, though poppies grow
In Flanders fields.

—John McCrae, "In Flanders Fields"[1]

On July 3, 1961, my dad and I drove back from the pole bean field in the pickup truck for lunch. It was an extremely hot day and I remember being bathed in sweat as we stopped at the mailbox. The newspaper came with the regular mail in those days and when I opened the Hendersonville *Times-News* the headline blazed across the top: "Ernest Hemingway Dead at 61."

I don't remember anything else about that day except what I read in the news story. The feature article described the world's most famous writer as having been depressed and sick. It said he had been killed by a shotgun blast to the head, and it quoted his wife Mary as saying, "This in some incredible way was an accident." There was a picture of the author standing beside a huge marlin.

I was sixteen years old at the time and bound for college that fall. That was my last summer working in the bean fields with my dad, plowing with a horse, saving my quarters and sweaty dollar bills to buy books and pay tuition. I was going to escape the small farm in the Blue Ridge Mountains of North Carolina to study science at a university. In those "Beat the Russians" years it seemed necessary for all young people to study nuclear engineering or aerospace engineering.

Like any ambitious sixteen-year-old I was interested in studying many things. I wanted to be a composer and a pianist. I wanted to study philosophy and higher mathematics. I wanted to attend West Point and become a pilot but was told I was too nearsighted to even qualify for the appointment. I wanted to fly B-52s.

But the subjects I was most possessed by were reading and writing. But the greatest discovery of the year before I went away to college had been Thomas Wolfe's *Look Homeward, Angel*. I read passages from the book so many times I had them by heart: "Each of us is all the sums he has not counted: subtract us into nakedness and night again, and you shall see begin in Crete four thousand years ago the love that ended yesterday in Texas."[2] At the end of the novel, as Eugene Gant walks in the square in the morning sun after hallucinating that the stone angels in his father's monument shop have come alive and Ben has returned as a ghost to talk with him, he exhorts himself to set out on his journey: "I shall find no door in any city. But in the city of myself, upon the continent of my soul, I shall find the forgotten language, the lost world, a door where I may enter, and music strange as any ever sounded; I shall haunt you, ghost, along the labyrinthine ways . . . "[3]

This was the rhetoric with which I had been inebriated for many months when I discovered the work of Ernest Hemingway in 1961. Oddly enough I had just begun to read Hemingway a few weeks before his death. I had discovered several of the Michigan stories and had begun *A Farewell to Arms*. And I had begun to appreciate a new kind of poetry. Hemingway's prose was as powerful as Wolfe's, but in a very different way. Hemingway's diction was plain and spare, his sentences stripped down, his observations understated. I found that Hemingway could achieve his most powerful effects with quiet language and—something new to me—Irony. After the tidal waves of Wolfe's language, it was a revelation and education to read sentences such as these from *In Our Time*:

We were in a garden at Mons. Young Buckley came in with his patrol from across the river. The first German I saw climbed up over the garden wall. We waited till he got one leg over and then potted him. He had so much equipment on and looked awfully surprised and fell down into the garden. Then three more came over further down the wall. We shot them. They all came just like that.[4]

And in the collection's first story "Indian Camp" Nick asks his father, "Is dying hard, Daddy?" The father responds, "No, I think it's pretty easy, Nick. It all depends."[5]

I began to be thrilled with a different kind of writing and a different kind of sensibility. Where Wolfe had celebrated emotion through overstatement and explicitness, Hemingway drove home the emotions by suggestion, by implicitness. For a young reader perhaps the most impressive thing about Hemingway's style is the way it evokes emotional and spiritual depth under a surface of fact and control, even nonchalance. Hemingway's style and tone evoke a special sense of character and integrity. To a young reader the style implies a rigor similar to science, to good newspaper and sports reporting, to the playing of dangerous sports, even when the voice is clearly British, not American:

> It was a frightfully hot day. We'd jammed an absolutely perfect barricade across the bridge. It was simply priceless. A big old wrought-iron grating from the front of a house. Too heavy to lift and you could shoot through it and they would have to climb over it. It was absolutely topping. They tried to get over it, and we potted them from forty yards. They rushed it, and officers came out alone and worked on it. It was an absolutely perfect obstacle. Their officers were very fine. We were frightfully put out when we heard the flank had gone, and we had to fall back.[6]

Reading Hemingway's stories, I discovered how a voice can evoke character, and how a few carefully chosen sentences can imply a whole world of attitude and experience.

Growing up in rural North Carolina I attended schools so old-fashioned they required a lot of memorization and recitation. Beginning in about the fifth grade, we had to memorize poems as well as patriotic texts such as The Preamble to the Constitution and The Gettysburg

Address, and say them before the class. One of the poems we had to memorize in the fifth or sixth grade was Alan Seeger's "I Have a Rendezvous
with Death."

> I have a rendezvous with Death
> At some disputed barricade,
> When Spring comes back with rustling shade
> And apple-blossoms fill the air—
> I have a rendezvous with Death
> When Spring brings back blue days and fair.
>
> It may be he shall take my hand
> And lead me into his dark land
> And close my eyes and quench my breath—
> It may be I shall pass him still.
> I have a rendezvous with Death
> On some scarred slope of battered hill,
> When Spring comes round again this year
> And the first meadow-flowers appear.
>
> God knows 'twere better to be deep
> Pillowed in silk and scented down,
> Where Love throbs out in blissful sleep,
> Pulse nigh to pulse, and breath to breath,
> Where hushed awakenings are dear ...
> But I've a rendezvous with Death
> At midnight in some flaming town,
> When Spring trips north again this year,
> And I to my pledge word am true,
> I shall not fail that rendezvous.[7]

Along with learning Seeger's poem and "In Flanders Fields" and a few
other poems from World War One, we were taught a little about the history of the war, the fighting in the trenches, the evil Kaiser. My teacher
passed along to us as history propaganda stories about Germans marching
through Belgium in 1914 and cutting off the right arms of all male children
so they could not grow up to be soldiers. She told us King Arthur was seen
riding a white horse above the no man's land, leading the Allies to quell
the Hun. She had been a little girl during the Great War, but she described

the breaking of the Hindenburg Line as though she had been there. In her version the war was a story of good smashing evil, of heroism and sacrifice. She also had us memorize Rupert Brooke's "The Soldier." Brooke was her favorite poet. She showed us a picture of him with his curly locks on both sides of his forehead, looking dreamy and romantic.

> If I should die, think only this of me:
> That there's some corner of a foreign field
> That is for ever England. There shall be
> In that rich earth a richer dust concealed:
> A dust whom England bore, shaped, made aware,
> Gave, once, her flowers to love, her ways to roam,
> A body of England's, breathing English air,
> Washed by the rivers, blest by suns of home.
>
> And think, this heart, all evil shed away,
> A pulse in the eternal mind, no less
> Gives somewhere back the thoughts by England given;
> Her sights and sounds; dreams happy as her day;
> And laughter, learnt of friends; and gentleness,
> In hearts at peace, under an English heaven.[8]

The week after Hemingway's death *Life* magazine published a famous portrait of the grizzled author on its cover. Inside was a feature on the career of Hemingway, with many photos and a tribute by Archibald MacLeish. I pored over MacLeish's article until I knew much of it by heart. He talked about Hemingway's fame as an athlete, soldier and boxer, big game hunter and fisherman, enthusiast of bull fighting, fighter with the Resistance. He described the influence of newspaper editors, and Sherwood Anderson and Gertrude Stein. This was the first time I heard the name Ezra Pound, who MacLeish quoted as saying about the young Hemingway in Paris, "The son of a bitch's *instincts* are right."[9] He described Hemingway living in a garret in Paris in the early 1920s, writing sentence after sentence and revising them endlessly. He described Hemingway's style as carving walnut, tough and lean. He "[w]hittled a style for his time from a walnut stick / In a carpenter's loft in a street of that April city."[10] I read more Hemingway stories, and I read *A Farewell to Arms,* and I reread MacLeish's article, and I began to think about writing in a new way:

In the late summer of that year we lived in a house in a village that looked across the river and the plain to the mountains. In the bed of the river there were pebbles and boulders, dry and white in the sun, and the water was clear and swiftly moving and blue in the channels. Troops went by the house and down the road and the dust they raised powdered the leaves of the trees. The trunks of the trees too were dusty and the leaves fell early that year and we saw the troops marching along the road and the dust rising and leaves, stirred by the breeze, falling and the soldiers marching and afterward the road bare and white except for the leaves.[11]

Here was a voice that was firm and fresh and authoritative. But it was also poetic, almost hypnotic in its repetitions and simplicity. The passion was caught in the restraint of the voice. And the tragedy of the story was caught in the tone of the voice from the first sentence. At the age of sixteen I was struck by the photographic quality of the writing, even the cinematic quality of it. Hemingway gave his narration the authority and seeming directness of a document. He was giving the facts of the story. I would later study modern poetry and see how Hemingway had put into fiction writing the tenets of Imagism in poetry as defined by Ezra Pound around 1912:

1. Direct treatment of the "thing": whether subjective or objective.
2. To use absolutely no word that does not contribute to the presentation.
3. As regarding rhythm: to compose in the sequence of the musical phrase, not in sequence of a metronome.[12]

Other tenets of Imagism as defined by Pound were: "An 'Image' is that which presents an intellectual and emotional complex in an instant of time. . . . It is better to produce one Image in a lifetime than to produce voluminous works . . . use no superfluous word, no adjective which does not reveal something . . . the natural object is *always* the adequate symbol. . . . Go in fear of abstractions."[13]

There was already a model for the kind of precision and economy and rigor of poetic style in classical American literature, in the prose and much of the poetry of Henry David Thoreau. Thoreau had already shown how to communicate his passion, his commitment to accuracy, his white-hot allegiance to the truth of facts and expression in the simplest, most direct language. But, of course, I did not know that at the time.

And I certainly did not know that Thoreau had been influenced by the new art and technology of photography which had just become popular in America in the 1840s as Thoreau began work in his journals on the project that would become *Walden*. I believe the impact of photography on writing has been greater than we generally recognize. I know photography had a profound effect on Walt Whitman's poems about the Civil War, and I know that Whitman's *Drum Taps* and Matthew Brady's photographs had a significant impact on the way later writers such as Stephen Crane would recreate battle scenes of the Civil War.

As a reporter Hemingway had taught himself to make words work as pictures. The challenge photography had brought to writing, as early as Henry David Thoreau, was the authority of its seeming objectivity and neutrality. Photography caught and fixed the details, the truth, the naked eye might have missed, or the brain forgotten. There was something clinical and factual and unarguable about a photograph. It was beyond mere opinion, subjectivity, and interpretation. It was the truth. "The camera does not lie" became an adage. "Prayer is the contemplation of the facts of life from the highest point of view," Emerson has written,[14] so "To the wise, therefore, a fact is true poetry, and the most beautiful of fables."[15] For Robert Frost, "The fact is the sweetest dream that labor knows."[16]

The camera saw with a lens a hundred times the size of the human lens. And the photographic plate was a hundred times the size of the human retina. I believe that the poise and the detailed rigor of Hemingway's description and narration were deeply influenced and inspired by the ethics and aesthetics of photography. Hemingway's style occurs like a great vowel shift in modern writing, and the art of narration has never been the same since.

Besides the tone of voice and the plain, naked details, one of the things that struck me from the very first about Hemingway's writing was his willingness, even his commitment, to look directly at pain, at the source of pain. When Frederic Henry is wounded in *A Farewell to Arms*, we are there, at the center of the experience:

> Through the other noise I heard a cough, then came chuh-chuh-chuh-chuh—then there was a flash, as when a blast-furnace door is swung open, and a roar that started white and went red and on and on in a rushing wind. I tried to breathe but my breath would not come and I felt myself rush bodily out of myself and out and out and out and all the time bodily in the wind. I went out swiftly, all

of myself, and I knew I was dead and that it had all been a mistake to think you just died. Then I floated, and instead of going on I felt myself slide back. I breathed and I was back.[17]

My feeling at the age of sixteen was that Hemingway had found a way to make writing in the old way obsolete. He had made the writing almost invisible and the experience everything. The first time you read a passage you are hardly aware of the cadence or the texture of the sentences. I would later discover that this is the way much of the best art works. Art that is most successful conceals its art. It was a considerable art that could make me feel there was no art, only the facts and intense experience. But I understood the power and newness of what Hemingway was doing, as many millions of readers had before me.

When I talked about Hemingway to my friends in 1961 the word I used most often was "honesty." I was in love with the confessional frankness of the narrator of *A Farewell to Arms*. The brutal candor had its own kind of eloquence: "I had been driving and I sat in the car and the driver took the papers in. It was a hot day and the sky was very bright and blue and the road was white and dusty. I sat in the high seat of the Fiat and thought about nothing. A regiment went by in the road and I watched them pass. The men were hot and sweating."[18]

Never had I seen anyone who wrote so well of wounds, of hospitals, of the love of God and the fear of God. Frederic Henry was willing to talk about the things no one else was willing to talk about, that I was unable to talk about. And the poetry, the poetry of description, the poetry of voice, the poetry of implicitness, were incomparable. Nowhere is this better shown than in the priest's description of his home region of Abruzzi:

There were bears on the Gran Sasso D'Italia but it was a long way. Aquila was a fine town. It was cool in the summer at night and the spring in Abruzzi was the most beautiful in Italy. But what was lovely was the fall to go hunting through the chestnut woods. The birds were all good because they fed on grapes and you never took a lunch because the peasants were always honored if you would eat with them at their houses.[19]

Critics from the first have singled out the narrative of the retreat from Caporetto in *A Farewell to Arms*. Many consider it the finest writing about warfare that Hemingway ever did. The fresh, surprising detail, the pacing, the matter of fact telling of extraordinary events, create a sustained experience of threat and disorientation, uncertainty, and desperate longing that has been a model for later writers. This art is demonstrated nowhere better than in the scene where Henry shoots the sergeant:

> "I order you to halt," I called. They went a little faster. I opened up my holster, took the pistol, aimed at the one who talked the most, and fired. I missed and they both started to run. I shot three times and dropped one. The other went through the hedge and out of sight. I fired at him through the hedge as he ran across the field. The pistol clicked empty and I put in another clip. I saw it was too far to shoot at the second sergeant. He was far across the field, running, his head held low. I commenced to reload the empty clip.[20]

Even more memorable is Henry's description of his escape after he has been arrested as a deserter and is about to be shot himself. The desperation and drama of the scene are heightened by the tense understatement of the narration. This is one of the most important lessons later writers have learned from Hemingway: when events are dramatic enough, when the issue at hand is a matter of danger, even life and death, the language must seem to disappear and the events unfold on their own. Of course, it is a sleight because the language is making the events unfold:

> I looked at the carabinieri. They were looking at the newcomers. The others were looking at the colonel. I ducked down, pushed between two men, and ran for the river, my head down. I tripped at the edge and went in with a splash. The water was very cold and I stayed under as long as I could. I could feel the current swirl me and I stayed under until I thought I could never come up.[21]

It is astonishing to think that Hemingway did some of his finest, most original writing when he was only twenty-four and twenty-five. He was the age of our graduate students when he carved out this style in Paris. He never had been to college. He never had been to a graduate writing workshop. When the century was young, he went off to the war and was wounded and he worked for the Toronto *Star*. And he met Sherwood Anderson in Chicago. I believe the example of Sherwood Anderson is as important as many biographers have suggested, and perhaps even more so. For what was special about Anderson was that he was a kind of regionalist, a member of the Chicago Renaissance with Carl Sandburg and Edgar Lee Masters and Vachel Lindsey and Theodore Dreiser. But he was also very much of a modernist, a friend and supporter of Gertrude Stein. There is a jazz-like quality of improvisation in Anderson's short stories. His voices have both the realistic idiom and an air of expressionistic distortion. Anderson's best writing has a unique blend of regional inflection and flavor combined with an almost abstract musicality. However real his characters may seem his language is clearly artifice.

One of the things young Hemingway must have learned from Anderson so early is that stories are not actual events transferred to the page, but the seemingly real created through artifice of language. Having understood that from the beginning, Hemingway was already ahead of most young writers, then and now.

I have found it interesting that Frederic Henry in *A Farewell to Arms* is described as an architecture student. Not a whole lot is made of this on the surface of the novel, but I think it is a significant connection. A few years ago, I thought of developing a course at Cornell that explored the inter-relationship of poetry and architecture from the Renaissance to the twentieth century. It was easy to see how the Palladian fashion of Elizabethan building could be paralleled to the classical style of Fulke Greville and Ben Jonson and the school of Jonson. Jonson even collaborated with the designer and architect Inigo Jones. And I saw how the Baroque poetry of the seventeenth century could be compared to the architecture of Christopher Wren, Vanbrugh, and Hawksmoor. Vanbrugh himself was a famous playwright and poet before he became known as an architect. And, of course, Pope was a friend of Burlington and wrote a famous poem to Burlington about neo-classical poetics and aesthetics. Similar comparisons could be made between Romantic poets and both the Greek Revival and neo-Gothic fashions in architecture.

But where my planning ran aground was in the twentieth century. If the most celebrated architect of the age was Frank Lloyd Wright with his "prairie style," where was the parallel in poetry? The obvious place to look was the Prairie School of poetry, but neither Sandburg, nor Masters, nor Lindsey seemed comparable to the originality and quality of Wright's buildings. It seems odd now that I did not think to connect Wright with that other former resident of Oak Park, Illinois, Ernest Hemingway. For now I can see that the plainness and boldness, the radical simplicity, the seeming naturalness of Wright's early work in the Oak Park houses, did indeed have their counterparts in Hemingway's prose. The poet who paralleled Wright's designs was not Sandburg but Hemingway. And whether it was conscious or not, I have no doubt that the famous presence of Wright's architecture in Oak Park, where Hemingway grew to manhood, influenced his thinking about style and design, about art and life. Hemingway's childhood home was just a few blocks away from Wright's studio and several of his classic houses. Hemingway set out to find the hard clean line in language that would match the hard clean line in Wright's buildings, and the bold clean lines of the new century. The difference was that Hemingway, coming two decades later, and having been to war, would apply those principles of design to the experience of war. And war would define much of the century just unfolding.

"Prose is architecture, not interior design, and the Baroque is over,"[22] Hemingway wrote in *Death in the Afternoon*. To write the true poetry of war one must put down the facts of the war. But putting down the facts can take on an irony all its own. Just stating the facts of horror can numb the reader on the one hand or take on a satiric edge on the other. It is this paradox of writing about war that Hemingway is addressing in his bitterly parodic story "A Natural History of the Dead," originally a section of *Death in the Afternoon*, but included in the 1933 collection *Winner Take Nothing*:

> Until the dead are buried they change somewhat in appearance each day. The color change . . . is from white to yellow, to yellow-green, to black. If left long enough in the heat the flesh comes to resemble coal-tar, especially where it has been broken or torn, and it has quite a visible tarlike iridescence. The dead grow larger each day until sometimes they become quite too big for their uniforms, . . . The individual members may increase in girth to an unbelievable extent and faces fill as taut and globular as balloons. . . . The smell of a battlefield in hot weather one cannot recall. You can remember that there was such a smell, but nothing ever happens to you to bring it back. . . .
>
> The first thing that you found about the dead was that, hit badly enough, they died like animals. Some quickly from a little wound you would not think would kill a rabbit. . . . Others would die like cats; a skull broken in and iron in the brain they lie alive

two days like cats that crawl into the coal bin with a bullet in the
brain and will not die until you cut their heads off.[23]

What comes through in this satire, where the speaker has a supposedly
clinical detachment, an educated, even British, voice, reporting as a scientist on the appearance of corpses on a battlefield, is that even the facts
won't give you the truth. The detailed description of the dead is one kind of
ghastly truth, but far from the main truth of the war, the experience of war.
The irony is brutal, the story unsettling, the truth skewed, partial, the effect
numbing.

A brutal, unsettling account of a soldier who has been gassed is given in
Wilfred Owen's poem "Dulce Et Decorum Est":

Dim, through the misty panes and thick green light,
As under a green sea, I saw him drowning.

In all my dreams, before my helpless sight,
He plunges at me, guttering, choking, drowning.

If in some smothering dreams you too could pace
Behind the wagon that we flung him in,
And watch the white eyes writhing in his face,
His hanging face, like a devil's sick of sin;
If you could hear, at every jolt, the blood
Come gargling from the froth-corrupted lungs,
Obscene as cancer, bitter as the cud
Of vile, incurable sores on innocent tongues, --
My friend, you would not tell with such high zest
To children ardent for some desperate glory,
The old Lie: Dulce et decorum est
Pro patria mori.[24]

Sweet and decorous it is to die for one's country. Owen is probably the
finest of all English war poets, and this poem is a landmark in the truthful
poetry of war. It is dramatic and authentic. But its designs on the reader are
clear almost from the beginning. It is bitter and moralistic, and it tips its
hand almost from the first line. It is a true poem of war but portrays only a
partial picture of war. Owen's poetry has a narrow, bitter intensity. It does
not even attempt wholeness, the larger picture.

One of the most intense experiences of the soldier is the longing for home, for the home place. He may be dissatisfied when he actually returns there, as in Hemingway's story "Soldier's Home." He may find home completely different from what he remembered and imagined in the army. But home is what he thinks about while he is lying awake in a faraway tent or hospital or abandoned building. In "Now I Lay Me" the soldier never sleeps. He lies listening to the chewing of silkworms, as if he is forced to listen to the spinning of the Fates. The gnawing of the silkworms is the noise of entropy, of the universe being chewed up and broken down to waste.

It is often noted that most of Hemingway's fiction about war is not about actual fighting, not about combat itself. It is about romance set against the backdrop of war and going home after war. War is the human condition. War is history. War is the fate against which an individual defines himself. Much of Hemingway's best writing is about convalescence, about waiting, and about insomnia. Hemingway is the poet of insomnia. "The Gambler, the Nun and the Radio" is a great ode to insomnia, as is the story "A Clean, Well-Lighted Place," as are many passages in *The Sun Also Rises* and *A Farewell to Arms*. From "Now I Lay Me":

> . . . all night you could hear them eating and a dropping sound in
> the leaves. I myself did not want to sleep because I had been living a
> long time with the knowledge that if I ever shut my eyes in the dark
> and let myself go, my soul would go out of my body. I had been
> that way a long time, ever since I had been blown up at night and
> felt it go out of me and go off and then come back. I tried never to
> think about it, but it had started to go since, in the nights, just at
> the moment of going off to sleep, and I could only stop it by a very
> great effort.[25]

While he lies awake in the dark Nick thinks of fishing whole trout streams, a pool and a shallow, and a log at a time. He thinks of finding the bait he would use, grubs and insects, grasshoppers. When he cannot fish mentally, he says his prayers. He tries to pray for everyone he ever knew, and he tries to recall everything that ever happened to him. He recalls his house and backyard, and the time his mother burned his father's arrowhead collection. When he can neither remember nor pray, he lies awake in the dark listening to the silkworms. One night he has a long conversation in the dark with a fellow soldier who urges him to marry.

The testimony of those who have been to war is that the experience has far more to do with waiting, with worry and boredom, than with actual combat. "Now I Lay Me" may be Hemingway's finest war story. It is certainly one of his best. The brilliance of the story is in the way it shows, by reflection, by indirection, how the experience of danger, how the proximity of death, strip away illusions. The soldier in the story occupies his mind through the dark hours remembering and reliving his favorite memories of trout fishing in all the streams he has known. He distracts himself by praying for all and by trying to relive his youth in detail. And he distracts himself by talking to his fellow soldier John, but all the time in the background the silkworms are chewing away and dropping excrement on the leaves below. They are the cosmic noise he is trying hard not to hear. They are the second law of thermodynamics, the impersonality of nature, the inexorable breakdown of all toward shit and meaninglessness.

I believe a fine paper could be written on the use of grasshoppers in this and some other Hemingway stories, notably "Big Two-Hearted River" and "A Way You'll Never Be." There is a great deal of loving detail in many of the stories about catching grasshoppers and using them for bait in trout fishing. In "Now I Lay Me" Nick Adams says: "Sometimes the stream ran through an open meadow, and in the dry grass I would catch grasshoppers and use them for bait and sometimes I would catch grasshoppers and toss them into the stream and watch them float along swimming on the stream and circling on the surface as the current took them and then disappear as a trout rose."[26]

That is one of the memories that sustains him through the long, sleepless nights. And in "A Way You'll Never Be" a wounded and shell-shocked Nick Adams, speaking compulsively and hysterically, says: "If you are interested in scars I can show you some interesting ones but I would rather talk about grasshoppers. What we call grasshoppers that is; and what are, really, locusts. These insects at one time played a very important part in my life."[27]

Nick goes on to describe in great detail to the alarmed adjutant the look of grasshoppers and how they are used for trout bait: "the medium-brown is a plump, compact, succulent hopper that I recommend as . . . something you gentlemen will probably never encounter. But I must insist that you will never gather a sufficient supply of these insects for a day's fishing by pursuing them with your hands or trying to hit them with a bat."[28]

Nick continues his breathless lecture on the proper way to catch grasshoppers, as though he were instructing troops. Driven over the edge emotionally, he keeps returning to the scenes and lore of his childhood. It is a scary performance, and one of the most dramatic, and one of the most memorable scenes in all Hemingway's stories about war.

Even greater attention is given to the catching and use of grasshoppers as trout bait in "Big Two-Hearted River," where we see Nick after he has returned from the war, physically recovered but still healing emotionally. In some of the finest descriptive writing Hemingway ever did he tells how the grasshoppers in the burned over tract of forest are now black: "he noticed a grasshopper walk along the ground and up onto his woolen sock. The grasshopper was black. As he had walked along the road, climbing, he had started many grasshoppers from the dust. They were all black. . . . They were just ordinary hoppers, but all a sooty black in color."[29]

As the burned over wilderness suggests the world severely damaged by the war, the black grasshoppers suggest the damaged men who have survived the war. In what was once a paradise of the river woods, only the sooty grasshoppers have survived. "Big Two-Hearted River" shows Nick's true homecoming: "Inside the tent the light came through the brown canvas. It smelled pleasantly of canvas. Already there was something mysterious and homelike. Nick was happy as he crawled inside the tent. He had not been unhappy all day. This was different though."[30]

After sleeping well that night in the tent, Nick goes looking for trout bait the next morning: "He found plenty of good grasshoppers. They were at the base of the grass stems. Sometimes they clung to a grass stem. They were cold and wet with dew, and could not jump until the sun warmed them. Nick picked them up, taking only the medium-sized brown ones, and put them into the bottle. He turned over a log and just under the shelter of the edge were several hundred hoppers. It was a grasshopper lodging house."[31]

All day Nick fishes and catches trout. It is a satisfying day. The man who could not sleep while he listened to the silkworms gnawing, who could not control his hysterical talking, is at ease with the river. He decides not to go to the swamp but to stay in the open country, fishing with grasshoppers. In the symbolism of the story, this suggests that he does not want yet to analyze the emotional trauma, does not want to go deeper into his mental problems. He prefers to heal himself by doing again the things he once did for pleasure. "Big Two-Hearted River" may be Hemingway's most perfect story. The descriptive writing is as good as any in Thoreau. It is a model of the poetics of sticking to the facts while suggesting a world of emotional and intellectual complexity and implying the drama of history, of war, beyond the horizon.

But why all the fuss about grasshoppers in this and the other stories?

Why would an author famous for shooting rhinos and catching giant mar-lins pay so much attention to grasshoppers? Certainly, the descriptions show his gift for vivid, intimate observation of the natural world. And to the disturbed soldier at war grasshoppers represent the world of childhood and nature he has left behind. I want to address this question by thinking about the popular connotations and associations grasshoppers have. Perhaps the most famous poem about grasshoppers is La Fontaine's "The Grasshopper and the Ant," translated here by Marianne Moore:

> Until fall, a grasshopper . . .
> . . . chirred a recurrent chant
> Of want beside an ant,
>
> Begging it to rescue her
> With some seeds it could spare
> Till the following year's fall. . . ."[32]

In this ancient fable the grasshopper is seen to be the hedonist, the irre-sponsible no-count who sings and fiddles while the ant prepares against the winter and the hard times to come. The grasshopper is the classic ne'er do well, the bohemian, the poet if you will. And think of the ant in Proverbs: "Go to the ant, thou sluggard; consider her ways, and be wise" (6:6).

But also remember the famous scene with ants in *A Farewell to Arms*. We see what happens to ants in the fire:

> Once in camp I put a log on top of the fire and it was full of ants. As it commenced to burn, the ants swarmed out and went first toward the center where the fire was; then turned back and ran toward the end. When there were enough on the end they fell off into the fire. . . . I remember thinking at the time that it was the end of the world and a splendid chance to be a messiah and lift the log off the fire and throw it out where the ants could get off onto the ground. But I did not do anything but throw a tin cup of water on the log, so that I would have the cup empty to put whiskey in before I added water to it. I think the cup of water on the log only steamed the ants.[33]

The ants are consumed without knowing they might just as easily have been saved by the indifferent Henry. But if they had been grasshoppers, they would have flown out of the flames and lived to sing another day.

It seems to me that the grasshoppers represent for Hemingway not just childhood and pastoral innocence, but also anti-puritan rebellion and relish of the present moment. The grasshoppers sing and die. They do not try to store up treasure for old age. Their treasure is every moment of every day lived before the cold and darkness come, before they are caught and eaten by a trout. They have the courage, and the wisdom, to live in the present. In a society where art itself is frowned on, where wine and liquor have been declared illegal, the grasshoppers may suggest art and joy and the courage to pursue pleasure, or at least the nonchalance to ignore the mean and timid, the moralistic smallness of middle-class society. The grasshoppers have a special meaning for the soldier who can't sleep, and the soldier who speaks compulsively, manically, and the soldier who returns to the wilderness scarred and still healing:

> He washed the trout in the stream. When he held them back up in the water they looked like live fish. Their color was not gone yet. He washed his hands and dried them on a log. Then he laid the trout on the sack spread out on the log, rolled them up in it, tied the bundle and put it in the landing net. His knife was still standing, blade stuck in the log. He cleaned it on the wood and put it in his pocket.
>
> Nick stood up on the log, holding his rod, the landing net banging heavy, then stepped into the water and splashed ashore. He climbed the bank and cut up into the woods, toward the high ground. He was going back to camp. He looked back. The river just showed through the trees. There were plenty of days coming when he could fish the swamp.[34]

The grasshoppers suggest freedom, escape from the confines of a pinched, restricted life. The grasshoppers suggest survival of the impractical, the poetic freedom to sing and fly. That is the greatest lesson the soldier may have learned. That, I believe, is Hemingway's truest poetry of war.

NOTES

1. John McCrae. "In Flanders Fields." *The Penguin Book of First World War Poetry*. ed. George Walter. New York: Penguin Classics, 2006. 155.

2. Thomas Wolfe, *Look Homeward, Angel*. 1929. New York: Scribner, 2006. 3.

3. Wolfe, *Look Homeward, Angel*. 508.

4. Ernest Hemingway. *In Our Time*. 1925. New York: Scribner's, 1996. 29.

5. Hemingway, *In Our Time*. 19.

6. Hemingway, *In Our Time*. 39.

7. Alan Seeger. "I Have a Rendezvous with Death." *The Penguin Book of First World War Poetry*. ed. George Walter. New York: Penguin Classics, 2006. 105–107.

8. Rupert Brooke. "The Soldier." *Rupert Brooke: Collected Poems*. Cambridge: The Oleander Press, 2010. 133.

9. Ezra Pound, quoted in Archibald MacLeish. "His Mirror Was Danger." *Life* magazine. Vol. 52, No. 2. July 14, 1961. 71. https://books.google.com /book?sid=glQEAAAAMBAJ&pg= PA71&source= gbs_toc_r&cad=2#v= onepage&q&f=false. Accessed 20 July 2024.

10. Archibald MacLeish, "His Mirror Was Danger." 71.

11. Ernest Hemingway. *A Farewell to Arms*. 1929. New York: Scribner, 1995. 3.

12. Ezra Pound. "A Few Dont's by an Imagiste." *Poetry*. Vol 1, No. 6 (March 1913). 200. www.gutenberg.org/files/43224/43224-h/43224-h.htm. Accessed 20 July 2024.

13. Pound, "A Few Dont's." 201–202.

14. Ralph Waldo Emerson. "Self-Reliance." *Essays & Lectures*. ed. Joel Porte. New York: Library of America, 1983. 275–76.

15. Emerson, "Nature." *Essays & Lectures*. 48.

16. Robert Frost. "Mowing." *Collected Poems, Prose, & Plays*. 26.

17. Hemingway, *A Farewell to Arms*. 54.

18. Hemingway, *A Farewell to Arms*. 33.

19. Hemingway, *A Farewell to Arms*. 73.

20. Hemingway, *A Farewell to Arms*. 204.

21. Hemingway, *A Farewell to Arms*. 225.

22. Ernest Hemingway. *Death in the Afternoon*. 1932. New York: Scribner, 1996. 191.

23. Ernest Hemingway. *Winner Take Nothing*. 1933. New York: Scribner's, 1970. 100–101.

24. Wilfred Owen. "Dulce et Decorum Est." *The Collected Poems of Wilfred Owen*. ed. C. Day Lewis. New York: New Directions, 1965. 55–56.

25. Ernest Hemingway, *Men Without Women*. 1927. New York: Scribner's, 1997. 145.

26. Hemingway, *Men Without Women*. 146.

27. Hemingway, *Winner Take Nothing*. 56.

28. Hemingway, *Winner Take Nothing*. 56.

29. Hemingway, *In Our Time.* 135.

30. Hemingway, *In Our Time.* 139.

31. Hemingway, *In Our Time.* 145.

32. La Fontaine. "The Grasshopper and the Ant." *Fables of La Fontaine.* Trans. Marianne Moore. New York: Viking Press, 1954. 13. archive.org/stream/in.ernet.dli.2015.150694/2015.150694.The-Fables-Of-LaFontaine_djvu.txt. Accessed 25 July 2024.

33. Hemingway, *A Farewell to Arms.* 327–28.

34. Hemingway, *In Our Time.* 155–56.

PART THREE

Uncommon Meters:
Vision, Craft, and the Authority of Poetry

THE MYSTERY OF EDGAR ALLAN POE

"It is not so much my method, as my air of method."

—Edgar Allan Poe[1]

From childhood's hour I have not been
As others were—I have not seen
As others saw—I could not bring
My passions from a common spring—
From the same source I have not taken
My sorrow—I could not awaken
My heart to joy at the same tone—
And all I lov'd—I lov'd alone—
Then—in my childhood—in the dawn
Of a most stormy life—was drawn
From ev'ry depth of good and ill
The mystery which binds me still—
From the torrent, or the fountain—
From the red cliff of the mountain—
From the sun that round me roll'd
In its autumn tint of gold—
From the lightning in the sky
As it pass'd me flying by—
From the thunder, and the storm—
And the cloud that took the form
(When the rest of Heaven was blue)
Of a demon in my view—.

—Edgar Allan Poe[2]

From this poem, which we assume is autobiographical in the sense that it shows the way Edgar Allan Poe thought of himself, or liked to present himself, we hear the voice of someone deeply alienated from those around him, and from his culture and times. It is a Byronic confession, an assertion of separateness, of uniqueness, and a cataclysmic sense of identity amid doom and suffering. The self-dramatization, the eerie, stormy atmosphere, the resounding couplets, portray not only a very peculiar voice, but a haunted and haunting point of view. This little poem is a view of Poe's life in miniature.

The writer we know as Edgar Allan Poe was born in Boston January 19, 1809, to traveling actors. His father, David Poe, son of an Irish-born Revolutionary patriot, from Baltimore, struggled to further his acting career in spite of a tendency toward drunkenness. Soon after Edgar's birth the father disappeared. His mother, the English-born Elizabeth Smith Arnold, was one of the most gifted actresses of the American stage, playing prominently in New York, Boston, Baltimore, Charleston and Richmond. Fighting consumption, the brave young thespian, who had an unusually fine singing voice, and had given birth to three children, succumbed to her disease in a boarding house in Richmond, Virginia, on December 8, 1811. It has been suggested by a number of scholars that watching his lovely mother die, seeing her last as a corpse, imprinted the future poet with a sense of essential connection between death and the poetic.

The three Poe children became wards of foster parents. Edgar was taken into the house of Frances and John Allan, a prosperous tobacco merchant born in Scotland. Though not legally adopted, he was raised as Edgar Allan amid affluence. These circumstances, of being reared among wealth, but having no legal entitlement as a mere foster child, would have a significant impact on the character and fortune of the future writer. It is thought the childless Frances Allan somewhat spoiled the bright and attractive boy who from an early age could entertain guests with recitations and dancing.

When John Allan moved to Scotland, and then to London, to further his business interests, Edgar was placed in an expensive boarding school called Manor House School at Stoke Newington, near London. From his years at that school Poe acquired a sense of himself as a gentleman, and memories of the place would figure vividly in the story "William Wilson," Poe's narrative of the alter ego. After the Allan family returned to Richmond in 1820, Edgar's education continued at private academies.

In his teens Poe fell in love with the mother of one of his friends, Jane Stanard, later describing her as "the first, purely ideal love of my soul."[3] All his life Poe would seek such an ideal love, in a world and among people far from ideal. In 1831 he would write one of his most memorable lyrics, titled "To Helen," to Mrs. Stanard's memory.

> Helen, thy beauty is to me
>   Like those Nicéan barks of yore,
> That gently, o'er a perfumed sea,
>   The weary, way-worn wanderer bore
>   To his own native shore.
>
> On desperate seas long wont to roam,
>   Thy hyacinth hair, thy classic face,
> The Naiad airs have brought me home
>   To the glories that were Greece,
>   And the grandeur that was Rome.
>
> Lo! In yon brilliant window-niche
>   How statue-like I see thee stand,
> The agate lamp within thy hand!
>   Ah, Psyche, from the regions which
>   Are Holy-Land![4]

This short poem, one of Poe's most popular, shows his intense idealization, combined with classical allusions, with mystery, ambiguity. No one has ever satisfactorily explained the charm of this poem, or explained exactly what it means or why it is so memorable. Already Poe was revealing his tendency to fall in love with women who for one reason or another were unavailable. The unavailability seems to be part of the attraction.

In 1824, John Allan's firm suffered such reverses it was dissolved. But the next year a rich uncle in Scotland died and left Allan a considerable fortune. He bought one of the finest houses in Richmond, and his ward, Edgar, fell in love with a pretty neighbor, Elmira Royster. The two became engaged, over the objections of her parents and his foster parents. As a mere foster son, Poe had few prospects, in spite of the affluence surrounding him. He and John Allan seemed always to quarrel.

To get the lovesick youth out of the way, and to give him an education, Allan sent Poe to Mr. Jefferson's University, the University of Virginia, then in its second year. At Charlottesville Edgar excelled at languages, both classical and modern, but indulged in partying and gambling, and acquainted himself with the mountainous countryside that would later figure in the story "A Tale of the Ragged Mountains." Explaining that he *had* to gamble since Allan gave him an inadequate allowance, Poe lost $2000 that Allan refused to pay. When Edgar was forced to return to Richmond, he discovered that Elmira, his betrothed, was now engaged to someone else.

In Richmond Poe quarreled bitterly with John Allan, and the young man, calling himself "Henri de Rennet" sailed for Boston, the city of his birth. There he persuaded a young printer to publish a thin volume called *Tamerlane and Other Poems* by "A Bostonian." Then he enlisted in the army as "Edgar A. Perry," and in November 1827 was transferred to Fort Moultrie, on Sullivan's Island near Charleston, South Carolina.

One of the many astonishing facts of Poe's life is his success as a soldier. The rebellious young man must have attended to his duties scrupulously, for he was rapidly promoted to the highest non-commissioned rank of sergeant-major. The record suggests that he was well liked by those he served with. Poe began to think of a military career, and reconciled with John Allan, who helped him secure an appointment to the United States Military Academy at West Point. Discharged from the army, and awaiting entry to the Academy, Poe was saddened to learn that his main advocate, Frances Allan, had died. He stayed with relations in Baltimore and published *Al Aaraaf, Tamerlane, and Minor Poems* there in December 1829. The book received a short but favorable review by the critic John Neil.

At the Military Academy Poe again excelled in languages and made a reputation among the cadets for his verse satires. When Mr. Allan remarried and severed relations with Poe, Poe got himself expelled from the academy for dereliction of duty. Now he knew he would never be Allan's heir, and in those days a man without a private income could ill afford a military career. Legend has it that Poe, to get himself kicked out of the academy, once appeared for drill on the parade ground wearing only his sword. An old joke goes: What are the three possible responses to an order at West Point: "Yes, sir," "No, sir," and "Nevermore, sir."

Before he left West Point in February 1831 Poe collected a subscription for his new book, *Poems: Second Edition.* Assuming it would be a volume of witty lampoons of officers at the Academy the cadets subscribed readily. But when the book was published in New York the cadets were disappointed to find it contained serious poems such as the classic "To Helen." The preface, "Letter to Mr. B—," shows Poe already developing his critical skills.

Some biographers have considered the three or four years after Poe left West Point as his "mystery years." At least one writer has suggested that he spent much of that time living in an attic room in Baltimore taking laudanum, and watching his brother, William Henry Poe, die of consumption. But, in fact, we know that he lived mostly with his aunt Maria Poe Clemm, her daughter Virginia, his brother William Henry, who was indeed dying from consumption, and his grandmother Elizabeth Cairnes Poe, whose meager pension from the government helped support the household. In this period Poe began to write short stories and published five tales in the *Saturday Courier* in 1832.

In 1833, at the age of 24, the young writer won a $50 prize from the *Saturday Visitor* for the story "MS Found in a Bottle."

The next year Poe broke into print in one of the most widely distributed periodicals of the time, *Godey's Lady's Book*, with the story "The Visionary." His foster father John Allan died in Richmond and left Poe nothing. However, John P. Kennedy, author of the classic *Swallow Barn*, and other books, and a judge for the *Saturday Visitor* contest that had awarded Poe the $50 prize, took an interest in the younger writer and recommended Poe to Thomas W. White, publisher of *The Southern Literary Messenger* in Richmond, where Poe began to publish poems, stories, and reviews. Poe was so poor he had to decline an invitation to dinner with Kennedy because he had nothing to wear, and Kennedy loaned him money for new clothes.

After Poe's grandmother died, and that slim support was lost, Poe moved to Richmond where White gave him freelance work, then hired him as assistant editor of the *Messenger*. Writing much of the critical content of the magazine, Poe earned a reputation as a "tomahawk man" for his sharp and witty reviews of contemporaries. He was particularly irritated by the trend of praising books by Americans simply because there were American. As he once wrote, "because, sure enough, its stupidity is American."[5] His trenchant reviews rapidly increased the circulation of *The Southern Literary Messenger*.

We do not know what the relationship was between Poe and his much younger first cousin Virginia Clemm before he left Baltimore. But when his aunt wrote that Virginia must go to live with another relation Poe emotionally begged to marry Virginia and proposed to bring her and Mrs. Clemm to Richmond. Already Poe had received a warning from his boss that he must curb his drinking or be fired from the magazine.

In October of 1835, Poe brought Virginia and her mother to Richmond, and married his cousin, not yet 14, on May 16, 1836. He became editor of *The Southern Literary Messenger*, which achieved ever-greater circulation, publishing the famous and soon to be famous. Also, Poe worked on a blank verse drama called *Politian*, which was never finished.

Poe's marriage to his first cousin "child bride" has been a source of gossip throughout his life and since. Beautiful cousin-lovers figure in much of his writing, from the Valley of the Many-Colored Grass of "Eleanora" to "Annabelle Lee" of his last year. Always the cousin is worshiped as an ideal, with what Poe called "a Uranian love." Always the young kinswoman dies. Sometimes the beloved woman is a sister, as in "The Fall of the House of Usher." Always she is sickly and dying.

It is thought by many biographers that the marriage between Edgar and Virginia was never consummated. Always she was his muse, his soul mate, his ideal "sister." Later, when Poe engaged in flirtations with various literary ladies, Virginia seemed not in the least jealous, but to approve of Poe's romantic friendships with women writers. And after Virginia's death, Poe's engagements to mature women were always broken off, before any marriage could take place. Only D. H, Lawrence has imagined that Poe's relationship with Virginia was intensely physical. Perhaps his comments say more about Lawrence than about Poe. We do know that Poe, in his "Preface" to the *Poems* of 1829, [later reworked into the poem "Introduction" in the *Poems* of 1831] acknowledged: "I could not love except where Death / Was mingling his with Beauty's breath / Or hymen, Time, and Destiny / Were stalking between her and me."[6] Freudian critics such as Marie Bonaparte have speculated not only on Poe's erotic fixation on beautiful dead women as the most inspiring subject of poetry, but also about the sublimation of his passion into ideal vision, into art. It is the "Uranian" attachment he returns to again and again, not the physical. It is physical passion that destroys the paradise of the Valley of the Many-Colored Grass in "Eleanora."

Informed by New York publishers that only novels, not short stories, would sell, Poe undertook a longer work of fiction, *The Narrative of Arthur Gordon Pym*, brought out by *Harper and Brothers* in 1838. While not considered a completely successful novel, *Pym* has been a treasure for critics and students of Poe, and for later novelists such as Herman Melville, who was deeply influenced by its story and its allegory of a voyage to the end of the world in Antarctica. The ambiguous whiteness of that frozen world would find its place in *Moby Dick* and would reveal Poe's awe and fear of the challenge and mystery of the blank page. Later Poe's novel would inspire H. P. Lovecraft to write *At the Mountains of Madness*, his greatest work of fiction.

In the meantime, Poe had been fired from the editorship of *The Messenger* for drinking. Now Poe began the period in which he did most of his best work. He took his little family to New York, hoping to make a career there as an editor and reviewer. But the New York literary world was not welcoming to this intruder from the South. Among the classic American authors of his era, Poe was *the* outsider. Writers of old Knickerbocker and Dutch families such as Washington Irving and Evert Duyckinck were the leading figures. Many editorial positions were held by pious men of the cloth who became prosperous men of letters, such as the Rev. Rufus Griswold, who later became Poe's executor and would one day work to tarnish Poe's reputation.

Poe, as he himself knew, was an outsider in several senses. He had not attended Harvard, Yale or Columbia. He did not belong to an old, distinguished family, nor was he connected to the church. Unlike any of the leading writers of his time, except for William Gilmore Sims, he was raised in the South and proudly referred to himself as "a Virginian." Poe was the first major writer in America of Irish descent. He had much in common with Nathaniel Hawthorne, but the author of *The Scarlet Letter* belonged to a distinguished old New England family that included judges and sea captains in its lineage. Hawthorne was a graduate of Bowdoin College, where he knew Longfellow and Franklin Pierce, a future president. Added to that, Poe's drinking, his unconventional marriage, his intense, volatile personality, and even his looks, made him seem alien in the polite Victorian society of literary New York.

Unable to support himself and his family in Manhattan, and with the novel *Pym* not yet published, Poe moved on to Philadelphia, then the center of American publishing. It would be in the City of Brotherly Love where Poe would first become famous, though he would never be prosperous or earn more than a subsistence. In Philadelphia he would do ghost writing and hack work, solve codes readers sent to *Alexander's Weekly Messenger*, and become editor of *Burton's Gentleman's Magazine*. To the latter he contributed anonymous reviews as well as masterpieces such as "The Fall of the House of Usher" and "William Wilson." Poe was now thirty years old, and the prose he was writing is among the most memorable in American literature. His colorful, macabre imagery, his cadence, his exotic vision, were like no one else's. Here is the first paragraph of "The Fall of the House of Usher":

During the whole of a dull, dark, and soundless day in the autumn of the year, when the clouds hung oppressively low in the heavens, I had been passing alone, on horse-back, through a singularly dreary tract of country; and at length found myself, as the shades of evening drew on, within view of the melancholy House of Usher. I know not how it was—but, with the first glimpse of the building, a sense of insufferable gloom pervaded my spirit. I say insufferable; for the feeling was unrelieved by any of that half-pleasurable, because poetic, sentiment, with which the mind usually receives even the sternest natural images of the desolate or terrible. I looked upon the scene before me—upon the mere house, and the simple landscape features of the domain –upon the bleak walls—upon the vacant eye-like windows—upon a few rank sedges—and upon a few white trunks of decayed trees—with an utter depression of soul which I can compare to no earthly sensation more properly than to the after-dream of the reveler upon opium—the bitter lapse into everyday life—the hideous dropping off of the veil. There was an iciness, a sinking, a sickening of the heart—an unredeemed dreariness of thought which no goading of the imagination could torture into aught of the sublime. What was it—I paused to think—what was it that so unnerved me in the contemplation of the House of Usher? It was a mystery all insoluble; nor could I grapple with the shadowy fancies that crowded upon me as I pondered. I was forced to fall back upon the unsatisfactory conclusion, that while, beyond doubt, there are combinations of very simple natural objects which have the power of thus affecting us, still the analysis of this power lies among considerations beyond our depth. It was possible, I reflected, that a mere different arrangement of the particulars of the scene, of the details of the picture, would be sufficient to modify, or perhaps to annihilate its capacity for sorrowful impression; and, acting upon this idea, I reined in my horse to the precipitous brink of a black and lurid tarn that lay in unruffled lustre by the dwelling, and gazed down—but with a shudder even more thrilling than before—upon the remodeled and inverted images of the grey sedge, and the ghastly tree-stems, and the vacant and eye-like windows.[7]

The firm of Lea and Blanchard in Philadelphia published late in 1839 Poe's *Tales of the Grotesque and Arabesque*. The "grotesque," coming from the word grotto, suggests Poe's Gothic imagination, and "arabesque" his colorful intricate fantasies with a hint of the Middle Eastern. Poe seemed to have a special affinity for Arabic words and Arabic themes and images. Though the volume was not a commercial success, Poe was kept on as editor of the *Gentleman's Magazine* when it was bought by George Graham in 1840, at the great salary of $800 a year.

In *Graham's Magazine* Poe would make literary history by publishing the first of his tales of "ratiocination," "The Murders in the Rue Morgue," in effect introducing the detective story to the world of letters. It was a period of intense work for Poe, as he published his classic review article on Hawthorne's *Twice-Told Tales*, going a long way toward defining the short story as we know it. This is the period in which he wrote the haunting sketch "The Masque of the Red Death," and the ever popular "The Pit and the Pendulum."

Hoping to somehow found his own magazine, Poe broke with Graham and went freelance. As one of the most successful editors and critics in the country, it made sense that he would want to have his own magazine. He hoped to call it *The Penn Magazine* and even printed a "Prospectus" for the publication. But nothing came of the plan.

In 1843, Poe published "The Tell-Tale Heart" in James Russell Lowell's new magazine *The Pioneer*, in Boston, and his first substantial critical essay on poetry and poetics, "The Rationale of Verse." And he made an even greater effort to create his own magazine, to be called now *The Stylus*. All he needed was a financial backer, and perhaps a well-paying sinecure with the government to enable him to publish the most outstanding literary journal in the United States. Having praised the poetry of Robert Tyler, son of President Tyler, and with the help of sympathetic friends, Poe applied for a job at the Philadelphia Customs House. But to secure the cushy position, he needed to go to Washington for an interview with the president.

Perhaps to celebrate his good fortune, and new prospects, Poe had a drink with a friend on the way to the capital, and later arrived drunk at the White House with his gray West Point overcoat—the only one he ever owned—on wrong-side out. He was escorted out of the executive mansion, and friends had to put him on the train back to Philadelphia. End of his hopes for a government sinecure.

We know that Poe had a serious problem with alcohol that got him fired from more than one editorial position. Some have speculated that he was diabetic, and more adversely affected by alcohol than most. And while this may be true, there seems to have been other forces working on this most gifted individual. Throughout his career Poe sabotaged many opportunities that came his way. In a romantic sense we can see that he had a Byronic or aristocratic disdain for mere worldly success. While penniless he could comport himself like a nobleman. But the fact is Poe lived through real poverty and need and humiliating failures, giving pain not only to himself but to those dear to him such as Virginia and Mrs. Clemm. Modern biographers have seen in Poe what might be called a "death-wish," a compulsion, a desire to fail, to escape worldly, vulgar success. Sometimes in anguish he no doubt rationalized his failures that way. However that may be, and whatever the psychological explanations, we know he relentlessly *tried* to find success, and again and again botched the opportunities that came his way.

Poe's first national fame came when he published "The Gold Bug," the most popular of his detective stories in his time, in the Philadelphia *Dollar Newspaper* in January 1843, winning the $100 short story prize. The story was reprinted again and again in newspapers around the country, making the author one of the most popular writers of the decade. "The Gold Bug" was also dramatized by others, and Poe became a household name. He began his career as a lecturer at this time with "Poets and Poetry of America."

Now, with his new fame, Poe was ready to take on New York City again. He moved his family back to Manhattan, even as the health of his wife Virginia, who had broken a blood vessel in her throat while singing, began to decline. He had not given up on the idea of *The Stylus*, which would have an audience across the South and the Western states. But unable to find a backer for his own magazine, he joined the staff of the New York *Evening Mirror*.

For some time, Poe had been working on the poem called "The Raven," and when it was published in the January 1845 *Evening Mirror*, "The Raven" enjoyed an enormous popularity. Never before had a single American poem made such an impact on readers. Other magazines reprinted "The Raven," and readers memorized the trochaic verse. Poe wrote to a friend

"The Bird beat the Bug . . ."[8] School children memorized and recited the stirring lines. "The Raven" ends:

> "'Prophet!' said I, 'thing of evil!'—prophet still, if bird or devil!
> By that Heaven that bends above us—by that God we both
>   adore—
> Tell this soul with sorrow laden if, within the distant Aidenn,
> It shall clasp a sainted maiden whom the angels name Lenore—
> Clasp a rare and radiant maiden whom the angels name Lenore."
>   Quoth the Raven 'Nevermore.'
>
> 'Be that word our sign of parting, bird or fiend!' I shrieked,
>   upstarting—
> "Get thee back into the tempest and the Night's Plutonian shore!
>   Leave no black plume as token of that lie thy soul hath spoken!
>   Leave my loneliness unbroken!—quit the bust above my door!
> Take thy beak from out my heart, and take thy form from off my
>   door!"
>   Quoth the Raven 'Nevermore.'
>
> And the Raven, never flitting, still is sitting, *still* is sitting
> On the pallid bust of Pallas just above my chamber door;
>   And his eyes have all the seeming of a demon's that is dreaming,
>   And the lamp-light o'er him streaming throws his shadow on
>   the floor;
> And my soul from out that shadow that lies floating on the floor
>   Shall be lifted—nevermore![9]

Partly because of the fame of "The Raven" Poe began to be invited into the polite society of literary New York. He proved to be an impressive performer, reciting "The Raven" and other poems in darkened drawing rooms. He flattered hostesses, edited poems of the rich, and flirted with beautiful literary ladies. *The Raven and Other Poems* was published, and a volume of twelve stories called *Tales* was brought out to much acclaim. Poe borrowed money to buy the *Broadway Journal* and at last had his own magazine. He also conducted a romance, mostly in verse, with the lovely Frances Sargent Osgood.

But just as Poe seemed to have achieved many of the goals he had aspired to, fame, invitations to lecture and recite, surrounded by admiring and important women, he began to undermine his own success. First, he began to accuse fellow authors of plagiarism, including the eminent Longfellow. Poe's outbursts of defensiveness and paranoia, his attacks and accusations, began to alienate important friends such as the patrician James Russell Lowell. His flirtations with women in Victorian New York did not help either. He insulted an audience at the Boston Lyceum by seeming to patronize or mock them. He referred to Emerson and the Boston literary elite as "frog-pondians." Emerson would return the favor, calling Poe "the jingle man." Poe quickly undercut the reputation he had worked so hard to achieve. And more than once he was seen staggering drunk on the streets of New York, so helpless he had to be driven home.

To aggravate his woes, Virginia's health continued to decline. It became clear she was suffering from advanced consumption. By late 1845, as Poe was becoming the butt of jokes and subject of choice gossip, Virginia went into rapid decline. Depressed, uncertain, Poe let his *Broadway Journal* fold and moved out of New York City to the village of Fordham. Virginia was now an invalid, nursed by a saintly volunteer Marie Louise Shew, a friend who helped the Poes financially also. Newspapers published reports of the family's plight, further humiliating the proud writer. Seriously ill himself, Poe wrote to Virginia, "You are my *greatest* and *only* stimulus now, to battle with this uncongenial, unsatisfactory, and ungrateful life."[10]

Nevertheless, in these unfavorable conditions Poe managed to publish one of his most notable tales, "The Cask of Amontillado," as well as a series of sketches called "The Literati of New York." I have often quoted the opening of *Cask* to students to show how Poe can grab the readers' attention from the first sentence and draw them into the story: "The thousand injuries of Fortunato I had borne as best I could; but when he ventured upon insult, I vowed revenge."[11]

The death of Virginia on January 30, 1847 sent Poe into a further tailspin. However unconventional his marriage may have been, it is clear that Virginia was the emotional center, the stabilizer, of his erratic life. After she was gone, he spent weeks and months in bed, nursed by Mrs. Clemm and Mrs. Shew, and he visited Virginia's grave repeatedly. And yet even in these conditions he revised his review of Hawthorne's tales for publication, wrote two of his most memorable poems, "To M.L.S" and "Ulalume," and one of his most important story-essays, "The Landscape Garden," later revised as "The Domain of Arnheim." And he began to make notes for his longest nonfiction work, which he called a prose poem, the cosmological theory exploration that became *Eureka*. Nothing Poe ever wrote is more distinctive and eerie than the poem "Ulalume":

> The skies they were ashen and sober;
> The leaves they were crispéd and sere—
> The leaves they were withering and sere—
> It was night, in the lonesome October
> Of my most immemorial year:
> It was hard by the dim lake of Auber,
> In the misty mid region of Weir: —
> It was down by the dank tarn of Auber,
> In the ghoul haunted woodland of Weir.[12]

In "The Landscape Garden" Poe would begin to formulate one of his most important aesthetic theories. For him the landscape garden is one of the ultimate works of the imagination, where art is carried so far, transforming nature, and to such a perfection, that the garden, though completely man-made, artificial, looks "natural."

In 1848 Poe began to regain his physical health, but perhaps not his emotional health. He blamed his bouts of drinking on insanity caused by Virginia's death: "It was in the horrible, never-ending oscillation between hope and despair which I could *not* longer have endured without total loss of reason. In the death of what was my life, then, I receive a new but—Oh God! How melancholy an existence."[13]

Still hoping to found *The Stylus*, Poe lectured to raise funds and find subscribers, reading from notes called "The Universe," drafts of the later *Eureka*. While lecturing in Lowell, Massachusetts, he formed an attachment to a married woman, Mrs. Annie Richmond, and in Providence, Rhode Island, he became engaged to the poet Mrs. Helen Whitman, a widow who was comfortably well off. Mrs. Whitman insisted that Poe stop drinking, and when she was informed by friends of Poe's bad behavior in New York, he attempted suicide with a heavy dose of laudanum, which he managed to throw up. The whole affair became a melodramatic farce, and Poe returned to New York and Mrs. Clemm. In Providence Poe had delivered the lecture "The Poetic Principle" and read the poem "The Bells."

In 1849 Poe seemed to recover his stability, somewhat. Writing mostly for a Boston publication called *Flag of Our Union*, he criticized James Russell Lowell for omitting Southern writers from his "A Fable for Critics" and exclaimed "Literature is the most noble of professions. In fact, it is about the only one fit for a man."[14] In the late spring he left for Richmond, the place of his youth, still hoping to find backers for *The Stylus*. At a stop in Philadelphia friends were astonished at Poe's obsession with persecution, and his manic behavior. A friend named Charles Barr paid for his train fare on to Richmond.

In the Virginia capital Poe was welcomed as a native son and celebrity. He gave several well-attended lectures, visited his sister Rosalie, joined a temperance society, and became engaged to his former sweetheart Elmira Royster Shelton, now a well-off widow. Poe's problems once again seemed solved. Insisting he must return to New York to bring Mrs. Clemm to Richmond, he took a boat to Baltimore, where he was found delirious outside a polling booth on October 3, 1849. Taken to a hospital he died on October 7 of "congestion of the brain." In his final hours he called out for Reynolds, the sailor and author whose story had served as the inspiration for *The Narrative of Arthur Gordon Pym*, where he had approached the ultimate great white mystery. Perhaps Poe hoped that Jeremiah N. Reynolds once again could serve as his guide into the vast unknown. In an obituary by Rufus Griswold, Poe was accused of drunkenness, dishonesty, and plagiarism, setting the tone for much criticism of the author for decades to come.

In the 160 years since, scholars have speculated endlessly on the cause of Poe's death. Many have said he went on a drunken binge and was led from poll to poll to vote, given drinks and told how to vote by his handlers. According to this theory he died of alcohol poisoning or delirium tremens. Others have suggested he was bitten by a rabid dog or rat while lying in the gutter and died the painful death of rabies. Still others have decided it was diabetes that caused his delirium. We may never know for sure. Another guess is encephalitis brought on by exposure. The poet Charles Baudelaire would write that Poe's death was, in effect, a suicide.

What we do know is that Poe's fame grew, even as his reputation was blackened by the Reverend Rufus Griswold and others. While Victorian scholars continued to describe Poe as a drunk or drug addict, a womanizer and a plagiarist, his stories and poems found an ever-larger reading public. The supposed scandals about Poe did not hurt the sales of his books one bit. Edition after edition of his poems and stories began to appear, and no anthology of American poetry was seen without "The Raven" or "Annabelle Lee" or "To Helen." School children memorized the poems, and Poe's verses were recited in declamation contests throughout the 19th and into the 20th century.

The real beginning of Poe's international reputation occurred in France where one or two of his stories appeared in translation in magazines in the 1840s, while Poe was still alive. The young poet Charles Baudelaire read them and was swept away. He later said that discovering Poe's work was like reading his own dreams of years before. Baudelaire was observed in the train station in Paris, stopping anyone who looked like an American, and asking if they knew "Edgar Poe," and if they had any copies of his work. For the rest of his life Baudelaire, perhaps the greatest modern European poet, devoted himself to translating Poe's prose and introducing the American to the French reading public. Of the gossip about Poe's drinking Baudelaire commented one might "believe that all the authors of the United States, Poe alone excepted, are angels of sobriety."[15] In his journal Baudelaire tells us that he prays to the spirit of Poe every day.

The great French symbolist poet Stéphan Mallarmé translated several of Poe's poems into French and wrote the poem "Le Tombeau de Edgar Poe" to be read at the dedication of the monument over Poe's grave in Baltimore. The only American poet present at that ceremony was Walt Whitman, but he chose not to say a word. Almost every major French poet or critic since has written an essay or other tribute to Poe. There has been a good deal of discussion about the extraordinary admiration the French have for Poe, in contrast to the grudging recognition by American critics. One explanation has been French poets such as Baudelaire and Mallarmé hardly knew English, therefore projected onto Poe's work a sophistication of their own imagination. But Baudelaire knew English from childhood: his mother had lived in Ireland as a girl. And Mallarmé was a professor of English in the lycee system. Others have suggested that the French, with their tradition of *sadisme* and literature of cruelty, took to Poe because of the very decadence of their culture. Few American scholars have been will- ing to concede to the French a far greater critical maturity about modern writing than existed in the Anglophone world of the 19th century. Poe was a modernist writer long before the age of modernism. Compared to Poe's best work many of the stories of Hawthorne, his closest rival in American, creak with heavy-handed moralism and allegory.

The novelist and critic Marilynne Robinson, writing in the *New York Times* a few years ago, suggested that the controversy about Poe's place in the canon of American literature derives from his use of familiar genre conventions, the Gothic horror story, the exotic romance. Because he was working with conventions so familiar and so much imitated since, his stories are seen as vulgar clichés by some. But she points out Poe is the original, and in his hands these conventions are raised to the level of high literary art.

Others have speculated that Poe's aestheticism is inimical to a critical tradition with its roots in Puritan New England and evangelical Protestantism, where universities were founded as theology schools to produce ministers and missionaries. American literary studies and graduate work could be seen as extensions of Sunday School, teaching us how to do the right thing and lead virtuous lives. Today, almost all literary studies are didactic. Poe despised the didactic, and it is hard to fit Poe's work into such a culture. And many may be embarrassed by Poe because they read him so avidly when young and know so many of his poems by heart. Poe is something we feel we must outgrow.

Writers in other cultures have no such reservations. The authors of Latin America, including those called the Magic Realists, adore Poe. I remember talking with the Mexican novelist Carlos Fuentes at a party in New York. The subject of Poe came up and Fuentes began quoting long passages from Poe's stories verbatim. Those who know the work of Borges already know of his affinity with Poe.

One of the leading experts on Poe in the United States is the poet Richard Wilbur, who in his many essays on Poe's work describes Poe's vision as Gnostic, meaning he seeks to escape the painful, fallen, physical world of time into the spiritual, the ethereal, the eternal. Several years ago at Cornell, I taught a course called "Poe and Emerson: Contrasting Strains of American Romanticism." I told students that Emerson had the greatest influence on American literature of any writer, and Poe had the greatest influence on world literature of any American writer. I described the similarities of the two founders of American poetry and poetics. Both were born in Boston in the first decade of the 19th century, both were deeply influenced by Coleridge and the Neo-Platonists, and the German Romantics. Yet their talents and vision took them in very different directions. Emerson was inspired by the Wordsworthian side of Coleridge's thought, expansive, hopeful, looking out toward nature as the language of the soul. Emerson had started out as a preacher, and he spent his life exhorting listeners and readers to see the divine all around them and in themselves. Poe was inspired by the Gothic side of Coleridge's imagination, by "The Rime of the Ancient Mariner," "Kubla Khan," "Christabel." Instead of looking outward to health and hope, Poe saw sickness, evil, madness and death.

Art and beauty, the imagination, were the means to escape from the travail of the world and time: "Inspired by an ecstatic prescience of the glories beyond the grave, we struggle, by multiform combinations of things and thoughts of Time, to attain a portion of Loveliness whose very elements, perhaps, appertain to eternity alone."[16]

Poe did not believe this world or people could be improved. The deep melancholy and loneliness in Poe are two of the things we respond to in his work. For we recognize that hopelessness and alienation in ourselves and are comforted to find a kindred spirit so imaginative, transcending the shallow optimism and cliches and facile promises all around us, in political cant, in self-help manuals. Besides the great artistry, the memorable music, the haunting images, the ingenious plots of Poe's work, it is this deep sorrow we respond to. As Baudelaire says in his poem "Bènèdiction," "I know sadness is the only nobility."[17] It is a recognition that stirs us deeply. The novels of my late Cornell colleague, Vladimir Nabokov, including *Lolita* and *Ada,* are threaded through with allusions to Poe's work.

But there is no particular need to defend Poe. He is the most widely read American author in the world. He *was* prickly, defensive, at times paranoid. He was an alcoholic, bi-polar, was sometimes delusional, and conducted silly flirtations. But the originality of his talent and the vastness of his achievement and influence are hard to deny. If you are asked to recite a line of poetry, what comes to the tip of your tongue? It would be hard to exaggerate Poe's influence on Symbolist, therefore modern poetry, in several languages, on the short story, the detective story and science fiction and fantasy, on the psychological thriller, the horror story, and ultimately on films, including the horror films, and on modern, analytical literary criticism. Poe would brag about how meticulously and scientifically he created the effects of "The Raven." But we know he had the ability and the inspiration also to sit down and write *ex tempore* a poem such as this to his saintly benefactor Marie Louise Shew:

> Not long ago the writer of these lines,
> In the mad pride of intellectuality,
> Maintained "the power of words"—denied that ever
> A thought arose within the human brain
> Beyond the utterance of the human tongue;
> And now, as if in mockery of that boast,
> Two words—two foreign soft dissyllables—

> Italian tones made only to be murmured
> By angels dreaming in the moonlit "dew
> That hangs like chains of pearl on Hermon hill"—
> Have stirred from out the abysses of his heart,
> Unthought-like thoughts that are the souls of thought,
> Richer, far wilder, far diviner visions
> Than even the seraph harper, Israfel,
> Who has "the sweetest voice of all God's creatures,"
> Could hope to utter. And I! My spells are broken.
> The pen falls powerless from my shivering hand.
> With thy dear name as text, though bidden by thee,
> I cannot write—I cannot speak or think,
> Alas I cannot feel; for 'tis not feeling,
> This standing motionless upon the golden
> Threshold of the wide-open gate of dreams,
> Gazing, entranced, adown the gorgeous vista,
> And thrilling as I see upon the right,
> Upon the left, and all the way along
> Amid empurpled vapors, far away
> To where the prospect terminates—*thee only*.[18]

The final lines of the poem remind us of the passage in "The Domain of Arnheim" where the hero Ellison is described as living in his artistically created perfect estate, with his bride "whose loveliness and love enveloped his existence in the purple atmosphere of paradise."[19] Ellison, the author says, had found the four essential conditions of happiness: "free exercise in the open air. . . . second . . . the love of woman. . . . third, and most difficult of realization, was the contempt of ambition. . . . fourth . . . an object of unceasing pursuit; and he held that, other things being equal, the extent of attainable happiness was in proportion to the spirituality of this object."[20]

It has been said that if you split a photograph of Poe's face down the middle you can see the dividedness of his character. One side looks confident, alert, and the other exhausted, sad, disheveled. While this may be true and explain some of the contradictions and struggles of his life, it does not diminish the quality of the work he left, or his legacy. His cosmological speculations in the prose poem *Eureka* anticipate in a surprising way the theories of modern physics such as the Big Bang. In his essay "The Poetic Principle" Poe asserts that a long poem is a contradiction in terms, great poems being so intense they must be short enough to read at one sitting. What are called long poems are mostly short poems strung episodically together. Much as we want to dispute him, it is hard to come up with exceptions to his assertion.

One of the finest critical essays on Poe in the 20th century was written by the poet William Carlos Williams in his 1925 volume *In the American Grain*. Williams tried to describe a cultural tradition in America far more inclusive than the academic one that focused primarily on Puritan New England. Williams saw Poe as the definitive American writer of his time, who actually portrayed the complexity and violence and contradictions around him: "It is to save our faces that we've given him a crazy reputation, a writer from whose classic accuracies we have not known how to escape..."[21] Williams continues his praise, "His attack upon the difficulty that faced him was brilliantly conceived, faultlessly maintained and successful...."[22] and declares "On him is founded a literature."[23]

Though we think of Poe as the master of the detective story, the Gothic romance and horror story, the psychological thriller, the science fiction and fantasy short story, haunting lyrical poetry, and groundbreaking analytical criticism, it is interesting to consider him also as a regional writer. Poe is arguably the most popular and influential American writer in world literature and culture, but his identity as a Southerner was never forgotten by him. Born in Boston to itinerant actors on January 19, 1809, the same year as Abe Lincoln and Alfred Tennyson, Poe grew up in Richmond as a foster child in the Allan family. He always described himself as a Virginian and planned to return to that city on the James to live just before his mysterious death in Baltimore in October of 1849.

Many of Poe's stories have an English or European setting and flavor. His great landscape tale "The Domain of Arnheim" is set in some imagined country, a paradise on earth of architecture and gardening design. But Poe's story "A Tale of the Ragged Mountains" may be the first work of classic short fiction set in the Southern Appalachian Mountains where Poe had once been a student at the University of Virginia. It is appropriate that he set this story of mystery, hypnosis, and transmigration of souls, in the foothills of the Blue Ridge Mountains, in a world of dark coves and ancient, majestic trees. Poe's story is a phantasmagoria of enigmas and splendors, as he gives a realistic treatment to what is apparently supernatural.

In American literature of the nineteenth century Poe is the distinct outsider, a Southerner, an orphan of Irish-American descent, with a reputation for drunkenness, among New England Brahmins and New York aristocrats. In every way he failed to fit into the literary world of his time, except for the popularity of his stories and poems. From then until the present, he has held an uneasy place in the American literary canon, more respected by foreign critics than native ones. Much of his work is peculiarly modern and is known by heart by millions around the globe, cherished especially by the French and the South American Magic Realists. And oddly enough, in this one tale, he belongs to the Appalachian canon, and I for one, am proud to claim him as one of us.

Poe ends his essay "The Poetic Principle," one of his final attempts to define his aesthetics, by conceding the difficulty of defining poetry, but he lists some things that inspire poetry and song and suggests the inspiration of the poet. I will end by quoting parts of his vivid catalogue:

> [The Poet] recognizes the ambrosia which nourishes his soul . . . —in the volutes of the flower—in the clustering of low shrubberies—in the waving of the grain-fields—in the slanting of tall, Eastern trees—in the blue distance of mountains—in the grouping of clouds—in the twinkling of half-hidden brooks—in the gleaming of silver rivers—in the repose of sequestered lakes—in the star-mirroring depths of lonely wells. He perceives it in the songs of birds . . . in the sighing of the night-wind—in the repining voice of the forest—in the surf that complains on the shore—in the fresh breath of the woods—in the scent of the violet—in the voluptuous breath of the hyacinth—in the suggestive odour that comes to him, at eventide, from far-distant, undiscovered islands, over dim oceans, illimitable and unexplored. He owns it in all noble thoughts . . . in all chivalrous, generous, and self-sacrificing deeds. He feels it in the beauty of woman—in the grace of her step—in the lustre of her eye—in the melody of her voice . . . in the harmony of the rustling of her robes . . . —but above all—ah, far above all—he kneels to it—he worships it in the faith, in the purity, in the strength, in the altogether divine majesty—of her love.[24]

NOTES

1. *The Collected Letters of Edgar Allan Poe: Volume I: 1824–1846*. ed. John Ward Ostrom. 1948. Rev. Burton R. Pollin and Jeffrey A. Savoye. New York: Gordian Press, 2008. 1:595.

2. Edgar Allan Poe. *Poetry and Tales*. ed. Patrick F. Quinn. New York: Library of America, 1984. 60.

3. Edgar Allan Poe. *The Collected Letters of Edgar Allan Poe: Volume II: 1846–1849*. Pollin and Savoye. New York: Gordian Press, 2008. 2:694.

4. Poe, *Poetry and Tales*. 62.

5. Edgar Allan Poe. *Essays and Reviews*. ed. G. R. Thompson. New York: Library of America, 1984. 506.

6. Poe, "Introduction." *Essays & Reviews*. 55.

7. Poe, *Poetry and Tales*. 317–18.

8. *The Collected Letters of Edgar Allan Poe: Volume I*. 1:505.

9. Poe, *Poetry and Tales*. 85–86.

10. Poe, *Collected Letters, Volume I*. 1:578.

11. Poe, *Poetry and Tales*. 848.

12. Poe, *Poetry and Tales*. 89.

13. Poe, *Collected Letters, Volume II*. 2:641.

14. Poe, *Collected Letters, Volume II*. 2:426.

15. Charles Baudelaire. "Edgar Allan Poe: Life and Works, from the French of Charles Baudelaire." Trans. H. Curwen. *The Works of Edgar Allan Poe*. London: John Camden Hotten. 1873. 17. www.eapoe.org/papers/misc1851/1873000m.htm. Accessed 11 June 2024.

16. Poe, "The Poetic Principle." *Essays and Reviews*. 91.

17. Charles Baudelaire. *Baudelaire: Selected Verse with an Introduction and Plain Prose Translations by Francis Scarfe*. Baltimore: Penguin Books, 1961.

18. Poe, "To ---- ---- ----." *Poetry and Tales*. 88.

19. Poe, *Poetry and Tales*. 858.

20. Poe, *Poetry and Tales*. 856.

21. William Carlos Williams. "Edgar Allan Poe." *In the American Grain*. New York: Albert and Boni, 1925. 216.

22. Williams, *In the American Grain*. 220.

23. Williams, *In the American Grain*. 222.

24. Poe, *Essays and Reviews*. 93–94.

CARL SANDBURG

POPULIST AMONG THE MODERNS

PRAIRIE

> I was born on the prairie and the milk of its wheat, the red of its
> clover, the eyes of its women, gave me a song and a slogan. . . . The
> prairie sings to me in the forenoon and I know in the night I rest
> easy in the prairie arms, on the prairie heart.[1]

Carl Sandburg was born in Galesburg, Illinois, on January 6, 1878, the son
of Swedish immigrants, his father a blacksmith who worked for the railroad. As a boy Sandburg labored at many menial jobs and also traveled
around the country as a hobo, experiences that deeply influenced his later
writing. In 1898 he volunteered for the US Army and served in Puerto Rico
during the Spanish American War. Returning home, he entered Lombard
College where he began to write poetry and published three hand-printed
volumes. Out of college he worked as an organizer for the Wisconsin Social
Democratic Party, served as secretary to the mayor of Milwaukee, and married Lilian Steichen.

To support his family Sandburg took up journalism and became a reporter and then an editorial writer for *The Chicago Daily News*. *Chicago
Poems*, published in 1916, made him internationally famous. Besides other
books of poems, he published an insightful volume on the Chicago race
riots of 1919, and *Rootabaga Stories* in 1922. Traveling with his guitar he
became one of the best-known bards and troubadours of his time.

In 1926 Sandburg published a biography, *Abraham Lincoln: The Prairie
Years,* a phenomenal bestseller that made him even more famous, followed
by *Abraham Lincoln: The War Years*, awarded a Pulitzer Prize in 1940. He
was also celebrated for his collection of folk songs called *The American
Songbag.*

During WWII Sandburg was paid more than $140,000 for a screenplay, and with the money he bought Connemara, an estate in Flat Rock, North Carolina, built by Christopher Memminger, Secretary of the Treasury of the Confederacy. There his wife bred prize winning goats, and he turned his unproduced screenplay into the epic novel *Remembrance Rock*. For the last 21 years of his life Sandburg, who died in 1967, lived in the mountains of western North Carolina.

I grew up four miles away, just across the mountain from Sandburg's home. I never met the poet, but my dad, a carpenter and house painter, worked at Connemara from time to time. He considered Sandburg, with his long white hair falling over his forehead, a strange bird. But I was very much aware of the poet while growing up. His picture was often in the newspaper. I remember saying to a cousin once, "How much you reckon he gets for one of them poems?" We decided Sandburg might be paid as much as fifty dollars for a poem. I was indeed fortunate to have such a role model so close, so famous, a poet of the people, working people, right there in the Southern Appalachian Mountains.

A well-known scholar from Johns Hopkins recently called me and asked if I knew of a really good history of American poetry. In reply I mentioned Roy Harvey Pearce, Hyatt Waggoner, and Albert Gelpi. "That's just what I mean," she said. And I had to agree: there isn't any adequate history of American poetry. There isn't even a really good anthology. And it is not enough to say simply that the canon of American literature is still defining itself, is still developing so rapidly it cannot be easily summarized. The problem seems far deeper and more elusive than that. The source of the difficulty is in the very diversity of American culture, the creative pluralism, as well as the uncertainty of identity and opposing definitions. From the beginning we have been a nation of both Federalists and Democrats, neo-classicists and populists. In American poetry there was from the first the symbolist gothic interiors of Poe and the expansive natural idealism of Emerson and Whitman. The question of what is American poetry leads quickly to the question of what is America. And we are still answering that, in the hope that out of the many will emerge a definitive one.

For classes in American poetry, I often present, not a definition, but a series of traits and continuities to look for. It goes something like this: 1. Attention to nature as language, sign; 2. Love of the homemade as opposed to that imported from Europe; 3. Celebration of solitude; 4. Seeing the extraordinary in the ordinary; 5. Use of many vernaculars, including terms of trades and professions; 6. Love of science and technical things; 7. Use of rhetoric from the Bible; 8. Ahistorical interests only; 9. Romantic emphasis on self-hood; 10. Celebration of plain living and high thinking; 11. Poetry of the city as well as the country; 12. Moral seriousness; 13. The myth of American destiny; 14. Contradictions, lack of consistency.

Reading Carl Sandburg this year I have been struck by his love of paradoxes, and by the paradoxical character of much of his work and career. First, he was known as the poet of Chicago, of the Midwest, with Vachel Lindsay and Edgar Lee Masters, one of the "Prairie Poets," and yet he lived much of his life in Flat Rock, in the "Little Charleston" in the Blue Ridge Mountains, in the antebellum mansion which was his residence for the last two decades of his life. No poet in American literature is more a figure of combinations and contradictions. If he is the poet of the rough and brawling modern city, as in "Chicago," the global "Hog Butcher" ("Tool Maker, Stacker of Wheat, / Player with Railroads and the Nation's Freight Handler; / Stormy, husky, brawling, / City of Big Shoulders"), he is also the poet of elusive gentleness, of fogs and moonlight, of wind in orchards, and the delights of children[2]. He is at times a political poet, a poet of war and public issues, and yet many of his best lines capture the most private moments of vision, evanescent moods, and nuances of memory and reverie.

Nowhere do we find the paradoxes more pronounced than in the consideration of his reputation. Sandburg began as one of our radical experimentalists of the 'teens, contributing to *Poetry* in Chicago along with Ezra Pound and T. S. Eliot, Wallace Stevens, and William Carlos Williams, then became perhaps the most familiar poet of his time, memorized by school children, friend of governors and presidents, spokesman to Congress, and American's most famous biographer. In his early poems I still find the freshness and surprise his first readers and listeners must have experienced. There is a futuristic electricity in his lines about working people and streets and railroads, industrial America, and there is a cubist color and fragmented sharpness in the images of many of his poems. You only need to recite the titles of his first four books to feel the rush of discovery of the American landscape, and the landscape of the new vernaculars: CHICAGO POEMS, CORNHUSKERS, SMOKE AND STEEL, SLABS OF THE SUNBURNT WEST.

At the same time, we remember that Sandburg began his career as a Chautauqua speaker, a union organizer, a salesman of stereoscopes, and a journalist, and all his works have the best virtues of journalism: immediacy, directness, relevance. He never wrote a book, poem, address, or commentary which anyone with a high school education could not understand and enjoy.

The son of immigrants, largely self-educated, a onetime hobo, fireman, he lived to rub elbows with the mighty of the land and world. No other American poet except Archibald MacLeish has been so at home with legislators, cabinet members, public figures, or so recognized and loved by those in public life. He is the only American poet I know of who has addressed a joint session of the United States Congress.

Beginning as an imagist, as a poet of the most delicate instants of perception, the briefest sparks of language, with almost asiatic quickness, he lived to write the most popular multi-volume biography in our history, and one of the most substantial and fascinating epic novels in modern American literature, *Remembrance Rock*. Known often for his short poems, his collected works would fill a library shelf and then some, and his *The People, Yes* is one of the longest American poems.

Nowhere is Sandburg more typically American than in his contradictions. This very hemisphere was stumbled on by a European hoping to get to the East by going West. In American poetry of the nineteenth century, Walt Whitman, the would-be poet of the masses, was read mostly by Emerson and a few Eastern and English intellectuals, while the aristocratic Longfellow sold hundreds of thousands of copies of his books to ordinary people and was a household name. Sandburg was well aware that part of the character and glory of this country *was* in its complexities.

> The people is a polychrome,
> a spectrum and a prism . . .
> a console organ of changing themes . . .[3]

I feel very fortunate to have grown up in Henderson County when Carl Sandburg lived here. Not many places in the Blue Ridge Mountains could offer to a hopeful young writer the example of a great and famous poet living just over the ridge. And I feel lucky that it was Sandburg we had among us, because he was such a splendid and charismatic model of what a poet could be: a man without pretensions, for all his fame and accomplishments, who could speak to ordinary people, as one of them. I have always regretted that I never met him personally, but my sister was at Flat Rock High School when he visited there once, and she told us about him.

I learned most from the wonderful sense of freedom and openness in his poems. They are spoken so naturally they just seem to form themselves without effort from the American language and landscape. It is one of the signs of true art to conceal the artistry so successfully. His poems spoke of the dignity of working people, and compassion for the suffering of others. Reading him in high school I discovered that poetry could be found everywhere, and could be made from ordinary language, that nothing was wasted or irrelevant for poetry. In his short poems he expressed the sense of longing and mystery about existence the young have, as in "Under the Harvest Moon":

> Over the garden nights,
> Death, the gray mocker,
> Comes and whispers to you . . .[4]

Sandburg understood the restlessness and curiosity of the young, and their glimpses of destiny. This from "Wind Song:"

> Who can ever forget
> listening to the wind go by
> counting its money
> and throwing it away?[5]

For a young reader there is such relish in Sandburg's humor and air of careless ease. He inspires confidence and nonchalance, attentiveness, and a democratic hopefulness. His music seems to be on the tongue and in the air already, a discovery of something we had forgotten that we had.

I also feel fortunate to have had the model of Sandburg from an early age because of his interest in history, in Lincoln, and in the American past. It has been said that Americans, and American writers, do not have a strong sense of the past. We are descended from people who came here from somewhere else to begin new lives, to dwell on neither the past nor planning for the future, but to live in the present. But Sandburg is a poet with a very immediate sense of history, and the way the past works into the present, and he feels the presence of the past, and the absence. Here are a few lines from his short poem called "Buffalo Dusk:"

> The buffalos are gone.
> And those who saw the buffalos are gone.[6]

And beyond the detail and paradox of the process of history he saw the even greater natural processes and cycles stretching back into the farthest memory and beyond that into the timeless, which poets feel in every hurried instant of their lives. Consider the perspective of the poem "Cool Tombs."

> ... Tell me if the lovers are losers ...
>   tell me if any get more than the lovers ... in the dust ... in the
> cool tombs.[7]

No poet moves the young so much as a love poet, and Sandburg was first and always a love poet. He never forgot the intense sense of loss the lover feels even at the moment of fulfillment, and how the ideal and the unattainable slip away in the actual experience. Sandburg is a poet for the young because he himself was always young.

When Sandburg's *Chicago Poems* appeared in 1916 the book was greeted as one of the most remarkable examples of the "new poetry." The title poem had been published two years before in *Poetry* magazine and made the newspaperman famous in the Windy City and across the poetry-reading world. Sometimes he was an imagist, as in "Nocturne in a Deserted Brickyard":

> Fluxions of yellow and dusk on the waters
> Make a wide dreaming pansy of an old pond in the night.[8]

At other times he is a Whitman-like prophet, poet of the city and industrial landscape, bard of the common man. Sandburg was at the heart of the radical experimental school of the Chicago Renaissance which included Theodore Dreiser and Sherwood Anderson, Ben Hecht, Margaret Anderson and *The Little Review*, as well as Edgar Lee Masters and Vachel Lindsey, Harriet Monroe, and Mrs. William Vaughn Moody. The Boston poet Amy Lowell wrote an enthusiastic review of his first book and became his friend. Ezra Pound wrote from London, "Dear Sandburg, the 'Chicago Poems' have come at last. *Complimenti miei*! The thing that strikes me most is that you have kept the whole book down to brass tacks ... The address to Billy Sunday is refreshing. There is a great deal in the book I had not seen ... I think you are right in the main."[9] I take this as very high praise from the man who dared edit Yeats' and Eliot's new poems.

In those early years of his fame Sandburg was recognized as one of the leading innovative poets. He received warm praise from the newly celebrated Robert Frost among others. It was only in the aftermath of World War I, and in the Twenties, that modern American poetry began to separate itself into schools and factions, the emerging leader being T. S. Eliot with his Metaphysical traditionalism. Yet, in the Roaring Twenties, in the Jazz Age, Sandburg wrote some of the most jazzy and improvisational poetry of the time. As Chicago was the great center of jazz music and smart speakeasies, the Chicago poet was the inventor and leading exponent of the daring and playful new word music. Here are lines from "Jazz Fantasia":

> Drum on your drums, batter on your banjoes,
> sob on the long cool saxophones.
> Go to it, O jazzmen.[10]

Sandburg always had a special feeling for black culture and the African American community, and I find it appropriate that many members of the Harlem Renaissance of the Twenties share with him the art of a jazz or "blues" poetry. That kinship can be seen especially in the rhythms of Langston Hughes.

But Sandburg and his Chicago contemporaries could not have foreseen in 1920 the impact of the new criticism of I. A. Richards and T. S. Eliot and the new classicism of Eliot and Pound were to have on the future of American poetry. As William Carlos Williams said, "*The Waste Land* wiped out our world,"[11] meaning the world of local American experimental poetry. Not only was the poetry of disillusionment and pessimism in fashion, as well as the cynicism about America and self-consciousness about the European past, but difficulty became one of the marks of excellence. The recondite literary allusions of *The Waste Land* and Pound's *Cantos* became the model and manner for the young poets of the 1920's and 30's. Poetry was subsumed more and more into the world of scholarship and criticism, and into the classroom. For the next forty years American poetry would be dominated by brilliant poet-critics such as Eliot, John Crowe Ransom, Yvor Winters, R. P. Blackmur, Allen Tate, as well as the British Richards and William Empson. One measure of the new poetry was the way it provided grist for explication in essays and graduate seminars. In the parlance of the day, it was the "critic who completed a poem." The Whitman and Sandburg vision of a poetry for everybody, a democratic literature, seemed to vanish from the pages of the little magazines, replaced by a poetry for the elite intellectual few. Or as Eugene Jolas said in the manifesto for his magazine *transition*, "The common reader be damned."[12]

But meanwhile the reading public did not turn away from Sandburg. His books continued to be bought and read by the general readers, quoted, and even anthologized throughout the New Critical era. He was always a favorite with actors, musicians, and the press. In fact, both he and Frost became even more popular as the years passed, white-haired celebrities recognized by every school child. One reason for this great success was their ability as speakers and reciters of their own verse. Sandburg became a modern troubadour, crossing and re-crossing the country every year to thrill audiences with his reading and singing. He helped revive a folk heritage with his concerts and his *American Songbag*. And as the biographer of Lincoln, he became known to millions who had never heard of the "objective correlative" or the "fallacy of affective form."

True to the paradoxical nature of American culture, the 1930s seemed a time when the mind of American poetry was divided and neither side was in communication with the other. The critical essays written in that decade have become an essential part of our tradition but seem to have little to do with the equally interesting radical literature of the time. Sandburg was almost a cult figure for the political poets and songwriters of the Depression era. His *The People, Yes* seemed to sound the keynote for a whole decade of documentary films, photographs, radio plays, the songs of Woody Guthrie, even parts of James Agee's *Let Us Now Praise Famous Men*. If there was a true national poet it was Carl Sandburg, however little he was discussed by Cleanth Brooks and Robert Penn Warren in the most famous textbook of the day, *Understanding Poetry*.

I have always found it odd that the critics' fascination with William Carlos Williams in the 1950s did not extend to Sandburg. Williams' interest in the free verse line, his focus on American speech and the local and realistic, his concern with the broad spectrum of American humanity, seem so close to Sandburg's themes you wonder how the connection could have been missed. My only guess is that Sandburg seemed to lack the theoretical interests that Williams formulated in concepts such as "composition by field" and "the variable foot," which helped draw the young poets and critics to the author of *Paterson*. Also, Sandburg's poetry is primarily oral, and many critics are not sensitive to the sound of poetry. For Ransom and Tate, Sandburg lacked "the tragic view of life." The truth is that Sandburg is as much the forerunner of the Beats as Williams and Whitman. Ginsburg's *Howl* owes as much to the rhythms of "Chicago" as it does to the cumulative detail of *Paterson* or the rhetoric of *Song of Myself*. It seems to me that Sandburg has often been used without acknowledgment. Many of his poems are so familiar they are recalled perhaps unconsciously as sources of gesture and tone. Many of the radical poets of the Sixties were in debt to Sandburg for their rough-hewn poetics and delicate, colorful images, more than to the translations of Latin American poetry they claimed as their inspiration. And almost fifty years before the Vietnam War Sandburg had written war poetry, and anti-war poetry. The Deep Imagists of the Midwest, such as Robert Bly and James Wright, with their evocative lyrics of cornfields and steel mills, grain elevators and lonely towns, their attacks on corrupt and corrupting political life, have their roots in the poems of Sandburg, however much they talk of Pablo Neruda or Georg Trakl. An early poem by Robert Bly is "Watering the Horse":

> Suddenly I see with such clear eyes
> The white flake of snow
> That has just fallen in the horse's mane.[13]

And James Wright's poem "A Blessing" begins:

> Just off the highway to Rochester, Minnesota,
> Twilight bounds softy forth on the grass.
> And the eyes of those two Indian ponies
> Darken with kindness.[14]

And the poet of North Dakota, Thomas McGrath, a former union-organizer and populist epic writer, author of *Letter to an Imaginary Friend*, is equally in the Sandburg tradition. A younger poet, Ted Kooser, of Garland, Nebraska, is right now writing splendid poems about deserted farmhouses and interstate highways cutting through wheatfields, and the unemployed of the freight-handling cities.

I think it is time the critics and historians of American poetry, who have pretty much ignored Sandburg while the rest of us read and memorized his poems, look again at his work. I suspect that such a re-evaluation is already beginning. I think the critics need Sandburg more than he needs them, and that perhaps his poetry represents more permanent values than the values of modernism. It is even conceivable that the great Moderns are the aberration, and that Sandburg and Frost represent the true mainstream of American poetry. It is always hard to predict how the future will revise the canon of literature, but I would guess there will be some surprises for us all. Let me quote from an early poem by Sandburg called "Four Preludes on Playthings of the Wind":

> The feet of the rats
> scribble on the doorsills;
> the hieroglyphics of the rat footprints . . .[15]

So much of our perspective on modern poetry is the result of a generation of canonization by textbooks and anthologists. Something told often enough comes to seem inevitable. I suggest it is time to re-examine our literature, and Sandburg is a good place to start that examination.

Nowhere will we find a more colorful or musical poet, with a love of the places and faces and names of our world, with such a profound understanding of the dignity of work, with such an accurate ear for the evolution and inflections of our speech, for the multiplicity and paradox of our cities and towns, countryside, and wilderness.

Sandburg has the strength of simplicity and quiet alertness and attention, as well as stirring Sousa-like parade music, and the many voices of a carnival ventriloquist. He speaks from the peripheral glance, the nuance, the overheard fragment, the surprise in the most ordinary detail. He is interested in absolutely everything and everyone. At one time a vaudeville performer, a salesman, soldier, hobo, lecturer, politician, he answers Emerson's call in "Self-Reliance" for "a sturdy lad . . . who in turn tries all the professions, who teams it, farms it, peddles, keeps a school, preaches, edits a newspaper, goes to Congress, buys a township, and so forth in successive years, and always like a cat lands on his feet, worth a hundred of these city dolls. He walks abreast with his days and feels no shame . . . for he does not postpone his life, but lives already."[16]

Sandburg has the American love of fact, of the sciences, of the homemade. He was a minstrel, a humorist, a showman, and a philosopher, a phonographer of language. From the nation's heartland, he always wrote to and from the nation's heart. More than any of our poets since Whitman he seems to touch the collective wisdom of the people. For all his roughness there is a peculiar delicacy to his poetry. It comes to us directly, without the need of quotes and interceding critics and explainers, with no need of gloss. You could make a poem almost of his titles. To be appreciated his poems have to be heard, because he found the true cadence of his times, and as Archibald MacLeish says, "The People listened."

I will end by quoting from the poem "Grass," and then from "Limited" from *The People, Yes.*

Pile the bodies high at Austerlitz and Waterloo.
Shovel them under and let me work –
I am the grass; I cover all . . .[17]

And "Limited."

I am riding on a limited express, one of the crack trains of the
nation . . .
I ask a man in the smoker where he is going and he answers:
'Omaha.'[18]

NOTES

1. Carl Sandburg, *Complete* Poems. 79.

2. Sandburg, *Complete Poems.* 3.

3. Sandburg, "The People, Yes." *Complete Poems.* 616–17.

4. Sandburg, *Complete Poems.* 49.

5. Sandburg, *Complete Poems.* 217.

6. Sandburg, *Complete Poems.* 256.

7. Sandburg, *Complete Poems.* 134.

8. Sandburg, *Complete Poems.* 55.

9. Quoted in Penelope Nivens. *Carl Sandburg: A Biography.* New York:
   Charles Scribner's, 1991. 211.

10. Sandburg, *Complete Poems.* 179.

11. William Carlos Williams. *The Autobiography of William Carlos Williams.*
    New York: New Directions, 1967. 174.

12. Eugene Jolas. "Transition: An Occidental Workshop, 1927–1938." *Critical
    Writings, 1924- 1951.* eds. Klaus H. Kiefer and Rainer Rumold. Evansville:
    Northwestern UP, 2009. 122.

13. Robert Bly. *Silence in the Snowy Fields.* Middletown, CT: Wesleyan Univer-
    sity Press, 1962. 133.

14. James Wright. *James Wright: Collected Poems.* Middletown, CT: Wesleyan
    University Press, 1971. 135.

15. Sandburg, *Complete Poems.* 183.

16. Ralph Waldo Emerson. *Essays & Lectures.* 275.

17. Sandburg, *Complete Poems.* 136.

18. Sandburg, *Complete Poems.* 20.

CONCORD CONSTRUCTIVIST AND YANKEE DOODLER

The Poetry of William Harmon

A few years ago, I was reading through a little magazine, skimming the examples of loose free verse and confessional open forms, when suddenly I turned the page to a tiny poem, terse and crystalline in formal perfection, delightful in rhyme, luminous in wit and wordplay. It was a short lyric by William Harmon, neat as a madrigal. I remember saying spontaneously, "Thank goodness for the *mind*."

I have now been reading William Harmon's poetry for over thirty years, and I am still surprised by the range and daring of his work. His voice is distinctive yet varied and evolving through many changes and permutations. Whenever I encounter a new Harmon poem, I know I'll discover unexpected patterns, vast reaches of reference, lyrics of wordplay and depth. His poems celebrate high culture and low culture, science and linguistics, barbeque, and stock car racing. The poems may embody and enact themselves in long Isaiah lines or in crisp, exact rhymes, and meters.

Twenty years ago, I wrote that "William Harmon's voice is unique. No one else has quite his range of playfulness, improvisation, vastness of reference. He is a poet of thunderstorms and hymns, as well as 'the retail sublime.' He combines the vision and rhetoric of a revival preacher with the new high tech, high-rise, shopping mall world of the Sun Belt. He is one of the smartest, funniest, most serious poets I know."[1]

One of the things I noticed when I read Harmon's first book of poems, *Treasury Holiday* (1970), was the way he found poetry in the most unexpected places, in commercial language, ads, technical jargon. He delights in the spoken vernacular and the visual vernacular, in polka dots and Styrofoam peanuts. He finds a Pythagorean numerical dimension in the most ordinary and everyday things, and he sees the anagram of "canoe" in "ocean." He takes the language of television and therapy and turns it into found poems, shape poems, concrete poems, and epigrams.

It was the dream of the Russian Constructivists to create from the common artifacts of the Industrial Age new images and forms, often abstract or at least nonrepresentational, but always pleasing and fresh with surprise. In many of his early poems Harmon is very much a Constructivist, creating out of the ordinary, our throw-away culture, the jargon of literary theory and self-help manuals, a poetry of celebration, of large architectonic ambition and soaring wit and bold irony.

But while Harmon's poetics may remind us of the Constructivists or Cubo-Futurists, his language and images, details and reference, rhetoric, and allusions, are quintessentially American, even patriotic in an alternately serious and self-deprecating way. In his love of high rhetoric and a sweeping, inclusive, democratic poetics, Harmon can remind of us Emerson, native to that famous Concord to the north. But Harmon is a native of Concord, North Carolina, a textile town near Charlotte known for its cotton mills, barbeque, stock car racing and high school football. He is our Piedmont Charles Ives.

Harmon's second book of poetry, *Legion: Civic Choruses* (1973), is a book of anthems and fanfares, parade music, pep rally music. The poems glory in the spirit of the Fourth of July and Memorial Day ceremonies, Sousa music and the high-stepping majorettes, flashing brass and the 21-gun salute, and all the while undercutting themselves with cunning asides and sly puns. The words are bright as surgical steel, alert as a cell phone key.

There is a driving military music to many of the "civic choruses." We hear reveille and taps, parades and tattoos, close order drill, and marches. Many of the choruses are anthems and carols for the industrial and retail world combined with military salutes and commands:

> General merchandise the old testament.
> wares notions sundries dry goods ready to wear candy hats cash &
> carry
> 		Harry Truman making change thanks.
> cut-rate kickshaws ten cents each three for a quarter &Jeremiah
> shifts
> 		to turn his burnt eyes from the living zenith to our
> grain elevator

temple of the wounded the dead.
poor people.
general rank & file matrix of merchandise womb of goods left left
left
      right left.
      halt.
      fallout.[2]

You can start reading *Legion* anywhere and find yourself swept up and laughing at the asides and observations: "form from morf," the hymns of P. P. Bliss, the hamming and auctioneer chants, wordplay the equivalent of glossolalia:

so I say unto thee Thomas I say emerald platinum mink orchid
whole deal dovetailed dado the Elephantine Papyrus eagle lion &
last & least least the cerebrations of stellar Kant the Alexanderissi-
mus of metaphysics.[3]

One of the delights of *Legion* is the sense of improvisation on a cluster of themes, variations and permutations, shufflings and turnings, launching out and returning:

the twice-tolled tropic of excrement where love's strafed tent leans
in the steady wide wind of will & blind pain in the jail of ringing
            rain rain.
the seedy birth the windy birth gapes like an open glove
compartment.
a steady wind because it turns to stone when it disdains to turn
at all.[4]

The Intussusception of Miss Mary America (1976) is Harmon's third book of poems. The themes are again patriotic, but this book shows Harmon at his most Rabelaisian. It is a poetry of Paul Bunyan scale, of America itself as a giantess getting married, a poem of Gargantuan hyperbole, scatologi-cal, pornographic, satiric, parodic, ostensibly a wedding hymn, an epithala-mium. It is a celebration of the multiplicity and contradictions and vulgar-ity of American culture, American self-image, American destiny. The poem reads like a carnival, a five-ring circus, a music of body parts and machine parts, garbage, exploded dictionaries and ripped encyclopedias, a mosaic of music notes and motes of dust bowl storms and Chicago fires, perfumes and industrial vapors. Reading *The Intussusception of Miss Mary America* I kept thinking, this poet is a Yankee Doodler, a tinkerer, a Yankee Doodle Dante. He updates Sandburg's *The People, Yes* in a festival and ceremony from a fever dream in outer space:

> Mary America's nostrils are the business end of a doublebarreled
> tengauge shotgun & Her chin a crag of 20 Mule Team Borax
> Her elbows are the stinking zoos & public schools & and disin-
> fected jails . . .
> . . . The universal joints of Her wrists are the banjos of Xmas &
> brain
>
> > damage.[5]

William Harmon's fourth book of poems, *One Long Poem* (1981) reveals a marked change of tone and style. The poems are elevated, poised, and eloquent. Many are sustained, poised lyrics. The subjects are of a piece with the earlier poems, but the voice is now cool, even restrained in compression. The poems speak more calmly and draw out their thoughts and arguments more consistently:

> Now the only thing the house has ever really wanted to do is fly,
> but it is
>
> > unable to.
> It has wings, east and west, but they are wings of occidental hard-
> wood fastened to lead beams by means of mortal nails.[6]

We find the same sparkling wordplay in this book, "larval lar," "the elegy is dead," "dotted dog," but the voice is lower, almost *sotto voce* at times. The poet is still celebrating the aesthetics of the retail world:

> A vast magnificent civilization founded on retail merchandising,
> Every man a middleman, every beast, even, a middlebeast.
> I bark a bit myself, inside. The insects' number is beyond me.[7]

One of Harmon's best poems is "Sentimental Etude on Dogeared Foolscap." It is a salute to a character named Succotash, a kind of Everyman, but Everyman as con man, as showman:

He is said to dive straight as a die from unearthly heights
Like an Olympic medalist, ski like mad or anything, swim
Endlessly, swallow swords, produce presto a full deck
From thin air or your ear, eat fire from a short spoon,
Geronimo nonchalantly out of barrel-rolling Cessnas, and
With a quelling gesture that marries modesty to understanding
Coax inflamed tigers into supine docility.[8]

The book includes "Interoffice Memorandum to Jim Seay" which is a detailed memoir about Harmon's grandfather, Lee Anderson Pickerel, in his old age. It is one of Harmon's finest poems, a sustained and affectionate narrative, hilarious in places:

I was there (Motley community, near Hurt,
Pittsylvania County) for his ninety-fifth.
He exhaled eleven or twelve treasured breaths
Through his trembling harmonica, surprisingly *Presto.*
One of my aunts said, "Dad, play 'Home Sweet Home.'
He said, 'I just did.'[9]

There is another distinct voice shift in Harmon's fifth book of poems, *Mutatis Mutandis: 27 Invoices.* Here the verse is metrical, iambic, and the poems read like dances. The pleasure of dance is the repetition of the steps with evolving variations. In these poems we find the same kind of wordplay and allusive thought that characterize the earlier poems, but here the zaniness and flamboyance, the goofiness, are contained and restrained in blank verse, villanelles, and sonnets. The narrator pokes fun at "mindless mildness" and the inherent confusions of our language: "Rare earths, my dear, are neither rare nor earths."[10] We also find the poet breaking new ground in a poem such as "Invoice No. 22: The Fallacy of Experience" with its sustained meditation on one of our culture's favorite assumptions, that we learn from experience:

I wonder why we worry so about it.
You can't *not* have experience, you know. . .
. . . Emily Dickinson
Knew all about the world firsthand without
Even leaving the kitchen.[11]

"Mutatis mutandis" means "the necessary changes having been made." It is a book of change, of growth, of varied perspectives. Though a communicant of no known church, by turns a self-proclaimed agnostic, atheist, skeptic, renegade, the poet Harmon is clearly haunted by the sacred, by ritual, by the quest for meaning, by the beliefs of the past, by hymns and sermons, by the Psalms and the rhetoric of the Old Testament. He protests again and again his secular-ness, and in poem after poem reaches out for the spiritual, the numinous, the inspired connection. In the searching playfulness of his unbelief, he is often more authentically religious than many so-called devotional poets. His fifth book ends with a benediction:

> You are here and now
> Awake—O vivid invisible center of my homely homily!—
> Then it must have to be the case,
> It must, that is, befall that you are wholly blessed,
> Under the aegis, under the auspices, under something
> That has sponsored you and sheltered you forever.
>
> Make no mistake:
> You could not let a second's breath
> Without the unanimous permission of the one universe.
> And you have that. You do.
> You have it all the time, all tides, all times,
> But never quite so much and perfectly
> As when you absolutely least expect it,
> Between two bites (say) of a Milky Way.[12]

NOTES

1. Robert Morgan. Unpublished essay.

2. William Harmon. "Store." *Legion: Civic Choruses*. Middletown, CT: Wesleyan University Press, 1973. 33.

3. Harmon, "Ifs & Cans." *Legion: Civic Choruses*. 40.

4. Harmon, "Triple Hymn." *Legion: Civic Choruses*. 51.

5. William Harmon. *The Intussusception of Miss Mary America*. Santa Cruz: Kayak Books, 1976. 19.

6. William Harmon. "The House." *One Long Poem*. Louisiana State University Press, 1982. 6.

7. Harmon, "The Lillies of the Field Know Which Side Their Bread is Buttered On." *One Long Poem*. 33.

8. Harmon, *One Long Poem*. 30.

9. Harmon, *One Long Poem*. 49.

10. Harmon, "Invoice No. 15: Pieces of Speech." *Mutatis Mutandis: 27 Invoices.* Middletown: Wesleyan University Press, 1985. 23.

11. Harmon, *Mutatis Mutandis*. 35.

12. Harmon, "Invoice No. 27: He-Who-May-Say." *Mutatis Mutandis*. 45.

THE REIGN OF KING STORK

GEOFFREY HILL'S EARLY POETRY

There seems to have been a new beginning in British poetry in the past few years. It has happened quietly, with little fanfare, at least in America, and from separated points in the counties and along the Celtic fringe. Though rooted in the rich compost of English poetry, the work of each new poet seems to have evaded in its own way the dead ends of Imagism and the plainly though adroitly tilted cliche of Auden that stymied and insularized British poetry for several decades. Hill in the north, Alasdair Maclean in Scotland, and Seamus Heaney in Ulster, especially, are all writing poetry of originality and vigor, each in his own style already a master. But of them all Hill is the most gifted, the most ambitious, the most accomplished. He exhibits a kind of literacy and comprehensive imagination the rest lack. He is in command of a profound moral sophistication and maturity rare among the poets writing in the language anywhere.

On first reading any of Hill's poems one is struck by his fresh and functional use of forms, and by the dense connotative textures. There is little that is obvious in either his best rhymes or his meaning. Beginning with *Somewhere is Such a Kingdom*, his collected poems through 1971, and the first trade edition of his books available in the United States, the surprise is how early he achieved his style. The first poem, "Genesis," was written when he was nineteen and published in a pamphlet in Donald Hall's Fantasy Poets series when Hill was twenty. This kind of precocity is unheard-of in the United States, where most great poets write their first good poems in their thirties. It is clear that Hill mastered the traditional forms very early and by 1952 was making them dance to his own ideas and voice. "Genesis" was originally subtitled "a ballad of Christopher Smart," and though that has been dropped here the echoes of Smart's mania and genius in *Jubilate Agno* and *A Song to David* are in the text, especially when read aloud. Where Smart with his sometimes splendid obsession tried to rewrite the liturgy there, Hill has him in the ballad redacting the book of creation from a Christian point of view. It is a haunting poem—"There is no bloodless myth will hold"[1]—and the last few lines present the kind of charged ambiguity, the grim paradox sensually posed, that Hill so much delights in. Hill is a fallen stoic whose only redemption is found perhaps (he is not sure) in language:

> And by Christ's blood are men made free
> Though in close shrouds their bodies lie
> Under the rough pelt of the sea;
>
> Though Earth has rolled beneath her weight
> The bones that cannot bear the light.[2]

I will just note in passing the multiple and evocative readings possible for the last line. The flesh cannot reveal truth or enlightenment, nor, by pun, give birth to, survive, or carry it. Both this and the dead bodies lying "Under the rough pelt of the sea" tie this first poem with the central image of Hill's first collection, *For the Unfallen*, which is reprinted complete in the *Collected Poems* and in the more recent *Broken Hierarchies*. It is this early work that contains the grain of truth leading Harold Bloom to assert erroneously in the introduction that "Hill has been the most Blakean of modern poets."[3] This would be accurate had he written nothing but "Genesis," but almost immediately Hill became another kind of poet entirely, as we shall see.

In this early work Hill is obsessed with the metaphor of the drowned, of the sea giving up its dead at the Resurrection. In "Requiem for the Plantagenet Kings" he draws on his acute sense of history, especially the history of England, and his unusual ability to somehow make guilt physical, and to sculpt mythic figures: "Sleeked groin, gored head, / Budge through the clay and gravel, and the sea / Across daubed rock evacuates its dead."[4] The act of horrific resurrection, the mangled body freed from its drowning in love, chaos, corruption, and time, recurs often. Shipwreck is the end of sex and marriage.

> Grant the detached, pierced spirit could plunge, soar,
> Seeking that love flesh dared not answer for,
> Nor suffers now, hammocked in salt tagged cloth
> That to be bleached or burned the sea casts out.[5]

In "The Guardians" the old, watching the young sail out for recreation, and having seen "Packed harbors topple under sudden gales," and "yachts burn at the wharf / That on clean seas pitched their effective sails," know they will later have to "wade the disturbed shore; / Gather the dead as the first dead scrape home."[6] Nature is a kind of Titanic on which we are all booked. In fact, Hill has a poem, section V of the suite called "Of Commerce and Society," titled "Ode on the Loss of the 'Titanic,'" where the "ignorant sea" is seen as an avenging god not to be appeased.[7] In "The White Ship," where the Melvillean allusion is perhaps closest, evil is the flesh itself and those in time are "Creatures passed through the wet sieve / Without enrichment or decay."[8] But is there any compensation, any understanding gained by drowning?

> What paradises and watering-places,
> What hurts appeased by the sea's handsomeness![9]

The sea is seductive, and like Nature itself, cruelly confused about the role and possibility of men:

> And the sometimes-abandoned gods confuse
> With immortal essences men's brief lives,
> Frequenting the exposed and pious: those
> Who stray, as designed, under applied perils . . .[10]

Not only does Hill have an unromantic distrust of nature and "generative process," he seems suspicious, even ashamed, of art which cultivates and feeds on the violence, waste, and suffering of human experience. At the same time, he keeps returning to the gesture of summoning time and drowning and decay into the permanence of form and language. The poem seems for him a kind of verbal garden where the expulsion is reversed by hard-won saying. Though he is not sure how far he should trust it, the gesture is made again and again, a deep structure he finds wherever he turns, as he will later make of the concentration camps of World War II an inverted Eden.

The other major theme of the early poems is marriage, closely related to the drowning image and perhaps as complex. In at least one poem, if I read it correctly, "Asmodeus," the demon from the *Apocrypha*, is recognized as the true Cupid who cannot be expelled or tamed into a hearth deity without destroying the marriage.[11] "The Turtle Dove" could be an eloquent and concise telling of Dylan and Caitlan Thomas's most stormy years.[12] In Hill's poetry there is always a "distant fury of battle," the title of a poem here and a phrase he uses later in a note for one of his most important sequences.

Wherever he looks the battle, the same battle, is being fought, in history, theology, love, politics, nature, art. A short poem that seems to unite all these preoccupations is "The Re-birth of Venus," where the sea is now a *vagina dentata.*

> And now the sea-scoured temptress . . . approaches all
> Stayers, and searchers of the fanged pool.[13]

A long article could be written on this one eight-line poem. An interesting implication is, for instance, that in the modern world love has been driven into hiding in the cunt, out of experience at large, ". . . having failed / to scoop out of horizons what birds herald."[14] Now human love can make no landings on firm ground, or pass on the open sea, but lurks shark-like, threatening those who would find it in sex. And one could talk about the brilliant understatement, as in the choice of the verb "approaches." Technically the poem demonstrates Hill's superb ability to strike memorable tough lines out of long sinuous sentences, breaking in the most unexpected places, and then starting again, as in line four, and the near seamless fusing of the parenthesis with the forward moving thesis in the second stanza. The rhymes here are some of his most accomplished.

A motif that begins to emerge more and more clearly in the later poems of *For the Unfallen* is the sharp-edged ambiguity about art, including the art of words. This could best be described as a suspicion, a skepticism, expressing alternately reverence and contempt. It appears in the carefully selected phrase "artistic men" which appears twice, first describing the Magi in "Picture of a Nativity" and later in "Of Commerce and Society." What the poet has begun to suspect is that art, no matter how well-executed, begins to betray what it would uphold. The prime example of this for him, both here and in later poems, is the language's, and culture's, inability to prevent, even comprehend, the atrocities of Nazi Germany:

> . . . Many have died. Auschwitz,
> Its furnace chambers and lime pits
> Half-erased, its half-dead . . .[15]

There is the fear that art, even when trying most conscientiously, evades and subverts, because of its very nature. Realizing the full impossibility of Milton's stated task (and hence his or any poet's), Hill offers the poem as apology rather than as adequate elegy. In fact, he becomes so unbearably conscious of the limitations and falsifications of poetry in the actual world that he feels guilty for his own gift to make art, and only art, of the agony of others.

There are two other ideas in the first collection which I want to mention quickly, and they are both related to the central theme. In section VI of "Of Commerce and Society," which is subtitled "Homage to Henry James," he compares the sorry state of America with the sorry state of Europe.

> Enlarged and deep-oiled, America
> Detects music, apprehends the day-star
>
> Where, sensitive and half-under a cloud,
> Europe muddles her dreaming...[16]

In one sweep he takes care of romantic poetry, including the America Whitman heard singing, and Thoreau's ultimate equation of possibility— "The sun is but a morning star"[17]—and Shelly's euphoric idealism. But Hill is not just a stoic; he is a fallen stoic, and his salvation, which is his formidable power as a maker, throws him always back into the tragedy of the actual world, which language must amplify. "In Piam Memoriam" celebrates the glass saint "Exposing his gifted quite empty hands, ... Of worldly purity the stained archetype"[18]—admire the pun on "stained,"—but turns at the end in a passage foreshadowing the majestic music of *Mercian Hymns*, to the decaying and generative world of nature, a fact as inexplicable as the renewals language enacts and elicits:

> The scummed pond twitches...
> The common, puddled substance: beneath,
> Like a revealed mineral, a new earth.[19]

The poems from *King Log*, Hill's second volume, are at once some of his finest and most infuriatingly obscure. He had spent the year 1959–1960 in America, lecturing at the University of Michigan. It may have been while there that he came particularly under the influence of Allen Tate's poetry, because, whereas the interest was there before, as in the epigraph to "Of Commerce and Society," the new poems show a dominant likeness in both music and ideas to Tate's work. Contrary to Bloom's statement, already mentioned, what we find in *King Log* could be called unromantic, unBlakean, and certainly un-apocalyptic. Not only has Hill taken over the tortured, overloaded line from Tate, he has been deeply stirred by Tate's ideals and strictures. Perhaps the word is not "influenced" but a "recognition" of kinship. I suspect that Hill used Tate's poetry as a clarification and confirmation of his own ideas, and what he made of that agonizingly conscientious line and allegiance to form, the guilt of history, the sad failure of American progressivism, and Tate's love of the "Mediterranean," the catholic, the lucid, and controlled, is something very much his own, indeed unique in contemporary poetry. We would have to go back to Baudelaire, and maybe earlier to find the classical precision, depth, and ease of surface this all leads to in "The Songbook of Sebastian Arrurruz." But more on that later.

The title of *King Log* comes from Aesop, the fable where the frogs are given a log for a king. When they complain to Zeus that their monarch is unresponsive to their needs, he gives them a stork for king instead, and the stork eats them. It is a brilliant choice of title for Hill at this point in his career because it expresses his skepticism of social and religious progress, and idealistic reformation in general. History is the correlative of guilt and reformers at best fail to comprehend its burden, at worst aggravate and abet its cruelty. Yet, in such a world, no bystander is innocent either and "innocence" is a liability, even at times a threat. In these poems Hill is master of a clear and two-edged irony. "Ovid in the Third Reich," a confession of helplessness to alleviate or even understand evil, self-justification, must be read as accusation. Hill plays on the disarming sophistry of the modern intellectual, the use of irony to avoid responsibility, self-incrimination. In the poem "Annunciations," when the Word returns from abroad "with a tanned look,"[20] we know that any "announcing" can be taken ironically, and that the "announcer" will plead seriousness or jest, depending on the accusation, and beyond that will plead the times, and the world which tends to corrupt what it hears. "Ovid's" defense is deceptively simple:

> Too near the ancient troughs of blood
> Innocence is no earthly weapon.[21]

Hill turns his attention to America in the three poems called "Locust Songs" dedicated to Allan Seager, his colleague at Michigan and the biographer of Theodore Roethke. These poems show as much as any here the impact of Tate and Tate's revulsion for Emerson, Whitman, and populistic rhetoric. Going back to Jonathan Edwards, and forward through the Transcendentalists and Whitman, we find an obsession in the New World with discovering divinity in everything, from the commonplace and humble, to the continent itself, and the destiny of the new nation. To Tate and Hill this easy optimism is evidence, if not of insanity, of a crippling heresy, ignoring the fallen state of nature, and leveling all being, so the mud and detritus of the riverbank and sewer are infused with the same deity as the rituals of the Church; and the miracles are denied any special significance or efficacy, no more important than the annual resurgence of grass or the copulation of birds. To Tate the refusal to recognize the fallen, tragic condition of man only deepens suffering and invites madness. What is especially disturbing to this kind of sensibility is the American ideal of establishing and maintaining a paradise here on the savage continent, or rather several million paradises in each of which the individual man will be his own king and pontiff. Though I have no particular sympathy for their side of the argument, (they have much in history to support them) it is impressive what currency Hill can give this view in his poetry.

> So with sweet oaths converting the salt earth
> To yield, our fathers verged on Paradise:
> Each to his own portion of Paradise,
> Stung by the innocent venoms of the earth.[22]

The "innocent" here is one of the outstanding examples of Hill's gift for choosing adjectives. I think of it as a buried allusion to Whitman's wonderful poem, "This Compost." The last of the "Locust Songs" is titled "Shiloh Church, 1862: Twenty-three Thousand," and we are reminded, by the name of the battlefield, of the village in the Old Testament so often mentioned as the scene of destruction visited by Jehovah for wickedness and false worship, and of Melville's great poem "Shiloh." In America it is the work of "Geneva's tribe, outlandish, and abhorred":

> Whose passion was to find out God in this
> His natural filth, voyeur of sacrifice, a slow
> Bloody unearthing of the God-in-us.[23]

No longer the young visionary speaking for Christopher Smart—"There is no bloodless myth will hold"[24]—he now sees only the carnage wrought by fervor and extreme idealism. Because he is certainly aware of the strain in himself, he is now increasingly sensitive to phrases like "voyeur of sacrifice," and the luxuriating in brutality in his own poems.

In "September Song" Hill returns to his preoccupation with the German death camps, this time with an elegy for someone born a day later than himself and gassed in September of 1943. Thus, he is a kind of surviving twin: "I have made / an elegy for myself it / is true."[25] But the lament is for the survivors like himself as well as for the dead, though the speaker is worried by that easy paradox.

> September fattens on the vines. Roses
> flake from the wall. The smoke
> of harmless fires drifts to my eyes.
>
> This is plenty. This is more than enough.[26]

At times in his vision, suffering is equated with paradise. The last line reads so double it functions as a refrain. Indeed, the whole poem is binary, including its own echo, or inverted reflection. It mirrors the ambiguous duality of the fallen world, in which the concentration camp can be seen as a kind of Eden from which we the non-victims have been expelled and sentenced to live out our exile in guilt. One of the best marks of Hill's greatness as a poet is his attention to the conscience of and for history. His confessions are not confessional poetry in any personal sense only but speak for the race and species. What seems to alarm him most is looking into the fallen world and seeing people pretend not to know they are fallen, though he grants they may be helpless to act on that knowledge. At one extreme is the self-righteous preaching and at the other a satisfied surrender to corruption. The concentration camp is the world itself, an island of the condemned. To pretend the sentence has not been passed is the graver blasphemy.

But the martyrdom is nihilism, and the assumed sainthood of the modern intellectual, is equally offensive. Of what use is intoxication with one's insight into nothingness, the celebration of negative triumph? "An Order of Service" ends:

> Let a man sacrifice himself, concede
> His mortality and have done with it . . .[27]

This kind of renunciation of understanding is only another manifestation of the romantic hubris. The visionary void is no more authentic than the visionary plenitude of Whitman, and it is that emptiness, Hill would say, on which the Transcendentalists of the Twentieth Century have built their gospel, as confused and misled as the Romantics of the century before. To seize on the void as the unifying metaphor is, in Hill's mind, to evade the whole question. The nothingness is certainly there but will not suffice now any more than four thousand years ago.

In the tradition of Yeats' "The Scholars" and Roethke's "Academic," Hill gives us "The Humanist," lest anyone think he is advocating for that failed movement. The humor here arises from the scholar's blindness to the carnality, even cannibalism, of his surgical enterprise. The schoolman by the tedium of his manner, the sense of superiority to his subject, denies the full-fledged reality of what he examines. He denies by his rhetoric and gesture that he shares the common clay.

> The *Venice* portrait: he
> Broods, the achieved guest
> Tired and word-perfect . . .[28]

The first of the two great sequences of *King Log* is "Funeral Music." In a short essay appended to the collection, the poet describes the group as attempting "a florid grim music broken by grunts and sighs. . . . One finds the chronicler of Croyland Abbey writing that the blood of the slain lay caked with the snow that covered the ground and that, when the snow melted, the blood flowed along the furrows and ditches for a distance of two or three miles."[29]

These blank verse sonnets are an homage to the reign of King Stork. The language wallows and revels in violence, intrigue, betrayal, gore. Passages anger by their very complexity and obscurity. Others are among the best Hill has ever written. Some remind me of Hopkins' bitter sonnets, and of Dickinson's indictments of God. A priest at the scene of a beheading prays, his "voice fragrant with a mannered humility."[30] A participant, perhaps one of the condemned, meditates, "we are dying / To satisfy fat Caritas, those / wiped jaws of stone."[31] Soldiers dying in each other's filth on the battlefield—and the image seems to include us all in the mortal combat of conscience with experience—"Tup in their marriage-blood, gasping, 'Jesus.'"[32] "Tup" means to come into heat, and to copulate, and the Christian connotations of "marriage blood" are clear.

Among this brutality and meaningless conflict, the speaker turns with wrenching nostalgia toward the Platonic world of Mind as the exclusive reality. But he cannot believe it, though, as always, it is the nonbeliever who can apprehend the full glory of what he rejects.

> . . . Averroes, old heathen,
> If only you had been right, if Intellect
> Itself were absolute law, sufficient grace.[33]

But experience fractures and obliterates the most complete and appealing mental architecture. Stripped of faith, even in experience itself, one anonymous voice concludes, "I believe in my/ Abandonment, since it is what I have."[34] The image that we hold longest, from this poem more spoken than seen, more whispered than spoken, is this after-battle landscape in section seven.

> Reddish ice tinged the reeds; dislodged, a few
> Feathers drifted across; carrion birds
> Strutted upon the armour of the dead.[35]

A key entry in *King Log* is the short lyric "History as Poetry." More than any modern poet in English, Hill feels a deep responsibility to address the reality of history. Where most of his contemporaries stay with their personal experience for subject matter, or play with fantastic and vague textures, practicing an emotional nominalism, Hill works with the biography of state and race, language, the neuroses of empire, actuality of wars. His title here reverses the well-known equation of the Marxists and phenomenologists, that all relevant literature participates in and clarifies history. "History as Poetry" says something entirely different, bringing collective events sharply into the foreground of his text. We already know of Hill's awe of his own and others' gifts, how the imagination through "the knack of tongues"[36] will always salute and celebrate, perhaps can only praise and celebrate, no matter what the case, the suffering and waste of history. As the world of experience is pathetically undeserving of praise and salutation so the human spirit may be unfit for the "resurgence," the turnings over and renewals out of the carnage of history. Poetry with its love of the dramatic, the violent paradox, may be the truest image of history, and "the tongue's atrocities."[37] Hill is skeptical of the practice of his own art. Even when attempting the opposite, trying to peel away illusion and present truth, indictment, not praise, the craft and medium subvert the intentions.

> Poetry . . .
> . . . Unearths from among the speechless dead
> Lazarus mystified, common man . . .[38]

The second sequence, and the crowning work of *King Log*, bears the unlikely title, "The Songbook of Sebastian Arrurruz," and purports to be a translation from the work of a Spanish poet of that name, dates 1868–1922. It is with this group that Hill came to his full powers as a poet, shedding the labored obscurities of many of the early poems. Whereas before his lines often clogged and tangled in both syntax and meaning, were loaded so heavily with ironies they sometimes collapsed, he now wrote with a classic simplicity of surface. According to some of the reviewers of the original volume in 1968 the name "Sebastian Arrurruz" is meant to suggest first the martyrdom of St. Sebastian and then the arrows that kill him, as well as the arrowroot which is an herb for drawing out poison from wounds made, for instance, by venomed arrows. Playing that game further I would say that "Arrurruz" embodies the hum of the released bow string and the whisper and thud of the arrow going home. But I believe it far more worthwhile to go immediately to the poems themselves, and the martyred lover who is their speaker and subject. In the group of eleven poems the speaker meditates on his loss of a mistress to someone else a few years before. As the title implies, he is still receiving and trying to heal his wounds. This may sound sentimental when summarized, but the sequence reads dry as rioja, and crisp and cool as sea wind on glaring rocks. They could be the finest erotic poems published in recent years.

One of the things I have admired most about contemporary British poets such as Philip Larkin and Hill is their ability to choose the inspired adjective. This genius is used to better advantage than ever in the "Songbook." The choices are always startling, always accurate, "refreshed trivia,"[39] "glandular blooms."[40] This is one of the reasons that Hill can write at such a high level of generalization and connotation. His statements are sensuous, his images significant, often because of happy modification. I don't have space here to quote much from the sequence but let me give at least three examples. Section Four:

> See how each fragment kindles as we turn it,
> At the end, into the light of appraisal.[41]

And section two, titled simply "Coplas," or stanzas, begins:

> "One cannot lose what one has not possessed."
> So much for that abrasive gem.
> I can lose what I want. I want you.[42]

Significantly section seven is titled "From the Latin." It is perhaps the finest single lyric here. It is an example of the plain style cut in jade.

> There would have been things to say, quietness . . .
> And at night my tongue in your furrow.[43]

I don't want to leave the sequence without quoting the final lines from "A Song from Armenia."

> Your mouth, and your hand running over me,
> Deft as a lizard, like a sinew of water?[44]

Here all of Hill's talents come together at once, with none of his worst. His tendency toward the tropical and sensuous is controlled by astringent wit, like a dry desert wind across the Mediterranean. There is a wholeness to the imagination here, a luminous classic quality, catholic in the best sense, a demonstration of what Tate had in mind all along but had not quite realized in poetry. The sequence reads like a short novella, distal yet vivid. The poems remind me a little of Antonio Machado, but no one has ever translated anything like this into English. This is the original.

The last section of the first *Collected Poems* is *Mercian Hymns,* originally published in 1971 and Hill's most accessible book. It is the one that is making his name widely known, even popular. Luckily, it also contains some of his best poetry. It could be described as a fantastic autobiography, a reverie of historic scope. The epigraph from C. H. Sisson explained Hill's concern with the interrelationships of the personal and the historical. It begins, "The conduct of government rests upon the same foundations and encounters the same difficulties as the conduct of private persons."[45] Hill takes the example of Offa, King of Mercia (757–796), as "the presiding genius of the West Midlands"[46] and dramatizes the history of England and the character of state through this personalization. The "hymns" are a kind of dense, clear prose, colored with unexpected humor and astonishing juxtapositions in terms of time, superimposing the present on medieval landscape, creating a deep texture of history and language. There is lightness, and thickness with regard to reference and association. The ambience created is at once modern, medieval, and timeless. You could say that the sequence resembles something of David Jones's *The Anathémata* in thirty sharply etched miniatures, but that would not be completely fair to either Jones or Hill. The distances of history melt inside the powerful field of Hill's linguistic energy.

Like many of the earlier works, the diction, the substitutions, the modifica-tions, are stunning and masterful. But it is the overall effect, incorporating comic relief, that is most memorable. That relief is not found so much in the earlier grim poems. Though there is no narrative as such, there is a sense of sweep, of leaping into obscure corners of history and the psyche and dis-covering crucial documents. The poems thrill, not with patriotism exactly, but with a loving knowledge of the physical, linguistic, cultural hearth on which we live. Both the peripheral and direct vision are coordinated and focused. *Mercian Hymns* is a sign that Hill has at least partially won his struggle with his own talent and hypersensitivity to experience. His field of vision is amazingly wide and these poems consolidate the fullness of his talent realized in the "Songbook."

Again, the fabric here is woven of brutality and beauty twisted tightly together, but remaining distinct. Though at one point the speaker seems to feel that the poems are a kind of grave-robbing of language and psyche, Hill has learned better to live with his ugly fascinations and obsessions. I think a better analogy here would be archeology or numismatics. There is a digging out and cleaning into definition of objects such as coins from old wells, from the mold and bone-heaps. Hill successfully rejuvenates the cliché of "coining," by striking from the ancient but permanent substance both new and ancient features. In fact, Hymn XIII is about examining old "coins" from Offa's time. "Draw, one by one, rare coins to the light. Ringed by its own lustre, the masterful head emerges, kempt and jutting, out of England's well."[47]

If there is a central image in the book, it is grubbing into the com-post and refuse, the midden heaps, among "night-soil, tetanus"[48] plowing, grave-digging, archeology of flues from Roman times, root systems, tear-ing out of stumps, shoveling into the detritus of empire and church. "Their spades grafted through the variably-resistant soil. . . . They ransacked epiph-anies, vertebrae of the chimera, armour of wild bees' larvae."[49] And after the great ceremonies of state, what is left on the land? "Wine, urine, ashes."[50]

There is a wonderful honoring of craftsmanship, the anonymous arti-san, "this master-mason as I envisage him, intent to pester upon typanum and chancel arch his moody testament, confusing warrior with lion, drag-on-coils, tendrils of the stony vine."[51] This is followed directly by one of the masterpieces of the group, an attack upon the industrial parody of crafts-manship. Here again, Hill makes the historical personal, summoning to the forefront fragments of modern ugliness.

> Brooding on the eightieth letter of *Fors Clavigera*
> I speak this in memory of my grandmother, whose
> childhood and prime womanhood were spent in the
> nailer's darg.[52]

The choice of the word 'darg' for hire sends a shiver down the spinal well. The last stanza is the first defiantly repeated, and with a very different effect because of what precedes it.

Hill is one of the two or three best poets writing today in English, and he seems to be getting better. The poems I have seen in magazines since *Mercian Hymns* seem original even for him. This is especially true of the group of sonnets published in *Agenda* called collectively "Lacrimae."

Section XVII of *Mercian Hymns* is among Hill's very best work, a brief account of a contemporary, perhaps Hill himself, driving south through France, and narrowly avoiding a collision with some villagers on bicycles in the Vosges. "His maroon GT chanted then overtook. He lavished on the high valleys its *haleine*."[53] The notes, which are helpful, even indispensable, explain that the final word is an allusion to *The Song of Roland*.

Probably the single finest "coin" in this collection is number XXVII. I will end by quoting its conclusion.

> Earth lay for a while, the ghost-bride of livid
> Thor, butcher of strawberries, and the shire-tree
> dripped red in the arena of its uprooting.[54]

NOTES

1. Geoffrey Hill, "Genesis." *Broken Hierarchies: Poems, 1952–2012.* ed. Kenneth Haynes. Oxford: Oxford University Press, 2016. 4.
2. Hill, "Genesis." *Broken Hierarchies.* 4.
3. Harold Bloom. "Introduction" to *Geoffrey Hill: Collected Poems.* Oxford: Oxford University Press, 1986. xiii.
4. Hill, *Broken Hierarchies.* 15.
5. Hill, "Metamorphosis V." *Broken Hierarchies.* 18.
6. Hill, *Broken Hierarchies.* 21.
7. Hill, *Broken Hierarchies.* 30.
8. Hill, *Broken Hierarchies.* 22.
9. Hill, "Wreaths." *Broken Hierarchies.* 23.
10. Hill, "After Cumae." *Broken Hierarchies.* 25.

11. Hill, *Broken Hierarchies*. 16–17.

12. Hill, *Broken Hierarchies*. 12.

13. Hill, *Broken Hierarchies*. 18.

14. Hill, *Broken Hierarchies*. Ibid.

15. Hill, "Of Commerce and Society, IV." *Broken Hierarchies*. 29.

16. Hill, *Broken Hierarchies*. 30.

17. Thoreau, Henry David. *A Week on the Concord and Merrimack Rivers, Walden; or Life in the Woods, The Maine Woods, Cape Cod*. ed. Robert F. Sayre. New York: Library of America, 1985. 587.

18. Hill, *Broken Hierarchies*. 34.

19. Hill, *Broken Hierarchies*. Ibid.

20. Hill, "Annunciations." 40.

21. Hill, "Ovid in the Third Reich." *Broken Hierarchies*. 39.

22. Hill, "The Emblem." *Broken Hierarchies*. 41.

23. Hill, "Shiloh Church, 1862: Twenty-Three Thousand." *Broken Hierarchies*. 42.

24. Hill, "Genesis." *Broken Hierarchies*. 4.

25. Hill, *Broken Hierarchies*. 44.

26. Hill, *Broken Hierarchies*. Ibid.

27. Hill, *Broken Hierarchies*. 45.

28. Hill, "The Humanist." *Broken Hierarchies*. 46.

29. Hill, *Collected Poems*. 201.

30. Hill, "Funeral Music." *Broken Hierarchies*. 47.

31. Hill, *Broken Hierarchies*. 48.

32. Hill, *Broken Hierarchies*. 49.

33. Hill, *Broken Hierarchies*. 50.

34. Hill, *Broken Hierarchies*. 52.

35. Hill, *Broken Hierarchies*. 53.

36. Hill, "History as Poetry." *Broken Hierarchies*. 61.

37. Hill, *Broken Hierarchies*. Ibid.

38. Hill, *Broken Hierarchies*. Ibid.

39. Hill, *The Songbook of Sebastian Arrurruz. Broken Hierarchies*. 75.

40. Hill, *Broken Hierarchies*. 76.

41. Hill, *Broken Hierarchies*. 72.

42. Hill, *Broken Hierarchies*. 70.

43. Hill, *Broken Hierarchies*. 75.

44. Hill, *Broken Hierarchies*. 77.

45. Sisson, C. H. *A C. H. Sisson Reader*. eds. Charlie Louth and Patrick McGuinness. Manchester, UK: Carcanet Press Limited, 2014. xiv.

46. Hill, *Collected Poems*. 201.
47. Hill, "Hymn XIII: Offa's Coins." *Broken Hierarchies*. 95.
48. Hill, "Hymn XV: Offa's Bestiary." *Broken Hierarchies*. 97.
49. Hill, "Hymn XII: Offa's Coins." *Broken Hierarchies*. 94.
50. Hill, "Hymn XVI: Offa's Sword." *Broken Hierarchies*. 98.
51. Hill, "Hymn XIV: Offa's Laws." *Broken Hierarchies*. 96.
52. Hill, "Hymn XXV: Opus Anglicanum." *Broken Hierarchies*. 107.
53. Hill, "Hymn XVII: Offa's Journey to Rome." *Broken Hierarchies*. 99.
54. Hill, "Hymn XXVII: The Death of Offa." *Broken Hierarchies*. 109.

JEFF DANIEL MARION

POET ON THE HOLSTON

My first contact with Danny Marion came in the fall of 1974 when I received a letter postmarked Jefferson City, Tennessee, dated October 14, inviting me to send poems to a new magazine called *The Small Farm*. The letter was written neatly in brown ink on beige letterhead. The writer, Jeff Daniel Marion, said a review of my most recent book of poems, *Red Owl,* would appear in the first issue of the new magazine. It was a special thrill to get this invitation from my home region, the Southern Appalachians. At the time I was still adjusting to living in Ithaca, New York, and teaching at Cornell University. A magazine called *The Small Farm* was a journal after my own heart.

Of course, I sent a sheaf of poems to Mr. Marion for his new magazine. He accepted several and a correspondence and friendship began that has now lasted almost forty years. He wrote me that he planned to devote the third issue of *The Small Farm* to a celebration of my poetry. That's the kind of letter a young poet likes to receive. I could not have been more pleased. We gave ourselves a year to plan the issue. There would be a batch of new poems, a bibliography, interview, critical essays on my work, and a selection of excerpts from my notebooks. I had never worked on a project with more excitement. In those days before email, we kept the US Postal Service humming with exchanges of poems, suggestions, drafts of articles.

As part of our planning, I agreed to visit Danny and his family in the late summer of 1975 while on my annual trip to see my folks in western North Carolina. We agreed to meet at Big Creek in the Smoky Mountains early one August morning and fly fish most of the day, then move on to Danny's house in Jefferson City to work on the Robert Morgan issue of *The Small Farm.*

It was a very hot late summer day and Mr. Leatherwood, at Leatherwood's Store where we bought our fishing licenses, said, "You won't catch nothing: fish don't bite in this weather." But we brushed aside his warning, calling him a sourpuss and a spoilsport. We parked our cars at the entrance to the park, and, carrying our rods and flies and picnic lunch, marched deep into the Smoky Mountains. The water of Big Creek was so clear we could see huge trout hovering near the bottoms of the pools. We cast our flies and they ignored us. There is nothing more humiliating than for a large trout to look you in the eye with contempt. We tried one kind of fly after another. We moved farther up the creek to fresh pools, where even larger trout hung motionless in the clear water. But they defied us to interest them in the trifles and baubles we cast on the surface.

Still, Danny and I persisted with good cheer. We told ourselves we just hadn't used the right flies or the correct technique. We cast upstream and downstream. We cast near rocks, and we cast into the center of pools. We tried wet flies as well as dry flies. The trout were so visible, magnified in the still pools, and we might have caught them with grapple hooks. We got on our knees and begged the trout to at least notice what we threw at them. Occasionally a big trout would glance toward us and wave its tail in derision. We prayed we would not be totally embarrassed and have to return home with empty creels.

Around noon we took a break and had a fine lunch at Brakeshoe Spring. To keep up our spirits and refuse to be defeated we decided after lunch to try bait fishing. I told Danny I wouldn't tell if he wouldn't tell. Overturning rocks, we soon found some fat earthworms and slipped them on our hooks. Danny had some shot sinkers that we squeezed on our leaders. But when we cast the bait into the pools the trout showed no more interest in the worms than they had in the dry flies. They were torpid and they remained torpid.

Refusing to concede that old Leatherwood had been right, we walked farther upstream toward the headwaters, where the stream was coldest, fed by mountain springs. Determined to catch fish one way or another we hardly noticed that the sky had clouded up. Thunder cracked the air above us, and soon rain began to pound the trees and ground. We were sweaty and exhausted, and the rain felt delicious. We decided to call it a day, and began trudging downstream, back to the cars.

I stayed that night with Danny's family in Jefferson City, and the next day was as successful as the fishing trip had been a failure. Danny offered to show me around the area near Jefferson City. We visited the Hermit's Cave on the Holston River, saw the peak called Devil's Nose, the community called Choptack, the Ebbing & Flowing Spring, the Amis House, part of

Cocke County, home to Mildred Haun, author of *The Hawk's Done Gone*, and best of all Nance's Ferry.

Wilson Nance was napping on a bench under a tulip tree when we arrived. We drove onto his ferry and he took us across the Holston. I had never heard of a current powered ferry before and was intrigued to see how it worked. Attached to cables, the ferry could be turned to the left or to the right so the current would propel it, like wind pushing a sail, across the river. Reversing the angle, he could then navigate back in the other direction. Mr. Nance said his family had operated the ferry here for almost two hundred years. But he was the last. He had no sons interested in staying on the farm by the river to provide ferry service. Later I wrote a poem called "Nance Ferry," for Danny Marion.

> Through the geometry of turbines that
> Hot August day they were
> Emptying half the French Broad River
> Onto the Holston below the Cherokee
> Project. We saw the black crowned night
>
> Heron on a snag lift off into
> The sycamores and princess trees over
> The rampant water. Back on the bluffs
> Hermit's Cave aimed a muzzle, blackened since
> The Civil war by campfires, at the north.
>
> A few miles down we came on
> Wilson Nance asleep in the shade of
> A great poplar near the water's edge, his cattle
> Drifting on the hills above.
> The ferry rode thirty feet off shore
> Pulling at its high cable like an animal.
> He woke easily and drew it in so we could
> Drive aboard. "Works by current power," he said
> And with the big helm winched it
> Aslant the stream on its lines like a sail
>
> The water hit and drove trolleying along
> The cable. "This power was give to man to work
> By his strategies," he said of the water. We rocked

> Toward the yon landing. His family's ferried
> Here two hundred years, but he's the last,
>
> No sons and no more than three cars a day
> Generally come down, at least to cross, though others
> Come to look. Most take the bridge twelve miles
> Below since nothing major's either side
> Close by. We paid the fifty cents
>
> And drove out on the gravel ramp between cedars,
> Then stopped to watch him, sweating seriously
> In the awful sun, haul the flat around
> And fly it like a water kite back to his own
> Shore and to the bench under the big tulip tree.[1]

My visit with Danny and his family in 1975 seemed to open a whole new world for me. I had spent little time in Tennessee before that. I knew a little about the Alleghenies and the Cumberlands, and the settlement of that region. I loved the hilly pastures of eastern Tennessee, the cedars along ditches and in gullies, the limestone outcrops, the old churches among sycamore groves, the intimate sense of history of the region, of the TVA, the Cherokee, and figures such as Davy Crockett and John Sevier.

I learned a lot from talking with Danny because he knew so much about the history of the region, the families who had settled there, and he knew the scholarship of the frontier era. As I listened to him and wrote down the names of books I should read, I realized I was entering a new phase in my writing and thinking. Other than Jim Wayne Miller, Danny was the first person I ever heard talk about "Appalachian Writing." The term was new to me. I had grown up in the mountains of North Carolina and we thought of ourselves as mountain people. But I had hardly been aware of the term "Appalachia." I had lived in the Blue Ridge Mountains, the eastern chain of the Appalachians.

Talking with Danny gave me a new perspective on the region and on writing. It was like making a new start. Along with Jim Wayne Miller, Danny had seen a brave new future for the writing of and about our area. It was Danny who first suggested I read Cormac McCarthy. It was Danny who really introduced me to the essays of Wendell Berry. In part, it was Danny's interest in the Southern Appalachian region that got me interested in writing fiction again. For more than ten years I had concentrated on poetry. But slowly I realized I wanted to write in voices other than my own, which I had not been able to do in verse. And I wanted to tell some of the stories I'd heard growing up from my grandpa and parents and aunts and uncles, stories about panthers and mad dogs, snakes and bears, ghosts, the Civil War, the Native Americans, herbal medicine, folk stories, family stories. In the early 1980s I began to write fiction again, mining the material that had been in my memory all along.

Though it never had a wide circulation, and didn't last for many years, *The Small Farm* had a vast impact on the writing in the region, and certainly on my own writing. Think back to a time when there were no Appalachian Studies programs in the colleges and universities, when there were only a few literary publications in the region. There was an emphasis on Southern writing, on Faulkner and Flannery O'Connor, but little on the writing of the Southern Highlands. That is the context in which Danny Marion began to publish *The Small Farm*. With Jim Wayne Miller and a few others, he cleared and broke the new ground.

Now there are dozens of programs, publications, associations, conferences, festivals, and fellowships devoted to Appalachian literature. One reason that has happened is that Danny Marion had a vision. He conceived and created, or helped create, a new field of literary activity that is now booming. His little magazine sent out ripples that are still stirring in our region.

While Danny was launching *The Small Farm*, and helping to create the field of Appalachian Studies, he was also launching his career as a poet. Beginning with a book called *Out in the Country, Back Home*, and then a book titled *Tight Lines,* Danny quickly established himself as one of the leading poets of the region. He also began to work at mastering the art of the letterpress.

In *Out in the Country, Back Home* Danny revealed his lively sense of humor, as well as his allegiance to the land, and the people of the land. In "A Mountain Fable of a Sort" he tells the story of the day "money washed down out of the mountain / in mason jars . . .":[2]

> Brother Blazer slapped his leather
> backed Bible across his knee &
> shouted: "It's the Lord's manna
> from above—we never had it so good.
> Amen & keep it coming Lord."

And the whole town gathered—
lines, fishhooks, nets & long distance swimmers—
on the bank of the Little Pigeon.
So Sally Stipes bought a new
washing machine for her front porch
(the old one now rests less than
a fathom down on the bottom
of Sinking Creek) . . . .[3]

In these early poems there is also a wonderful delicacy of tone, a refined sense of the music and texture of words, a pace of perfected attention. Here is the lyric called "Brakeshoe Spring":

past Crestmont on the way up
to Walnut Bottoms

a brakeshoe wedged into the bank
as spillway

watershed
for the logging engineer
whose train passed daily
over 50 years ago

now a flume
padded by moss
breaking the slow arrival
of water

tongue whose words
trickle downward
into

crescendo
that nourishes the names
of galax & laurel

earth & sea.[4]

In the handsome letterpress book *Tight Lines* (1981) Danny explores farther and deeper into his art of memory and place. In "The Chinese Poet

Awakens to Find Himself Abruptly in East Tennessee" we hear a somewhat different voice in a new context of association. The poetic horizon has
been expanded, yet the sense of place has deepened.

> I have come home
> heavy from the day's labor:
> how the words of others fail
> to bear up, droop their shoulders.
> even the mountains seem to sag
> in this blue light.
>
> Han Shan knew,
> giving his poems to trees & rocks,
> letting them stay home to weather
> alone.
>
> No escape:
> Everything settles into dust.
>
> Suddenly from behind
> the goat who had waited
> all day to be fed,
> charges—butts me forward
>
> I am moved.
> The old bearded one knows his master.[5]

And we hear a new dramatic voice in a poem such as "The Farm Wife's
Aubade." And a new lyricism also:

> Let this land's corduroy,
> an apron of brown
> plowed fields & green rows,
> always wear its colors
> in blessed light
>
> Whenever darkness falls,
> let it be sown with moon & stars,
> a zodiac to guide
> the labor of these hands.

Let the rooms that house my labors
be sweet with a lingering incense:
yeast of daily bread,
cinnamon
& the scent of hickory smoke.

Let my song be a kitchen window,
dipper & water bucket on the sill,
filling with the world outside.

And let my life pour
across these days in honeyed light
slow & rich as the dawn of May.[6]

There is an acute sense of wordplay, and of the resonance of words in these poems. "The Garden" begins, "A season comes to attention in these rows . . ."[7]

Over the years Danny has continued to develop the mode of the dramatic. Many poems are spoken in the voices of characters. He has also expanded his sense of geography. Many of the newer memory poems in the volume *Letters Home* are set in Detroit, where Danny and his parents lived during WWII. They are poems of culture shock, of uprootedness, of surprise. This is "November 1943":

No welcome to my mother,
our basement two rooms little
better than a stall, our heat
a gas range, its oven door
left open through the night, my
father hugged himself, danced
on the cold concrete floor before
leaving for work. Welcome said
winds whistling down Great Lakes to
mountain wife hanging their one
set of bedsheets on clothesline,
sails she lifts to catch the fresh
bloom of air, let sun bleach clean
these wet flags of truce.[8]

There is a painful sense of out-of-placeness and difference in the suite of Detroit poems. They are about learning as well as remembering. This from "Cleaning Lady 1944":

> Twice a week we go, Mother
> and I, to the Strastsma's where
> our world opens wider, to
> row upon row of fine books
> lining shelves to the ceiling, rugs
> rich with swirls of color, words
> calling to me from spines whose
> crisp letters awaken
> a hunger I cannot name.
> My mother lets me sit on
> the plush couch, opens a book
> in my lap, and I turn pages...
> rags to riches my mother
> mops the floor, her sweat a shine.[9]

I believe Danny reaches his deepest level of meditation and self-searching in the poems collected in *Father* (2009). These are poems of great affection, loyalty, and bonds of kinship. But they are also poems of profound honesty, less confessional than testimonial, poems of coming to terms with memory. There is a relentless clarity of vision in poems such as "Prayer to a Dead Father":

> Father I never forgave you
> those lessons to learn my ABC's
> at three, trembling and peeing
> my pants in fear of not
> pleasing you, your scowl a red
> welt stinging. Not till fourth grade
> could I say them through, lined
> like wooden blocks A-Z,
> just as your loops with shoe
> laces never quite fit my hand,
> granny knot the usual failed
> attempt—to this day give me

boot, slipper or buckle—what holds
without a line to grip me in knots.
At eight I would prove a man,
leaning to sight along the barrel
of the 12-gauge you held smiling,
the group of men squatted, waiting
the shot that sent me breathless,
reeling backwards from the silent,
knowing faces, my shoulder stinging
into ache beyond the worst kick,
that purple patch of betrayal
hanging for weeks above my heart.
At thirteen my buddies the two beagles
you brought home as pups, penned
out back, hungry to break free,
lay back their ears in a lope,
trail every luring scent:
a mile from home, noses to ground,
you found them, jerked each up
by an ear, swung them like feed sacks,
yelps and howls worse than my screams,
rage doubled by your threat to swing
me by the ear if I didn't shut up.
Was it their yen for freedom
you hated, the leap to wild abandon
beyond your discipline forever?
So I believed returning home
from college when a friend told
me your belief that I was
ruined by books, words you claimed
were back talk and sass, so set free,
no longer to be the son
you wanted, words burning my ears
all these years. So forgive me, father;
for even now I cannot forgive you.[10]

These later poems are not only elegiac, they are also narratives of growth, of survival, of the ways we age and adjust. They are poems of the knowledge of time passing. Here are lines from "To My Father Ten Years Later":

Six months later you visited:
a hospital bed in a windowless
room, you lay beneath the white
sheet of final winter, a stillness
I could not fathom. You rose, slinging
the sheet back and I ran to
your side, both hands pushing you down,
back onto the bed where
you belonged: I've got to
get out of here, harsh words
ringing as I woke and stumbled
from my bed into the summer
night, cold and distant light of stars
still burning, river still whispering.

III

The same year you visited again:
we drove the old '47 Chevrolet,
you and I in front,
Uncle Gene in back, and
arrived at the vacant lot,
neighborhood gathering place
for tag football, Sunday softball.
It was late fall, almost November, grass
still green, a cool crisp afternoon,
but I was snug in my dreams
of fourteen, wondering where my friends
were, waiting for the game to begin.
I heard your voice and turned
to see that you and Gene were
outside: Let the bear out, you had said.
I felt its black bulk push past me,
slime of drool on my arm,
heavy earthiness of bear's odor filling the car. . . .

Left in the car, I did not belong
in that field beyond time where
you had wandered, your world safe
from me, the drowsy sprawl of
afternoon, the long sleep coming on.

IV

I don't hear from you much anymore,
the three of you leaving no forwarding
address. I am left here with my words,
those black birds gathering on this field
of white, wings ready for the long flight,
homing signals stirring darkly within.[11]

We owe a great debt to Danny Marion for editing *The Small Farm*, for encouraging and calling attention to a new generation of poets, for helping to call attention to the writing of the region and the field of Appalachian Studies. In his own poems Danny has been at the forefront of a remarkable renaissance. From the first his poems revealed an exciting new voice in Southern poetry, a vivid sense of place, a powerful use of memory. His later poems show a deepening and expanding of his craft as he confronted and met the challenges of a rapidly changing community, a disappearing past and a radically changing present.

The first recipient of a Literary Fellowship from the Tennessee Arts Commission in 1978, Danny received the 2004 Independent Publisher's Award for Poetry for *Ebbing & Flowing Spring*. That volume was also named "Appalachian Book of the Year" by the Appalachian Writers Association. In the almost forty years we have been friends I have never known anyone with a more intense knowledge of a region, its people both good and bad, charged with both erudition and affection.

Danny Marion's poems are memorable for their startling imagery, wit, precision of craftsmanship, lyrical speech, and sense of humanity. It is an honor to celebrate his life and work.

NOTES

1. Robert Morgan, "Nance Ferry." Unpublished poem.
2. Jeff Daniel Marion. "A Sort of Mountain Fable." *Out in the Country, Back Home*. Winston-Salem: Jackpine Press, 1976. 43

3 Marion, *Out in the Country, Back Home.* Ibid.

4. Marion, *Out in the Country, Back Home.* 53.

5. Jeff Daniel Marion. *Tight Lines.* Emory, VA: Iron Mountain Press, 1981. np.

6. Marion, *Tight Lines.* np.

7. Marion, *Tight Lines.* np.

8. Jeff Daniel Marion. *Letters Home.* Abingdon, VA: Sow's Ear Press, 2001. 7.

9. Marion, *Letters Home.* 12.

10. Jeff Daniel Marion. *Father.* Nicholasville, KY: Wind Publications, 2009. 68–69.

11. Marion, *Father.* 66–67.

JIM WAYNE MILLER

A RADIATING PRESENCE

It is a special privilege to introduce *The Jim Wayne Miller Reader*. But I must concede at the start that anyone introducing Jim Wayne Miller will have trouble deciding how to describe him. He was a poet, short story writer, novelist, playwright, essayist, critic, lecturer, professor of German, translator, teacher of workshops and summer seminars. He was a roving ambassador for literature and culture of the Appalachian region, a friend and encourager of many other writers, mentor to dozens if not hundreds of younger writers, editor, anthologist, historian. He was a connoisseur of the fine arts and the popular arts. He was a man of many contradictions. It has been said that at one time one of the most important archives of Appalachian studies was carried in boxes and folders in the back seat and trunk of Jim's gray Buick as he traveled from one conference, one festival, one lecture or symposium to another. He was a wandering scholar, a bard, in the age of super-highways and community colleges, arts councils, and the awakening awareness in the Southern Appalachians to its heritage, history, and literature.

Because Jim had so many hats, and wore each so effectively, it is impossible to describe him in a sentence, or in a paragraph. But I recall that Robert Frost, one of Jim's most important heroes and models, when asked to explain his role as writer-in-residence at the University of Michigan, called himself a "radiator." I can think of no better word to describe Jim's presence. Like Frost, he was first and last a poet, but among his students, fellow writers, readers, faculty colleagues, he was a radiator giving off the energy of a passion for words, for word play, for humor (including racy jokes), for history and folkways, for music and musical instruments, for film, for stories, always stories. Whenever you saw Jim, he was surrounded by friends, by students, by folks he had just met. If you listened you would hear outbursts of laughter from time to time, as he grinned and drew on a cigarette, and offered yet another story or anecdote from his vast and always growing memory hoard.

Jim was a close friend of the Appalachian scholar Loyal Jones, another native of western North Carolina who lived and taught in Kentucky. I was first introduced to Loyal by Jim at the Kentucky Book Fair in Frankfort. Assuming a serious mien Loyal said, "Have you heard, they've canceled the faith healing service?" Taken aback, I wondered where his question was leading. Then Loyal added, still poker-faced, "The preacher's sick."

It was always a thrill to see Loyal and Jim together, as they traded jokes and anecdotes, scurrilous gossip from academia, one punch line after another. I don't think any of the Borscht Belt comedians could have topped them.

"How does your family feel about your writing?" Loyal said to Jim.

"Somebody asked my dad if he had read Jim's last book," Jim said. "My dad answered, 'I hope so.'"

The first time I taught at the Appalachian Writers Workshop in 1988 I got almost no sleep for a week. It was impossible to go to bed as long as Jim and Ed McClanahan and others were telling story after story, delivering punch line after punch line, then talking serious for a while about other writers, politics, history. And usually there was singing, if somebody had a guitar or banjo, which they always had. Far into the night we sang old ballads, Carter family numbers, hymns, protest songs. In the crowd around Jim everyone seemed to know each other, the poets and playwrights, teachers and musicians, the journalists and humorists, the arts administrators and even politicians. It was a warm and lively company.

Jim was the first person I ever heard talk about such a thing as Appalachian writing. My first contact with him had occurred way back in 1963–64 when I was an undergraduate at UNC-Chapel Hill and serving as fiction editor of *The Carolina Quarterly*. I selected some very short stories that had been sent by someone named Jim Wayne Miller. One story was later included in one of Jim's longer works of fiction, the 1989 novel *Newground*. Two brothers are attending a country school and the story is told by the older brother. When the teacher asks the students what they had for breakfast most of the students lie, telling the teacher what she wants to hear: "They recited: bacon, eggs, toast, milk, cereal, all lovely approved things."[1] But the younger brother Eugene doesn't understand the game and blurts out that he had biscuits and sawmill gravy, and then he adds, "and *new* molasses."[2] The older brother says, "A half-mad, hysterical laugh rose to the high ceilings of the gym and bounced back before I realized that it was I who had laughed. I cringed down, ashes inside, and looked to see whether anyone on either side of me knew that Eugene was my brother."[3]

My second contact with Jim came the next year, in 1964, when a thin crisp volume of poems called *Copperhead Cane* arrived at the office of *The Carolina Quarterly*. I was just beginning to discover contemporary poetry then, and the bright young poets were talking about Robert Lowell, John Berryman, Robert Bly. But here was a collection of poems about the mountains where I had grown up. It had never occurred to me one could make poems about the Blue Ridge Mountains. Fiction, yes, but not poems. Not only were Jim's poems authentic and colloquial, they were in rhyme and meter. Many were sonnets. "Endings have a wile, a mountain cunning, / and only seem to sleep, like groundhogs sunning / on rocks," a poem called "In a Mountain Pasture."[4]

I was struck at once by the voice, and by the formal mastery. With a shiver of recognition, I read: "Catch up the hound by collar and scruff, / And drop the cattle gate! / The fox has holed in Reynolds' Bluff, / The moon is up, it's late!"[5]

Going back to Jim's early poems I have been struck again and again by how much his own man he was from the beginning. These poems shine as brightly as if they were written this morning. They do not reflect the fashions of 1964, but have a timeless, crafted quality. They have the authority of form and the authority of felt experience. They are true in detail and natural in speech.

From the very first Jim showed his independence from the fashions of the academic poetry establishment. As I reread his poems I keep thinking of his courage in the face of indifference. He had the courage to be himself over the decades with little concern for the whims of the creative writing industry. The fact that he made what he wrote seem natural, even inevitable, shows the success of his intense concentration and talent. Rereading his poems, I feel again what a brave man he was.

From the first Jim's poems showed a fascination and even intimacy with death. His second book of poems was called *Dialogue with a Dead Man*. The poems reveal his vivid sense of history, and the way poems speak across time, across generations, to the past, to the future. The poems are dialogues with the past, with American history, as well as with the interior self. Also, we begin to see Jim celebrate and honor, and lament, the passing of a way of life.

One of Jim's great subjects, in his poems, in his fiction, his essays, and his lectures, is the rapid changes in the Appalachian region in the last half of the twentieth century. In haunting lyrics, with telling detail, he dramatized the shifts and evolution of the older rural culture into the American mainstream in the post WWII era, his era. It would become the theme of much of the writing from the region, in the work of Lee Smith, Bobbie Ann Mason, and many others. But Jim was one of the very first to address the subject. As early as the 1970s he began to call attention to the drastic disruptions in the region in his essays, reviews, lectures, workshops, and through his editing.

For many writers of my generation Jim served as a living link between the Appalachian writers of the past, and the exploding community of writers of the 1970s and 1980s and beyond. He was friends with and wrote about the work of Jesse Stuart, James Still, Harriette Arnow, Wilma Dykeman. He was tireless in his efforts to call attention to these writers, some with roots in the populist writing of the 1930s, the age of *The Grapes of Wrath*. If Cratis Williams had been the "radiator" in the generation before him in establishing Appalachian literature as a popular subject at universities and summer workshops, such as the Appalachian Writers Workshop at Hindman Settlement School, Jim was very much Williams' heir and successor, bringing that excitement to a new generation. Because Jim was an outstanding writer himself, and because of the surge of interest in the culture of the region, Jim helped create an audience that probably exceeded any Williams had dreamed of.

Jim's later poems, especially the Brier poems in *The Mountains Have Moved Closer*, are studies of deracination. They are among the best known and the most loved poems of our region. No one has been able to better describe and enact the sense of loss, the paradoxes of identity in the mountains. The narratives, the dramas, the monologues, and multiple voices, have captured for all time the ironies of our place in geography and history. Many lines are the most quoted in Appalachian poetry. In *Brier, His Book* we see Jim take his place in the populist tradition that runs from Whitman and Mark Twain, Carl Sandburg, Bill Monroe and Woody Guthrie, to Gary Snyder, Ted Kooser, and Thomas McGrath. He is bardic and he is prophetic. He speaks in tongues and sings deep-down blues. But he also makes us laugh and delights us with adroit wordplay and ingenious conceits.

Jim's poems are witty, clear-eyed, dramatic, and unsentimental. He is often a very experimental poet, trying new things with voice and form. His poems are charged with a relish for improvisation. I love the way he recovers the out-of-the-way and forgotten and celebrates the wisdom of work with hands. He can shout like a revival preacher or caller of a square dance. At the same time, he is a poet of informed political conscience and consciousness. Rereading his poems reminds us that he is not only the poet of the mountains, but of the planet.

Even those of us who have been familiar with Jim's work for forty years or more are often surprised by the turns and insights when we reread him. He is always more complex than we remember. While a major exponent and theorist of regional writing and culture, Jim was the one who, amid the controversy over the play *The Kentucky Cycle* and the amount of time the author had spent on research in Kentucky, asserted that whether the author had spent ten days or ten years or no time at all in Kentucky was irrelevant. Only the quality of the work mattered.

And recently looking at Jim's introductory essay in the anthology *Southern Appalachian Poetry* I found this statement: "I don't wish to impute a mystique to any particular place. And I hope no one finds any witless yodeling about mountains in my poems just because I come from the mountains of North Carolina. . . . I have no literary enthusiasm for mountains and am not interested in them as mere landscape. . . . What interests me is people in the place—how they coped, what they have come to as a result of living in that place."[6]

I would add that the one element of Jim's writing not emphasized enough is the comic. Many of his most serious insights are delivered with humor. In poem after poem, he leads the reader or listener into a trap of recognition, through irony, the subtle aside or punch line.

As a youth Jim was a neighbor and admirer of the lawyer, song collector, musician and impresario, Bascom Lamar Lunsford. He attended the folk festival Lunsford produced every summer in Asheville, often hitchhiking from Leicester to Asheville in the 1940s and 1950s. This musical tradition is very much a part of the legacy Jim was keen to pass on to the students and writers younger than him. It was a mission he took on with relish, wry humor, and tireless energy.

I must confess that I did not understand at first the importance of what Jim was attempting as a scholar and critic. It was only in the early 1980s that I began to see how essential his work on Appalachian writing was, how necessary and unprecedented. He saw the need to collect, publish, and define what was going on in the region, what had gone on before, and he saw how necessary it was to place Appalachian writing in the context of American culture and history. As a scholar of European languages and literatures and folklore, Jim's vision was at once local and universal. What he did was critical for me, for us, and for contemporary literature. As we say in the mountains, he was clearing some new ground.

Knowing Jim helped me know myself better. Through his historical and critical work, I was able to see what I was doing in a new light. Listening to, or reading, his critical prose was a special delight. Jim had a subtle and illuminating sense of the advantages and limitations of the regional, and of the way poetry discovers and defines place, and reaches beyond place. One of Jim's most important themes is the way we live in two or three overlapping cultures at once, one foot in the past and one in the present rapidly becoming the future.

Jim could not have been an authority on the regional if he had not also been an authority on the non-regional. He was deeply learned in the history of ideas, and he knew how to place his insights about the mountains in the context of wider and older cultures. He loved popular culture also, especially movies and country music. He was an expert on modern languages, and he knew Heidegger as well as shape notes.

It should not be forgotten that Jim spent his professional life as a teacher and scholar of German language and literature, of German and European folklore and intercultural studies. Perhaps many think his two careers, as Appalachian poet, novelist, critic and editor, and scholar of German were unrelated. But, in fact, they were closely related, and I believe his two careers stimulated and nourished each other. I think the connection between Jim's poetry and German culture is very deep. German poetry and poetics informed much of his creative and critical work. I don't think it was just an accident that an NDEA fellowship to Vanderbilt drew Jim to the study of German and German culture and folklore. Shall I say, his work in German was germane to all his other work?

The way German culture and poetry are earth-rooted and blood-rooted fascinated and inspired Jim. And the German interest in folklore and folk music must have stimulated him early on to look back at his own region, at the music he had heard since a boy from his neighbor Bascom Lamar Lunsford. It must have been a pleasure to encounter the seriousness and depth German scholars gave to *volkslieder* and *volkskunde*.

Like Thomas Wolfe, Wilma Dykeman, and John Ehle, Jim was a native of Buncombe County, North Carolina, next door to my own Henderson

County. To me he was a contact and connector to many of those I did not know, some of whom I could never know. Jim took the responsibility of teaching us about ourselves, and through his influence, through his writing, through his poems and stories, he is *still* teaching us. Even as I write this, I can hear his laughter at some wordplay, some wicked turn of phrase.

A friend once told me that one of her favorite memories was of seeing Jim dance with his wife Mary Ellen at a party after a literary festival. As Jim held Mary Ellen in his arms and they circled on the dance floor, oblivious to those around them, my friend said the look of delight and affection on their faces made her wish that she herself, and every woman, could have a lover so attentive, so devoted, so alert, and lively and happy.

It seems unthinkable that Jim is no longer here to consult. I last saw him at the Kentucky Book Fair in the fall of 1995 and we sat behind the Gnomon Press table most of the day catching up on gossip and news of the region. When I got back home, I received a package from him containing articles, poems, bibliographies that had come up in our discussion.

I would like to celebrate the way Jim kept to the large perspective, as well as the local and personal. It was his sense of cultural history that enabled him to create a field, to clear a new ground, where little had been done before. Jim had what he called "a nostalgia for the future."
I would like to celebrate how he encouraged and supported so many young and so many of the not so young. I would like to honor his loyalty and versatility.

"He was the most generous human being I ever met," the poet Dana Wildsmith said after his death.[7]

I would like to celebrate his sense of connectedness, his allegiances, and his sense of humor. He was an example to which to aspire. He actually liked people, and liked to be with people. Jim tells us in "Regional Identity and the Future" from *Appalachia Inside and Out*: "We have moved many times, and I believe we can find the gap and migrate to the future as a people with a common history and heritage. Our history, which is our burden and our affliction, is also our source of strength. Our past has a future."[8]

One of my fondest images of Jim is from a late-night session in the lounge of one of the dormitories at the Hindman Settlement School, during the week of the writers' workshop. The room was filled with people clapping and singing old protest songs. There was a guitar, a banjo, and a dulcimer. In those days before air conditioning the room was boiling hot, though the night was cooling off outside. Jim had taken a chair to the open door and was sitting in the doorway, smoking a cigarette. What I remember best is the smile of profound pleasure on his lips, as he savored the cigarette, took a sip from the glass of bourbon and ice in his left hand, listening to the music of his friends inside the room, and the extraordinary fanfare of katydids in the dark trees outside. To understand Jim we have to understand that deep delight, that *loyalty*, that love.

NOTES

1. Jim Wayne Miller. *Newfound.* New York: Orchard Books, 1989. 83.
2. Miller, *Newfound.* 84.
3. Miller, *Newfound.* 84.
4. Jim Wayne Miller. "In a Mountain Pasture." *Every Leaf a Mirror: A Jim Wayne Miller Reader.* eds. Morris Allen Grubbs and Mary Ellen Miller. Lexington: University Press of Kentucky, 2014. 19.
5. Jim Wayne Miller. "After the Hunt." *Dialogue with a Dead Man.* Athens: University of Georgia Press, 1974. 11.
6. Jim Wayne Miller. "Preface." *Southern Appalachian Poetry: An Anthology of 37 Poets.* ed. Marita Garin. Jefferson, NC: McFarland, 2007. vii.
7. Dana Wildsmith. *Appalachian Journal.* Vol. 33, No. 2 (Winter 2006). 160.
8. Jim Wayne Miller. *Appalachia Inside Out: Culture and Custom.* Vol. 2. eds. Robert J. Higgs, Ambrose N. Manning, and Jim Wayne Miller. Knoxville: The University of Tennessee Press, 1995. 738.

THE AUTHORITY
OF POETRY

When we first experience the best art, there is surprise, a sense of strangeness, and then the opposite, a certain *déjà vu*, or recognition of something we had forgotten that we knew. This is true of poetry as well as the other arts, including music. The truest art may seem, at first, aberrant, and later strike us as familiar, inevitable. For this reason, we resist the new, then claim it as the standard by which to measure other examples and honor its authority.

Much of the authority of poetry resides in mystery, the quality that eludes paraphrase. That which is too readily explained is readily forgotten. Think of a sonnet by Hopkins or Mallarmé. They are haunting in part because they evade easy translation. Whitman proclaims, "I too am untranslatable."[1] Every day we read words or hear words in the air that don't detain us, but slip away, escaping memory. "I placed a jar in Tennessee" stays fresh, in part because we're never sure exactly what is said. Should it be taken literally? Did Wallace Stevens mean for us to believe he actually set a jar on a ridge in the 16th state, or is the gesture suggestive, and, if so, suggestive of what? The image leaps at you, but in an important way you can never be certain of interpretation. We know perfectly well what each word means semantically, but we can never be sure of their intention, and in that way the image remains alive, an unsolved mystery.

Yet an element of the satisfaction of poetry is also in the experience of rightness of its expression, the accuracy of word choice and sound. Yeats, for example, in "Leda and the Swan," in the fifth and sixth lines, says, "How can those terrified vague fingers push / The feathered glory from her loosening thighs?"[2] *Vague* can be read in several ways. The fingers might be "vague" because the woman is stunned and not in control of her actions, or "vague" because she can't feel them in her terror. But "vague" can also suggest she is resisting less as her thighs loosen. She is uncertain how to respond to the overwhelming force that is about to penetrate her.

Poe's first poem called "To Helen" is on the surface easily accessible. It is one of the most popular poems in American literature, often found in high school textbooks. Once memorized, it's hard to forget. Yet when described or paraphrased the poems seem to slip away. We can't explain what is meant by the phrase "Lo! in yon brilliant window niche."[3] A window is not a niche. In mansions statues stand in lighted niches in walls. Is Poe telling us that Helen is a statue: "the agate lamp within thy hand."[4] Is this Helen of Troy? Why would Helen of Troy be like a ship bearing "weary, way-worn wanderers"[5] to a native shore? When we first read or hear the poem it seems perfectly accessible, but on closer inspection the poem becomes more and more elusive of explanation. But we are persuaded, that somehow this Helen draws the weary travelers to a paradise called home.

Some of the power of poetry lies in the accuracy of its statement. Poetry restores our experience, or memory of experience of the things of this world. When Frost in "After Apple Picking" reminds us of "the instep arch" that "keeps the pressure of the ladder-round,"[6] we go "ah" with the pleasure of remembering, or seeming to remember, the pressure of a ladder rung while climbing to pick apples. The phrase seems so perfect we don't have to have picked apples on a ladder ourselves to feel its rightness. Poetry delights by making our world, and our memory, more immediate. When Whitman points out "water-plants with their graceful flat heads,"[7] we are given perception of those again, as the child might see them for the first time. The vision of poetry can be Edenic.

Poetry can demonstrate its authority in seemingly contradictory ways. Shakespeare's 73rd sonnet is perfect in voice, cadence, images, resolution. The similes could not be improved on. The poem is like sculpture, consummate, complete:

> That time of year thou mayst in me behold
> When yellow leaves, or none, or few, do hang
> Up on those boughs which shake against the cold,
> Bare ruined choirs, where late the sweet birds sang.[8]

But there is also the delight of openness, of larger, dynamic flow, not contained in any compact closure. Always arriving and leaving, as in *Job,* or *Revelation*, in *Leaves of Grass*, Ginsburg's *Howl*, Smart's *Jubilate Agno*. The energy of such poetry can seem uncontrollable even as it demonstrates a different kind of control, reaching forward, higher. We experience energy that seems not to be contained, sometimes frightening, bardic, manic, at the brink of the rational, somewhat like glossolalia:

For the tides are the life of God in the ocean, and he sends angels
to trouble the great DEEP.
For he hath fixed the earth upon arches & pillars, and the flames of
hell flow under it . . .
For MATTER is the dust of the earth, every atom of which is life.[9]

Everyone knows poetry is the oldest literary art, far antedating the written word. Poetry is the mother art of all writing. Our ancestors sang and said and carried poetry in their memories and on their tongues for tens of thousands of years before anyone learned to scratch sounds and sentences on surfaces of clay, stones, and skins. And most of us know something about the glorious history of poetry, from Sumer and ancient China to the Greeks, to Shakespeare, to Walt Whitman, to the splendors of Wallace Stevens. But is there a role for poetry in our digital age, of instant communication, as we drown in information, numbers, dates, and quotes, at our fingertips?

From our creative writing programs to our self-publishing culture, there is a flood of verse around us. It would be foolish to argue there is no longer interest in poetry. In a way there seems to be more attention than ever. But when you ask students, or anyone, to quote a line or two of poetry, they at first look startled. And then, if they comply, they call up a fragment of poetry from the past: "Whose woods these are I think I know"[10] or "Once upon a midnight dreary . . . "[11] It's rare for anyone to recall a line of free verse.

There are many reasons for this. Obviously rhymed and metered verse sticks in the mind more easily than free verse. But sometimes people do quote Sandburg's "City of the Big Shoulders,"[12] or Whitman's "I celebrate myself."[13] So, it's not only a matter of rhyme and meter; it's also an issue of sound and voice, a sense of words spoken memorably, with intensity and personality behind the words. Poetry is as much about architecture of sound and voice as it is about image, and the geography of association and metaphor.

We live in a visual, not an oral culture, spending our days studying screens, TV screens, computer screens, phone screens, and sometimes even paper pages. Most of us think of poetry as something seen, not listened to in the air, not attending words with our ear. But when asked to quote something, certain phrases and lines do come to mind. These words and phrases we carry with us, along with advertising slogans and pop lyrics.

What I want to discuss here is not just quotability, memorability of words, but the peculiar authority of poetry. We remember certain lines because of the rightness of sound and sense. Poetry has a special strength no other literary art has, not prose fiction, not essays. How many times have you heard the phrase "Do not go gentle into that good night"[14] worked into reviews or columns or conversations? How many times have you heard someone refer to the phrase "These fragments I have shored against my ruins?"[15] or "Something there is that doesn't love a wall?"[16] or "(I am large, I contain multitudes)."[17]

At moments of grief or stress, excitement or exuberance, lines such as these reassure; they are what we have in common, like quotes from scripture in former times. Much of their authority does come from memorability. These words are out there in the cloud we all have access to. Even in the digital age we reach back to the oral and aural memory for a telling expression.

There are almost as many definitions of poetry as there are poems. Wordsworth most famously stated in the Preface of *Lyrical Ballads*, Second Edition, "Poetry is the spontaneous overflow of powerful feelings; it takes its origins from emotion recollected in tranquility."[18] Emily Dickinson, writing to Thomas Wentworth Higginson, exclaimed, "If I feel physically as if the top of my head is taken off, I know that is poetry . . . is there any other way?"[19] In his great essay "The Poet" of 1844, Ralph Waldo Emerson declared, "For it is not metres, but metre-making arguments, that make a poem."[20] Wallace Stevens, heir to the High Romantic tradition in New England, addressing modern poetry, celebrated "The poem of the mind in the act of finding / What will suffice."[21]

To the Coleridge of *Biographia Literaria* we owe perhaps the definitive thought on the authority of the poetic imagination: "The primary imagination I hold," he writes, "to be the living power and prime agent of all human perception, and as a repetition in the finite mind of the eternal act of creation in the infinite I AM."[22] Having once practiced as a minister, as had Emerson, Coleridge expected the reader to hear the echo of the passage from Exodus 3:14, where the Burning Bush on Mount Sinai says to Moses, asserting supreme authority, "I AM THAT I AM." And later Jesus, in John 8:58, when his authority is challenged, answers, "Before Abraham was, I AM." Half a century after Coleridge, Baudelaire would echo his words: "C'est l' infini dans le fini" or "Beauty is the infinite in the finite."[23] Frost would make a contribution to the discussion also, arguing that a poem is "a momentary stay against confusion,"[24] observing that a poem "begins in delight and ends in wisdom," and that "Like a piece of ice on a hot stove the poem must ride on its own melting."[25]

But less romantic critics have also offered arresting descriptions of poetry. The Victorian Matthew Arnold defined poetry as the "criticism of life,"[26] and he added, "More and more mankind will discover that we have to turn to poetry to interpret life for us, to console us, to sustain us."[27] The New Critic Yvor Winters, concerned to counter the emotional excesses of Romantic poetics, proclaimed, "a poem says something in language about a human experience,"[28] stripping poetry to a bare essence of content. Even Coleridge could be austere, describing poetry as "the best words in the best order."[29] Carl Sandburg notoriously teased that "Poetry is the achievement of the synthesis of hyacinths and biscuits."[30]

All efforts to define poetry are attempts to explain the authority the best poems command. It has been said that poetry has never been as much an integral part of the culture of the United States as it has been in other countries and cultures. In Latin America, leaders and revolutionaries have sometimes been well-known poets. In France politicians announce their favorite poets while campaigning. Some have theorized that the near absence of poetry in our public life has its origins in our immigrant society, broken off from deep roots in classical and ancient poetic traditions. We look forward rather than backward, pragmatic, proud of our get-up-and-go. Poetry is a traditional art, as well as an *avant garde* one. Classical traditions from Europe may seem to have little connection to the way we live. Yet in moments of national crisis, or mourning, poetry is remembered and prized, even cherished, and lines from Frost or Dickinson, or Whitman, are recalled to offer consolation and promise of communality.

What exactly is it about poetry that makes it so appropriate, even necessary, at times of shock and grief? Along with quotes from scripture, the lines offer consolation. In our memorial services, in presidential addresses to the nation, after the assassination of President Kennedy, after 9/11, excerpts from poems were offered to bring us together, to enhance comments of hope and strength, a sense of community. More than sentences from philosophers or great novelists, cadences of poetry seem called for, commensurate with the gravity of the occasion, to reassure us of solidarity.

Some might say it's important at times of crisis that familiar words be spoken, affirming identity and kinship, often lost in a materialistic and selfish culture. No doubt, that is one of the values of poetry, especially traditional poetry. Others might say it's the *oldness* of poetry that reassures, the continuity of a shared culture and language, in a society that often seems centrifugal and broken, without center, evolving so fast there is little confidence of stability. In that way poetry recalls the religious service, phrases and cadences that have been heard so many times over the centuries, in different places, words of prayer and comfort, words of dignity.

The repetition of familiar words yields a special power: "The Lord our God is one God," "As it was in the Beginning, is now and ever shall be, World without end." Others might say it is, in part, metrical perfection and rightness of phrase that give a sense of affirmation and strength to the occasion.

Elizabethan playwrights such as Marlowe and Shakespeare knew that iambic pentameter lines command attention, have an almost magnetic effect on an audience. We are told that when someone speaks with great conviction or emotion, the words tend to fall into an iambic pattern, holding attention. No doubt metrics can be an important factor in the effect poetry can elicit.

But the impact of poetry at moments of emergency or crisis and important rituals may derive also from the way we view or understand poetry. Though caring little about verse in our everyday lives, we still feel it has significance, a more than usual potency, connecting us to mystery, to spiritual things we may resist understanding. Poetry is beyond and above, as well as within us. At momentous times we respond to its peculiar power. Our relationship to poetry is not unlike that of the tourist in Philip Larkin's "Church Going" where someone is forever surprising:

> A hunger in himself to be more serious,
> And gravitating with it to this ground,
> Which, he once heard, was proper to grow wise in,
> If only that so many dead lie round.[31]

Attempts to make poetry a familiar everyday thing has been more successful with those who attempt to write poetry themselves, less with readers. William Carlos Williams has a large following among those who write poems. But others seek in poetry the elaborate, the formal, the surprising. One of the attractions of poetry is that it is not just of the quotidian and familiar. Dylan Thomas is more popular than others because his poems are ritualistic, shamanistic, bardic. They seem to lift the listener to some other realm: "And death shall have no dominion."[32] Attempts to popularize poetry, to make it part of the usual and familiar have, I am told, almost always failed. Thomas's ceremonial poetry has possibly sold more books (and recordings) than any other modern poet.

If poetry drifts too far from evocative sound, it becomes prose-like, starved of its unique power. Prose can be poetic also, but it lacks the ritualistic energy of the best poems, the dance of repetition and variation, advancing and returning. As poetry has become more prose-like, the poetic spirit has survived in rock and roll, rap, country music, for the pleasures of rhyme and measure.

A colleague once said to me that she gave up writing poetry as an undergraduate because she found she had nothing to say. I told her poets find what they want to "say" in the process of writing. Playfulness with language, with images and sounds, with metaphor and voice and form, is a more effective way to get into writing poetry. Poets rarely begin with a thesis and compose a poem to illustrate an argument. Such a poem would have no surprise, once the reader saw where it meant to go. The ability to recognize and incorporate surprise is an essential gift.

Poets, when writing at their best, hear a low voice, which is also their own voice, but beyond their ego, beyond what is merely personal, transcending the individual, to find something more authentic, universal. The genuine is often encountered by seeing the ordinary in a new way and finding the extraordinary in the familiar. The voice of the poem can be the voice of memory, the voice of personality, the voice of craft. But most important is the voice of discovery, of recognition, finding the universal in the specific, while negotiating an arbitrary form, recovering the forgotten.

Oliver Wendell Holmes theorized that the four-beat line of common meter is nearly universal because the line's duration coincides with the length of human breath. In several psychological studies it has been found that the human mind can keep four things in mind at once, on average, though a few can retain as many as seven. These numbers have an analogy to the four accents of common meter, and the variant sometimes called "Poulters' Measure," with more accents.

The German neuroscientist Karl Popper has argued that the four-stress line represents the unit of information the brain can assimilate at once. All these findings seem to echo each other. Common meter is common in so many languages because it and its variants are instinctive. We sing, we recite, and, apparently, we think, in that measure. It has been suggested that even in iambic pentameter the ear recognizes only four strong stresses in each line, as though the ear tends to listen for the more universal pattern.

Even free verse often favors and approximates, tends toward, the four-stress line.

Many of the devices of poetry are effective because they remind us of our earliest perceptions of ourselves and the world around us. Metaphor is powerful because it connects us to the mental state of infancy and childhood where the parts of the world were not differentiated, but integrated. Then we saw things around us as extensions or transformations of ourselves, our bodies. The world we discovered was versions of toes, heads, torso. The world we found was also a body, a face, wonderful, various, and mysterious. Personification can be a powerful dimension of poetry. We speak of a hill's "shoulder." Wordsworth's daffodils toss "their heads in sprightly dance . . . in glee."[33] The water of Usher's tarn is "sullen."[34]

Equally notable is the way poetry reminds us of a time when our senses were not separated, but blended. The infant tastes colors, smells sight, hears flavors, touches music. Synesthesia is one of the most powerful devices of the poetic hoard, along with personification. For Czelaw Milosz, "the smell of silence is old."[35] For Rimbaud, silence is "perfumed";[36] for him, vowels have different colors. In Baudelaire's "Correspondences," all senses echo each other.[37] Several times in the Bible, death is referred to as something to "taste," as in Luke 9: 27. Dylan Thomas refers to "the light of sound."[38] Goethe refers to a cathedral as "frozen music."[39]

To see music, hear color, taste the textures of words, reminds us, psychologists suggest, of memories when all perceptions were fresh and sensations bold and every experience a discovery. Poetry reawakens memories of a time of original perceptions, when the world and we were new to each other, senses intense, and mingled. Poetry reaches back, beyond our education in demarcations, definitions, and logic, to an Eden of unmediated beholding. Poetry helps to recover a glimpse of what we once knew and may have forgotten.

It was Madison Smartt Bell who said the poetic imagination is inspired by "universal animism," universal because it connects everything with everything, animistic because it perceives rivers, wind, stones, stars, as alive.[40] Poetry belongs to a world before dissection, before we defined by difference instead of likeness. As Shelley says in "A Defense of Poetry," "Reason respects differences, and imagination the similitude of things."[41]

Wallace Stevens, in his final illness, liked to quote poetry to those who tended him in the Hartford hospital. It was not his own poems he recited— but Longfellow's. Maybe he thought the nurses and orderlies would respond to Longfellow's work better than to "The Idea of Order at Key West" or "Anecdote of the Jar." Or it may have been that in his final illness the words that came to his tongue were lines memorized in youth, called up at the end of life. The lilt of the dactyls of *Evangeline* and the trochaics of *Hiawatha* delighted him in those terminal days.

Authority is enhanced by the combinations of predictability and surprise. Whether it is in the Pledge of Allegiance, the Lord's Prayer, or the words of a Bar Mitzvah service, the expectation of familiar phrases, and cadences, are an important part of ceremonial energy. But in poetry the repetition of rhymes, parallel phrasing, are also strengthened by variation, difference, along with progression. The unexpected word, sound, or idea must seem unavoidable once encountered. Without variation, repetition becomes predictable; without repetition verse becomes only procession, more prose-like.

Words that stay in the memory have special authority, assurance of continuity, reaching across time and mood of any particular day. As poetry has evolved further from memorization, it has lost some of its original strength. What we carry within us and can recite is already above and beyond the ordinary.

There is the authority of the familiar, of what is already known, but there is also the authority of the strange. Poe often quoted Francis Bacon's observation that "there is no exquisite beauty without some *strangeness* in the proportion."[42] Modern poetry has concentrated on peripheral factors such as fragmentation, difficulty of interpretation, novelty, and randomness, abandoning the essential nature of poetry: rhythm, repetition, predictability *with* surprise, memorability. Modern poetry emphasizes the exceptional, not definitive characteristics. As a result, much of the general audience has slipped away. Poetry is restricted to the classroom, and to those who write it. In the age of the New Criticism poetry became a province for the interpretive elite. In our time poetry has been replaced in academia by the political.

One feature that attracts us to the poetry is its perfection of form. The best poems of the past have a crystalline exactness, an air of ultimate completion. We feel those poems exist in their final incarnation and could not be other than they are. We cannot imagine the 73rd sonnet in any alternate form. Poems rely on the *mot juste*, the supreme choice, and could not be otherwise, in the lattice of a structure set permanently, any more than a Mozart sonata could be corrected. Whether found in a yellowing, dust-covered volume, or in a freshly printed edition, the best lines shine as luminously and vividly as at the moment they were composed.

Poetry aspires to the sacred in a corrupt and confusing world. Poetry lets a reader or audience seek it out. Yet in contrast to perfection of form, or in conjunction with it, there is the spontaneous unfolding of language and voice, phrase by phrase, sentence by sentence, stanza by stanza, conveying the persona of a speaker. The voice must live, in language spoken by a living person to real readers and listeners. This paradox is at the heart of poetry, for the best poetry plays at least two games at once, perfection of arbitrary form, with authenticity of voice, sentences without loss of naturalness and character, passing through an artificial, imposed grid. Much of the delight of poetry derives from this contrast and playfulness, the voice hitting the marks of a chosen pattern, similar to the way a dance has prescribed steps, but refreshing, spontaneous variations.

Since the time of Dante, this combination has been central to European poetry, the classical form in partnership with the contemporary voice. Dante's treatise on poetics was written in Latin, *De Vulgari Eloquentia*, or "the vernacular eloquence." He composed his great poem in formal terza rima stanzas, but in the language of his own time. This pairing of formal pattern and living voice can be illustrated in Janet Lewis's "Helen Grown Old."

> When the last flame had faded from the cloud,
> And by the darkening sea
> The plain lay empty of the arméd crowd,
> Then was she free
> Who had been ruled by passion blind and proud?[43]

In an age of impermanence, when most things are meant to be used and discarded, when nothing is expected to last, whether clothes or electronics, software or hardware, words written decades or centuries ago, that linger in the mind, have a peculiar meaning and weight. As Shakespeare and others liked to brag, the right words in the right order can outlast brass and marble. It's a distinct privilege to attempt, or enjoy, an art that dates from prehistory and can be carried in memory without digital help, to be recited and passed on, generation to generation. In memory, poetry is intimate and vital as breath, pulse, heartbeat.

Ezra Pound's famous "Make it new!" inspired a century of poetry writing and comment about poetry. But more than anyone of his era, Pound prompted an interest in the poetry and ideas of earlier times, whether Confucian Chinese, classical Greek or Roman poetry, Medieval or Renaissance. It's ironic that Pound, the essential Modernist and theorist, who encouraged generations of young writers, had such deep roots in the past. Implicitly, when he tells the young to "make it new," he means "make it old." And it's true that the best new poetry, almost in spite of itself, rediscovers what is ancient in metaphor, in nature, in language itself. As Emerson says, "all language is fossil poetry."[44] Names are derived from other names. A poet benefits from learning the etymological strata in each word. By experiment, by moving forward, a poet often recovers the past. And by moving backward, we can sometimes touch the future.

Poets, and those who write about poetry, speak of the "necessity" of poetry. This is an ironic and provocative claim in the age of smart phones, advertising hype, social media. Most people lead lives with little thought of poetry, at least poetry in the traditional sense. (In a larger consideration, poetry is all around us, in rock and roll songs, industrial designs, scientific jargon.) People have long, productive lives with little thought of verse, except what they may have read in high school, or in some college class. Even educated people, if asked, will assert that they do not understand poetry, and the pieces they see in *The New Yorker* make little sense to them. Prize-winning books of poetry may sell just a few hundred copies and end up remaindered.

So, what is it that is so necessary about poetry? We do know that in the 19th century poets such as Tennyson and Longfellow sold books in the tens of thousands, if not hundreds of thousands. But that kind of popular poetry has long been replaced by prose fiction, television, film, and pop music. In the age of movies and video, poetry has a different pace, timing, a quieter voice, a welcome alternative. Poetry does work that film, novels, and essays cannot. Poetry is language at its quick essence, words that can be repeated, that prompt repetition.

William Carlos Williams famously asserted: "It is difficult to get the news from poems, yet men die miserably every day for lack of what is found there."[45] One way to address the question is to remind ourselves that not every decade or era is a great age of poetry. In the period after the American Civil War, after the explosion onto the scene of Emerson, Poe, Hawthorne, Melville, Whitman, and Thoreau, there were years when nothing of note seemed to appear. This was the age of the Robber Barons, who got their start by profiteering off the war. Emily Dickinson *was* writing great poems, but they would not be known until after her death.

It is indeed desirable that literate people have Whitman, Keats, Hopkins, and Dickinson to return to for pleasure and inspiration. It's important that students and journalists, teachers, all well-informed people who care about culture and language, have these examples to enjoy and remember, and maybe quote "Ozymandias" or "Annabel Lee."

But is it imperative to have contemporary poets and poetry? Who is paying attention? The answer has to be *yes*, because of the challenge to keep the language fresh and vigorous. Even if poets fail in their attempts to achieve great art, those attempts are important, for we learn from the struggle, from each other, in competition with each other, and learn even from failure, by falling short, and knowing it.

Poets benefit from imitation, but more by listening to an inner voice. Poets must go deep into themselves and into language until they hear something that seems their own. That's why poets are often loners. They learn from each other, but they learn more from themselves. That is the harder part; that's what you don't get from a workshop or textbook. Workshops encourage a poetry of facility, an air of mastery without mystery. Learning to listen is more important than learning to workshop, critique, or teach. Learning to see and listen is better than learning to sound smart. Acquiring patience and attention, and recognizing happy accidents, are hardest of all.

Young poets need readers who recognize not only what they have done but what they are capable of. The response is essential, even if it is from only one. Hopkins never published, but was read by Robert Bridges, and one or two others. Dickinson had a sister-in-law who responded to her poetry. The validation is necessary, but it doesn't have to come from a famous critic.

The necessity of poetry depends on the need for memorable language. People who never read poetry can recite parts of "The Raven" or Tennyson's "In the spring a young man's fancy lightly turns to thoughts of love."[46] Journalists and others like to quote from poems that readers and listeners recognize. Most of those who can read can quote from Frost's "The Road Not Taken," or Thomas's "Do not go gentle into that good night." Poetry is part of the glue that holds a culture and a language together, however unaware of it most may be. That doesn't mean that the latest book by a winner of the Pulitzer Prize is necessary. It does mean that a sense of the magic and memorability of words is valuable in a vital community.

To be effective, especially at their endings, poems should have "reach," connecting something close to the faraway, the small with the large, one sense with another, in an unexpected way. Much of the energy of poetry is generated by that reach, which, once encountered, seems unavoidable. My poem "Bellrope" ends:

> the wheel creaked up there as heavy
> buckets emptied out their startle
> and spread a cold splash to farthest
> coves and hollows, then sucked the rope
> back into the loft, leaving just
> the knot within reach, trembling
> with its high connections.[47]

A major test of poetry is that it resonates and resounds across time, raising the language of everyday above the ordinary. That's why it's so hard to judge contemporary work. Poetry is words that ask to be spoken and repeated, but so are advertising slogans. Politicians and advertising writers know that if a phrase is heard enough, it becomes memorable, therefore even memorability is not a sure sign of the quality of poetry.

The audience for novels, film, television, self-help books, cookbooks is much greater, but we look to Emerson, or Shelley, to Wallace Stevens, for the quote that will dignify an argument or an occasion. That authority is rare in contemporary poetry, but it is a power all poetry aspires to. Poetry returns to us at odd moments. Awaking from brain surgery, in a fog of disorientation, I kept repeating Auden's lines, "Follow poet, follow right / to the bottom of the night."[48] Saying the words over and over, I was delighted to discover that "bottom of the night" means just before dawn, and to see the pun on "right." That recognition anchored me in a time of confusion, pain, ambiguity. Repeating the words helped raise me from a cognitive miasma.

In Confucian culture, candidates for promotion to high office were evaluated by their knowledge of the classics. We have no such requirements for advancement in our society, except we do. A knowledge of poetry is still a mark of education and intelligence. Any kind of knowledge is impressive, but a familiarity with poetry is an indication of intelligence and memory, even in our superficial and hurried digital age.

Why does poetry need to be defended? As far back as Sir Philip Sidney, poets were writing treatises defending poetry. Shelley's "A Defense of Poetry" is one of the most inspired and inspiring essays on poetry. Wordsworth's preface to "Lyrical Ballads" and Whitman's introduction to *Leaves of Grass* may be considered breakthroughs in poetry and poetics. Perhaps the impression of a need to defend poetry goes as far back as Plato, a poet himself, who in *Republic* recommended expelling poets from the ideal state because they mislead citizens and destabilize a community. For some, poetry has been seen as, at best, useless, at worst, subversive, yet, even they, read, or maybe write, poetry.

One special feature of poetry, in contrast to prose, is that verse turns, while prose proceeds to the edge of the page until it hits a barrier. The name verse suggests turning. A poem advances and returns at once. The sentence, the unit of narrative or argument, goes forward, while each line of verse whips back on itself to start over. These doubling and contrasting motions give poetry an exceptional energy, not unlike the phrasing of music over the base rhythm, performing two motions simultaneously, proceeding and repeating, advancing and starting over.

A well-known statement of late 20th century poetics goes something like this: "Form is never more than an extension of content." This is yet another version of what was once called "the imitative fallacy," or "the fallacy of affective form," where a poem about the ocean might have wavy lines, or a poem about confusion might appear confusing. One weakness of this argument is that it implies only one dimension of form. The more important feature is the sound, the poem you hear. What do the words mean and suggest; what does the voice imply?

This contemporary idea of poetry leaves out the possibility of contrast and synergy between what is said and the choice of a pattern. A poem where structure only reflects the meaning of the poem would be simplistic and predictable, not taking advantage of the possibilities of verse, and concerned more with the appearance on the page than with the richness of the poem when spoken.

In one of the most memorable lines of Emerson's poem "Bacchus," the intoxicated poet claims to "hear far Chaos talk with me."[49] "Bacchus" is a companion poem to "Merlin," parts I and II. The poems seem to contrast wisdom with intoxication. We soon guess that intoxication can be more stirring than wisdom. Nietzsche would define this difference as Apollonian versus Dionysian. But even with the inspiration of words and perception there must be some control, some shape. Emerson concedes the exciting attraction of the irrational, the siren thrill of delirium, that invigorates the imagination, transcending the merely rational, what is known. The formal must feel the temptation of turbulence and the chaotic, yet pull back to control the energy with lucidity, benefiting at once from both excitement of wildness and the wisdom of form and restraint.

The authority of language has often been associated with political authority, as far back as history can go. In the mead hall of the Anglo-Saxons, in the longhouse of the Iroquois, the leader was most often the figure with the greater persuasive and rhetorical power. Tecumseh of the Shawnees may have been the most eloquent speaker in American history. He could mesmerize and persuade all in his audiences. The ring-giver of the Anglo-Saxons could also "talk the big talk." In modern times rhetorical energy has sometimes been associated with evil genius, the Mussolinis and Hitlers. We have seen this persuasive energy in revival preachers, in politics, and advertising. Sometimes poetry incorporates this kind of force, but more often the lyric poem speaks in a quieter voice, one individual to another. Poetry can be the still, small voice that connects person to person, and, therefore, humanity at large.

Poetry bridges time and the timeless, the flow of time, and the dimension out of time, in Jungian terms, the diachronic and the synchronic. Why was the discovery of Egyptian art and hieroglyphs so important to Walt Whitman in the 1850s? The art of ancient Egypt revealed to him the permanence of the human imagination, the vitality of the present, and the freshness and kinship of art stretching back to remote antiquity.

There is a sense in which the very uselessness of poetry is part of its appeal and value. We don't absolutely have to have music or film or fine cuisine on any given day. We don't have to have exciting architecture or great universities, but our lives are much richer because of them. Part of the appeal of poetry is that it is something extra. The dog does not have to bark at the moon, but doing so thrills it. A mockingbird does not have to imitate the sounds it hears on the breeze, but the variety of imitations seems to inspire it.

It has been said that art mirrors nature and the world of one's experience. But it is also claimed that our modern world is fragmented, no longer coherent. If that is so, does it follow that poetry or other arts must also be fragmented, similar to broken mirrors, each piece reflecting some facet of the shattered whole? By this analogy our poetry should be as shattered as our contemporary culture. But again, would that not be an example of the imitative fallacy? Should not the purpose of a work of the imagination be to make a coherent response to the shattered whole, even if it is a fictive whole? For a poem is not just a reflection, but a structure of imagination. The poet merely reflecting disorder has not done his or her work. If the world is truly broken, it's what we do with the slivers to make a mosaic that's significant. Poetry is not just a reflector of the zeitgeist, but an act of response and creation.

Besides the richness and depths and range of English, there are particular advantages to writing poems in the language. One is that iambics seem natural to this tongue. And buried deep in English is the power of alliteration. Going back to "Beowulf" and forward to Robinson Jeffers, the long lines are enlivened as repeated consonants thrust a voice at the listener, helping to dramatize action, statement, and observation. Alliteration adds to the vitality of the cadence. Deep within the structure of English that pulse waits to be heard, as in Gerard Manley Hopkins's "Duns Scotus's Oxford":

> Of realty the rarest-veinèd unraveller; a not
> Rivalled insight, be rival Italy or Greece.[50]

Much of the verve of modern times is related to science and technology. It's inevitable that poetry would incorporate some of this energy and ways of understanding. Having been raised in a fundamentalist family and congregation, I well recall the exhilaration of learning about Darwinism and evolution. Looking at the anatomy of birds and four-legged animals, I saw at once the logic of Darwin's ideas. Having been taught the world was created about six thousand years ago, I was thrilled to learn of geologic time, atomic time, of mountains and rocks hundreds of millions of years old, of the complexity of atoms and matter, of vast distances to and between the stars. It was music, as though doors were opening to other doors, and worlds opening to further worlds. I have never felt more relief, more delight of possibilities. The fundamentalist world gave me an appreciation of rigor, discipline, and sincerity. Science opened dimensions of depth to past and future, alternative paths of understanding, a larger community, both animate and inanimate.

Although I had learned to recite poems in school, my first personal encounter with poetry occurred when my sister brought home her college textbook, an anthology of American literature. I was in the ninth grade and had never seen such a treasury of writing. Flipping through the pages, one day I came upon Whitman's "Song of Myself" and was struck by the force of the voice:

> I celebrate myself, and sing myself,
> And what I assume you shall assume,
> For every atom belonging to me as good belongs to you.

> I loafe and invite my soul,
> I lean and loafe at my ease observing a spear of summer grass.[51]

It was a revelation that anyone could write that way. The words had such intimacy, and yet elevated music. No poem I had read before had that personal effect. Whitman's lines were raw, charismatic.

The language of poetry can seem either highbrow or lowbrow. But lowbrow incorporated into poetry becomes highbrow. For all the talk of common speech by Wordsworth and later writers, there is a paradox we can't ignore. Read a passage from the best poetry aloud and see if it sounds like common talk. It is common parlance raised to the second power by selection, compression, elevation, context. Poetry by its very nature is elevated. That's why people who are not poets remember Dylan Thomas's lines. We have "common speech" around us all the time. When we go to poetry, we want to hear something we associate with authority, something we can't find just anywhere. All the talk about "everyday language" is part of the paradox: we love poetry that is common language distilled, as fermenting matter is distilled to ardent spirits, or ore refined into metal. We could say that making poems in the language of everyday is part illusion, a trick of the craft. But then all art is illusion, making the artificial seem real, the stone seem to breathe, the paint appear alive. Lyric poetry compresses both language and subject without seeming to. All art is distortion appearing perfectly formed.

The poems we remember have a dimension of unconscious memory, of gatherings in forest shadows, reciting secret phrases, charms, looking into the shade, at light shone through the treetops. Poetry awakens in us something not to be found in daily speech, tapping into pre-consciousness and prehistory.

It has been said that art transcends both the Age and the ego. Any poet knows that when writing poetry at its best, words reach a dimension in language beyond the personal, recovering power buried or implicit in words and combinations of words, re-finding in new idioms what has been there all along, the poetry contributed by the millions who have spoken the words, accumulating etymological depth and richness. Even "autobiographical" poetry finds a universal bedrock beyond the personal. That's what makes poetry relevant to others, however individualistic it might seem.

A poet must let a poem unfold as it will, then revise later. Every poem has its own logic, and part of the challenge, and pleasure, is finding that logic, which may seem strange at first, then inevitable when understood. Young poets may see revision as betrayal of their inspiration. Older poets know revision is a privilege.

There are peculiarities about American poetry, recognized by Emerson as early as his essay "The Poet" of 1844. These peculiarities are caused in part by the unusual history of the United States, its lack of a classical past, its combinations of immigrants and indigenous people, the history of slavery, its irregular systems of education. Taking these factors into account, of both the wilderness and the newly arrived population, Emerson sought to describe what was at hand to inspire a new generation of bards. He exhorted his readers with pronouncements such as "For poetry was written before time was,"[52] and "The poet alone knows astronomy, chemistry."[53] The most radical statement in Emerson's essay occurs near the end as he addresses future poets: "Thou shalt lie close hid with nature, and canst not be afforded to the Capital or exchange . . . And this is thy Reward. The ideal shall be real to thee . . ."[54]

It is as though Emerson foresaw that the Whitmans and Dickinsons and Stevenses could be out of the contemporary literary mainstream, off to the side in their own seclusion, because of the fragmentation of American culture, its diversity and contradictions, its absence of coherence and literary center, yet speaking for all.

Emerson and other poets of the nineteenth century, recognized nature as the universal language of reference. Technologies change rapidly, as fashions alter overnight, with slang and name-brand products. But stars and flowers, rivers, woods, soil and gravity, reach across time, and through time. Stars and weeds belong to a permanent idiom, sustained even through different languages and translations. Nature, freshly seen, will always be the reference for the poetic imagination. T. S. Eliot's poetry embraces an intimacy with the natural world not often recognized.

It is difficult to discuss the so-called elitism of poetry. Some of the authority of poetry can lie in the fact that only a small portion of the population is actually engaged with or by poetry. For all Whitman's claims to be the poet of the masses, he was read mostly by the educated intellectuals of his time. Poetry can seem almost like a secret language, like pure mathematics, masonic symbols, ancient Latin or Greek. Many think of poetry as a feature of priest-craft, to be explicated in seminars and learned journals. And there is a satisfaction in knowing the "real" meaning of poems such as Hopkins's "Heraclitean Fire," which is hard to comprehend.

At the other end of the spectrum, we enjoy poems of classic plainness, poems with few metaphors or images, language stripped almost to bare statement, sometimes described as the "plain style." This may be the hardest poetry to write because a poet cannot hide behind ornament or obscurity, must have something of interest to say. Usually, these poems are metrical or pleasing with music in other ways. Examples include Ben Jonson's "To Heaven," Dickinson's "Success is counted sweetest," or J.V. Cunningham's "Epigram 43":

> In whose will is our peace? Thou happiness,
> Thou ghostly promise, to thee I confess
> Neither in thine nor love's nor in that form . . .
> . . . And if I rest not till I rest in thee
> Cold as thy grace, whose hand shall comfort me?[55]

Some poets write in several styles. Wallace Stevens can be spare and abstract, or elaborate and ornamental as a baroque cathedral. It is the former that is most difficult, beyond the reach of many readers, while seeming plain on the surface. A poem of plain statement can become more challenging with every reading.

As we grow older, we appreciate more and more the poetry of simplicity. Plainness requires the poet to be clear about what is said and how it's said. A poetry of clarity must have something to say. In its crystalline lattice of words, a poem should express thoughts worth repeating, and say them memorably. Over the years the poetry of simplicity, though harder to achieve, ages better, stays fresher, worthy of re-reading.

Luckily there are many mansions in the house of poetry, ranging from the ambiguity of a Mallarmé sonnet, and the obscurity of phrasing in Gerard Manley Hopkins, to the bold statements of Dickinson, and the sweeping rhetoric of Whitman. We love the learning woven into *The Waste Land*, the voice at play in Marianne Moore's work, the aestheticism of Wallace Stevens, and the seemingly plain surface of Robert Frost, often disguising darker strata. One kind of voice, one kind of poetics, does not cancel out all the rest. Dogmatic assertions of preference may be useful to a critic making a point, even useful to readers. Yet almost anything we pronounce about poetry can be contradicted, with plausible evidence.

When I worked as a laborer and house painter, I thought of poetry as something extra, something to cherish on holidays and weekends, in afterhours, something to treasure and hold in mind while my hands were busy with shovel or paint brush. Poetry added another dimension, and delight. Those who teach, or have freedom to write whenever they choose, may lose that recognition of the gift of poetry, the added value to their lives. Familiarity can erase the sense of wonder and reward.

In important ways we can see history as the biggest poem, an epic poem. After the natural world, history is our greatest standard of reference. One key to understanding Walt Whitman is the exuberance of the 1840s and 1850s. One clue to grasping T. S. Eliot is the horror of WWI and its aftermath. The poet touches and magnifies features of the past but cannot be overwhelmed by the sheer complexity and scale of history. The multiplicities of time may be revealed by shaping and selective editing.

Like all art, poems exist for their own time, as well as for all time. The Greeks believed the muses were the daughters of Memory. The poet draws on memory to recreate the discoveries of childhood, of the past, but depends equally on imagination to create what has not been thought of before, and make it seem always there, authoritative, inevitable, timeless. When all else seems mere entertainment, poetry remains.

NOTES

1. Walt Whitman, *Poetry and Prose.* 246.

2. William Butler Yeats. "Leda and the Swan." *Collected Poems of W.B. Yeats.* New York: The Macmillan Company, 1964. 211.

3. Poe, *Poetry and Tales.* 62.

4. Poe, *Poetry and Tales.* Ibid.

5. Poe, *Poetry and Tales.* Ibid.

6. Robert Frost. *Collected Poems, Prose, & Plays.* 70.

7. Whitman, "There Was a Child Went Forth." *Poetry and Prose.* 138.

8. William Shakespeare. "Sonnet 73." *The Riverside Shakespeare.* 2nd ed. Ed. G. Blakemore Evans. Houghton Mifflin, 1997. 1856.

9. Christopher Smart. *Jubilate Agno.* 1939. Westport, CN: Greenwood Press, 1969. 67.

10. Frost, "Stopping by Woods on a Snowy Evening." *Collected Poems, Prose, & Plays.* 207.

11. Poe, "The Raven." *Poetry and Tales.* 81.

12 Sandburg, *Collected Poems.* 3.

13 Whitman, *Poetry and Prose.* 188.

14. Dylan Thomas. "Do Not Go Gentle into That Good Night." *Dylan Thomas:*

Collected Poems, 1934–1953. eds. Walford Davies and Ralph Maud. London: Orion Books, 2000. 188.

15. T. S. Eliot. "The Waste Land." *Complete Poems, 1909–1962.* New York: Harcourt Brace & Company, 1991. 69.

16. Frost, "Mending Wall, *Collected Poems, Prose, & Plays.* 39.

17. Whitman, *Poetry and Prose.* 246.

18. William Wordsworth, and Samuel Taylor Coleridge. *Lyrical Ballads, 1798 and 1802.* ed. Fiona Stafford. Oxford: Oxford University Press, 2013. 99.

19. Emily Dickinson. *The Letters of Emily Dickinson.* eds. Christanne Miller and Domhnall Mitchell. Cambridge: The Belknap Press, 2024. 502.

20. Ralph Waldo Emerson. *Essays & Lectures.* 450.

21. Wallace Stevens. *The Palm at the End of the Mind: Selected Poems and a Play.* ed. Holly Stevens. New York: Vintage Books, 1972. 174.

22. Samuel Taylor Coleridge. *Biographia Literaria.* 1817. ed. Adam Roberts. Edinburgh: Edinburgh University Press, 2014. 205.

23. Charles Baudelaire. *The Painter of Modern Life and Other Essays.* ed. and trans. Jonathan Mayne. London: Phaidon, 1964. 97.

24. Robert Frost. *Selected Prose of Robert Frost.* eds. Hyde Cox and Edward Connery Latham. New York: Collier Books, 1966. 18.

25. Frost, *Selected Prose.* 20.

26. Matthew Arnold. "The Study of Poetry." *Victorian Poetry and Prose.* eds. Lionel Trilling and Harold Bloom. New York: Oxford University Press, 1973. 251.

27. Arnold, "The Study of Poetry." 234.

28. Yvor Winters. *Forms of Discovery.* Denver: Alan Swallow, 1967. xii.

29 Samuel Taylor Coleridge. *Specimens of Table Talk, July 20, 1827.* London: John Murray, 1836. 45.

30. Carl Sandburg. "Definitions of Poetry." *Complete Poems,* 319.

31. Philip Larkin. "Church Going." *Collected Poems.* ed. Anthony Thwaite. New York: FSG, 2003. 59.

32. Thomas. *Collected Poems,* 56.

33. William Wordsworth. "I Wandered Lonely as a Cloud." *William Wordsworth: Selected Poems.* ed. Stephen Gill. New York: Penguin, 2004. 164.

34. Poe, "The Fall of the House of Usher." *Poetry and Tales.* 320.

35. Czeslaw Milosz. *The Princeton Encyclopedia of Poetry and Poetics.* ed. Alex Preminger, et al. Princeton: Princeton University Press, 1965. 840

36. Arthur Rimbaud. "The Ladies Who Look for Lice." *Arthur Rimbaud: Complete Works.* Trans. Paul Schmidt. New York: HarperPerennial, 2008. 86.

37. Charles Baudelaire. "Correspondences." *Flowers of Evil.* 1857. Trans. George

Dillon and Edna St. Vincent Millay. New York: Washington Square Press, 1962. 161.

38. Thomas, "From Love's First Fever to Her Plague." *Collected Poems*. 21.

39. Johann Wolfgang von Goethe. *Conversations of Goethe with Johann Peter Eckermann*. Trans. John Oxenford. ed. J. K. Moorhead. Boston: Da Capo Press, 1998. 303.

40. Madison Smartt Bell. "Lecture." Chattanooga, Tennessee. Spring 1991.

41. Percy Bysshe Shelley. "A Defense of Poetry." *Romantic Poetry and Prose*. eds. Harold Bloom and Lionel Trilling. London: Oxford University Press, 1973. 746–762.

42. Poe, *Poetry and Tales*. 263.

43. Janet Lewis. "Helen Grown Old." *Poems Old and New, 1918–1978*. Athens: Swallow Press, 1981. 62.

44. Emerson, *Essays & Lectures*. 190.

45. William Carlos Williams. *Collected Poems II*. New York: New Directions, 1950. 318.

46. Alfred, Lord Tennyson. "Locksley Hall." *Alfred Lord Tennyson: Selected Poems*. ed. Christopher Ricks. New York: Penguin, 2007. 53.

47. Robert Morgan. "Bellrope." *At the Edge of the Orchard Country*. 30.

48. W. H. Auden. "In Memory of W.B. Yeats." *Collected Poems of W. H. Auden*. ed. Edward Mendelson. New York: Vintage International, 1991. 248.

49. Ralph Waldo Emerson. "Bacchus." *Emerson's Prose and Poetry*. eds. Joel Porte and Saundra Morris. New York: Norton, 2001. 453.

50. Gerard Manly Hopkins. "Dun Scotus's Oxford." *Gerard Manley Hopkins: Poetry and Prose*. ed. W. H. Gardner. London: Penguin, 1970. 40.

51. Whitman, *Poetry and Prose*. 188.

52. Emerson, *Essays & Lectures*. 449.

53. Emerson, *Essays & Lectures*. 456.

54. Emerson, *Essays & Lectures*. 467.

55. J. V. Cunningham. "Epigram 43." In *Quest for Reality*. eds. Yvor Winters and Kenneth Fields. Chicago: Swallow Press, 1969. 171.

AFTERWORD

HEALING

Robert Morgan

The epileptic brain has its own logic and reasons. Though dampened by Keppra or Vimpat or some other anti-seizure drug, it fires off random signals to leg and toes, to cramp and burn, to seethe and tremble, as though threatening the body. Without the drug the brain would trigger the body to attack itself full strength, firing neurons, resulting in a sense of falling, falling, until consciousness fades. The epileptic brain likes to conceal its causes even from experts. The brain wants to show its authority over both body and mind and over sleep. Even when subdued, the epileptic brain presides, and reminds us of its lurking presence, concealing its secrets, the rogue half of self that must be lived with.

2013 was my year of bad news. In February I was diagnosed with CML, Chronic Myeloid Leukemia. As frightening as that may sound, it turned out that the condition could be controlled by a drug called Gleevec or Imatinib, discovered a few years earlier by a doctor named Drucker. Without it I would have had chemo and possibly a bone marrow transplant. With the Gleevec I felt perfectly healthy.

In June of that year, I happened to be at my house in western North Carolina when I began to feel weak and dizzy, with pains in my torso. Realizing this was something serious, and that I knew no doctors in North Carolina, I packed my car at 2AM and drove all the way back to Ithaca, New York, a journey of thirteen hours. Hurrying to the emergency room, I was given an EKG because of the chest pains. Then I was taken to the hospital where for three days I was given test after test, including a stress test. Finally, the doctors conceded my heart was fine.

But before release I was subjected to an MRI. A tumor, a meningioma, was discovered on the top of my brain, on the left side. To break the news to me a team entered my room, a neurologist, a surgeon, a nurse, a social worker, and maybe a chaplain. They explained that the tumor was most likely benign and had been there for several years. I was told to follow up with a visit to the neurologist, and the next day I was sent home, still weak and with pain in my lower abdomen.

In the days that followed I continued to grow weaker. While in the hospital I had asked a nurse if I might have Lyme disease. She said no because I did not have a rash. I grew so weak I could hardly stand. Walking was a challenge.

After almost two months I called my GP and he gave me a blood test for Lyme disease, which proved positive. As I took the antibiotic, I slowly began to feel better. I'd lost forty pounds and had little energy. But I could walk and work again, and the pain in my lower abdomen faded. When on book tour for a new novel that September, people told me I looked like a ghost of myself.

But that still left the meningioma on the top of my head. The neurologist in Ithaca referred me to a neurosurgeon in Rochester. More MRIs were taken, and the neurosurgeon pointed out there had been little change in the tumor since it was first discovered. It was almost certainly benign, and I'd experienced no noticeable side effects. He recommended we just keep an eye on the meningioma by taking another MRI every six months. For the next six years that's what we did. The tumor seemed to have stabilized, or crystallized, and I experienced no recognizable problems. The Lyme disease had left me with only a little neuropathy in my left hand, and I expected to live to the age of ninety.

As the months and years passed, the meningioma came to seem like a friendly ghost, sitting on the top of my brain, but causing me no apparent difficulties. It was with me wherever I went, and it saw whatever I saw. I wondered if the tumor affected my dreams or interfered with my thought process.

Until April 7, 2020. The day before I had dug several wheelbarrow loads of wet soil to fill in the subsidence around a new septic tank. It was heavier work than I was used to at the age of seventy-five. I felt tired, but it was a good fatigue. I went to bed and slept soundly. But around one A.M. I woke with a searing fire in the calf of my left leg. I was helpless to stop it, and the pain was unbearable as the leg began to shake. The burning pain reached my abdomen and chest, and then a thousand Fourth of July fireworks exploded in my head, and I began to fall backwards, with nothing to hold onto, as if from forty thousand feet, falling and falling, and then I blacked out.

When I woke paramedics were hovering over me saying "We think you've had a stroke." According to my wife I had been unconscious for half an hour, and she was unable to wake me. Wearing only a housecoat, I was trundled in a kind of chair out into the cold night and loaded into an ambulance. By the time I was in the vehicle my head was clearing. At the hospital I was given a series of tests. To get out of the emergency room with its threat of coronavirus, I agreed to be admitted to the hospital. For three days I was subjected to more tests. A neurologist told me the *grand mal* seizure was almost certainly caused by the meningioma. I was given the anti-convulsive drug Keppra. After three days I was sent home.

What followed was caused by either my misunderstanding, or my lack of attention. I looked at the bottle of Keppra given me at the hospital and saw it was a thirty-day supply with no refills. For some reason that "No re-fills" suggested that I did not need to continue taking it after the bottle was used up. The seizure was one episode and now it was over.

Four days after the Keppra ran out I had another seizure, not quite as grand as the first, but painful and scary. I was only unconscious after the fireworks and sense of falling for about ten minutes. As soon as it was business hours, I called the neurosurgeon and got a prescription for Keppra.

But this time my experience with Keppra was very different. It made me shivery and shaky. I had chills and felt very fatigued. Once while mowing the lawn my legs began to tremble and buckle and I fell on the grass, assuming another seizure was coming on, but it never did. After a few minutes the trembling stopped and was I able to pull myself up on a fence post. But the shaking returned often. The neurologist suggested I double the dose of Keppra, and I began to take 2000 mg every day.

The extra Keppra made my legs feel encased in lead. I grew weaker and could only work in the yard for a few minutes. I lived in fear of another seizure. The neurologist suggested that I suffered from a combination: the brain trying to have a seizure suppressed by the Keppra, the side effects of the Keppra, and panic caused by fear of another seizure. Desperate, I called the neurosurgeon in Rochester. He referred me to one of his associates, the head of neurosurgery at the medical school. I drove up to Rochester for an appointment with the surgeon and another MRI. The MRI showed the meningioma had not changed very much, but apparently it had crossed over the center of the brain and now affected the left side because the first seizure had begun in the left leg. Now, fearing another *grand mal* seizure, I opted for surgery to remove the meningioma.

The neurosurgeon did not exactly recommend surgery but was ready to take on the job. I signed forms that admitted I knew such surgery could have side effects, including possible death. I was told there might be seizures after the surgery, but somehow that did not seem so significant, if I could get rid of the meningioma, and the odds were that all would be well. No one explained that because of my age the risks of motor control damage were increased. The meningioma had grown on a part of the brain that controlled motor functions.

From the MRIs it was clear there was a great deal of edema, or swelling, around the tumor. It was the swelling that was most dangerous and had probably caused the seizures. The swelling was blocking a major sinus on top of the brain. That was the detail that tipped the balance toward surgery. I did not want to risk further swelling. Another consideration was my age. If the meningioma had to be removed, better have it done while I was still young enough and healthy enough to recover.

Surgery was scheduled for June 23rd, 2020. In the days leading up to the operation I tried to put my manuscripts and affairs in order. I wanted to be calm and optimistic. The directions called for me to be at the hospital for prep by 5:30 a.m. Because of the coronavirus I did not want to risk staying in a motel near Rochester the night before. We left Ithaca at 3 a.m. Because of the pandemic no one could accompany me into the hospital nor visit later. I felt remarkably peaceful as we drove through small towns and countryside in the middle of the night. Familiar landmarks looked very different in the dark. As I strolled into the hospital, I didn't know it was the last time I would ever walk normally.

In the preparation room I had to take off all my clothes and change into a hospital gown. A team of anesthesiologists gathered and entertained me with cheerful banter. They assured me that from my point of view the surgery would last only seconds. I was wheeled into the bright operating room and hooked up to a least two IVs.

Sure enough, the next thing I knew I was waking in a dimly lit recovery room, and nurses were checking blood pressure and temperature and heart rate every few minutes. I was told I had been given three units of blood during the surgery. Another unit was transfused into me to prevent anemia. There was no pain. I had been given Tylenol, but throughout the aftermath of the surgery I would feel little if any pain. A drain had been placed in the side of my head and from time to time someone replaced the bottle that filled with red liquid. A catheter was in place, and periodically the bag of urine was exchanged for an empty one.

As I lay in bed with all that attention, I moved my limbs and found everything intact, except I couldn't wiggle the toes on my right foot. I tried again and discovered there was no feeling below the knee on my right leg. "You are in trouble," I said to myself. I touched my right hip and was relieved to feel the touch. At least the paralysis was only below the right knee. I touched my left foot to my right and could feel the topical contact.

Since the meningioma was on the left side of the brain, mostly, it made sense that if there was damage it would be on the right side of the body. When the surgeon came by, he agreed that motor control in the right foot had been damaged, but assured me I would recover it, or most of it, with Rehab. He promised me I would be astonished by the improvements following physical therapy. The doctor and all his team were extremely upbeat.

I was courteous to the medical staff, but I knew things were far from upbeat. As I lay in the step-down room, hooked up to many tubes and wire monitors of heart and breath, I knew I was in deep trouble. How much of my right side would be affected by the paralysis? Might the paralysis get worse instead of better? I thought of Walt Whitman whose stroke in 1873 had left him partly paralyzed for the rest of his life. I thought of Whitman's notes in *Specimen Days* about him hobbling into the woods and spending his days observing trees, birds, flowers, clouds and recalling his youth and service in the military hospitals during the Civil War. I thought of the writer Reynolds Price who spent his life in a wheelchair after radiation therapy left him paralyzed below the waist.

When I was moved to a ward for recovering from neurosurgery, I found myself curious about those suffering from long-term disability. I was looking at things from a new point of view. The nurses still took my temperature and blood pressure every hour and, for the first time, meals were brought to me. I found the hospital kitchen liked to offer sweet things, brownies, cake, maple syrup on pancakes and waffles. The catheter was extracted, and I was told to pee in a bottle. But out my window I found I could view the majestic medieval tower of the University of Rochester library with clouds floating beyond. The sight suggested timelessness, and the spirituality of another age.

But all was not peaceful in the ward. An elderly woman in the bed next to mine, behind a curtain, groaned and screamed throughout the day and night. She called for her daughter Judy and cursed the nurses when they tried to help her. I got little sleep as she moaned and swore hour after hour.

As I lay in bed with nothing to do, I began to explore memory. I picked through my earliest memories, of the days and nights when we lived in the old Morgan house when I was two or three. I recalled the smells of the smokehouse and spring house, the Irish junipers above the bank, a snake in the yard I almost picked up, the steps down to the outdoor toilet, the tractor that came to plow the bottomlands in spring, the ground fogs on the fields by the river in early morning, the biplane that swooped down in summer to dust the fields with insecticide, the looming presence of Cicero Mountain across the river.

On my third day in the ward, New York State lifted the ban of visitors in hospitals. My wife Nancy was allowed to bring some clothes and mail. This made a considerable difference, contact with the outside and more normal world. And I was told that the next day I would be discharged from the hospital wing and moved to the Rehab wing. The move occurred on a Saturday, and all was quiet on the Rehab floor. There was no therapy on Saturday.

In Rehab I had no window on a medieval tower, and my roommate, who had suffered a stroke, had difficulty speaking. I could not walk, but I could speak normally. As I lay in bed, I continued to investigate memory, thinking of incidents, both painful and pleasant, not recalled in years. Memory led to memory. Many incidents concerned my father, his failures in practical ways, his considerable kindness. My wife brought a notebook, and I began to list facts, images, and my feelings about him. I'd written poems and shorter memoirs about my dad. I decided I had not been completely fair to him and decided to write another essay about him, a longer memoir, stressing his virtues in a selfish world. Over the next two weeks I listed over three hundred facts recalled about him, for an article or longer memoir.

Rehab was helpful, but not as useful as it might have been. There were only two, or sometimes three, sessions each day, including occupational therapy where I practiced using my hands for ordinary tasks, taking showers, getting in and out of bed, speech therapy with tests of cognitive skills, physical therapy where I practiced standing, walking with a walker, mounting steps, strengthening leg muscles. Slowly I made progress, learning to walk further with the walker. But ninety percent of the time in Rehab was spent sitting in a wheelchair or lying in bed. The long stretches of time could have seemed lethal. I could watch television, or try to read, but my mind seemed in a fog following surgery. Yet my memories were clear, and I mostly made notes for my memoir.

Strangely, there were parts of my Rehab days that I enjoyed. I came to depend on the nurses and their associates who responded at all hours when I pressed the call button. They would bring me water or ginger ale and empty the urine bottle. They helped me dress in the morning and undress in the evening. They were courteous and usually attentive. When I switched on the TV most of the news was about the coronavirus and the many infections and deaths as the pandemic surged and people refused to wear masks. Oddly, I felt safe in the hospital, isolated from the raging disease and the violence on the streets, in a sanctuary. All the staff wore masks, and many wore shields over their eyes. I imagined I was in a monastery or convent, a place set aside.

I enjoyed the routines at times, the time to sleep and the time for waking, even the times I was wheeled to the bathroom. Luckily, I was soon able to dress myself, to wash myself, to shift from bed to wheelchair. I began to think of the process of recovery, and the many occasions when I had been healed of wounds or sickness. Despair was just under the surface, the knowledge that I might never be able to walk as before. But I was told that I *would* be able to walk again, with the walker and maybe I could one day graduate to a cane. Otherwise, I was healthy and strong.

I was told again and again that the brain could learn to "rewire" itself, teach itself to control the right leg below the knee, that step by step the motor control could come back. The word that dominated my thoughts was "healing," that wonderful ability of the body to bring itself back to health. It was a matter of patience, of hard work, of letting time do its work. In my childhood I had recovered from measles, whooping cough, mumps, scarlet fever, pneumonia, and later from eye surgery, Lyme disease, flu. Healing was a metaphor for life itself. We are always threatened by injury, disease. Often, we just have to stand back and let nature do its work.

As my discharge day approached, I felt a certain dread. Would I be able to function on the outside? I'd come to depend on the nursing and therapy staff. What would it feel like to be released on my own recognizance? Yet I wanted more than anything to escape the hospital, to be free to set my own hours and routines again. I was afraid and I was thrilled at the prospect of release. The question could I navigate on my own at home kept worrying me, though I knew perfectly well my wife would be there to help me.

I had been told by the Rehab doctor that I was subject to extreme apnea. She recommended a device called a CPAP machine with a mask that fitted over the nose and mouth. When breathing stopped the machine kickstarted it. I first tried the mask while in the Rehab wing of the hospital. The first night it felt intrusive and awkward. But on the second night I found I did sleep longer and better. It was mysterious that in the morning I was more alert, even in the mental fog caused by the surgery.

As we drove back to Ithaca from Rochester with my new walker on July 15th, 2020, the countryside seemed a revelation, as though I'd forgotten the green of fields and woods. Tractors were baling hay, the metal silos gleamed. The people in villages and small towns went about their business unaware that I'd had surgery and spent almost a month in the hospital. The world in no way depended on me or was aware of me. Whatever happened to me, things would continue in their own ways. It was exactly the middle of the summer, and the people were occupied with their seasonal work.

As we approached the house, I did feel trepidation. Would I be able to negotiate the steps into the kitchen with the walker? Nancy had had grab bars installed at that door. Would those help with my entry? To reach the laundry room from the garage I had to step across a threshold. To reach the kitchen from the laundry room I had to climb two steps, one sixteen inches wide. As it turned out, I did not have much trouble getting out of the car to the walker, or crossing the threshold, or even mounting the steps into the kitchen. The grab bars were in just the right places. It was only when I reached the dining room and sat down that I realized how worried I'd been; I was trembling, but I'd made it. I was home.

Now that I was in my own house, the real work of rehabilitation could begin. A therapist came the next day and gave me a set of exercises to perform at least twice a day. On her second visit she gave another, more difficult set, and added short walks with the walker. I probably had not had such workouts since Physical Ed in college. I was still weak from surgery and lying in the hospital for twenty-two days.

The threat of post-operative depression hovered near me. Would I spend the rest of my life hobbling around with a walker or maybe restricted to a wheelchair, unable to work outside or drive a car, stand up to lecture? Could I go to the bathroom by myself? Carry a drink from the refrigerator? Was my writing at an end? Would friends still contact me and visit when they learned I was disabled?

I recognized there was self-pity in such thoughts. Self-pity was a bath to luxuriate in. If I sank into it there would be no way back or out. Fortunately, I had the exercises, and the practice with the walker. I wanted more than anything to walk with the walker, and to regain my strength after the more than six hours under anesthesia. I walked every hour doing a two-step, right foot, left foot, move with the walker.

To my surprise, my strength began to return now that I was out of the hospital. From one day to the next I didn't notice the change, but from week to week it was obvious. I could stand holding to nothing but my balance. The therapist assigned me harder exercises and urged me to try walking continuously, pushing the walker ahead steadily as one step rolled onto the next. Gradually I found that possible to do if I set my right foot down firmly on the heel.

During the third week home I ventured outside with the walker and made my way down the driveway to the road and back. It was the first time I'd been outside in more than a month. Grasshoppers clicked and flicked around the garden. I heard a cicada in the trees. As I returned by the red shed a cricket signaled in the shade of the aspens, telling us that autumn was not that far away.

My ambition became to walk with a cane, the four footed quadcane, now that I could stand, and take a few steps holding to nothing. If I could walk with a cane so many other places would be accessible to me, in my study, library. When I tried the quadcane I saw this aid would have its own challenges. First, when the cane was moved forward, the four little feet would have to be set firmly on the floor before a step was taken. The walking had to be a two-step again, right foot, left foot, move the cane ahead, right foot, left foot, move the cane ahead. But I was out there on my own, left hand on the handle, moving forward in space.

Two months after leaving the hospital I found I could walk with a regular cane. All I had to do was concentrate on balance, with three points touching the floor or ground. That gave me a new sense of freedom, out in open space, independent. Next, I discovered that for short distances I could walk holding to nothing.

One of the mysteries of healing is that it is invisible. At any given time, you cannot see the act of healing any more than you can see the process of history unfolding. You can only witness the results, the wound scabbing over, the strength returned to a limb, like a stream clearing after pollution is reduced, a mind clearing after trauma. Healing takes place in time, a slow piece of music played silently. Healing is as much emotional as it is physical. We heal in part because we are determined to heal. Several times in my life I have put pain and trauma behind me simply by persisting and believing that I could and then waking later to realize that I had moved on. There is a saying that "ninety percent of life is just showing up," but sometimes it takes an act of will to show up. The existential and essential truth about healing is you let time and hope do their work.

What have I gained from this chapter of my life? I have learned that the world looks different from long days in a wheelchair, and that we must depend on others: we cannot grow just on our own. I have learned to appreciate the absence of pain, and to see things from the perspective of the disabled more than ever before. I have learned to see with fresh eyes the dedication of nurses and therapists. As I have come closer to my death, I have seen it is neither friend nor stranger, only a milestone, a fact. I have learned that life itself is a process of healing, emotional, physical, perceptual, cognitive healing. I have seen that even our worst moments are part of the adventure.

BIBLIOGRAPHY

Arnold, Matthew. "The Study of Poetry." *Victorian Poetry and Prose*. Eds. Lionel Trilling and Harold Bloom. New York: Oxford University Press, 1973. 233–254.

Auden, W. H. "In Memory of W.B. Yeats." *Collected Poems of W. H. Auden*. ed. Edward Mendelson. New York: Vintage International, 1991. 248.

Augustine. *Confessions*. Translated by F.J. Sheed. Indianapolis: Hackett Publishing Company, 1993.

Baudelaire, Charles. "Bènèdiction." *Baudelaire: Selected Verse with an Introduction and Plain Prose Translations by Francis Scarfe*. Baltimore: Penguin Books, 1961.

———. "Correspondences." *Flowers of Evil*. Dillon and Millay. 161.

———. *Baudelaire: Selected Writings on Art and Artists*. 1972. Trans. P. E. Charvet. New York: Penguin, 1993.

———. "Edgar Allan Poe: Life and Works, from the French of Charles Baudelaire." Trans. H. Curwen. *The Works of Edgar Allan Poe*. London: John Camden Hotten. 1873. 17. www.eapoe.org/papers/misc1851/1873000m.htm. Accessed 11 June 2024.

———. *The Painter of Modern Life and Other Essays*. ed. and trans. Jonathan Mayne. London: Phaidon, 1964.

Bell, Madison Smartt. "Lecture." Chattanooga, Tennessee, Spring 1991.

Bierstadt, Albert. "The Sierras Near Lake Tahoe, California." Oil on panel. 1865. https://www.wikiart.org/en/albert-bierstadt/the-sierras-near-lake-tahoe-1865. Accessed 11 June 2024.

Bloom, Harold. "Introduction" to *Geoffrey Hill: Collected Poems*. Oxford: Oxford University Press, 1986. xiii.

———. "Passionate Beholder of America in Trouble." *The New York Times*. 8 February 1987. Section 7, Page 13. www.nytimes.com/1987/02/08/books/passionate-beholder-of-america-in-trouble.html. Accessed 25 July 2024.

Blotner, Joseph. *Faulkner: A Biography*. 1974. One Volume Edition. New York: Vintage, 1991.

Bly, Robert. "Watering the Horse." *Silence in the Snowy Fields*. Middletown, CT: Wesleyan. University Press, 1962. 139.

Brooke, Rupert. "The Soldier." *Rupert Brooke: Collected Poems*. Cambridge: The Oleander Press, 2010. 133.

Coleridge, Samuel Taylor. *Biographia Literaria*. 1817. ed. Adam Roberts. Edinburgh: Edinburgh University Press, 2014.

———. *Specimens of Table Talk,* July 20, 1827. London: John Murray, 1836.

Cunningham, J. V. "Epigram 43." In *Quest for Reality*. eds. Yvor Winters and Kenneth Fields. Chicago: Swallow Press, 1969. 171.

Davies, Paul. "Is Nature Mathematical?" *New Scientist*. March 21, 1992. 34–40. www.newscientist.com/article/mg13318134-400-is-nature-mathematical. Accessed 20 July 2024.

DeVoto, Bernard. "Genius is Not Enough." *The Saturday Review of Literature* 13. April 25, 1936. 3–4, 14–15. www.degruyter.com/document/doi/10.4159/ harvard.9780674865488.c16/html. Accessed 11 June 2024.

Dickinson, Emily. "Poem 1400." *The Complete Poems of Emily Dickinson*. ed. Thomas H. Johnson. 1890. Boston: Little, Brown and Company, 1952. 599–600.

———. "Letter to Thomas Wentworth Higginson." *The Letters of Emily Dickinson*. eds. Christanne Miller and Domhnall Mitchell. Cambridge: The Belknap Press, 2024. 502.

Donald, David Herbert. *Look Homeward: A Life of Thomas Wolfe*. Boston: Little, Brown, 1987.

Dykeman, Wilma. *Family of Earth: A Southern Mountain Childhood*. Chapel Hill: University of North Carolina Press, 2016.

———. *Return the Innocent Earth*. New York: Holt, Rinehart and Winston, 1973.

———. *The Far Family*. New York: Holt, Rinehart and Winston. 1966.

———. *The French Broad*. Knoxville: University of Tennessee Press, 1965.

———. *The Tall Woman*. New York: Holt, Rinehart and Winston, 1962.

Eastlake, William. "Sense of Place." *South Dakota Review*. Volume 36, Number 1 (Spring) 1998. 144.

Eliot, T. S. *Complete Poems, 1909–1962*. New York: Harcourt Brace & Company, 1991.

Emerson, Ralph Waldo. *Essays & Lectures*. ed. Joel Porte. New York: Library of America, 1983.

———. "Bacchus." *Emerson's Prose and Poetry*. eds. Joel Porte and Saundra Morris. New York: Norton, 2001. 453.

Frost, Robert. "After Apple Picking." *Collected Poems, Prose, & Plays*. eds. Richard Poirier and Mark Richardson. New York: Library of America, 1995. 70.

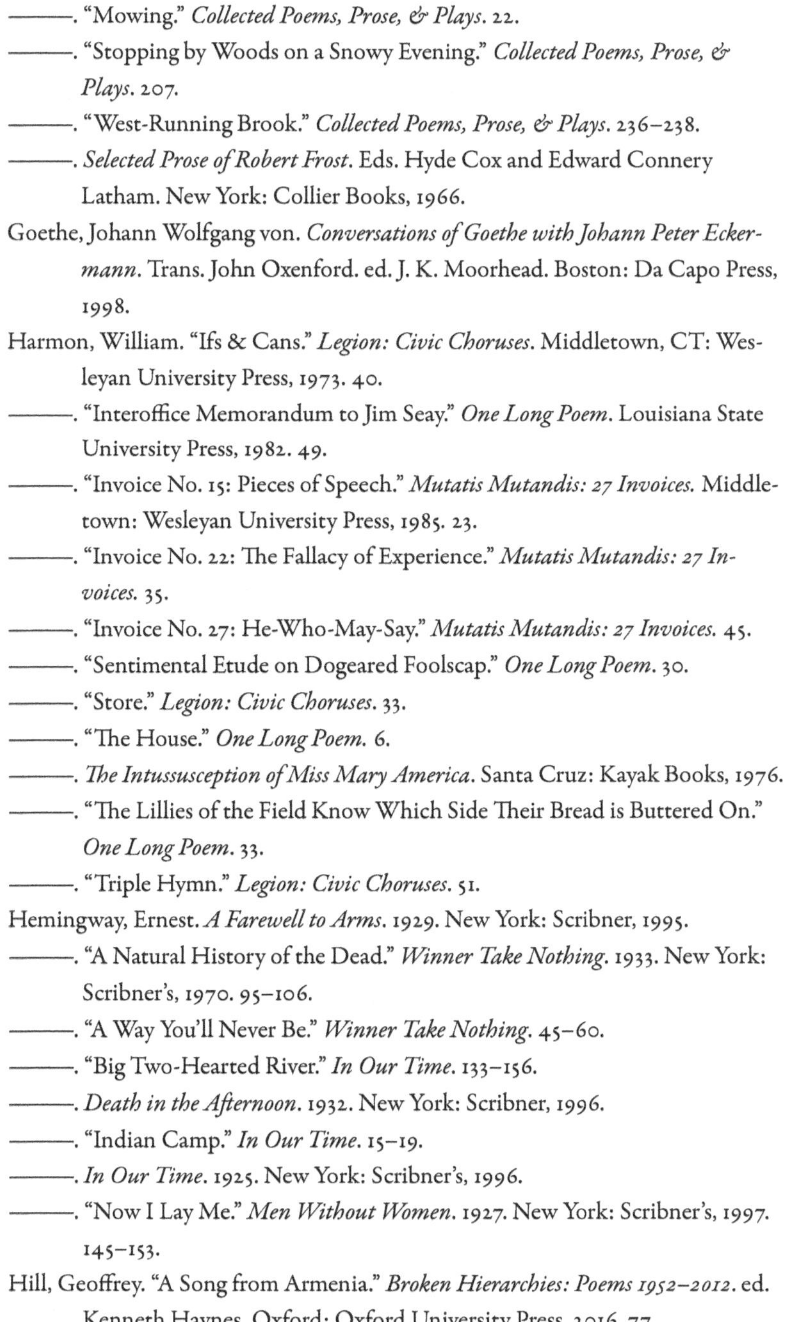

———. "Mending Wall." *Collected Poems, Prose, & Plays*. 39.

———. "Mowing." *Collected Poems, Prose, & Plays*. 22.

———. "Stopping by Woods on a Snowy Evening." *Collected Poems, Prose, & Plays*. 207.

———. "West-Running Brook." *Collected Poems, Prose, & Plays*. 236–238.

———. *Selected Prose of Robert Frost*. Eds. Hyde Cox and Edward Connery Latham. New York: Collier Books, 1966.

Goethe, Johann Wolfgang von. *Conversations of Goethe with Johann Peter Eckermann*. Trans. John Oxenford. ed. J. K. Moorhead. Boston: Da Capo Press, 1998.

Harmon, William. "Ifs & Cans." *Legion: Civic Choruses*. Middletown, CT: Wesleyan University Press, 1973. 40.

———. "Interoffice Memorandum to Jim Seay." *One Long Poem*. Louisiana State University Press, 1982. 49.

———. "Invoice No. 15: Pieces of Speech." *Mutatis Mutandis: 27 Invoices*. Middletown: Wesleyan University Press, 1985. 23.

———. "Invoice No. 22: The Fallacy of Experience." *Mutatis Mutandis: 27 Invoices*. 35.

———. "Invoice No. 27: He-Who-May-Say." *Mutatis Mutandis: 27 Invoices*. 45.

———. "Sentimental Etude on Dogeared Foolscap." *One Long Poem*. 30.

———. "Store." *Legion: Civic Choruses*. 33.

———. "The House." *One Long Poem*. 6.

———. *The Intussusception of Miss Mary America*. Santa Cruz: Kayak Books, 1976.

———. "The Lillies of the Field Know Which Side Their Bread is Buttered On." *One Long Poem*. 33.

———. "Triple Hymn." *Legion: Civic Choruses*. 51.

Hemingway, Ernest. *A Farewell to Arms*. 1929. New York: Scribner, 1995.

———. "A Natural History of the Dead." *Winner Take Nothing*. 1933. New York: Scribner's, 1970. 95–106.

———. "A Way You'll Never Be." *Winner Take Nothing*. 45–60.

———. "Big Two-Hearted River." *In Our Time*. 133–156.

———. *Death in the Afternoon*. 1932. New York: Scribner, 1996.

———. "Indian Camp." *In Our Time*. 15–19.

———. *In Our Time*. 1925. New York: Scribner's, 1996.

———. "Now I Lay Me." *Men Without Women*. 1927. New York: Scribner's, 1997. 145–153.

Hill, Geoffrey. "A Song from Armenia." *Broken Hierarchies: Poems 1952–2012*. ed. Kenneth Haynes. Oxford: Oxford University Press, 2016. 77.

———. "After Cumae." *Broken Hierarchies.* 25.

———. "Annunciations." *Broken Hierarchies.* 40.

———. "An Order of Service." *Broken Hierarchies.* 45.

———. "Asmodeus." *Broken Hierarchies.* 16–17.

———. *Collected Poems.* Oxford: Oxford University Press, 1986.

———. "Coplas." *Broken Hierarchies.* 70.

———. "Epigraph." *Mercian Hymns.*

———. "From the Latin." *Broken Hierarchies.* 75.

———. "Funeral Music." *Broken Hierarchies.* 47–50, 52–53.

———. "Genesis." *Broken Hierarchies.* 3–4.

———. "History as Poetry." *Broken Hierarchies.* 61.

———. "Hymn IX: Offa's Book of the Dead." *Broken Hierarchies.* 91.

———. "Hymn XII: Offa's Coins." *Broken Hierarchies.* 94.

———. "Hymn XIII: Offa's Coins." *Broken Hierarchies.* 95.

———. "Hymn XIV: Offa's Laws." *Broken Hierarchies.* 96.

———. "Hymn XV: Offa's Beastiary." *Broken Hierarchies.* 97.

———. "Hymn XVI: Offa's Sword." *Broken Hierarchies.* 98.

———. "Hymn XVII: Offa's Journey to Rome." *Broken Hierarchies.* 99.

———. "Hymn XXV: Opus Anglicanum." *Broken Hierarchies.* 107.

———. "Hymn XXVII: The Death of Offa." *Broken Hierarchies.* 109.

———. "In Piam Memoriam." *Broken Hierarchies.* 34.

———. "Locust Songs: The Emblem." *Broken Hierarchies.* 41.

———. "Metamorphosis V." *Broken Hierarchies.* 18.

———. "Ode on the Loss of the 'Titanic.'" *Broken Hierarchies.* 30.

———. "Of Commerce and Society, IV." *Broken Hierarchies.* 29.

———. "Of Commerce and Society: Homage to Henry James." *Broken Hierarchies.* 30.

———. "Ovid in the Third Reich." *Broken Hierarchies.* 39.

———. "Requiem for the Plantagenet Kings." *Broken Hierarchies.* 15.

———. "September Song." *Broken Hierarchies.* 44.

———. "Shiloh Church, 1862: Twenty-three Thousand." *Broken Hierarchies.* 42.

———. "The Guardians." *Broken Hierarchies.* 21.

———. "The Humanist." *Broken Hierarchies.* 46.

———. "The Re-birth of Venus." *Broken Hierarchies.* 18.

———. "The Songbook of Sebastian Arrurruz." *Broken Hierarchies.*

———. "The Turtle Dove." *Broken Hierarchies.* 12.

———. "The White Ship." *Broken Hierarchies.* 22.

———. "Wreaths, II." *Broken Hierarchies.* 23.

Hopkins, Gerard Manley. "Duns Scotus's Oxford." *Gerard Manley Hopkins: Poetry and Prose*. ed. W. H. Gardner. London: Penguin, 1970.

Idol, John L. *A Thomas Wolfe Companion*. New York: Greenwood, 1987.

Jolas, Eugene. "Transition: An Occidental Workshop, 1927–1938." *Critical Writings, 1924–1951*. eds. Klaus H. Kiefer and Rainer Rumold. Evansville: Northwestern UP, 2009.

La Fontaine. "The Grasshopper and the Ant." *Fables of La Fontaine*. Trans. Marianne Moore. New York: Viking Press, 1954. archive.org/stream /in.ernet.dli.2015.150694/2015.150694.The-Fables-Of-La Fontaine_djvu .txt. Accessed 25 July 2024.

Larkin, Philip. "Church Going." *Collected Poems*. ed. Anthony Thwaite. New York: FSG, 2003. 59.

Lewis, Janet. "Helen Grown Old." *Poems Old and New, 1918–1978*. Athens: Swallow Press, 1981. 62.

Longfellow, Henry Wadsworth. "My Lost Youth." *Poems and Other Writings*. New York: Library of America, 2000. 337–339.

———. *Poems, The Song of Hiawatha*. 1855. 141–278.

Ludlow, Fitz Hugh. "Among the Mormons." *Atlantic Monthly* (April 1864). 494–495. https://www.theatlantic.com/magazine/archive/1864/04/among -the-mormons/306013. Accessed 25 July 2024.

MacLeish, Archibald. "His Mirror Was Danger." *Life* magazine. Vol. 52, No. 2. July 14, 1961. 71–72. https://books.google.com. Accessed 20 July 2024.

Marion, Jeff Daniel. "A Mountain Fable of a Sort." *Out in the Country, Back Home*. Winston-Salem: Jackpine Press, 1976. 4–5.

———. "Brakeshoe Spring." *Out in the Country, Back Home*. 53.

———. "Cleaning Lady, 1944." *Letters Home*. Abingdon, VA: Sow's Ear Press, 2001. 12.

———. "November 1943." *Letters Home*. 7.

———. "Prayer to a Dead Father." *Father*. 68–69.

———. "The Chinese Poet Awakens to Find Himself Abruptly in East Tennessee." *Tight Lines*. Emory, VA: Iron Mountain Press, 1981. np.

———. "The Farm Wife's Aubade." *Tight Lines*. np.

———. "The Garden." *Tight Lines*. np.

———. "To My Father Ten Years Later." *Father*. Nicholasville, KY: Wind Publications, 2009. 66–67.

McCarthy, Cormac. *Child of God*. 1973. New York: Vintage International, 1993.

———. *Suttree*. 1979. New York: Vintage International, 1992.

———. *The Gardener's Son: A Screenplay*. 1976. Hopewell, NJ: The Ecco Press, 1996.

McConkey, James Rodney. *Court of Memory*. New York: Dutton, 1983. 1993

———. *Crossroads*. New York: Dutton, 1968.

———. *Night Stand: A Book of Stories.* Ithaca: Cornell University Press, 1965.

———. *The Telescope in the Parlor*. Philadelphia: Paul Dry Books, 2004.

McCrae, John. "In Flanders Fields." *The Penguin Book of First World War Poetry*. ed. George Walter. New York: Penguin Classics, 2006. 155.

Miller, Jim Wayne. "After the Hunt." *Dialogue with a Dead Man*. Athens: University of Georgia Press, 1974. 11.

———. "In a Mountain Pasture." *Every Leaf a Mirror: A Jim Wayne Miller Reader*. eds. Morris Allen Grubbs and Mary Ellen Miller. Lexington: University Press of Kentucky, 2014. 19.

———. *Newfound*. New York: Orchard Books, 1989.

———. "Preface." *Southern Appalachian Poetry: An Anthology of 37 Poets*. ed. Marita Garin. Jefferson, NC: McFarland, 2007. vii.

———. "Regional Identity and the Future." *Appalachia Inside Out: Culture and Custom*. Vol. 2. eds. Robert J. Higgs, Ambrose N. Manning, and Jim Wayne Miller. Knoxville: The University of Tennessee Press, 1995: 734–739.

Milosz, Czeslaw. *The Princeton Encyclopedia of Poetry and Poetics*. ed. Alex Preminger. et al. Princeton: Princeton University Press, 1965. 840.

Morgan, Robert. "Bellrope." *At the Edge of the Orchard Country*. 1987. Winston-Salem, NC: Press 53, 2014. 30.

———. "Books in the Attic." *At the Edge of the Orchard Country*. 17–18.

———. *Boone: A Biography*. Chapel Hill: Algonquin Books, 2007.

———. "Cellar." *Red Owl*. New York: W.W. Norton, 1972. 4.

———. "Double Springs." *Land Diving*. Baton Rouge: Louisiana State University Press, 1976. 5.

———. *Good Measure: Essays, Interviews and Notes on Poetry*. Baton Rouge: Louisiana State University Press, 1993.

———. "Mountain Bride." *Groundwork*. Frankfort, KY: Gnomon Press, 1979. 8–9.

———. "Mountain Graveyard." *Sigodlin*. 1990. Winston-Salem, NC: Press 53, 2014. 27.

———. "Mowing." *Topsoil Road*. Baton Rouge: Louisiana State University Press, 2000. 15–16.

———. "O Lost, and Found." *The Thomas Wolfe Review*. Volume 25, Number 2 (Fall 2000). 3–9.

———. "Purple Asters." *Sigodlin*. 5.

———. "Squirrel. Shadow." *Land Diving*. 42.

———. "Soreshin." *The Iowa Review*. Volume 8, Issue 1 (Winter) 1977. 41–43.

———. "Speaking." *Red Owl*. 18.

———. "Sunday Toilet." *At the Edge of the Orchard Country*. 33–34.

———. "Thaw." *Red Owl*. 19.

———. "The Gift of Tongues." *At the Edge of the Orchard Country*. 29.

———. *The Truest Pleasure*. Chapel Hill: Algonquin Books, 1995.

———. "Tool Shed." *Red Owl*. 36.

———. "Visitors." *At the Edge of the Orchard Country*. 62.

———. "When He Spoke Out of the Dark." *Sigodlin*. 64.

———. "William Harmon." Unpublished essay.

———. "Wire Grass." *Red Owl*. 16.

———. "Working in the Rain." *Topsoil Road*. 14.

———. "Writing Spider." *Sigodlin*. 49.

———. "Yellow." *At the Edge of the Orchard Country*. 20.

———. "Zircon." *Dark Energy*. New York: Penguin, 2015. 72.

———. "Zirconia." *Zirconia Poems*. Northwood Narrows, NH: Lillabulero Press,
     Limited, 1969. 33.

———. "Zircon Pit." *Groundwork*. 49.

Niven, Penelope. *Carl Sandburg: A Biography*. New York: Scribner's, 1991.

Nobel, James Dodman. "Refrain One." *Modern Trilogy*. Chicago: Broadside Press,
     1940. 1.

———. "Refrain Six." *Modern Trilogy*. 33.

Owen, Wilfred. "Dulce et Decorum Est." *The Collected Poems of Wilfred Owen*. ed.
     C. Day Lewis. New York: New Directions, 1965. 55–56.

Pasternak, Boris. *Doctor Zhivago*. Trans. Max Hayward and Manya Harari. New
     York: Signet, 1958.

Poe, Edgar Allan. "Alone." *Poetry and Tales*. ed. Patrick F. Quinn. New York:
     Library of America, 1984.

———. *Essays and Reviews*. ed. G. R. Thompson. New York: Library of America,
     1984.

———. "Introduction." *Poetry and Tales*. 54–55.

———. "The Cask of Amontillado." 848–854.

———. *The Collected Letters of Edgar Allan Poe: Volume I: 1824–1846*. ed. John
     Ward Ostrom. 1948. Rev. Burton R. Pollin and Jeffrey A. Savoye. New
     York: Gordian Press, 2008.

———. *The Collected Letters of Edgar Allan Poe: Volume II: 1846–1849*. Pollin and
     Savoye. New York: Gordian Press, 2008.

———. "The Domain of Arnheim." *Poetry and Tales*. 855–870.

———. "The Fall of the House of Usher." *Poetry and Tales*. 317–336.

———. "The Poetic Principle." *Essays and Reviews*. 71–94.

———. "The Raven." *Poetry and Tales*. 81–85.

———. "To———." *Poetry and Tales*. 88.

———. "To Helen." *Poetry and Tales*. 62.

———. "Ulalume." *Poetry and Tales*. 89–91.

Pound, Ezra. "A Few Dont's by an Imagiste." *Poetry*. Vol 1, No. 6 (March 1913): 200–206. www.gutenberg.org/files/43224/43224-h/43224-h.htm. Accessed 20 July 2024.

Quest for Reality, eds. Yvor Winters and Kenneth Fields. Chicago: Swallow Press, 1969.

Rimbaud, Arthur. "The Ladies Who Look for Lice." *Arthur Rimbaud: Complete Works*. Trans. Paul Schmidt. New York: HarperPerennial, 2008. 86.

Rubin, Louis D. *Thomas Wolfe: The Weather of His Youth*. Baton Rouge: Louisiana State University Press, 1955.

Sandburg, Carl. *Complete Poems of Carl Sandburg*. New York: Harcourt, Brace and Company, 1970.

———. "Buffalo Dusk." *Complete Poems*. 256.

———. "Chicago." *Complete Poems*. 3.

———. "Cool Tombs." *Complete Poems*. 134.

———. "Definitions of Poetry." *Complete Poems*. 317.

———. "Four Preludes on Playthings of the Wind." *Complete Poems*. 183.

———. "Grass." *Complete Poems*. 136.

———. "Jazz Fantasia." *Complete Poems*. 179.

———. "Limited." *Complete Poems*. 20.

———. "Nocturne in a Deserted Brickyard." *Complete Poems*. 55.

———. "Prairie." *Complete Poems*. 79–84.

———. *The People, Yes. Complete Poems*. 439–617.

———. "Under the Harvest Moon." *Complete Poems*. 49.

———. "Wind Song." *Complete Poems*. 217.

Seeger, Alan. "I Have a Rendezvous with Death." *The Penguin Book of First World War Poetry*. ed. George Walter. New York: Penguin Classics, 2006. 105–107.

Shakespeare, William. "Sonnet 73." *The Riverside Shakespeare*. 2nd ed. ed. G. Blakemore Evans. Houghton Mifflin, 1997.

Shelley, Percy Bysshe. "A Defense of Poetry." *Romantic Poetry and Prose*. eds. Harold Bloom and Lionel Trilling. London: Oxford University Press, 1973. 746–762.

Sisson, C. H. "Epigraph" from *A C. H. Sisson Reader*. eds. Charlie Louth and Patrick McGuinness, UK: Carcanet Press Limited, 2014. xiv.

Smart, Christopher. *Jubilate Agno*. 1939. Westport, CN: Greenwood Press, 1969.

Stevens, Wallace. "Domination of Black." *The Collected Poems of Wallace Stevens*. 1954. New York: Vintage, 2011. 9.

———. "Of Modern Poetry." *The Palm at the End of the Mind: Selected Poems and a Play*. ed. Holly Stevens. New York: Vintage Books, 1972. 174.

Tennyson, Alfred Lord. "Locksley Hall." *Alfred Lord Tennyson: Selected Poems*. ed. Christopher Ricks. New York: Penguin, 2007. 51–62.

Thomas, Dylan. "And Death Shall Have No Dominion." *Dylan Thomas: Collected Poems, 1934–1953*. eds. Walford Davies and Ralph Maud. London: Orion Books, 2002. 56.

———. "Do Not Go Gentle into That Good Night." *Collected Poems*. 148.

———. "From Love's First Fever to Her Plague." *Collected Poems*. 21.

Thoreau, Henry David. *A Week on the Concord and Merrimack Rivers, Walden; or Life in the Woods, The Maine Woods, Cape Cod*. ed. Robert F. Sayre. New York: Library of America, 1985.

Tolstoy, Leo. *War and Peace*. 1869. Trans. Constance Garnett. New York: Modern Library, 1962.

Vaughan, Henry. "To His Books." *Henry Vaughan: The Complete Poems*. ed. Alan Kudrum. New Haven: Yale University Press, 1981. 611.

Viramontes, Helena Maria. "Foreword." Robert Morgan, *The Oratorio That Was Time: Fourteen Poems and Three Stories*. New York. Audubon Terrace Press, 2022. vii-viii.

Wallace, Garry. "Meeting McCarthy." *Southern Quarterly*. Vol. 30, No. 4 (Summer 1992). 134–139.

Whitman, Walt. "Song of Myself." *Poetry and Prose*. ed. Justin Kaplan. New York: Library America, 1982. 188–247.

———. "There Was a Child Went Forth." *Poetry and Prose*. 138.

Wildsmith, Dana. *Appalachian Journal*. Vol. 33, No. 2 (Winter 2006). 159–162.

Williams, William Carlos. *Collected Poems II*. New York: New Directions, 1950.

———. "Edgar Allan Poe." *In the American Grain*. New York: Albert and Boni, 1925. 216–233.

———. *The Autobiography of William Carlos Williams*. New York: New Directions, 1967.

Winters, Yvor. *Forms of Discovery*. Denver: Alan Swallow, 1967.

Wolfe, Thomas. *A Western Journal*. Pittsburgh: University of Pittsburgh Press, 1951.

———. *From Death to Morning*. New York: Scribner, 1935.

———. *Look Homeward, Angel*. 1929. New York: Scribner, 2006.

———. *Of Time and the River*. 1935. New York: Scribner, 1999.

———. *The Complete Stories of Thomas Wolfe*. New York: Scribner, 1987.

———. *The Short Novels of Thomas Wolfe*. ed. C. Hugh Holman. New York: Scribner, 1961.

———. *The Web and the Rock*. New York: Grosset & Dunlap, 1939.

———. *You Can't Go Home Again*. New York: Dell, 1960.

Wordsworth, William, and Samuel Taylor Coleridge. *Lyrical Ballads, 1798 and 1802*. ed. Fiona Stafford. Oxford: Oxford University Press, 2013.

———. "I Wandered Lonely as a Cloud." *William Wordsworth: Selected Poems*. ed. Stephen Gill. New York: Penguin, 2004. 164.

Wright, James. "A Blessing." *James Wright: Collected Poems*. Middletown, CT: Wesleyan University Press, 1971. 135.

Yeats, William Butler. "Leda and the Swan." *Collected Poems of W.B. Yeats*. New York: The Macmillan Company, 1964. 211.

INDEX

Abrams, M. H., 1, 89, 177

Adams, Barry, 22, 98–99

Adams, Henry; *The Education of Henry Adams*, 117

aerospace engineering, 5, 19, 25, 67, 190

Aesop, 258

Agee, James, 117, 140; *Let Us Now Praise Famous Men*, 138, 184

Albee, Edward, 68

Allan, John, 212–15

Ammons, A. R. (Archie), 1, 94–96, 99, 145, 177

anagram, 95–96, 245

Anderson, Sherwood, 20, 193, 197, 238

Appalachia, 8, 22, 95, 38, 272

Appalachian Literature, 8, 272–73, 283–84, 286–88

Appalachian Mountains (southern), 5, 30, 179, 229, 234, 269

Appalachian Studies, 273, 280, 284, 286

architecture, 115, 198–99, 229, 293, 305

Arkansas, 179–80, 183

Arnow, Harriette, 143, 286

arrowheads, 16, 70, 151

"art of far and near," 100, 124

Asheville, North Carolina, 21, 32, 52, 67, 77–78, 94; in Dykeman, 143–44, 149; in Miller, 287; in Wolfe, 105–7, 109, 116, 127

Augusta, Georgia, 57, 71

Bach, Johann Sebastian, 33, 72; *Fifth Brandenberg Concerto*, 67

Bakersfield, California, 132

Baltimore, Maryland, 140, 213, 225

Barstow, California, 133

Bartram, William, 96; *Travels*, 93

Bavaria, Germany, 130

Bernstein, Leonard; *The Joy of Music*, 82

Berry, Wendell, 272

Berryman, John, 285

Betts, Doris, 107

Bible, the, 51, 56, 66, 71–72, 148, 175, 235; Exodus, 294; Job, 292; John, 294; Luke, 298; *Old Testament*, 250, 259; Proverbs, 204; Revelation, 292; Romans, 166

Big Creek, Tennessee, 269–70

Biltmore House, 32

biography, 9, 51, 66, 118, 144, 233, 236, 262

Bishop, Elizabeth, 28

Black Balsam, 62–63

Black Mountain, North Carolina, 78

Blok, Alexander, 175

Blue Ridge Mountains, 2, 4, 39–40, 57, 75, 81, 272; in Miller, 285; in Poe, 229; in Sandburg, 235–36; "small farm in," 16, 19, 30, 35, 45, 68, 71, 190; in Wolfe, 78, 127–30

Bob's Creek, North Carolina, 67

bookmobile, 4, 32, 67, 92, 105, 173

Boone, Daniel, 66, 119–20

Boston, Massachusetts, 107, 130, 212, 214, 222–23, 226, 229, 238

Boucicault, Dion; *The Octoroon*, 82, 84

Boulder, Colorado, 116, 130

Bowdoin College, 217

Bozeman, Montana, 136

Brakeshoe Spring, Tennessee, 270

Brevard, North Carolina, 62, 88, 96

Brigham, Utah, 135

Brooks, Cleanth, 34, 240

Bryant, William Cullen; "Thanatopsis," 34

Bryce Canyon, Utah, 135

Burlington, Richard Boyle, Earl of, 198

Byron, Lord George, 20; Byronic, 108, 212, 220; *Childe Harold*, 112

Caldwell, Erskine, 143

Camus, Albert, 81; *The Stranger*, 169

Canadian Rockies, 32

Canton, North Carolina, 21

Caporetto, Italy, 196

Capote, Truman, 116

Capps, Delia Johnson, 68

Carnegie Library, 92

Carolina Quarterly, 284–85

Carruth, Hayden, *The Voice That is Great Within Us*, 90

Cascades, 132

catalogue, 5, 110–12, 117, 127, 130, 230

Catawbas, 36

caves, 16, 66, 118, 167–68; Hermit's Cave, 270; Mammoth Cave, 185

Cellini, Benvenuto; *Autobiography*, 117

Cervantes, Miguel de, 114

Chappell, Fred, 21, 69, 97, 99, 107

Charlotte, North Carolina, 78–79, 82, 246

Charlottesville, Virginia, 213

Cheever, John, 184

Chekhov, Anton, 184–85; "The Student," 186

Cherokee, 2, 16, 22, 36, 61, 70, 145–47, 271–72

Chicago, Illinois, 52, 79, 81, 134, 197–98, 233, 235, 238–40, 248

childhood, 2, 4, 7, 9, 56, 144, 310, 319; Baudelaire, 225; in Hemingway, 199, 202, 204–5; in Hill, 266; Poe, 211

China, 60

Chinook Pass, Washington, 137

Choptack, Tennessee, 271

Chronic Myeloid Leukemia, 313

Cicero Mountain, 33, 42, 67, 318

Cincinnati, Ohio, 52

Civitan Club, 77, 84

Clemm, Mrs. 215, 220, 222–24

Clemm, Virginia, 215, 220, 222

Cocke County, Tennessee, 271

Cole, Thomas, 123

Colorado Springs, 7

Columbia, South Carolina, 163

Columbia River, 137

Columbia University, 217

Concord, North Carolina, 246

Conrad, Joseph, 178

Cornell University, 1–2, 5, 39, 65, 81, 89, 95, 97; invited reading, 22, 93–94; McConkey, 6, 179, 183–84; moving to, 25, 38; teaching at, 145, 165, 198, 226–27, 269, 177; visiting lecturer, 22, 98–99. *See also* Ithaca, New York

cotton mill, 6, 48, 53, 60, 161–62

Crane, Hart; "The Bridge," 130

Crane, Stephen, 195

Crater Lake, Oregon, 131

creative writing, 61, 68, 87, 94, 184, 285, 293

criticism, 82, 89, 114, 174, 224, 229, 239, 295; New Criticism, 295, 299

Crockett, Davy, 272

Cumberland Gap, 52

Curwood, James Oliver, 32

Czechoslovakia, 46–47

Dante Alighieri; *De Vulgari Eloquen-tia*, 300

Deep Creek, Tennessee, 8

Delaware, 88

Delius, Frederick, 95

desert, 41, 130, 132–35

Devil's Courthouse, 64

Dickens, Charles, 71, 92; *Bleak House, Great Expectations*, 112

Dickinson, Emily, 2, 4, 20, 29, 38, 249, 261, 294–95, 301–2, 308–9

Dostoyevsky, Fyodor, 6; *Crime and Punishment*, 173

Dreiser, Theodore, 177, 198, 238

Duluth, Minnesota, 52

Durand, Asher B., 123

Durham, North Carolina, 79

Duyckinck, Evert, 217

East Hessle, Yorkshire (England), 89

East Rosemary Street, Chapel Hill, North Carolina, 20

Edison, Thomas, 24

Ehle, John, 143, 288

Eisenstein, Sergei, 110

Emory College at Oxford, 5, 78

Epoch magazine, 1, 94, 174, 184

Erdrich, Louise, 170

farm, 18–19, 22, 35–36, 39, 45, 60, 65, 68, 71, 127, 190; in Dykeman, 146, 152–55; in McCarthy, 163; in Wolfe, 134

farmhouse, 87–88, 94, 98, 100, 145, 241, 271

farming, 22, 36, 38, 77, 90; Hathaway, 94; Clyde Morgan, 46, 53, 55, 57, 62, 71

Faulkner, William, 18, 20, 94, 107, 114, 117, 143, 169, 273

fiction, 1–2, 5–6, 294, 301; Dykeman, 143, 146, 151, 154, 158, 164; Hem-ingway, 194, 216–17; McCarthy, 167, 169–70; McConkey, 183–85; Miller, 284–86; Morgan, 20–21, 30, 41, 65, 67–69, 75, 78, 272–73; nonfiction, 116–17, 143, 145–46, 185, 222; Pasternak, 173–78; science fiction, 227, 229; Wolfe, 107, 109, 112–15, 130, 139

film, 82, 227, 283, 301, 303, 305; *Gardener's Son*, 163–65; Sandburg, 240; techniques in fiction, 110, 130

Finger Lakes, New York, 39

fishing, 8, 201–3, 269–70

Fitzgerald, F. Scott, 107, 117; *The Crack-Up*, 84; *The Great Gatsby*, 114; *Tender is the Night*, 174

Flat Rock, North Carolina, 18, 88; Flat Rock High School, 18, 173, 236; Sandburg, 7, 47, 234

folklore, 40, 77, 156, 288

Forster, E. M., 178

Foster, Stephen, 66

Francis, Robert, 90

free verse, 15, 60, 80, 240, 245, 293, 298

French Broad River, 5, 144

frontier, 2, 33, 48, 56, 119, 124, 272

Fuentes, Carlos, 226

Galesburg, Illinois, 233

Galilei, Galileo, 30

Gap Creek, South Carolina, 66

geography of language, 17, 30

German, 31, 81, 147, 183, 191–92, 256, 283, 288, 297

Germany, 180, 183, 256

ghost, 16, 314; Dickinson, 29, 42; "ghost-bride," 266; ghost stories, 30, 39, 65, 273; Lewis and Clark, 137; in Wolfe, 106, 190

Ginsburg, Allen; *Howl*, 240, 292

Glacier National Park, 87, 116, 136

Going to the Sun Pass, Montana, 136

Goldwin Smith Hall, 22, 93
gothic, 6, 198, 219, 225–26, 229, 234
Graham's Magazine, 219
Grand Canyon, 116, 133–34
Grand Coulee Dam, Washington, 137
grandfather, 30, 50; Clyde Morgan's grandfather, 66; Harmon's grandfather, 249
grandmother, 43, 49–50; in Hill, 266; Poe's grandmother, 215
Graniteville, South Carolina, 167
grasshoppers, 201–5, 321
great-grandfather, 49, 71
great-grandmother, 45, 68
great-great-grandfather, 16, 30, 33, 49, 65–66
great-great-grandparents, George W. and Rebecca Ann Johnson, 91
Green, Paul, 107
Green River, North Carolina, 2, 4–5, 23, 52, 65, 73, 91, 99; land bought, 16, 30, 66; as subject matter, 26, 33, 35, 39, 75
Green River Baptist Church, 32, 49, 71, 78
Greenville, South Carolina, 57, 71, 93, 162, 164, 173
Greville, Fulke, 198
Grieg, Edvard, "Peer Gynt," 81
Guthrie, Woody, 240, 286

haiku, 19, 69
Hardy, Thomas, 98
harmony, 33, 74, 82, 116, 230
Harvard University, 115, 217
Hathaway, Baxter, 1, 38, 94, 177
Haun, Mildred; *The Hawk's Done Gone*, 271
haunted, 2, 17, 42, 65; Dickinson, 29, 34; Harmon, 250; Native Americans, 16, 36, 38, 70; Poe, 212, 223; Wolfe, 106, 109, 124, 128–29, 137

haunting, 94; in Dykeman, 157; in Hill, 254; in Miller, 286; in Poe, 212, 219, 227, 229; in poems, 291; in Wolfe 128
Hawksmoor, Nicholas, 198
Hawthorne, Nathaniel, 7, 222, 225, 301; *The Scarlet Letter*, 217; *Twice-Told Tales*, 219
Haydn, Joseph, 81
Haywood County, North Carolina, 69
Heaney, Seamus, 253
Hecht, Ben, 238
Hendersonville, North Carolina, 5, 84, 87–88, 105–6, 145, 189
Herrick, Robert, 89
Hidden, William E., 24
Higginson, Thomas Wentworth, 20, 294
Hindman Settlement School, 286–89
history, 1–2, 17, 25, 35, 67, 111, 163, 192, 272, 310, 321; Clyde Morgan, 51, 56–57, 66; in Dykeman, 144–45, 151, 157–58; family, 40, 66; in Hill, 254, 256, 258–60, 262, 264–65; Hemingway, 199, 201, 203; literary, 9, 20, 219, 234, 293, 305, 307; military, 72–73, 75, 174–76, 178; Miller, 283–86, 288–89; Native American, 90, 94; oral, 168; Sandburg, 236–37; Southern, 77, 82, 84, 90; the West, 123; Wolfe, 112, 114–16
Holmes, Oliver Wendell, 297; "Old Ironsides," 34
Holston River, Tennessee, 270–71
Homer, 73, 105; *The Iliad*, 60, 67, 110; *The Odyssey*, 60
Horace, 60
hospital, 90, 119, 313, 315–21; Boone, 119; in Hemingway, 196, 201; in Marion, 279; in McCarthy, 163, 166; Poe, 224; Stevens, 298; Wolfe, 138

Howard, Richard, 96
humor, 6, 9, 51; Dykeman, 150, 153–54;
    in Hill, 261, 264; in Marion,
    273; in McCarthy, 7, 166, 168; in
    Miller, 283–84, 287, 289; Sand-
    burg, 237, 242; in Wolfe, 131

imagination, 2–4, 30, 32, 35, 112, 144;
    Bell, 113; Coleridge, 112, 294;
    Emerson, 304; Hill, 253, 262;
    McConkey, 180; and memory,
    9, 310; Poe, 219, 223, 225–27;
    Shelley, 298, 305, 308
Imagism, 7, 194, 253
Iroquois, 2, 38, 305
Irving, Washington, 217
Ithaca, New York, 1, 5, 22, 83, 93–94,
    96, 99, 145, 183, 269, 313–14, 316,
    320. *See also* Cornell University

Jackson Hole, Wyoming, 135
James, Henry, 68, 114, 257
James, William; *The Varieties of Reli-
    gious Experience*, 170
Jarrell, Randall, 69
Jeffers, Robinson, 306
Jefferson City, Tennessee, 269–70
Jones, David; *The Anathémata*, 264
Jones, Inigo, 198
Jones, Loyal, 284
Jonson, Ben, 89, 198; "To Heaven,"
    309

Keats, John, 89, 302
Kennedy, John Pendleton; *Swallow
    Barn*, 215
Kerouac, Jack, 139
Kimble Branch, North Carolina, 16
Kings Mountain, South Carolina
    (Battle of), 157
Kooser, Ted, 241, 286

Lake Tahoe, 123–24
Lakewood, Ohio, 183
landscape, 4, 21, 30, 32; American West,
    5, 115–16, 123–24, 131–33, 138;
    Boone, 118; Green River, 16, 35;
    Ithaca, 37–40, 94; macabre, 167;
    medieval, 262, 264; in Miller,
    287; in Poe, 218, 222–23, 229; in
    Sandburg, 235, 237–38
Lanier, Sidney, "The Marshes of Glynn,"
    34; "Song of the Chattahoo-
    chee," 60
Lawrence, D. H., 216
Leicester, North Carolina, 287
Levertov, Denise, 184
Lillabulero, 21, 89
Lima, Ohio, 52
Lincoln, Abraham, 229, 233, 237, 240
Lindsay, Vachel, 198, 235, 238
Linney, Romulus, 67–68, 107
Little Review, The, 238
Little Switzerland, North Carolina,
    77, 79
Logan, Utah, 135
London, England, 19, 71, 107, 109, 130,
    151, 212, 238
London, Jack, 32, 92
Long John Mountain, North Carolina,
    98
Lovecraft, H. P.; *At the Mountains of
    Madness*, 217
Lowell, Amy, 238
Lowell, James Russell, 219, 222
Lowell, Robert, 68, 89, 285

Maclean, Alasdair, 253
MacLeish, Archibald, 193, 206, 236, 242
Magic Realists, 228, 230
Mailer, Norman; *Armies of the Night*,
    116
Mallarmé, Stéphan, 21, 291, 309; "Le
    Tombeau de Edgar Poe," 225

Manhattan, New York, 217, 220; *See also, New York*

Marion, North Carolina, 78–79, 83

Marvell, Andrew, 89

Mary Washington University, 2, 7

Mason, Bobbi Ann, 286

Masters, Edgar Lee, 198, 235, 238

mathematics, 25, 67, 190; advanced, 5; applied, 19, 67; pure, 68

Matthews, William, 5, 21–22, 89, 93, 96, 100

Mayakovski, Vladimir, 175

McClanahan, Ed, 284

McGrath, Thomas, 240, 286

Meeting House Hill, North Carolina, 25

Melville, Herman, 110, 174, 216, 301; *Moby Dick*, 217; "Shiloh," 259

memory, 1–4, 7, 25, 29–30, 56, 60, 66, 291–92, 294, 297, 299–300, 303, 307; Augustine, 179; in Dykeman, 144, 153, 164; in Hill, 266; and imagination, 9, 310; Marion, 8, 273–74, 276–77, 280; McConkey, 178–80, 184–85; Miller, 9, 284; Poe, 213; Sandburg, 235, 237; in Wolfe, 112–13, 129

Merwin, W. S., 89

Michigan, 169, 181, 183, 190

Mills River Valley, North Carolina, 94

Milton, John, 73, 256; *Paradise Lost*, 67, 110

Milwaukee, Wisconsin, 233

Misenheimer, North Carolina, 79

Mississippi, 107

modernist, 7, 169, 195, 225, 230, 236, 241, 301; modernist poetry, 5, 60, 89, 194, 225, 239–40, 242, 254, 262, 294, 297, 299; modern dance, 77, 79–80, 84; modern music, 81

Mohave, California, 133

Monroe, Bill, 286

Monroe, Harriet, 238

Moody, Mrs. William Vaughn, 286

Moore, Marianne, 20, 204, 309

Morehead State College, 179, 183

Morgan, Ben, 87–88, 91–92, 98

Morgan, Clyde, 2; "Daddy," 45–53, 55, 57–64, 71–72, 78–79, 84, 90, 163

Morgan, Evangeline, 17, 78–79, 98

Morgan, Nancy, 87, 90, 92, 94, 97–98, 318, 320

Moscow, Russia, 19, 35, 73, 151, 176

mother, 4, 15, 18, 29–30, 32, 48, 50–51, 53, 56, 62, 67, 94, 161; Baudelaire's, 225; in Dykeman, 153–54, 157; in Hemingway, 201; Marion's, 276–77; McConkey's, 178, 180–83; in Poe, 212, 216; of poetry, 293; Wolfe's, 107, 109, 139

Mount Olivet, North Carolina, 16, 66

Mount Mitchell, North Carolina, 84, 148

Mount Rainier, Washington, 137

Mount Shasta, California, 132

mowing, 46–48, 134–35, 315

Mozart, 17, 72, 299

music, 15, 17, 49, 67, 190, 274, 298, 305–6, 321; classical, 33, 66, 81–82, 93; country, 288, 297; Harmon, 246–48; Hill, 257, 261; jazz, 198, 239; in poetry, 34, 194, 227, 246–47, 257, 291, 297, 304, 307, 309; Miller, 283–84, 287–90; pop, 293, 301; rock and roll, 165, 170, 297, 301; Sandburg, 7, 237, 239–40, 242; at Wildacres, 77–78, 80–84; Wolfe, 106, 108, 115, 119

mystery, 4, 33, 35, 237, 291, 296, 302; Poe, 211, 213, 215, 217, 224; Wolfe, 105, 109, 113

Nabokov, Vladimir, 1, 38; *Ada* and *Lolita*, 227
Nance Ferry, Tennessee, 271–72
Nation, The, 95–96
National Geographic, 66, 71
Native Americans, 2, 16, 32, 36, 61, 82, 84, 131, 273
Needles, California, 133
neurosurgeon, 314–15
Newport, Tennessee, 143
New York, New York, 96, 107, 226; Poe, 212, 214, 216, 221–24, 230; Wolfe, 109, 115–16, 130; *See also* Manhattan
New Yorker, The, 179, 184, 301
New York Philharmonic, 33
Nietzsche, Frederick, 304; *The Birth of Tragedy from the Spirit of Music* and *Thus Spake Zarathustra,* 81
North Carolina State University, 5, 35, 65, 67
North Dakota, 241
Norton Anthology, 89, 93

Oak Park, Illinois, 198–99
O'Brien, Tim, 170
O'Connor, Flannery, 273
Ogden, Utah, 115, 135
Old Faithful, 136
Old North State, 65
Olympia, Washington, 138
Oteen, North Carolina, 78
Owen, Guy, 68, 99, 107, 164

Pace, Daniel, 16, 30, 66
Pacific Northwest, 94
Park House, 81
Painted Desert, Arizona, 134
painting; fine art, 123–24; house, 5, 36, 55–56, 88, 90, 94, 101
Palmer, Samuel, 95

Paris, France, 19, 35, 109, 151, 193, 197, 225
Parkman, Francis; *La Salle and the Discovery of the Great West,* 179
Pascal, Blaise, 87
pasture, 4, 16, 24, 26, 30, 36, 47, 50, 60, 66, 88, 90, 96, 272
Percy, Walker, 184
Perkins, Maxwell, 113, 130, 138
Pfeiffer College, North Carolina, 79, 81
Philadelphia, Pennsylvania, 24, 66, 217, 219–20, 224; Orchestra, 66
philosophy, 9; German philosophy, 81
photography, 195
"Pickwick, The," 21, 69
Piedmont, 6, 78, 93, 162, 246
Pindar, 60–61
Pink Beds, North Carolina, 62
Pisgah, 62, 94, 124
Plato, *Republic,* 303–4; Neoplatonic, 38, 226
Pocatello, Idaho, 135
Poetry magazine, 45, 235, 238
pole-beans, 53–4, 90, 173
Pope, Alexander, 198
Popper, Karl, 297
Portland, Oregon, 131
Price, Reynolds, 68, 107, 317

Quo Vadis, 19, 173

Raleigh, North Carolina, 79; *News & Observer,* 65, 107
Ransom, John Crowe, 239–40
"reach of poetry," 2, 17, 26, 101, 250, 292, 298–99, 302–3, 307
Rehab, 317–20
religion, 3, 17, 150, 154, 170; Baptist, 50, 151, 185; Hardshell, 50; Old Regular Baptist, 49; Pentecostal, 35, 49–51, 94

revision, 101, 308

Richmond, Virginia, 148, 212–16, 223–24, 229

Riverside Cemetery, North Carolina, 138

Robinson, Marilynne, 225

Rochester, New York, 314–17, 320

Rocky Mount, North Carolina, 53

Roethke, Theodore, 258; "Academic," 261

Romantics, 81, 119, 198, 220, 226, 235, 257, 260, 294–95

Roosevelt, Teddy, 51, 66

Rousseau, Jean-Jacques; *Confessions*, 117

Royster, Elmira, 213–14; Royster-Shelton, 224

Russian, 6, 67, 72, 110, 173, 175, 185, 246

Sacramento Valley, California, 132

Salem College, 21, 87, 89–90

Salt Lake City, Utah, 134–35

Sartre, Jean-Paul, 81, 92; *Nausea*, 169

Schiller, Frederick, 20

science, 7, 22, 25, 67, 72, 77–78, 94, 115, 190, 229; Harmon, 245; and poetry, 91, 235, 306; rigor of, 7, 191; Sandburg, 242

Scientific American, 26

Scotland, 212–13, 253

Seattle, Washington, 137–38

seizure, 313, 315–16

Sequoyah National Forest, 87, 116, 132

Settle, Mary Lee, 143

Sevier, John, 272

Shaw, George Bernard, 81

Shaw's Creek Church, North Carolina, 90

Shew, Marie Louise, 222, 227

Skyland Hotel, 84

Sims, William Gilmore, 217

Siskiyous, 132

Slatoff, Walter, 1, 94, 177

Small Farm, The, 8, 269, 273, 280

Smith, Lee, 170, 286

Snake River, 135

Snyder, Gary, 20, 68, 286

soil, 2, 22, 25, 38, 54, 66, 69, 91, 118, 146, 149, 155, 265, 314

Song of Roland, The, 266

Southern Literary Messenger, 215–16

spring (mountain), 22–23; in Dykeman, 146–47, 151–53, 155, 158; in Marion, 270, 274; *See also* water

Stanard, Jane, 212–13

stars, 4, 29–30, 41, 100, 275, 279, 298, 306, 308

Stein, Gertrude, 193

Steinbeck, John, 117, 139; *The Grapes of Wrath*, 286

Stendahl, 71; *The Charterhouse of Parma*, 174

Still, James, 143, 286

Stokely, James, Jr., 157; Jim Stokely, III, 143, 157; Dykeman Stokely, 157; Stokely-Van Camp, 150

Stoke Newington, England, 212

Stuart, Jesse, 286

sublime, 8, 17, 111, 123, 155, 170, 218, 245

Swannanoa, North Carolina, 78

Tar River, North Carolina, 53

Tasso, Torquato, 73

Tate, Allen, 69, 97, 239, 259

teaching, 60, 87, 96–97, 165, 176, 226; Cornell, 1, 22, 39, 99, 161, 165, 269; Jessie Rehder, 69; McConkey, 183; Miller, 289; Miss Mary Sue Waters, 18; Mr. Dean Ward, 32, 67; Mrs. Julia Lappin, 18; Salem College, 21, 87, 89

Temple of Zeus, The, 22, 93

Tetons, Grand, 135–36

Thompson's Falls, Montana, 136
Toledo, Ohio, 52–53
"tomahawk man," 215
Tompkins County, New York, 38, 40
trapping, 53, 55, 61–62
trout, 16, 61, 201–3, 205, 270
Troy, 110
Tuxedo Elementary School, 60, 67, 72
Twain, Mark, 286; *Adventures of Huckleberry Finn*, 174

"universal animism," 113, 298
University of Iowa, 183
University of Michigan, 257–58, 283
University of North Carolina-Chapel Hill, 2, 19, 21, 67–68, 79, 99, 107, 169, 284; intellectual beauty, 82–83
University of North Carolina-Greensboro, 69, 107
University of Tennessee, 145
University of Virginia, 213, 229
Upstate New York, 38, 40, 161

Vanbrugh, John, 198
Vanderbilt University, 288
Vergil, 73
voice, 3–8, 19–20, 25, 39, 50, 65, 69, 74–75, 84, 92, 99, 101, 109, 116, 292–93, 297, 300–302, 304–6, 309; in Dykeman, 143, 156; female voice, 109, 139, 154, 230; in Harmon, 245, 248–49; in Hemingway, 191, 194–96, 198, 200; in Hill, 253, 262; in Marion, 273, 275–76, 279–80; in McCarthy, 165–70; in McConkey, 179; in Miller, 285–86; in Poe 212, 228; in Sandburg, 242; in Wolfe, 116, 129–30, 132

walking, 29, 32, 62, 88, 100, 314, 318
Walterboro, South Carolina, 68
war, 6–7, 35, 37, 47, 57, 151, 199, 201–3, 205, 235, 262; anti-war, 97, 241; Civil War, 19, 148, 195, 271, 273, 317; Napoleonic, 73, 75; post-war, 154; Russian Revolution, 173–76; Spanish American, 233; Vietnam, 241; World War I, 191–93, 196–97, 238, 310; World War II, 143, 180, 183, 185, 234, 255, 276, 286
Warren, Robert Penn, 97, 240; *All the King's Men*, 139
Washington, George, 17, 51, 66
water, 5, 29, 39, 50, 53, 91, 100, 238, 318; baptism, 50; boiling, 136; clear, 146, 152, 156, 194, 270; in Dykeman, 146, 148–49, 153, 156; in Hemingway, 194, 197, 204–5; in Hill, 264; in Marion, 270–72, 274, 276; in McConkey, 185–86; in Poe, 298; stagnant, 48; in *The Truest Pleasure*, 41–42; water-bucket, 59, 99; water-plants, 292; watershed, 145–47, 274; in Wolfe, 108, 118, 123–24, 132, 135–36. *See also* spring (mountain)
waterfall, 22, 36, 69, 94, 132
weeds, 21, 37, 40, 46–48, 51, 54–56, 66, 88–89, 91, 99–100, 123–24, 152, 308
Welty, Eudora, 143, 184
Wessie, Aunt, 98
Western Reserve University, Ohio, 83
West Point, US Military Academy at, 67, 190, 214–15, 219
whetrock, 46
Whitman, Helen, 223
Wilbur, Richard, 226
Wildacres, 4, 77–79, 82–85

Wilder, Laura Ingalls; *Farmer Boy*,
    32, 92; *Little House on the Prairie*,
    67
wilderness, 32–33, 36, 51, 61, 129, 147,
    203, 242, 308
Wildsmith, Dana, 289
Willamette, Oregon, 131
Williams, Cratis, 286
Williams, Jonathan, 93, 95
Wilson, Colin; *The Outsider*, 81
Winston-Salem, North Carolina, 80,
    87, 98

Woodland tribes, 16, 36, 70
Wren, Christopher, 198
Wright, Frank Lloyd, 198–99
Wyatt, Sir Thomas, 60, 89

Yale University, 217
Yellowstone, 87, 136
Yosemite, 87, 132

Zion National Park, 135
zircon, 16, 24–26
Zirconia, North Carolina, 26